A COMMENTARY ON
THE NEW
CODE OF CANON LAW

By THE REV. P. CHAS. AUGUSTINE, O.S.B., D.D.
Professor of Canon Law

BOOK III

De Rebus, or Administrative Law

VOLUME IV

On the Sacraments (Except Matrimony)
and Sacramentals

(Can. 726-1011, 1144-1153)

SECOND, REVISED EDITION

B. HERDER BOOK CO.

17 SOUTH BROADWAY, ST. LOUIS, MO.
AND
68, GREAT RUSSELL ST., LONDON, W. C.

1921

NIHIL OBSTAT

Sti. Ludovici, die 15. Feb. 1921

F. G. Holweck,
Censor Librorum

IMPRIMATUR

Sti. Ludovici, die 16. Feb. 1921

✠Joannes J. Glennon,
Archiepiscopus
Sti. Ludovici

VAIL-BALLOU COMPANY
BINGHAMTON AND NEW YORK

CONTENTS

iv   CONTENTS

CONTENTS

CONTENTS

THE NEW CODE OF CANON LAW

BOOK III

ECCLESIASTICAL THINGS

PRELIMINARY REMARKS

The third book of the Code treats of "things" *(de rebus)*. The provisions which it embodies may be called *administrative law*, because the "things" comprised therein together form the object of ecclesiastical administration, either in the merely spirtual or the mixed domain. Besides, since *a potiori fit denominatio,* and the Sacraments constitute the most important part of this Book, the sacred ministry of the Church here becomes most conspicuous. But even mixed things, such as benefices and temporalities, must be assigned to the administrative section. One doubt only, at least for a moment, arose in our mind, *viz.,* concerning the *magisterium ecclesiasticum,* whether it has found its proper place. However, we must admit that the place for it was properly chosen. For although the teaching office may be reckoned among the personal rights of jurisdiction, yet, considering its objects (such as the censorship of books, seminaries, and schools), it is manifest that these fall under the heading of *res.* The Code, therefore, in Book III, treats in 827 canons of the following subjects:

Part I. Sacraments and Sacramentals.
Part II. Sacred Places and Times.
Part III. Divine Worship.
Part IV. The *Magisterium Ecclesiasticum.*
Part V. Ecclesiastical Benefices.
Part VI. Church Property.

THINGS IN GENERAL

CAN. 726

Res de quibus in hoc libro agitur quaeque totidem media sunt ad Ecclesiae finem consequendum, aliae sunt spirituales, aliae temporales, aliae mixtae.

The things of which this book treats, and which are as many means by which the Church attains her end, are either spiritual, or temporal, or mixed. *The end of the Church* is foremost and above all spiritual. But since the society founded by Christ is visible, and a moral or artificial person with corporate rights, the Church as such, as well as her members, cannot abstract from temporal or bodily things. The very notion of a sacrament, a thing sacred *par excellence,* implies a visible sign, which presupposes an inherent right to the appropriation and use of such material things as are necessary for the proper and divinely established administration of these visible signs. Furthermore divine worship requires buildings and ground on which to erect them, as well as sacred furniture to be used for the divine service. Moreover, the ministers of the Church are entitled to a decent support. Lastly, charitable institutions, which are the natural offspring of the Church, require material aid and subsidy. All of which goes to show that many objects or things, no matter how temporal or material they may appear, become hallowed by the use to which they are put in the Church, who, as it were, transfers them into a higher sphere.

But it must never be lost sight of that temporal things claimed by the Church are but means to realize the end for which she has been founded *(media sunt ad Ecclesiae finem consequendum),* and consequently are not sought by her for their own sake, but only as far as her end requires. The scope of these requirements, needless to say, is wide, and the needs are enormous, especially now-a-days, when Christian charity is overwhelmed with all sorts of demands.

The Code treats of three kinds of things: spiritual, temporal, and mixed.

First, let us answer the question, what is a thing, a *res?*

The reader may remember that the division adopted by the Code rests on the old trilogy: *personae, res, actiones.* After having treated of the rights and duties as annexed to the *persons* of men, the legislator now inquires into the objects of right or law *(obiecta iuris)*, leaving actions to be dealt with in the last two books, in connection with the penal code.

A *thing (res)* is an object that exists outside, though it may be strictly connected with, a person, and is perceived by the senses. When we say " perceived by the senses," this phrase must be understood in the way a human being reasons. There are *corporeal* things, i. e., such as affect the senses, and *incorporeal* things, which are not the object of sensation and can neither be seen nor handled, as, for instance, a hereditary right, an advowson, a usufruct.[1] The latter, in some way, are objects of sensation, else they would not be mentioned in the law.

The Roman law[2] took cognizance of divine things *(res divini iuris)*, and things appertaining to men *(res humani iuris)*. The divine things it divided into *res sacrae,* places or objects set apart and solemnly conse-

---

1 L. 1, Dig. 1, 8; Blackstone-Cooley, *Commentaries on the Law of England,* Chicago, 1879, Vol. 1, § 17.

2 Dig. *l. c.;* Ramsay-Lanciani, *Manual of Roman Antiquities,* 1901, p. 300.

crated to the gods by a deliberate act of the State, such
as groves, altars, chapels, temples; and *res religiosae sive
sanctae*, places or objects which acquired a sacred character from the purposes to which they were applied,
such as sepulchres and the walls of a fortified city.

Our Code adopts a somewhat different division, though
the distinction of the Roman law is still apparent. But
one thing is certain: all "things" dealt with here are
ecclesiastical *(res ecclesiasticae)*. The division adopted
may be illustrated by the subjoined diagram:

$$\text{Res ecclesiasticae} \begin{cases} \text{1. } \textit{spirituales} \begin{cases} \text{a) } \textit{stricte spirituales} \\ \text{b) } \textit{sacrae} \\ \text{c) } \textit{religiosae} \end{cases} \\ \text{2. } \textit{temporales} \\ \text{3. } \textit{mixtae} \end{cases}$$

1. *Spiritual things,* in the strictest sense, are such as
directly refer to the salvation of souls and their supernatural end, such as, *e. g.,* the Sacraments, the sacramentals, prayer, fasts and feasts, indulgences, ecclesiastical offices.

Res sacrae are things made sacred by a special dedication, blessing, or consecration, such as churches, cemeteries, sacred vessels,[3] etc.

Res religiosae are things connected with the religious
life or such as bear a religious character without a special
blessing or consecration, for instance, religious houses,
hospitals, etc.

2. *Temporal things* are such as are employed for the
temporal support of the Church and her ministers, or
for other necessities, for instance, dowries, funds, salaries, collections, subscriptions, etc.[4]

3. *Res mixtae* are such things as combine a temporal

---

[3] See can. 1154; can. 1497.
[4] Cfr. Devoti, *Institut. Canonic.,* l. iv, Leodii, 1874, t. 1, p. 308 f.

with either the strictly spiritual or the sacred or religious character, as, *e. g.,* ecclesiastical benefices and the *ius patronatus,* also churches and sacred vessels in so far as a distinction may be made between the consecration or blessing and the material value of the consecrated or blessed object. All these things, then, in so far as they fall under ecclesiastical jurisdiction, form the subject-matter of the third book.

SIMONY

Can. 727

§ 1. Studiosa voluntas emendi vel vendendi pro pretio temporali rem intrinsece spiritualem, ex. gr., Sacramenta, ecclesiasticam iurisdictionem, consecrationem, indulgentias, etc., vel rem temporalem rei spirituali adnexam ita ut res temporalis sine spirituali nullo modo esse possit, ex. gr., beneficium ecclesiasticum, etc., aut res spiritualis sit obiectum, etsi partiale, contractus, ex. gr., consecratio in calicis consecrati venditione, est simonia iuris divini.

§ 2. Dare vero res temporales spirituali adnexas pro temporalibus spirituali adnexis, vel res spirituales pro spiritualibus, vel etiam temporales pro temporalibus, si id ob periculum irreverentiae erga res spirituales ab Ecclesia prohibeatur, est simonia iuris ecclesiastici.

Can. 728

Cum de simonia agitur, emptio-venditio, permutatio, etc., late accipiendae sunt pro qualibet conventione, licet ad effectum non deducta, etiam tacita, in qua scilicet animus simoniacus expresse non manifestetur, sed ex circumstantiis colligatur.

Can. 727, § 1, *defines simony iuris divini* as a deliberate eagerness to buy or sell for a temporal price anything either intrinsically spiritual, or temporal with a spiritual thing attached to it in such a way that the temporal without the spiritual object could not exist at all, or the spiritual object itself, though only in a partial way, is intended in the bargain.

1. *Studiosa voluntas,* or the deliberate will, externally manifested, here implies not only the essential malice of a sin against the virtue of religion, but also the juridical element of external manifestation. For, as the Gloss [5] says, unless simony is external, it can be neither proved nor punished. Hence merely *mental simony,* if it is not manifested in any shape or form, does not enter the canonical realm. Different from this is the state of mind which prompts one to give or offer something temporal, not as a real price, but as a motive for attaining or causing something spiritual, or if the spiritual is given by way of gratuitous compensation, or *vice versa.* [6] This may happen when a gift is presented under the pretext of just remuneration, although the real motive is to obtain a spiritual favor, and *vice versa.* [7] However, if there is no intention to commit simony, and the sentiment of gratitude prevails, no simony can be construed.

Another kind of simony is called *conventional,* namely, when a pact intervenes, although the object of the simoniacal contract has not yet been delivered, or delivered only by one of the parties. Simony is *real* not only when a formal agreement has been made, but when

---

[5] Ad. c. 1, C. 1, q. 1, *s. v.* "*Quidem.*" The malice consists in this that a spiritual thing is treated as if it were menial and entirely dependent on man's will, and not on God's grace and power. Cfr. St. Thom., i–ii, q. 100, a. 1.

[6] *Prop. damn. ab Innoc. XI,* n. 45 (Denzinger, *Enchiridion,* n. 1062).

[7] Layman, *Theologia Moralis,* l. iv, tr. 10, c. 8, n. 66.

the object of that agreement has been delivered by both parties.

Confidential simony is that committed by the resignation of a benefice without regard to the ecclesiastical law.

2. The next element of simony is *sale or purchase.* Hence there must be a contract as understood by common law or custom. Can. 728 says:

When there is question of simony, purchase, sale, and other similar terms must be taken in a wide sense as signifying any stipulation, even though not fulfilled, and made only in a tacit manner, i. e., one in which the simoniacal intention was not explicitly manifested, but could be gathered from the circumstances of the case. Hence the stipulation required to render a transaction simoniacal may be any kind of onerous contract, sale or exchange, bailment, hiring, borrowing, or debt.[8] It is not required that the pact be *carried into effect.* Therefore if one would promise to give $1000 for a certain ecclesiastical office, for instance, a pastorship, he would be guilty of simony. Lastly, the agreement may be only *tacit, i. e.,* without a written or oral understanding as to the sort of benefit, whether spiritual or temporal. All that is required by law is a probable conjecture as to the simoniacal intention (*ex circumstantiis colligatur*). Such conjectures[9] may be based on the quality of the person who gives or receives, the quantity of the gift, and the time. Thus a poor person who gives a large sum to a prelate in order to obtain a spiritual favor, may justly be suspected of acting from a wrong motive, whereas a rich person need not be suspected,

---

[8] One of the four species of *contractus innominatus: do ut des, facio ut facias, do ut facias, facio ut des.* Cfr. Engel, V. 3, n. 4.

[9] Cfr. c. 18, X, V, 3 de simonia; Suarez, *De Relig.* l. iv, *de sim.,* c. 36, n. 12 (ed. Paris, 1859, t. 13, 843 f.).

because he or she may intend merely to make a present. Besides, the persons who give and those who take may be bound by friendship, blood-relationship, etc.,— reasons which would make simony a rather remote motive. Again, the reputation of giver and recipient must be taken into consideration.

The *quantity* of the gift must also be weighed. A large and disproportionate sum might cause suspicion, whereas an insignificant sum would not. The proportion between the price paid and the spiritual benefit received may also be indicative of the underlying intention. Consumable gifts (eatables, etc.) are not to be reckoned. Lastly, the *time* may offer a basis for conjecture. If the price is offered long before or after the spiritual benefit is bestowed, simony can not easily be presumed. The circumstances of the person should also be taken into account,— whether he is in need or not, etc. At any rate, some sort of agreement must be made, and consequently presents made out of liberality, pious donations, or charitable subsidies cannot be branded as simoniacal.[10]

3. *The temporal price* is generally comprised by the threefold kind mentioned in the Decree of Gratian: [11]

(a) *Munus a manu,* or pecuniary advantage, which comprises money and other movable as well as immovable things, the remission of debt, easements, etc.;

(b) *Munus a lingua,* which implies recommendations, praise, adulation, flattery, of a kind which is a matter of stipulation and procures a benefit;

(c) *Munus ab obsequio,* which involves service of any kind, either habitual or actual, not due by reason of mutual obligation, hire or pay, but rendered with respect to a spiritual favor, for instance, an office. Here again

10 Cfr. cc. 3, 18, 34, X, V, 3; Layman, *l. c.,* n. 8.   11 C. 114, C. 1, q. 1; c. 8, C. 1, q. 3.

it must be noticed that free and voluntary service, rendered, *e. g.*, by a friend or relative to a Cardinal or Bishop, though in the hope of obtaining a spiritual benefice, is not simony. Of course, there may be room for suspicion in such cases.

It may not be amiss to state that there is no simony involved if parents or ecclesiastical superiors promise talented boys a collegiate or seminary course, in order to induce them to embrace the ecclesiastical state, or if parents promise their children some temporal benefit to induce them to frequent the Sacraments. There is no real compact or mutual stipulation between the parties.[12]

4. Finally, the *spiritual element* must be considered. Our Code mentions two kinds of spiritual things: — such as are intrinsically spiritual, and such as are annexed to something spiritual.

(a) *Intrinsically spiritual* things, the Code says, by way of example, are the Sacraments, ecclesiastical jurisdiction, consecration, indulgences, etc. Hence to administer the Sacraments for the sake of money would be an act of simony.[13] Thus also the administration of the sacramentals for filthy lucre's sake would be simoniacal. The same must be said concerning acts of jurisdiction, absolution, delegation, grant of faculties,[14] if performed solely for a material reward. As to consecration, it is well known that the bishop is not allowed to charge anything, either for the sacred chrism or for consecration. But compensation for expenses is not forbidden.[15] Selling indulgences is simony in the truest sense of the word, but no simony is implied if a contribution is demanded in

12 Layman, *l. c.*, n. 11.
13 Cfr. C. 1, q. 1; X, V, 3 *passim.*
14 C. 14, X, V, 3.
15 C. 22, C. 1, q. 1; c. 21, X, V, 3.

the shape of an alms, as a requisite for gaining an indulgence.[16]

Simony is committed by *religious* if they charge a price for admittance to the religious state, because the latter is something intrinsically spiritual.[17] But dowries, victuals or compensation cannot be looked upon as a price for entering, but are necessary means of support. Intrinsically spiritual is the act of *preaching the word of God* and *teaching the catechism,* and hence to receive a temporal remuneration for performing these functions would be simony, according to S. Thomas.[18] However, preachers and teachers may lawfully be paid for administering their office.

These are the chief intrinsically spiritual things, i. e., such as are spiritual by their very nature and purpose, as well as by their divine origin.

(b) There are, besides, certain *temporal things* distinguished by a spiritual character attached to them *(res temporalis rei spirituali adnexa).* The Code speaks of a twofold connection of the temporal with the spiritual:

(1) That which is necessary to make the thing what it is supposed to be, for the one supposes the other. This is the case in all ecclesiastical benefices, pensions, and in fact all religious things. Hence the adage, *"Beneficium propter officium,"* which means that the material element necessarily presupposes the spiritual. This is what the authors [19] call subsequent or consequent connection.

(2) The other connection is present when the *spiritual character or thing is the object, though only partial, of the contract.* This is what is styled antecedent connec-

---

16 Layman, *l. c.,* n. 40.

17 Cfr. cc. 8, 19, 30, X, V, 3.

18 *Summa Theol.,* II–II, q. 100, a. 3, ad. 2; Suarez, *l. c.,* c. 18, n. 22 f.

19 S. Thom. II–II, q. 100, a. 4; Suarez, *l. c.,* c. 13.

tion, for instance, the consecration in the sale of a consecrated chalice. For the chalice is made and is such before it receives any consecration, and therefore the material element exists prior to the spiritual. Note, however, the wording of the Code: the spiritual must be intended in the bargain; in other words, *because* it is a consecrated chalice, I buy or sell it. Since consecration is intended *in recto,* and is something essentially spiritual, therefore the bargain is an act of simony *iuris divini.* On the other hand, as shall be seen in Can. 730, even a consecrated chalice may be bought or sold. The same rule is to be applied not only to consecrated vessels, but also to churches, oratories, cemeteries and blessed graves. It matters little whether the spiritual element is of strictly divine origin or of ecclesiastical institution, so long as it is spiritual in itself and attached to the temporal element by the lawful authority. The hieratic or sanctifying element is essentially spiritual or divine by reason of the divine power of the Church.

§ *2 of Can. 727* provides that it is simony *iuris ecclesiastici* to give temporal objects annexed to spiritual for other objects annexed to spiritual, or spiritual objects for spiritual objects, or temporal objects for temporal objects, when forbidden by the Church on account of the danger of irreverence for spiritual things. This law is evidently new, as the lack of quotations proves; but the matter itself is old.

First note the term *dare,* to give, which, as the particle *pro* indicates, here means to exchange. The exchange must be of the same objects, *e. g.,* if you exchange one set of holy oils for another set of holy oils; or one consecrated chalice for another; or one Mass for another; or if you preach for another who says Mass in your place; or exchange one piece of church property for another.   But as there seems to be no sinful agreement in these cases, what is it that renders the act simoniacal?   It is the express prohibition of the Church. Yet, as Suarez [20] appropriately says, this would not be sufficient; therefore another reason is added by the Code: *ob periculum irreverentiae,*— because these acts, though not evil in themselves, concern sacred things and may lead to irreverence.   In order to remove this danger, the Church, by positive legislation, prohibits even such acts as are not in themselves sinful.   This is especially the case in the exchange of ecclesiastical benefices and in selling holy oils or minor church offices.[21]

PENALTIES AGAINST SIMONY

Can. 729

Firmis poenis in simoniacos iure statutis, contractus ipse simoniacus et, si simonia committatur circa beneficia, officia, dignitates, subsequens provisio omni vi caret, licet simonia a tertia persona commissa fuerit, etiam inscio proviso, dummodo hoc non fiat in fraudem eiusdem provisi aut eo contradicente.   Quare:

1.° Ante quamlibet iudicis sententiam res simoniace data et accepta, si restitutionis sit capax nec obstet reverentia rei spirituali debita, restitui debet, et beneficium, officium, dignitas dimitti;

2.° Simoniace provisus non facit fructus suos; quod si eos bona fide perceperit, prudentiae iudicis vel Ordinarii permittitur fructus perceptos ex toto vel ex parte eidem condonare.

Apart from the penalties established by law (see Book V, Canons 2371, 2392), every simoniacal stipulation is

---

20 *De Rel.,* l. IV, de simi., c. 7.   X, V, 3; Ferraris, *Prompta Bibliotheca, s. v. "Simonia,"* n. 6.
21 Cfr. c. 8, C. 1, q. 3; c. 8,

null and void, and simony committed in connection with
benefices, offices, and dignities renders the appointments
null and void, even though the simoniacal act was perpetrated without the knowledge of the beneficiary, by a
third person, provided, however, it was not done in order
to defraud the one thus provided, or against his protest.
Therefore:

1.° Prior to any judicial sentence the thing simoniacally given and received must be restored, if restitution is
possible and feasible without irreverence to the spiritual
object, and the benefice, office or dignity must be sur-
rendered;

2.° The beneficiary of a simoniacal transaction cannot
receive the revenues of his benefice, but if he has accepted them in good faith, it is left to the discretion
of the judge or Ordinary to condone the income thus
received, either totally, or in part.

Since no other penalties are now in force except those
mentioned by the Code,[22] the penalties of simony are:

(a) Those mentioned in can. 2371, 2392.

(b) The simoniacal contract is null and void. This
occurs in resignations of office, as stated in can. 185.
Furthermore *no simoniacal stipulation is binding in the
ecclesiastical court and in the court of conscience.*
Hence, if one has given a sum of money to a bishop in
order to obtain a certain ecclesiastical office, the contract,
even though made in writing, would be devoid of judicial
force. A simoniacal compact obliges neither in the *forum
externum* nor in the *forum internum.*

A reasonable doubt may be entertained with regard to
entering religion. The act is complete only after profession has been made, and hence one may ask: Is
the profession invalid? The Code does not give a direct

[22] Cfr. can. 6, 5°.

answer to this question, nor do the Decretals [23] insinuate or the authors [24] assert its invalidity.

As to *indulgences* it has been decreed [25] that all objects endowed with indulgences must be delivered to the faithful gratis; if anything is demanded for them, no matter under what pretext, whether by way of price, exchange, gift, or alms, the indulgences are *eo ipso* lost. *Simple blessings,* without indulgences, are not subject to this decree, so far as we know. We may add that the Sacraments are valid, even though administered simoniacally, for the Code only says that the contract, not the thing stipulated therein, is invalid. Thus the blessing remains, though the Church, by positive law, exempts indulgences from the effect of a simoniacal act. The same must be held as to *acts of jurisdiction* tainted by simony; they are valid unless special provision is made to the contrary.

(c) Such provisions are here made concerning *benefices,* offices, and dignities. Benefices are accurately defined in can. 1409. Offices have been described in can. 145. By dignities are understood here, we think, not only those mentioned in can. 394 (diocesan chapters), but all which combine jurisdiction with preëminence, such as a prelacy, to which class belong bishops and abbots as well as the *superiores maiores* of religious communities. The text says that if simony is committed in connection with these benefices (presentation, appointment, election, postulation, nomination, etc.), the *subsequent provision is null and void.*[26]

(d) This penalty follows even if the simoniacal act was

[23] Cfr. cc. 8, 19, 30, X, V, 3.

[24] Cfr. Ferraris, *Prompta Bibliotheca, s. v. "Simonia,"* art. 1, n. 7.

[25] S. C. Indulg., July 16, 1887, ad 3 (*A. S. S.,* t. 20, 63 f.).

[26] Cfr. c. 12, X, I, 6; c. un. X, III, 12; cc. 2, 11, 12, 13, X, V, 3; c. 2, Extrav. Comm., V, 1; Paul IV, "*Inter caeteras,*" Nov. 27, 1557; Pius V, "*Cum primum,*" April 1, 1566; "*Intolerabilis,*" June 1, 1569.

committed by a *third person*. Hence if a relative or friend endeavors to put a person into office, or to obtain a dignity for him, the appointment, if made, is void, no matter whether the person thus appointed had knowledge of the simoniacal act or not.[27] The case is different, however, if the appointee protested against the simony, or if a third person committed the crime to prevent one from getting the office *(ex odio)*.[28]

A *moral and juridical consequence* of this penalty is that the thing simoniacally given and accepted must be restored, provided, of course, restitution is possible. A Sacrament administered simoniacally cannot be returned, but the administrator must restore the price received to the person who has paid it.[29] An act of jurisdiction, if validly performed, cannot be " restored." Nor, according to the text, is restitution required or admissible if it involves *irreverence* to some spiritual thing. This would be the case if sacred relics, *Agnus Deis*, blessed objects or consecrated vessels had passed through irreverent hands and been sold, as happened not infrequently in the ninth century.

In making restitution the rules of justice and equity must be conscientiously observed. Thus a consideration for the bodily or physical exertion made in imparting spiritual things, *v. g.*, in the administration of a Sacrament, preaching, etc., may be deducted from the amount to be restored.

As to *benefices, offices and dignities*, the text says that persons simoniacally in possession of them must be *dismissed* at once.[30] Dismissal is not resignation, and there-

---

27 Cfr. cc. 25, 33, X, V, 3.

28 Cfr. c. 27, X, V, 3: *per fraudem — in dispendium — malitiose* — hence envy may prompt a competitor or enemy to act simoniacally, in order to damage the other.

29 C. 115, C. 1, q. 1; c. 23, X, V, 3.

4 Suarez, *l. c.*, n. 15.

30 C. 27, X, V, 3 and the Con-

fore no right, or compensation, or consideration can be claimed in such a case. Both restitution and dismissal must be completed before any declaratory or condemnatory sentence, because the law itself declares such simoniacal transactions null and void.[31]

The second consequence, that a simoniacally provided person *cannot claim any revenues,* is perfectly logical; not having the right claimed, he cannot appropriate the object of that right.[32]

It may be added that these penalties and their consequences follow real simony only; almost all canonists exempt mental and conventional simony from these penalties.[33] As to confidential simony, which is committed in benefices, we shall recur to it under that heading.

WHEN THERE IS NO SIMONY

CAN. 730

Non habetur simonia cum temporale datur non pro re spirituali, sed eius occasione ex iusto titulo a sacris canonibus vel a legitima consuetudine recognito; item cum datur res temporalis pro re temporali, quae tanquam subiectum habeat adnexum aliquid spirituale, ex. gr., calix consecratus, dummodo pretium non augeatur propter adnexam rem spiritualem.

Here the Code considers two cases which apparently constitute simony, yet do not.

1. *There is no simony if a temporal object is given, not as an equivalent for a spiritual thing, but on the occasion thereof, for a reason acknowledged as just by*

stitutions of Pius V, already quoted.

31 C. 8, X, I, 35; c. 41, X, V, 3.

32 C. 115, C. 1, q. 1; c. 23, X, V, 3.

33 Cf. Layman, *l. c.,* n. 68; Ferraris, *l. c.,* art. 3, n. 1 ff.

either canon law or custom. Under this heading falls
the necessary and decent support of the clergy who administer spiritual things unto the faithful and receive
temporal things in return. Natural justice dictates that
the laborer is worthy of his hire, and that one who works
and occupies himself for another should receive his due.
There is no simony here because the salary is not given
as a temporal equivalent for the spiritual office and
there is no equalization or proportion intended between
the two.[34]

Canons who come to choir because of the daily dis-
tributions which are established by law precisely as an
inducement, do not commit simony; unless indeed, as St.
Thomas says, they purposely exclude every other intention.[35]

Mass stipends do not involve simony because they are
not given as a price for the holy Sacrifice, or for the
intrinsic or concomitant labor involved in saying Mass,
but merely as an alms intended to contribute to the necessary support of the sacred ministers.[36]

Legacies and foundations are not simoniacal because,
partly, they bear the character of benefices, and partly
involve a merely material obligation not intrinsically
connected with the spiritual character, and partly partake
of the nature of Masses or salaries.[37]

From this it may also be seen that clergymen may,
without danger of committing simony, treat with bishop
or congregation for a just and sufficient support.[38]

There is no simony committed if something is demanded for a plot or lot in a cemetery, for the purpose

34 Layman, *l. c.*, n. 60.
35 *Quaest. Quodlib.*, 8, q. 6.
36 Cfr. *prop. dam. Wicliff.*, n.
25 (Denzinger, n. 501).

37 Suarez, *l. c.*, c. 39, n. 17.
38 Cfr. c. 11, X, III, 5; Layman,
l. c., n. 15.

of meeting the necessary expenses of maintenance. To sell the right of burial in consecrated ground, of course, would be simony.[39]

Taxes established according to the rules of justice and custom are not simoniacal.[40]

2. *There is no simony involved when a temporal object is given for another temporal object which has some spiritual benefit attached to it,* as, for instance, a consecrated chalice, provided, however, that the price be not raised on account of the spiritual benefit. The reason for this ruling lies in the fact that the connection between the spiritual benefit and the material is antecedent, and not intrinsically necessary, whilst, on the other hand, the material and workmanship of the object has a price. Hence churches, sacred vessels, and vestments may be materially valued, provided the consecration or blessing attached to them is not prized, nor the price augmented on account of the spiritual benefit.[41]

---

[39] C. 15, X, III, 28; c. 41, X, V, 3.
[40] S. C. C., June 10, 1896 (*Coll. P. F.*, n. 1939).

[41] Layman, *l. c.*, n. 37; Suarez, *l. c.*, c. 14, n. 12.

PART I

THE SACRAMENTS

CAN. 731

§ 1. Cum omnia Sacramenta Novae Legis, a Christo Domino Nostro instituta, sint praecipua sanctificationis et salutis media, summa in iis opportune riteque administrandis ac suscipiendis diligentia et reverentia adhibenda est.

§ 2. Vetitum est Sacramenta Ecclesiae ministrare haereticis aut schismaticis, etiam bona fide errantibus eaque petentibus, nisi prius, erroribus reiectis, Ecclesiae reconciliati fuerint.

§ 1. As the Sacraments of the New Law, instituted by Christ our Lord, are the chief means of sanctification and salvation, the greatest care and reverence must be taken that they be suitably and properly administered and received.

The law is concerned mainly with the *administration* of the Sacraments. They must be administered *opportune et rite,* says our canon. *Opportune* refers not only to time and circumstances, but also to worthiness. Hence the minister must beware of two extremes: extreme severity and too great leniency. An instruction of the S. C. de Propaganda Fide [1] enjoins mercy and

1 April 29, 1784 (*Coll.*, n. 569).

kindness, especially towards the newly converted and those who live in places whither missionaries go but rarely. The clergy, though perhaps compelled to impose a public and protracted penance, should not deprive sinners, if really repentant, of the benefit of absolution, nor refuse them the Holy Eucharist. Besides, a distinction must be made between different crimes and criminals, especially if excommunication is involved, although the latter penalty renders them incapable of receiving the Sacraments. *Excommunicati tolerati* may be treated more leniently than *vitandi*.

Rite signifies, properly speaking, with due regard to the use of the rite prescribed. This point is treated more fully in can. 733. *Rite* may also refer to the *intention* of the minister and the recipient. This, according to the common teaching of theologians and canonists, must be *virtual, i. e.*, one which, though not present here and now, continues to exert its influence by virtue of an intention previously had and never retracted, on the part of the minister. On the part of the recipient, a *habitual* intention, *i. e.*, one that proceeds from the inclination of the mind and routine, but without actual reflection or even with distraction, suffices.[2]

But *rite* may also have another meaning, *viz., without simulation*. Simulation is an act by which one utters the form required over valid matter, but directly excludes the intention of effecting a Sacrament. This is strictly prohibited, and the contrary proposition, "Grave and urgent fear is a reason for simulating the Sacraments," has been formally condemned.[3] Entirely different from

---

[2] Cfr. Devoti, *Institut. Can.*, 1874, Vol. I, p. 319 f.; Lehmkuhl, *Theol. Moralis* II, n. 22; Marc, *Institut. Morales Alphonsianae*, II, 1412 ff.

[3] *Prop. dam. ab Innoc. XI*, March 4, 1679, n. 29 (Denzinger, *Enchiridion*, n. 1046).

fictitious or feigned administration is *dissimulation, i. e.,* the act of pretending to administer the Sacraments, which is rather a concealed refusal, and is not only licit, but at times may be necessary.[4]

On the care and reverence with which the Sacraments must be treated, we shall say what is necessary when dealing with the single Sacraments. The same holds good concerning juridically worthy reception. It must be remembered that we write on *law.*

§ 2 of our canon forbids the administration of the Sacraments to *heretics and schismatics,* even though they may be in good faith and ask for them. It is necessary that they first renounce their errors and become reconciled to the Church.

The penitential canons were rather strict on this subject.[5] Somewhat milder was the later theory as to those who relapsed into heresy and then repented; these were not to be denied penance and the Eucharist.[6]

The rules to be followed are these:

(a) *Before the age of fourteen, heretics and schismatics* must pronounce the profession of faith, but need not formally abjure heresy, provided, of course, they are sufficiently instructed in the Catholic faith. After that age, the profession of faith must be accompanied by abjuration of heresy or schism, otherwise they cannot be admitted to the Sacraments.[7]

(b) It is never permitted to absolve heretics or schismatics, even though they may never have thought of heresy or schism and profess to believe in only one Christian religion, in which they are ready to live and

4 Lehmkuhl, *l. c.,* II, n. 44 f.

5 C. 91, C. 24, q. 1, dictates one year of penance, if administered *nescienter;* ten, or seven, or five years if administered *scienter.*

6 C. 4, 6°, V, 2.

7 S. O., March 8, 1892 (*Coll. P. F.,* n. 2012).

die.[8] Such are merely material non-Catholics, but they cannot be absolved before making formal abjuration, if they have completed the fourteenth year of age.

(c) Such material heretics or schismatics may not be admitted to the Holy Eucharist, and no Catholic priest can absolve them or permit them to receive the Holy Eucharist in a schismatical temple.[9]

(d) Even in danger of death neither absolution nor the holy Viaticum can be administered to material heretics or schismatics, for instance, in a hospital, unless there is a solid presumption that they are members of the Catholic Church, or if they showed signs of willingness to be reconciled, but always under condition that the danger of scandal be removed.[10]

Of *apostate* Catholics it is required that they abjure their apostasy, and if they survive, they must make a written abjuration before the faithful, or at least permit the confessor to make their abjuration known to the faithful.[11]

(e) If persons who mix up with the faithful in church (soldiers, etc.) are suspected of heresy or schism, the Sacraments may be administered unto them only after they have given proof that they never had fallen away from the faith, or after formal abjuration.[12]

THE THREE SACRAMENTS WHICH CANNOT BE REPEATED

Can. 732

§ 1. Sacramenta baptismi, confirmationis et ordinis, quae characterem imprimunt, iterari nequeunt.

8 *Ibid.*

9 S. O., Aug. 28, 1669 (*Coll.*, n. 185).

10 S. O., Jan. 13, 1864 (*Coll.*, n. 1246).

11 S. O., July 25, 1630; May 7, 1822 (*Coll.*, nn. 57, 771).

12 S. O., July 30, 1806 (*Coll.*, n. 688).

§ 2. Si vero prudens dubium exsistat num revera vel num valide collata fuerint, sub conditione iterum conferantur.

The Sacraments of Baptism, Confirmation, and Holy Orders, which imprint a character, cannot be received twice — *i. e.,* absolutely; — but if a prudent doubt exists whether they were in fact, or whether they were validly conferred, they may be repeated.

The general rule is that if the matter and form required for these three sacraments have been properly applied by the respective minister, they are supposed and presumed to have been conferred validly.

As to the *intention* of the minister, all that is necessary is that he intends to do what the Church does, no matter what he may personally think or believe about the Sacraments,[13] and that he connects matter and form in such a way that the form may be referred to the matter and both constitute a specific act.

With regard to *Baptism* it is the rule, always insisted upon by the Roman Congregation, that *each single case must be investigated* when Baptism is to be conferred at all, or conditionally.[14] If there is no doubt that Baptism was never conferred, the Sacrament must be administered absolutely with the usual form: "*Ego te baptizo,*" etc. If the validity of a Baptism administered by non-Catholics is doubtful, the same rule must be followed. The rituals of the resp. sect should be examined and their customs observed, as stated under mixed marriages. Note that conditional Baptism is

---

13 Cfr. *Decretum pro Armenis;* S. C. P. F., June 23, 1830; S. O., Jan. 30, 1833 (*Coll. P. F.,* nn. 814, 830). The schismatic minister in this case, out of hatred for the Catholic Church, had no intention to baptize the children of Catholic parents, yet did everything correctly according to his own rite.

14 S. O., Nov. 20, 1878 (*Coll.,* n. 1504).

more easily admissible if no marriage is involved. For here the rule *baptismus est validus in ordine ad matrimonium* does not hold good. Therefore the golden mean must be observed: not too lenient and not too strict.[15] As to the *testimonies* in favor of the fact or validity of Baptism, see can. 779.

Indiscriminate rebaptizing of non-Catholics is not founded on the law,[16] though it may perhaps be called a safe theory, especially in our country, where there are so many sects which have discarded the doctrine that Baptism is necessary for salvation. But this holds good only in cases where no marriage is involved.

It is noteworthy that our Code has no *ruling as to irregularity being incurred by rebaptizing.* Hence this irregularity may now be regarded as abolished.

Concerning *Confirmation* there is not so much necessity or temptation for useless repetition. There are some decisions on this point, which, however, all concern schismatic confirmation. This is intelligible, because most heretical sects have thrown this Sacrament overboard. The general tenor of all the decisions *in casu* is that persons once confirmed by schismatic priests are not to be reconfirmed, unless they intend to receive tonsure and holy orders, or if they themselves or their parents ask for it, in which case Confirmation must be administered secretly and conditionally.[17] One decision, how-

---

15 S. C. P. F., June 23, 1830 (*Coll.*, n. 814).

16 The instruction just quoted mentions Calvinists, Presbyterians, and Anglicans, and apparently favors the validity of Calvinistic Baptism over that of the Anglicans and Presbyterians, who may therefore be more readily rebaptized.

17 S. O., July 5, 1853 (*Coll. P. F.*, n. 1095). This decision enjoins bishops to inquire whence the converts hail; if from Bulgaria, Cyprus, the Maronites of Mount Lebanon, Italy or the adjoining islands, absolute Confirmation is required; if from Walachia, Moldavia, or Asia, *acquiescent.*— Cfr. also S. O., March 16, 1872; April 2, 1879; January 14, 1885 (*Coll.*, nn. 1381, 1515, 1630).

ever, says that if Baptism was repeated conditionally, Confirmation should also be administered conditionally, to clergymen as well as laymen. The reason is, not that Confirmation is absolutely necessary, *necessitate medii*, but because the unconfirmed suffer a loss of perfection; although they would not be damned, unless perhaps by reason of contempt.[18]

As to Holy *Orders*, nothing need be said here, except that matter and form must be properly employed lest scruples arise and cases be proposed to the Holy Office, as we read of several.[19] The intention may be defective in the *ordinandus*. This happened in a certain seminarian, who had positively made up his mind not to be ordained, though he permitted the ceremonies to be performed over him. He had to be reordained privately and secretly.

RITES TO BE OBSERVED

CAN. 733

§ 1. In Sacramentis conficiendis, administrandis ac suscipiendis accurate serventur ritus et caeremoniae quae in libris ritualibus ab Ecclesia probatis praecipiuntur.

§ 2. Unusquisque autem ritum suum sequatur, salvo praescripto can. 851, § 2, 866.

In the celebration, administration, and reception of the Sacraments, the rites and ceremonies prescribed in the liturgical books approved by the Church must be accurately observed, and every one must follow his own rite, with due regard to canons 851, § 2, and 866.

18 S. O., June 20, 1866, *ad Gallas*, n. 40 (*Coll.*, n. 1293).

19 S. O., Sept. 7, 1892; Jan. 14,

July 6, 1898 (*Coll.*, nn. 1811, 1988, 2008); see can. 1007.

Conficere sacramentum means to effect or produce a Sacrament, to cause it to exist. As Christ our Lord is the efficient cause of the Sacraments, the word here signifies to produce a sacrament instrumentally, and is applied in its proper sense to the Holy Eucharist alone, because all the other Sacraments are effected or produced when *administered*. What *reception* means requires no explanation.[20]

Rites are the prayers which must be observed in the celebration of Mass and the administration of the Sacraments, or the formulas to be used according to the prescribed rule. *Ceremonies* are the gestures, acts, or bodily movements and signs which accompany the prescribed prayers, or the things over or with which the words are pronounced, such as blessings, lights, incense, vestments, and so forth.

The rites and ceremonies prescribed by the Church must be so observed that nothing is taken, or omitted from, or added to them. For they were introduced into the Church in order that the external worship of God might be performed with due reverence, that the sublime mysteries should appear more venerable, and that the faithful might be edified and their devotion enhanced.[21] This, however, does not mean that common sense or lawful custom [22] must be set aside. All that is necessary is that the essentials be strictly observed. On the other hand, *uniformity of ceremonies* — also among Regulars — is certainly an edifying spectacle. This is easily brought

20 *Trid.*, sess. 212, *de missae sacrif.*, c. 5; S. C. P. F., June 30, 1830 (*Coll.*, n. 817); Van der Stappen, *Sacra Liturgia*, 1898, t. 1, p. 3.

21 S. C. P. F., June 30, 1830 (*l. c.*).

22 Thus the S. Rit. C., Sept. 26, 1868 (*Dec. Auth.*, n. 3185) permitted a stole to be worn while preaching, if "custom permits." Sometimes futile doubts are proposed, especially to the S. Rit. C., whence the famous answer that the S. Congregation was not established for the purpose of fostering scruples.

about if all use and follow the *liturgical books approved by the Church*. These books, for the *Latin Rite*, are: (1) the *Missal*, which contains the rubrics for the proper celebration of Holy Mass; (2) the *Roman Ritual*, which contains the rites and prayers to be observed in the administration of the Sacraments and at other ecclesiastical functions; and (3) the *Roman Pontifical*, which contains the rites and prayers for episcopal functions. To the Latin Rite also belong the *Ambrosian Liturgy*, which is observed in some churches of the archdiocese of Milan, and the *Mozarabic Liturgy*, now observed only in one chapel of the Metropolitan Church of Toledo.[28]

§ 2 of canon 733 enacts that each one must *follow his own rite*. That the Roman Pontiffs were anxious to preserve the various rites is evident from the variety of Oriental liturgies. A variety of rites is not incompatible with unity of faith, nay it sheds new lustre and majesty upon the Church and proves her readiness to admit reasonable customs. The main *Oriental Liturgies* are:

(1) The *Greek*, based on the so-called liturgies of SS. Basil and John Chrysostom. It has two branches: the *pure Greek*, used at Athens and Constantinople and by Italian Greeks; the *Greek Rumenian*, the *Greek Ruthenian*, the *Greek Bulgarian*, and the *Melchite*, which latter is employed by the Patriarch of Antioch and his suffragans.

(2) The *Syrian*, which is the Syrian translation of the Antiochene and is used by the Syrian Patriarch of Antioch and his suffragans, by the Syro-Chaldæan Patriarch of Babylon and his suffragans, by the Syro-Maronite Patriarch of Antioch, and the adherents of the Malabar or Syro-Sorian Rite.

---

28 Van der Stappen, *l. c.*, p. 20 f.

(3) The *Armenian,* chiefly borrowed from the Greek and in use among the Armenians of Cilicia, Alexandria, Artum in Russia, and Lemberg in Galicia.

(4) The *Coptic,* which is in vogue in Egypt (Coptic-Egyptian) and Abyssinia (Coptic-Ethiopian).[24]

Some decisions may here find a place. If *children of both rites are to be baptized* in the same church, the Greek priest may validly baptize his subjects with water blessed according to the Greek rite, nor is he to be molested if he does not use water blessed according to the Latin rite. But the Ordinaries should see to it that baptismal water is kept in all churches blessed according to the Latin rite, and the Latin priests must use this water when baptizing their subjects, except in case of necessity.[25]

An Armenian or a Maronite priest may distribute Holy Communion which has been consecrated in unleavened bread, but he must use the language and ceremonies of his own (Armenian or Maronite) rite.[26] (Cfr. also can. 866.)

Priests of the Oriental Rite must make use of their own formulas and language in *absolving* faithful of the Latin Rite.[27]

THE HOLY OILS

CAN. 734

§ 1. Sacra olea quae quibusdam Sacramentis administrandis inserviunt, debent esse ab Episcopo benedicta feria V *in Coena Domini* proxime superiore; neque adhibeantur vetera, nisi necessitas urgeat.

24 Van der Stappen, *l. c.,* I, 18 f.
25 Benedict XIV, "*Etsi pastoralis,*" May 26, 1742, § II, n. VI.
26 S. C. P. F., April 30, 1866 (*Coll.,* n. 1288); cfr. can. 851, § 2.

27 S. O., Sept. 6, 1865 (*Coll.,* n. 1275). The form of the Greek Rite is either the subjunctive or the optative (*forma deprecatoria*), but never the indicative mood.

§ 2. Mox deficienti oleo benedicto aliud oleum de olivis non benedictum adiiciatur, etiam iterato, minore tamen copia.

CAN. 735

Parochus olea sacra a suo Ordinario petere debet et in ecclesia in tuta ac decenti custodia sub clavi diligenter asservare; nec ea domi retineat, nisi propter necessitatem aliamve rationabilem causam, accedente Ordinarii licentia.

The Holy Oils to be used in the administration of the Sacraments of Baptism, Confirmation, Extreme Unction, and Holy Orders, must be blessed by the bishop on Holy Thursday of each year, and old ones may not be used except in case of urgent necessity. Should the blessed oil be about to give out, other olive oil that is not blessed may be added, even repeatedly, but in smaller quantities than the holy oil.

Each pastor must ask his Ordinary for the holy oils and keep them in a safe and becoming place under lock and key in church. He may not keep them in his house except in case of necessity, or for some other plausible reason, and only by special consent of the Ordinary.

The custom of *renewing the holy oils* and chrism is ancient, even if we prescind from the spurious document which Gratian [28] (or rather Pseudo-Isidore) ascribes to Pope Fabian (236-250). The text of our canon is taken from the Roman Pontifical and Ritual. Cases in which the use of old oils is permitted, according to Benedict XIV, are: if there be no Catholic bishop near at hand, because priests are not allowed to receive the holy oils from a schismatic bishop; if the distance be so great

---

[28] C. 18, Dist. 3, *de cons.;* cfr. c. 12, X, III, 1.

that the oils can not arrive in time; or if there be any other impediment.[29] As to distance, one decision declares that a month's waiting would be sufficient.[30] This may happen in turbulent times, or when a serious strike interrupts communication. In future no special indult [31] is required for using the old oils if the case of necessity is verified. The law itself grants the right.

The renewal of the holy oils must be understood of the *blessing,* not of the oils themselves, as if the oils would have to be of the same year in which the blessing is given. It is the mystery that is to be renewed, not the oil.[32] Should it happen that a priest has not received the holy oils and must administer Baptism, he may use the old oils; he must not omit the anointment in order to supply that ceremony later with the oils recently received.[33]

§ 2 of can. 734 is plain enough. The addition of unblessed olive oil is permitted only in case of necessity. It is not permitted to bless part of the oil on Holy Thursday and mix this with unblessed oil immediately after.[34] The mixture should not exceed the proportion of 3:2, *i. e.,* only one-third of common olive oil may be added.

Can. 735 rules that the pastors must obtain the Holy Oils from *their own Ordinary.* This is an acknowledgment of the Ordinary's jurisdiction and their own dependence and shows the organization of the diocese. The old canons [35] already insisted upon this rule. Benedict XIV enjoined the Greek priests to receive the Holy

---

29 " *Anno vertente,*" June 19, 1750, § 5.

30 S. C. P. F., July 5, 1841 (*Coll.,* n. 924).

31 S. C. P. F., Sept. 27, 1835 (*Coll.,* n. 840) mentions an indult.

32 S. C. P. F., Aug. 13, 1669 (*Coll.,* n. 183); S. Rit. C., March 22, 1862, ad V (*Dec. Auth.,* n. 3114).

33 S. Rit. C., Sept. 23, 1837 (*Dec. Auth.,* n. 2773).

34 S. Rit. C., Dec. 7, 1844 (*Dec. Auth.,* n. 2882).

35 C. 122, Dist. 4, *de cons.*

Oils from their own, not from a schismatic, bishop, or from the Latin Ordinary under whose jurisdiction they are placed.[86]

As to the *keeping of the Holy Oils*, in our country the custom of keeping them in the rectory is rather widespread. It is safe to assert, however, that the S. Cong. of Rites would not approve of this custom, except where there are special reasons for it. Such a reason would be great distance between church and parsonage.[87] But the mere fact that the church is separated from the rectory has never been acknowledged as a sufficient reason.[88] The custom, however, is not formally reprobated in our text. If the Holy Oils are kept in the house, it goes without saying that a decent and becoming place must be set aside for the purpose.[89]

NO UNLAWFUL EXACTIONS PERMITTED

CAN. 736

Pro administratione Sacramentorum minister nihil quavis de causa vel occasione sive directe sive indirecte exigat aut petat, praeter oblationes de quibus in can. 1507, § 1.

What is here stated must be taken in the light of what has been said concerning simony, and be compared with can. 1507, § 1, which provides that the stole fees should be regulated by a provincial council or meeting of the bishops, whose enactments are to be submitted to the Holy See. Besides the fees thus established, says the present canon, the minister of a Sacrament is not allowed

---

86 "*Etsi pastoralis*," May 26, 1742, § IV.

87 S. Rit. C., Dec. 16, 1826 (*Dec. Auth.*, n. 2650).

88 S. Rit. C., June 23, 1892 (*Dec. Auth.*, n. 3779) and *passim*.

89 S. Rit. C., Dec. 16, 1826 (*Dec. Auth.*, n. 2650).

to charge or demand anything, for whatever motive or on whatsoever occasion, either directly by exaction, or indirectly by insinuation, for the administration of a Sacrament.

TITLE I

BAPTISM

Can. 737

§ 1. Baptismus, Sacramentorum ianua ac fundamentum, omnibus in re vel saltem in voto necessarius ad salutem, valide non confertur, nisi per ablutionem aquae verae et naturalis cum praescripta verborum forma.

§ 2. Cum ministratur servatis omnibus ritibus et caeremoniis quae in ritualibus libris praecipiuntur, appellatur *sollemnis;* secus, *non sollemnis* seu *privatus.*

Baptism is called the *gate to, and the foundation of, the other Sacraments,* because without it no other Sacrament can be validly received. The Church has ever taught that Baptism is absolutely necessary for salvation, — either really or by desire [1]— and that consequently no other sacrament can be validly received without it. Thus ordination would be invalid and imprint no indelible character if the *ordinandus* had not been baptized.[2] This necessity of Baptism is called *necessitas medii,* necessity of means, because without it salvation cannot be obtained. The reason for this absolute necessity [3] lies in the words of Our Lord, John III, 5. Either *in re* or *in voto* signifies that the *baptismus fluminis* or *flaminis* or *sanguinis* is sufficient.

[1] C. 3, C. 15, q. 1; cfr. Dist. 4, de cons.

[2] Cc. 1, 3, X, III, 43.

[3] "*Lamentabili,*" July 4, 1907, prop. damn., n. 42.

33

Baptism is *validly conferred*, the text further says, by *ablution with true and natural water combined with the prescribed form of words*. Here matter and form are clearly stated. The *matter* is true and natural water.[4] Water is *true* if no doubt exists as to its aqueous quality. A very thin liquor, the sap of trees, water made of rose leaves, etc., would be dubious. *Natural* water is that taken from wells, cisterns, ponds, rivers, or gained from ice, snow, drizzle, also mineral water.[5] Water mixed with ingredients that change its nature cannot be validly used.[6] A mixture of one part of chloride of mercury with two parts of natural water may be validly, and, in case of necessity, especially to spare a mother pains, licitly employed.[7]

The water must be applied in the form of an *ablution*, which is called *the proximate matter*. This is done either by pouring the water over the head or forehead of the one to be baptized, or by immersing him in the water (pond or river), or by sprinkling (*aspersio*) his head. In the Catholic Church pouring (*infusio*) is more common, at least in our country, although immersion and aspersion, too, are perfectly legitimate.[8] The water must touch the skin, not the hair only, of the head. If the head cannot be reached, some other principal part of the body,— chest, neck, hand or arm,— must be touched. In case of extreme necessity a wet sponge or rag may be used.[9]

The essential thing in the application of the matter is

---

[4] *Decretum pro Armen.* (Denzinger, n. 591); *Rit. Rom.*, tit. II, c. 1, n. 3.

[5] Cfr. Lehmkuhl, *l. c.*, II, n. 58 f.

[6] S. O., Nov. 8, 1770; July 9, 1779 (*Coll.*, nn. 480, 536).

[7] S. O., Aug. 21, 1901 (*Coll.*, n. 2121).

[8] *Rit. Rom., l. c.* n. 10.

[9] S. O., Nov. 8, 1770; July 9, 1779 (*Coll.*, nn. 480, 536); to apply the water in the form of a drink renders baptism invalid; *ibid.*

that the ablution is verified and signified. This may be done with a greater or lesser quantity of water, though one drop could hardly be said to express ablution.

The *form* of baptism is: "I baptize thee in the name of the Father, and of the Son, and of the Holy Ghost." These words must be pronounced simultaneously with the application of the water, without repetition or mutilation,[10] in the present tense indicative, though the imperative form is also valid; for instance, "*Baptizetur*," or "*Baptizare talis*," or "*Baptizet manus mea in nomine*," etc. But to use the perfect tense in order to signify a present action ("*Baptizatus est talis*") would render the ceremony invalid, unless the minister would not be aware of using the wrong tense, or if the language of the respective nation would permit the use of the perfect tense to signify a present action.[11] Mere slips of the tongue do not render the formula invalid. The forms: "I will administer unto thee the sacrament of baptism of sins in the name, etc.,"[12] has been declared invalid. Also the form: "*Ego te lavo nomine Patris, et Primogeniti, et Spiritus Sancti*." The form: "*Ego te lavo in nomine Patris, et Filii et Spiritus Sancti*,"[13] on the contrary, is valid, as is also the form which substitutes for "*Spiritus Sancti*," "*Spiritus boni*" or "*sacri*."[14]

§ 2 defines *solemn* and private or *non-solemn Baptism*. The former is administered with all the rites and ceremonies prescribed in the liturgical books. Where these are not employed, the Baptism is called *private*. The essential form remains the same, but there is a difference

10 *Prop. dam. ab Alex. VIII*, Dec. 7, 1690, n. 27 (Denz., n. 1184).

11 S. O., Sept. 8, 1633; S. C. P. F., March 27, 1631 (*Coll.*, nn. 74, 68).

12 S. O., June 23, 1840 (*Coll.*, n. 901).

13 S. O., Feb. 17, 1897 (*Coll.*, n. 1959).

14 S. O., April 30, 1904 (*Coll.*, n. 2191); for Japanese forms, see *Coll.*, n. 1323.

in the matter, in as much as for solemn baptism water especially blessed either on Holy Saturday or the Saturday preceding Whitsunday must be used.

Note that if a baptismal font can be kept neither in church nor in a private house, and no baptismal water can be gotten, natural water must be used rather than holy water.[15] Should the baptismal water have become putrid, natural (not holy) water should be used, although Baptism conferred with putrid water would be valid.[16]

[15] S. O., April 6, 1741; S. C. P. F., April 17, 1758 (*Coll.*, nn. 325, 411).

[16] S. O., April 17, 1839 (*Coll.*, n. 885).

CHAPTER I

THE ORDINARY MINISTER

CAN. 738

§ 1. Minister ordinarius baptismi sollemnis est sacerdos; sed eius collatio reservatur parocho vel alii sacerdoti de eiusdem parochi vel Ordinarii loci licentia, quae in casu necessitatis legitime praesumitur.

§ 2. Etiam peregrinus a parocho proprio in sua paroecia sollemniter baptizetur, si id facile et sine mora fieri potest; secus peregrinum quilibet parochus in suo territorio potest sollemniter baptizare.

CAN. 739

In alieno territorio nemini licet, sine debita licentia, baptismum sollemnem conferre ne sui quidem loci incolis.

CAN. 740

Ubi paroeciae aut quasi-paroeciae nondum sunt constitutae, statutorum peculiarium et receptarum consuetudinum ratio habenda est, ut constet cuinam sacerdoti, praeter Ordinarium, in universo territorio vel in eius parte ius insit baptizandi.

These three canons treat of the *ordinary minister* of the Sacrament of Baptism. He is, can. 738 says, the

37

priest, with regard to solemn Baptism. The reason is that by virtue of ordination the priest has received the power to confer this Sacrament.

But, continues the text, the right of baptizing is reserved to the *pastor* or another priest commissioned either by him or by the local Ordinary. In a case where the canons of a cathedral church had obtained from their Ordinary permission to baptize, the custom was declared legitimate, provided the stole fees were turned over to the Archpriest.[1] The Vicar-General may baptize without the consent of his Ordinary, provided the latter has not limited that power.[2] The Roman Congregations have insisted that Ordinaries should but rarely and only for urgent reasons give permission to priests who are not pastors to baptize,[3] because this is a strictly parochial right. Yet our canon says that in case of necessity *permission may be lawfully presumed*. A case of necessity — not convenience or friendship or relationship — would exist if a child were ill, if the priest visited a mission only at long intervals, if the distance from the parish house amounted to several miles, etc. But attention must be drawn to can. 463, § 3, concerning the duty of refunding the stole fee.

§ 2 concerns the case of *peregrini, i. e.*, persons who reside outside their own domicile or quasi-domicile, without, however, having given it up.[4] Such a person should be solemnly baptized by his own pastor in his own parish, if it can be easily and conveniently done; if not, any other pastor may solemnly baptize such a *peregrinus* in his own parochial district. If the *peregrinus* is a baby,

1 S. Rit. C., May 9, 1606 (*Dec. Auth.*, n. 213).

2 S. Rit. C., April 16, 1639 (*Dec. Auth.*, n. 672).

3 S. C. C., Sept. 27, 1687; Feb. 21, 1888; S. C. EE. et RR., Aug. 21, 1580; Dec. 14, 1604.

4 Can. 91.

the domicile or quasi-domicile of the father, or in case of an illegitimate or a posthumous child, that of the mother is decisive.[5] Hence a child born outside the parish in which his father or mother have their domicile or quasi-domicile, should be brought to the pastor of the father's or mother's parish, but only in case it can be done easily and without delay. *Easily* may be taken to mean without expense or conveniently. A distance of three leagues, or about thirteen miles, some[6] say, would excuse. However, now-a-days an automobile may easily be had, and travels smoothly, at least over good roads. The physical condition of the child, too, must be considered. *Sine mora*, without delay, must be understood according to can. 770, which says: *quam primum*, as soon as possible.

Can. 739 rules that neither the pastor nor another priest may solemnly baptize, even his own parishioners or subjects, in a *district not his own, unless he has obtained proper permission*. To do so would be setting aside all local organization. Of course the Ordinary and his vicar general may baptize anywhere in the diocese, but if he wishes to baptize one living outside his diocese, he needs the permission of the respective local Ordinary. This permission is required also when one of his diocesan subjects gives birth to a child in another diocese. The same rule applies to pastors and other priests who, when outside their own district, are asked to baptize one belonging to that district by reason of domicile or quasi-domicile.

Can. 740 provides for *parishes or quasi-parishes not yet established*. In such cases special statutes and prevailing customs must be observed, in order to make sure which priest, besides the Ordinary, is entitled to baptize either in the whole territory or in a particular district

---

5 Can. 90, § 1.   6 Lehmkuhl, *l. c.*, II, n. 66.

thereof. We could find no diocesan regulations[7] on this head by either the Baltimore Councils or any other American council or synod. The text is plain enough, alluding as it does to can. 216 on the establishment of regular parishes or quasi-parishes; where there are no diocesan statutes regulating the matter, custom must be followed, and the custom is that the *sacerdos excurrens* baptizes the children of his station or mission and is entitled to the fees.

But what about *linguistically distinguished parishes?* If the children belong to parents who are members of a, say German or Italian parish, there is no doubt as to the right of the pastor of that parish to baptize them. But there are doubtful cases, such as this: A couple moves into a parish, and before they have decided what parish to join, a baby is born to them. The Italian pastor is asked to baptize the child, because the mother is an Italian and would rather belong to the Italian congregation, whereas the father, though also of Italian descent, cares for no parish at all. In that case, we believe, the Italian pastor would be entitled to baptize the child and keep the fee. The pastor of the English speaking congregation could not claim the mother, nor could he insist upon territorial rights, because we suppose that the Italian parish lies within the limits of the English speaking congregation. But suppose an Italian mother comes to the pastor of a *German* speaking congregation, which is within the boundaries of an English speaking congregation, and begs the German pastor to baptize her child, either because he speaks Italian or is personally known to the family. Is the German pastor bound to refuse her request? We hardly think so, because, by reason of the

---

[7] At least the *Collectio Lacensis,* which we perused, seems to contain no such regulations.

territory or parochial district, he may claim as much right as the English pastor, and as far as pastoral rights go, he is as much entitled to perform the ceremony as the English pastor. However, if an Italian congregation is near, the English as well as the German pastor should tell the woman to go to the Italian pastor.

What about a *convert* who has been instructed by the pastor of a German congregation? He is an American of other than German ancestry, while his wife belongs to the German nationality. Or perhaps he is not yet married. In both cases we believe that, in justice, the pastor who instructed the convert is also entitled to baptize him, no matter whether he has a wife of German descent or is unmarried, because the pastor of the English speaking congregation cannot claim anyone as his subject before Baptism. This we say conditionally, *i. e.*, provided there are no diocesan regulations or lawful customs to the contrary.

EXTRAORDINARY MINISTERS

CAN. 741

Extraordinarius baptismi sollemnis minister est diaconus; qui tamen sua potestate ne utatur sine loci Ordinarii vel parochi licentia, iusta de causa concedenda, quae, ubi necessitas urgeat, legitime praesumitur.

CAN. 742

§ 1. Baptismus non sollemnis, de quo in can. 759, § 1, potest a quovis ministrari, servata debita materia, forma et intentione; quatenus vero fieri potest, adhibeantur duo testes, vel saltem unus, quibus baptismi collatio probari possit.

§ 2. Si tamen adsit sacerdos, diacono praeferatur, diaconus subdiacono, clericus laico et vir feminae, nisi pudoris gratia deceat feminam potius quam virum baptizare, vel nisi femina noverit melius formam et modum baptizandi.

§ 3. Patri aut matri suam prolem baptizare non licet, praeterquam in mortis periculo, quando alius praesto non est, qui baptizet.

The deacon is the extraordinary minister of solemn baptism, but he should not use this power without the permission of the local Ordinary or pastor, to be granted for a just reason; in case of necessity this permission may be lawfully presumed.

Hence a deacon, by virtue of his ordination,[8] may employ all the ceremonies and rites prescribed for the administration of Baptism by the Roman Ritual. However, as ecclesiastical legislation[9] has reserved this right to the pastor, the deacon is not the ordinary minister of the Sacrament of Baptism, but needs the permission of the Ordinary in whose diocese, or of the pastor in whose parish, he wishes to baptize. In case of necessity this permission need not be asked for. A case in point occurs in the Decree of Gratian,[10] where the " necessity " arose through absence of, or long distance from, the bishop or priest. The reasons mentioned in can. 738 would also be sufficient.

Can. 742, § 1, rules that, in case of *danger of death, private baptism may be administered by anyone,* provided he or she uses the proper matter and form and has the

[8] *Pontif. Rom.,* " *De ordinatione diaconi:*" " *Oportet ergo diaconum . . . baptizare,*" with a reference to Acts VIII, 12.

[9] C. 13, Dist. 93; c. 19, Dist. 4, de cons.
[10] *Ibid.*

right intention. Wherever possible, two witnesses should be called, or at least one, to testify to the act.

The first part of this paragraph embodies an article of faith,[11] and consequently binds the Greek as well as the Latin Church.[12]

The *rite* to be observed in administering Baptism privately consists in pouring natural water (not blessed) over the head of the subject, simultaneously pronouncing the words: " I baptize thee in the name of the Father, and of the Son, and of the Holy Ghost." The *intention* must be to " do what the Church does," no matter what one may believe about the Church. A superstitious intent or purpose does not necessarily exclude the right intention.[13] In the way described anyone may baptize, but only in *case of necessity,* or danger of death, as can. 759, § 1, explains. The phrase " danger of death " may be taken in a pretty wide sense, for several decisions of the Roman Court have approved the custom of baptizing privately if the missionary is absent for more than eight days,[14] or if there is danger that a baby may be smothered because placed in the same bed with his parents.[15]

§ 2 determines the order of precedence to be followed according to the Roman Ritual.[16] If a priest is present, he should be preferred to a deacon; a deacon to a subdeacon; a clergyman to a layman; a man to a woman (unless decency would demand preference for the woman or unless the woman knows the form and manner of baptizing better than the man).

11 *Trid.,* Sess. 7, can. 4, *de bapt.*
12 Benedict XIV, *" Nuper ad nos,"* March 16, 1743, § 6: *Forma professionis Maronitis praescripta.*
13 S. O., Sept. 19, 1671 (*Coll. P. F.,* n. 201). A mother was told by another woman to baptize her child in order to avoid future pregnancy.
14 S. C. P. F., Jan. 16, 1804; Sept. 11, 1841 (*Coll.,* nn. 674, 939).
15 S. C. P. F., Jan. 21, 1788 (*Coll.,* n. 593).
16 Tit. II, c. 1, n. 13.

A suspended or interdicted priest may never baptize
solemnly, but only privately.[17]   But since the question
here turns about private baptism, even a suspended priest
would have to be preferred to a deacon, etc.   Schismatic
monks may privately baptize only when there is no Catholic person at hand.[18]

§ 3 provides that *father or mother are not allowed to
baptize their own child* except there be case of danger of
death and no one else is at hand who could baptize *(qui
baptizet)*, *i. e.*, who is capable and willing to baptize.
Incapable would be, *e. g.*, a bigotted Baptist who does
not believe in infant baptism and, moreover, flatly refuses
to perform the ceremony.

Can. 743

**Curet parochus ut fideles, praesertim obstetrices,
medici et chirurgi, rectum baptizandi modum pro casu
necessitatis probe ediscant.**

The pastor shall take care that the faithful, especially
midwives, physicians, and surgeons, are thoroughly instructed in the manner of administering Baptism in
cases of emergency.[19]   For this purpose some special lec-
tures would be helpful.   The subject may also be mentioned at retreats.

BAPTISM OF ADULTS

Can. 744

**Adultorum baptismus, ubi commode fieri possit, ad
loci Ordinarium deferatur, ut, si voluerit, ab eo vel ab
eius delegato sollemnius conferatur.**

[17] S. C. P. F., Jan. 21, 1789
(*Coll.*, n. 598).
[18] S. O., Aug. 20, 1671 (*Coll.*, n. 198).

[19] S. C. P. F., Sept. 11, 1841
(*Coll.*, n. 939): especially intelli-
gent laymen and catechists.

When adults are to be baptized, the local Ordinary should be notified, if it can be done conveniently, in order that, if he so desires, he himself or a priest delegated by him may administer the Sacrament more solemnly.   No strict obligation can be read into this canon, as is evident from the term *deferatur* as well as from the subjunctive form employed.

CHAPTER II

CAN. 745

§ 1. Subiectum capax baptismi est omnis et solus homo viator, nondum baptizatus.

§ 2. Cum agitur de baptismo:

1.° Parvulorum seu infantium nomine veniunt, ad normam can. 88, § 3, qui nondum rationis usum adepti sunt, eisdemque accensentur amentes ab infantia, in quavis aetate constituti;

2.° Adulti autem censentur, qui rationis usu fruuntur, idque satis est ut suo quisque animi motu baptismum petat et ad illum admittatur.

Three conditions are required for the valid reception of Baptism: the subject must be a human being living and in the wayfaring state, and not previously baptized (*nondum baptizatus*). If these three conditions are verified, it matters nothing whether the subject be male or female, white, black or red, young or old, rich or poor, high or low (*omnis homo*). The reason is the absolute necessity of Baptism for wiping away original sin.[1] The limitation expressed in "*solus*" is based upon the same doctrine, but has a wider scope, inasmuch as there may be a doubt concerning deformed or doubtful human creatures, as will be seen in the following.

[1] C. 3, Majores, X, III, 42; *Trid.*, sess. 5, can. 3, *de peccato orig.;* sess. 7, can. 12 f., *de baptismo.*

§ 2 of can. 745 says that with *regard to Baptism, parvuli* or *infantes* (infants) are those who have not yet attained the use of reason,[2] and also those who have been insane from infancy, of whatsoever age they may be; whereas the term *adulti* (adults) comprises all who enjoy the use of reason; which qualification is sufficient to enable them to ask for Baptism of their own accord and to be admitted to it. *Infancy,* as a rule, is completed after the seventh year has been reached.[3] However this age limit must not be urged with regard to Baptism. It is no more than a guiding norm which permits presuming the use of reason. If this is attained earlier the child may be baptized even against the will of his parents.[4] If, on the other hand, the use of reason has not been attained after the seventh year, the subject must be treated as an infant. Generally speaking, however, the use of reason may be presumed after the seventh year unless certain signs point to its absence or there is at least room for a solid doubt.

On the same level with infants are those who have been *insane from infancy* (see canon 754). Medical authorities[5] say that insanity is a common condition, but it has not been satisfactorily defined. It supposes an appreciable unsoundness of the will, memory, and understanding, or of any one or two of these faculties. Where shall the line be drawn between the weak but responsible will and the insane will? What degree of opacity between intellect and cosmos separates the ignorant man from the lunatic? The extremes of both sanity and insanity are readily recognizable, but the intermediate de-

2 Can. 88, § 3.

3 S. O. Sept. 3, 1877; S. C. P. F., March 3, 1703 (*Coll.,* nn. 1480, 255).

4 Benedict XIV, " *Postremo mense,*" Feb. 28, 1747, n. 32.

5 Cfr. O'Malley-Walsh, *Essays in Pastoral Medicine,* 1911, pp. 106, 212 ff.

grees are often hard to perceive. There is no rule that may be applied to all cases; each must be diagnosed from its peculiar symptoms. The symptoms of idiopathic insanity — a phrase which medical men use to conceal their ignorance of the cause of the disease — are not readily recognizable unless looked for especially. Besides almost any form of mania is likely to recur. We are told that among a thousand cases of acute mania only one was observed in which the symptoms did not recur. These professional statements may give the priest a hint as to the treatment of such unfortunate patients. Concerning Baptism we shall see under can. 754 an Instruction of the S. C. Propaganda, which is in keeping with these statements.

Adults is here simply used to designate those who enjoy the actual and habitual use of reason, without regard to a fixed age limit. All such persons, if they ask for Baptism of their own accord, may be baptized, even against the will of their parents, because the divine does not depend on the human law.[6]

THE WAYFARING STATE

Can. 746

§ 1. Nemo in utero matris clausus baptizetur, donec probabilis spes sit ut rite editus baptizari possit.

§ 2. Si infans caput emiserit et periculum mortis immineat, baptizetur in capite; nec postea, si vivus evaserit, est iterum sub conditione baptizandus.

§ 3. Si aliud membrum emiserit, in illo, si periculum immineat, baptizetur sub conditione; at tunc, si natus vixerit, est rursus sub conditione baptizandus.

§ 4. Si mater praegnans mortua fuerit, fetus ab iis

6 Benedict XIV, " *Postremo mense,*" n. 32.

ad quos spectat extractus, si certo vivat, baptizetur absolute; si dubie, sub conditione.

§ 5. Fetus, in utero baptizatus, post ortum denuo sub conditione baptizari debet.

Can. 747

Curandum ut omnes fetus abortivi, quovis tempore editi, si certo vivant, baptizentur absolute; si dubie, sub conditione.

Can. 748

Monstra et ostenta semper baptizentur saltem sub conditione; in dubio autem unusne an plures sint homines, unus absolute baptizetur, ceteri sub conditione.

One essential condition for the administration of Baptism is that the subject be born,[7] not only conceived, *i. e.,* an individual subsisting by itself and no longer *enclosed in the womb*. No one enclosed in the maternal womb can be baptized, as long as there is a probable hope that he may be properly brought forth and then baptized. The decisions referred to by Cardinal Gasparri merely state that a baby, no part of whose body has been brought forth, and which was conditionally baptized with a syringe, must be rebaptized conditionally.[8] There is no word about *rite editus,* but about "*reserato materni uteri ostio,*" in which case conditional Baptism would have to be conferred.

§ 2 says that if the infant puts forth his head, he may

---

[7] John 3, 5: "*nisi quis renatus fuerit.*"

[8] S. C. C., July 12, 1797, referred to by S. C. C., March 16, 1897, reads: "*Servetur decretum S. C. Concilii diei 12 Julii 1794, viz: Si reserato materni uteri ostio, infans cujus corpusculi nulla pars adhuc in lucem prodivit, per siphunculum piaculari lavacro sub conditione fuerit tinctus, postquam ille natus fuerit, Baptismus erit sub conditione iterandus.*" (Cfr. Coll. P. F., n. 1962).

be baptized on the head, and shall not be rebaptized conditionally if he survives.

§ 3 provides that if he puts forth some other limb than the head, he may be conditionally baptized on this limb if there be danger; but in that case he must be rebaptized conditionally if he survives.

According to § 4, if a mother dies in pregnancy, the fetus, after being extracted by those who are obliged to perform that act, should be baptized absolutely if certainly alive, conditionally if there are only doubtful signs of life.

§ 5 declares that a fetus baptized in the mother's womb must be rebaptized conditionally after birth.

The last two sections call for some medico-pastoral remarks. The duration of pregnancy, from the fertilization of the ovum to full-term delivery is 280 days. This period is divided either into 10 months of twenty-eight days each — a lunar month — or into nine calendar months. During the first week the ovum remains in the Fallopian tube. Having entered the upper part of the tube and become impregnated, it slowly moves down, meanwhile beginning a process of repeated division or cleavage, known as the "*segmentation of the ovum*." After the sixth week the name *fetus* is applied to what was before called *embryo*, because after the sixth week the form is distinctly human. The greatest danger of miscarriage occurs at three months. In the course of the fourth month the sex can readily be distinguished. A fetus born at the termination of the sixth month may breathe feebly, but will die within a few hours.[9] When does animation take place? At the moment when the

9 Crusius, A. M., M. D., *The Antikamnia Foetation and Parturition Chart*; Kirke, *Handbook of*   *Physiology*, 8th Am. edit., 1914, p. 747 f.

pronucleus of the spermatozoon fuses with the pronucleus of the ovum in the Fallopian tube and makes the segmentation nucleus, the soul of the child enters, and personality exists as absolutely as it does after birth.[10] This, as we have said above, happens during the first week of pregnancy. It may be added that the fact that a fetus does not breathe is no proof it is dead. It is not unusual for a full-term child not to breathe for an hour or longer after birth.[11] These are valuable hints for those concerned. Who are they? After the mother's death, when the Cæsarean section is not only permissible, but required in order to baptize the child or fetus, a surgeon is to be called in to perform the operation. He should not be easily believed if he asserts that the child is dead. In that case any one else who has the skill and courage to extract the fetus may be invited, provided it is not against the law.[12] Whether the fetus is *certainly alive* can be discovered by diagnosis in the earlier stages of pregnancy, and by breathing in the later stages, although, as stated above, non-breathing is not an absolute proof of death. At any rate, as long as putrefaction has not set in, conditional baptism is to be administered.

We have deliberately abstained from passing judgment on the vexed question of the licitness of the Cæsarian section, as § 4 of can. 746 simply takes for granted the fact of the mother's death, and therefore leaves the controversy *in statu quo.*[13]

Can. 747 declares that all abortive human fetuses, if certainly alive, should be baptized absolutely; if it is doubtful whether they are alive or dead, Baptism should be administered conditionally.

---

10 O'Malley-Walsh, *l. c.*, p. 3.
11 *Ibid.*, p. 11.
12 Lehmkuhl, *l. c.*, II, n. 75.

13 Cfr. *Am. Eccl. Rev.*, Vol. 9; Lehmkuhl, *l. c.*, I, n. 844, 849; O'Malley-Walsh, *l. c.*, p. 11.

Can. 748 lays down the rule concerning the treatment of *monsters, i. e.,* misshaped human terata or products of erroneous development. Of such there are various kinds. Some of the autositic monstra show a strong resemblance to lower animals, but there is no record that could claim to be scientific of a hybrid between a human being and a lower animal. The omphalisitic single monsters are either dead when born, or die as soon as the placental circulation is cut off. The composite monsters, or species of twins, have various types according to the various combinations of the limbs: double-faced, double-headed, two-armed, etc.[14]

Such *monstra,* says the text, should always be baptized, at least conditionally. When there is doubt whether there are one or several persons, one must be baptized absolutely, the others conditionally.

There is no difficulty as to hermaphrodites, because sex does not affect the validity of Baptism.

Can. 749

Infantes expositi et inventi nisi, re diligenter investigata, de eorum baptismo constet, sub conditione baptizentur.

Infants that have been abandoned and found should be baptized conditionally, unless careful research makes it evident that the Sacrament has already been administered to them. One trustworthy witness, man or woman, especially the baptized subject himself, is sufficient to give evidence of Baptism having been conferred.[15] A slip of paper appended to the neck of the child is not

---

14 O'Malley-Walsh, *l. c.,* p. 69 ff.
15 S. C. C., Dec. 18, 1723; Jan.

15, 1724; Benedict XIV, "*Postremo mense,*" Feb. 28, 1747, n. 31.

sufficient proof if the writer is unknown or hidden,[16] and when there is no other evidence, conditional baptism must be administered.

CHILDREN OF INFIDELS

CAN. 750

§ 1. Infans infidelium, etiam invitis parentibus, licite baptizatur, cum in eo versatur vitae discrimine, ut prudenter praevideatur moriturus, antequam usum rationis attingat.

§ 2. Extra mortis periculum, dummodo catholicae eius educationi cautum sit, licite baptizatur:

1.° Si parentes vel tutores, aut saltem unus eorum, consentiant;

2.° Si parentes, idest pater, mater, avus, avia, vel tutores desint, aut ius in eum amiserint, vel illud exercere nullo pacto queant.

The Church has always insisted upon the necessity of Baptism and the fulfillment of the baptismal vows, which require an education that is in keeping with the principles of the Christian religion. On the other hand she wishes to uphold and recognize the natural rights of parents, and hence she does not permit Baptism to be indiscriminately administered to infants.

§ 1 of our canon repeats what Benedict XIV pointed out so clearly, that the children of infidels may *be lawfully baptized against the will of their parents only when they are in danger of death.* This danger must be such that there is little or no hope of their surviving to the age of discretion. Thus a nurse may baptize the dying child of Hebrew parents, a missionary acting as a physi-

---

[16] S. O., Jan. 5, 1724 (*Coll. P. F.,* n. 299).

cian may baptize a child in the same condition.[17]   If the illness is so grave that the physician judges the child will not live, there is sufficient reason for administering Baptism.   On the other hand, the Holy Office has decided that a great mortality among children,— as in China, where two-thirds die from various causes — does not warrant the administration of Baptism, unless the children can be withdrawn from parental control.[18]

§ 2 rules that, even *when there is no danger of death,* children of infidels may be lawfully baptized, provided their Catholic education is guaranteed, in the following two cases:

(1) If the parents or guardians, or at least one of them, consent to the baptism; (2) If there are no parents, *i. e.,* no father, mother, grandfather, grandmother, or guardians, or if they have forfeited the right to keep the child or are unable to exercise that right.

This rule is taken in the main from Benedict XIV's Constitution, "*Postremo mense,*" of Feb. 20, 1747.   It is based upon the *favor fidei,* which dictates that the supernatural right should prevail[19] over the natural. Hence if one of the parents consents, Baptism may be lawfully administered.

The same rule applies to *guardians,* because the parental power is supposed to devolve[20] upon them.   However it is a necessary condition that the children be brought up in the Catholic religion, and that the hope of Christian education be well-founded.[21]   The Holy Office decided that the children of the nomadic tribe of the Goayiros

---

[17] S. O., July 18, 1894 (*Coll. P. F.,* n. 1877).

[18] S. O., July 6, 1898; July 22, 1840; May 4, 1853; S. C. P. F., Jan. 13, 1783 (*Coll.,* nn. 2007, 902, 1090, 558).

[19] Benedict XIV, *l. c.,* n. 16.

[20] *Ibid.,* n. 14.

[21] S. O., Feb. 13, 1867 (*Coll.,* n. 1302).

(Colombia) might be baptized if there were any hope that they would be instructed in the Catholic religion [22] later on, or a well-founded expectation that the parents, who had expressed the desire of Baptism, would afterwards receive it.[23]

When Catholic godparents offer a child of infidel parents for Baptism, the Sacrament can be administered only if there is a solid hope that he will receive a Christian education.[24] How, if the grandparents give this promise? These are expressly mentioned under n. 2, but not under n. 1. Benedict XIV vindicated this right to the grandfather and grandmother if the parents were unwilling. But we hardly think that the legislator wishes to extend it to the grandparents when the parents are opposed to the child's Baptism, else the grandparents would be mentioned also under n. 1. N. 2 obviously supposes that there are neither parents, nor grandparents, nor guardians, or else that they have *forfeited their claim to the child*. This happens when children are exposed or forsaken by inhuman parents, who by such conduct lose their rights. Vagrant or rambling children should not, as a rule, be baptized without the consent of their parents.[25] The parents' right in the matter is practically lost when they are unable to claim it, *e. g.*, on account of insanity, utter destitution [26] or imprisonment for life.

[22] S. O., Sept. 6, 1899 (*Coll.*, n. 2068).

[23] S. O., Dec. 11, 1850, n. 4 (*Coll.*, n. 1054).

[24] S. O., Nov. 29, 1764 (*Coll.*, n. 457).

[25] Benedict XIV, *l. c.*, n. 9 f.

[26] S. C. P. F., April 17, 1777 (*Coll.*, n. 522, n. VII, VIII).

CHILDREN OF NON-CATHOLICS

CAN. 751

Circa baptismum infantium duorum haereticorum
aut schismaticorum, aut duorum catholicorum qui in
apostasiam vel haeresim vel schisma prolapsi sint, generatim serventur normae in superiore canone constitutae.

The same general rules apply to the children of heretics,
schismatics, and fallen-away Catholics, on account of the
danger of perversion and profanation,[27] which is almost
certain if both parents are non-Catholics. Hence if
parents, relatives or friends should offer for Baptism a
child that belongs to heretics, schismatics or apostate
Catholics, the priest must gently but firmly decline to
baptize it, unless he is morally certain that it will be
educated in the Catholic religion,[28] for instance, in a
Catholic college or academy, or by Catholic relatives.
Concerning the children of apostates the Holy Office has
decided[29] that Baptism may be administered to them only
if there is a well-founded hope that they will be separated
from their unworthy progenitors and entrusted to Catholics, as to which probability the minister must inquire. If
one of the parents is a Catholic and the other a Protest-
ant, the Catholic party must be seriously admonished to
tell the non-Catholic that Baptism was conferred and
the child must be given a Catholic education.[30] When

27 S. O., Jan. 21, 1767 (*Coll.*, n.
465): "*cum manifesto profanationis
periculo.*"

28 S. O., March 6, 1844, Americ.
Sept. (*Coll.*, n. 986); Aug. 26, 1885
(*Coll.*, n. 1643). If the parents refuse to assume any obligation to that
effect, Baptism may not be administered.

29 Jan. 28, 1637 (*Coll.*, n. 90).

30 S. O., Nov. 29, 1672; Nov. 18,
1745 (*Coll.*, nn. 205, 353); Benedict
XIV, "*Inter omnigenas,*" Feb. 2,
1744.

children of non-Catholic parents are baptized at home, no ceremonies are to be used.[31]

BAPTISM OF ADULTS

CAN. 752

§ 1. Adultus, nisi sciens et volens probeque instructus, ne baptizetur; insuper admonendus ut de peccatis suis doleat.

§ 2. In mortis autem periculo, si nequeat in praecipuis fidei mysteriis diligentius instrui, satis est, ad baptismum conferendum, ut aliquo modo ostendat se eisdem assentire serioque promittat se christianae religionis mandata servaturum.

§ 3. Quod si baptismum ne petere quidem queat, sed vel antea vel in praesenti statu manifestaverit aliquo probabili modo intentionem illum suscipiendi, baptizandus est sub conditione; si deinde convaluerit et dubium de valore baptismi collati permaneat, sub conditione baptismus rursus conferatur.

Adults who are physically and mentally normal, cannot be baptized except with their own knowledge and free will and after having been duly instructed and exhorted to be sorry for their sins. This law is based upon the necessity of coöperation in the work of salvation.[32] The Popes have frequently admonished missionaries to instruct candidates before Baptism, if need be by native ministers, and not to admit anyone to this Sacrament unless he were well instructed and imbued with Christian manners.[33] This rule applies to all, including negroes and

31 S. O., Jan. 21, 1767 (*Coll.*, n. 465).

32 *Trid.*, sess. 6, *de justif.*, c. 6; sess. 14, *de poenit.*, c. 1.

33 Alexander VII, "*Sacrosancti*," Jan. 18, 1658; Clement IX, "*In excelso*," Sept. 13, 1669; Clement XII, "*Compertum*," Aug. 24,

other infidels who are capable of embracing the Christian religion.   No one is to be baptized or abandoned after Baptism has been administered before he knows the truths necessary for salvation.[34]   Old people whose memory is failing may be baptized if they give assurance of their belief and profess it.[35]   Savages and nomads may be baptized if their mode of life does not conflict with religion or morality.[36]   Deaf-mutes may be baptized if they give some signs of religious knowledge.[37]   Now-a-days there are adequate means of instructing these unfortunates, and conclusive methods of ascertaining a person's religious training.

Concerning the *extent of this instruction,* the Roman Ritual [38] demands that neophytes " be carefully instructed in the Christian faith and holy manners."   By *Christian faith* are to be understood the principal mysteries, *i. e.,* those which must be believed *necessitate medii, viz.:* the Blessed Trinity and the Incarnation.   Express belief in our Lord Jesus Christ is specifically mentioned in one decision of the Holy Office.[39]   The *Apostles' Creed,* which is enjoined in an Instruction of the S. C. Prop. Fide,[40] contains the principal mysteries of the faith.   The Holy Office (*l. c.*) also urges instruction regarding the Holy Eucharist, unless the priest deems it better, for a prudent motive, to postpone this truth till after Baptism. Furthermore the " *Our Father,*" the effects of Baptism, and the acts of faith, hope, and charity, are to be incul-

---

1734; " *Concredita Nobis,*" May 13, 1739; Benedict XIV, " *Omnium sollicitudinum,*" Sept. 12, 1744; S. C. P. F., Sept. 12, 1645 (*Coll.,* nn. 129, 187, 347, 114).

[34] S. O., March 20, 1686 (*Coll.,* n. 230).

[35] S. O., March 8, 1770, n. 2 (*Coll.,* n. 477).

[36] S. O., Sept. 18, 1850 (*Coll.,* n. 1050).

[37] S. O., Dec. 11, 1850 (*Coll.,* n. 1054).

[38] Tit. II, c. 3, n. 1.

[39] S. O., May 10, 1703, ad 2; Jan. 25, 1703 (*Coll.,* nn. 256, 254).

[40] Oct. 18, 1883 (*Coll.,* n. 1606, n. XVII).

cated, and an act of contrition, or at least attrition, is required.[41]

Concerning *Christian morality* the aforesaid decision of the Holy Office insists upon all the divine precepts which, according to the Instruction of the S. C. Prop. mentioned, are included in the Decalogue. The last-named Instruction also demands the teaching of the precepts of the Church.[42] This insistence may cause some embarrassment, especially in cases of polygamy. For if one has many wives, he must dismiss all but the one with whom he has contracted a valid marriage. If he married all at one time, either as wives or concubines, he must dismiss all except one, with whom he must contract anew by renewing the matrimonial consent.[43] A girl of Catholic parents who is engaged to a pagan cannot be baptized unless she is ready to break off the engagement if no dispensation can be obtained.[44] Girls not yet betrothed to pagans may, however, be baptized,[45] even though there is danger that they will marry gentiles.

§ 2 of our canon deals with the Baptism of *adults in danger of death*. Such as cannot be carefully instructed in the principal mysteries of the faith, may be baptized if in any shape or form they show their readiness to assent to the truths of the Catholic religion and promise to observe its precepts. A noteworthy Instruction of the Holy Office [46] says, that adults in danger of

---

41 S. C. P. F., *ibid.*; S. O., May 10, 1703, ad 5 (*Coll.*, n. 256).

42 S. C. P. F., Oct. 18, 1883; another instruction, Sept. 12, 1645 (*Coll.*, n. 114) prescribes that they be enlightened on idol and devil worship, the cult of ancestors, the necessity of restitution, the abuse of opium, and polygamy.

43 S. O., May 10, 1703, ad 6 (*Coll.*, n. 256).

44 S. O., June 12, 1769 (*Coll.*, n. 472).

45 S. O., June 20, 1866, ad 10 (*Coll.*, n. 1293). These rules must evidently be applied to concubinage and other scandalous conduct, until signs of repentance are given and a promise of reform is made.

46 S. O., Aug. 3, 1860 (*Coll.*, n. 1198).

death may be baptized if they have faith, repentance, and the intention of receiving the Sacrament. Faith and repentance alone are necessary for the licit administration of Baptism, whilst an (at least habitual) intention is required for its valid administration. Hence, in case of doubt as to whether a dying person is sufficiently instructed in the mysteries of the faith, or whether he has the required attrition, the Sacrament may be administered absolutely; but if there is a doubt as to the intention, Baptism must be given conditionally. Concerning doubts as to sufficient instruction, or faith, or repentance, or amendment of life, the Holy Office [47] has declared that if the priest is morally certain that the patient answers his questions only to avoid contradicting his interrogator, or to please him, Baptism may not licitly be administered even *sub conditione*. But if the priest is morally certain of the patient's belief and the seriousness of his repentance, Baptism must be administered absolutely. In case of prudent doubt, when no time is left for further instruction, Baptism must be given conditionally. Signs (*e. g.* nodding of the head) or a simple " yes " are sufficient, especially if the patient had expressed a desire of being baptized before the danger of death supervened.[48] Old people who have given up the practice of idolatry and are in danger of death may be licitly baptized, even though their defective memory will not permit of proper instruction.[49]

From this may be easily understood the rule laid down in § 3, that if an adult can no longer ask for Baptism, but has, either previously or in his present state, in some probable way expressed his intention of receiving *Bap-*

[47] S. O., May 10, 1703, ad 1 (*Coll.*, n. 256).

[48] S. O., Sept., 1850; March 8, 1770 (*Coll.*, nn. 1050, 477).

[49] S. O., Dec. 11, 1850, ad 2 (*Coll.*, n. 1054).

tism, the Sacrament should be administered conditionally.
If he recovers and there is a doubt as to the validity of
the Baptism conferred, he must be rebaptized conditionally, *i. e.*, the minister must use some such words as:
" If thou art capable, *i. e.*, if sincerely thou wilt be
baptized, I baptize thee in the name, etc."

When baptisms thus conditionally administered are to
be investigated, inquiry must be made regarding the
presence of the right intention, of faith, and attrition.
If all three of these dispositions were wanting, Baptism
must be conferred absolutely; if there is doubt, the subject must be rebaptized conditionally.[50]

DISPOSITION FOR BAPTISM

CAN. 753

§ 1. Tam sacerdotem qui adultos baptizaturus est,
quam ipsos adultos qui sani sint, decet esse ieiunos.

§ 2. Nisi graves urgentesque causae obsint, adultus
baptizatus statim Missae sacrificio assistat et sacram
communionem percipiat.

It is becoming that a priest who baptizes an adult, as
well as the adult himself, if he be in good physical condition, should be fasting.[51]　This condition supposes that
Baptism of adults should, if possible and convenient, be
administered in the morning, as § 2 confirms when it says
that, except when grave and urgent reasons excuse, the
baptized adult should immediately assist at the Holy
Sacrifice of the Mass and receive Communion.[52]

50 S. O., Aug. 3, 1860; March 30,
1898, ad 3 (*Coll.*, nn. 1198, 1993).
51 *Rit. Rom.*, tit. II, c. 3, nn. 8,
9.
52 *Ibid.*, tit. II, c. 4, n. 51
(Pustet's ed., 1913, p. 37): " *Si hora
congruens fuerit, celebratur Missa,*

*cui neophyti intersunt, et SSm. Eu-
charistiam suscipiunt.*" But　no
grievous obligation can be read into
either this text or the Code. Custom may dispense from the obligation here inculcated.

BAPTISM OF INSANE PERSONS

CAN. 754

§ 1. Amentes et furiosi ne baptizentur, nisi tales a nativitate vel ante adeptum rationis usum fuerint; et tunc baptizandi sunt ut infantes.

§ 2. Si autem dilucida habeant intervalla, dum mentis compotes sunt, baptizentur, si velint.

§ 3. Baptizentur quoque, imminente periculo mortis, si, antequam insanirent, suscipiendi baptismi desiderium ostenderint.

§ 4. Qui lethargo aut phrenesi laborat, vigilans tantum et volens baptizetur; at si periculum mortis impendeat, servetur praescriptum § 3.

Insane persons and *maniacs* should not be baptized unless they have been so afflicted from birth or before they attained the use of reason, in which case they are to be baptized like infants.

If they have lucid intervals, they may, if they wish, be baptized in the course of one of these intervals, *i. e.*, while they enjoy the possession of reason.

They may also be baptized when in imminent danger of death, if they have expressed a desire for Baptism before they became insane.

Amentes is a general name for every form of insanity, mild or severe, temporary or permanent. *Furiosi*, properly speaking, are such as are frantic or violent, while *amentes* may be merely suffering from melancholia. "Originally, of course, mania meant any form of madness. Then it became gradually limited to those forms of insanity which differ from melancholia. Now it has come to mean an acute attack of mental exaltation."[53]   § 3

53 O'Malley-Walsh, *l. c.*, p. 222.

of our canon embraces all kinds of habitual madness. The insane, as St. Thomas says,[54] must be treated like infants because they are in the same state of danger. Therefore, when a physician says there is no hope of recovery, they must be baptized like children — *formâ parvulorum* — provided they were born in this condition or at least have suffered from the disease since their infancy,[55] *i. e.*, in round figures, before the seventh year of age, which limit admits of presumption.

Besides *amentia* proper there may be distinguished different degrees of mental dullness or feebleness, which may exist in an almost normally developed body. An adult who is incapable of distinguishing between good and evil must be treated like an infant, but may be baptized only in case of danger. When he is in no danger further development should be awaited, because such persons often outgrow their mental debility. A weak-minded adult who is capable of forming moral judgments must be treated like any normal person. When there is doubt as to a person's mental condition, the priest may judge in favor of Baptism.[56]

§ 2 says that insane adults who enjoy occasional lucid intervals, may be baptized during one of these, if they so desire. When in that state of mind they are supposed to possess will-power. However, too rigid a rule should not be applied to such unfortunates on account of the freakish nature of the malady.

§ 3 needs no explanation, except the remark that the intention of receiving Baptism is supposed to have been expressed before, and not retracted after melancholia or mania set in.[57]

54 *Summa Theol.*, III, q. 68, a. 12 (suppl.).

55 S. C. P. F., April, 1777, ad I, 1 (*Coll.*, n. 522).

56 *Ibid.*, n. II.

57 C. 3, X, III, 42; Benedict XIV, "*Postremo mense*," n. 46.

§ 4 mentions two diseases: *lethargia* and *phrenesis*. The former is the sleeping sickness prevalent around Lake Victoria, in Africa,[58] and elsewhere. It is often fatal. *Phrenesis* (phrenitis) is brain fever or wild delirium (frenzy). Persons suffering from these diseases may be baptized only when they are awake and desire to receive the Sacrament, except when in danger of death; then they may be baptized even when not awake, provided only that they expressed a desire for Baptism before the attack.[59]

[58] It is caused by the Tsetse fly; see *Scientific American Supplement,* Aug. 16, 1913, p. 104 ff. A similar disease (hook-worm) has lately stirred the medical authorities in our own country.

[59] C. 3, X, III, 42; *Rit. Rom.,* tit. II, c. 3, nn. 11–13.

CHAPTER III

CAN. 755

§ 1. Baptismus sollemniter conferatur, salvo praescripto can. 759.

§ 2. Loci Ordinarius potest gravi et rationabili de
causa indulgere ut caeremoniae praescriptae pro baptismo infantium adhibeantur in baptismo adultorum.

Baptism should be solemnly administered in all cases
except the one mentioned in can. 759. But the local
Ordinary may, for weighty and plausible reasons, permit
the ceremonies prescribed for infant Baptism to be used
in the Baptism of adults.

The Popes and the Roman Congregations have always
enjoined the use of solemn ceremonies in the administration of Baptism because it would betray grievous negligence to omit the ancient and imposing rites of this
Sacrament without cause.[1] For weighty reasons, however, Paul III granted to the missionaries of the West
Indies permission to shorten the baptismal ceremonies,
e. g., because of too great fatigue or lack of time.[2] Leo
XIII, in 1897, gave to the Ordinaries of Latin America
the faculty of using the short or infant formula.[3] Furthermore it has been a custom, at least tolerated, in our
country to use the short formula also at baptisms of

---

1 Benedict XIV, "*Inter omni-*
genas," Feb. 2, 1744, n. 19: "*Ne*
leves sint aut inanes causae pro
omittendis caeremoniis praescriptis."

2 "*Altitudo*," June 1, 1537.
3 "*Trans Oceanum*," April 18,
1897, n. VI.

65

adults. Now the legislator grants the Ordinaries power by law to employ this form whenever there is a grave and solid reason. Long-standing custom may be called such a reason.[4] Ordinarily the long formula must be used in baptizing adults, *i. e.*, all who have attained the use of reason, even if baptism is conferred at home,[5] provided there is no danger of death. A grave reason would be, as stated above, fatigue or lack of time, or great anxiety, especially on the part of scrupulous persons.

RITE

Can. 756

§ 1. **Proles ritu parentum baptizari debet.**

§ 2. **Si alter parentum pertineat ad ritum latinum, alter ad orientalem, proles ritu patris baptizetur, nisi aliud iure speciali cautum sit.**

§ 3. **Si unus tantum sit catholicus, proles huius ritu baptizanda est.**

This canon merely applies can. 98 to the particular case of Baptism. Children must be baptized according to the rite of the parents, either Latin or Oriental. If one of the parents belongs to the Latin and the other to the Oriental rite, the rite of the father is decisive, unless a special law provides otherwise, but if only one of the parties is Catholic, the child must be baptized according to the rite of the Catholic party.

This, in substance, has been the Roman practice since Benedict XIV laid down with great prudence and justice

---

4 It would not be amiss if synodal or provincial statutes would insert this permission.

5 S. Rit. C., Jan. 17, 23, 1914 (*A. Ap. S.*, VI, 32, 75). The arch-bishop of Paris had obtained permission to baptize boy neophytes who were admitted to Catholic schools with the short formula. S. O., May 19, 1879 (*Coll. P. F.*, n. 1520).

the rules here codified.[6] A special provision was made by S. C. Prop. Fide[7] for the ecclesiastical province of Leopolis (Lemberg). We do not know of any special provisions having been made for the United States,[8] wherefore the general law must be followed here.

BAPTISMAL WATER

CAN. 757

§ 1. In baptismo sollemni adhibenda est aqua ad hoc benedicta.

§ 2. Si aqua benedicta in baptisterio adeo sit imminuta, ut minus videatur sufficere, alia non benedicta admisceatur, etiam iterato, minore tamen copia.

§ 3. Si vero corrupta fuerit, aut effluxerit, aut quovis modo defecerit, parochus in fontem, bene mundatum ac nitidum, recentem aquam infundat ac proprio ritu in suis liturgicis libris praescripto benedicat.

§ 1. In administering *solemn Baptism* water especially blessed for the purpose must be used. This is the so-called *baptismal water,* which is blessed with special ceremonies on Holy Saturday and the Vigil of Pentecost. It should be kept in a neat and clean font, and the remainder poured into the *sacrarium* (waste-hole) when new water has been blessed.[9] Of course, Baptism would be valid even if other water were used.[10] Where there is danger that the baptismal font may be profaned, the baptismal water may be kept in any decent movable vessel.[11] In one case the Holy Office allowed the use of common

6 " *Etsi pastoralis,*" May 26, 1742, § II, nn. VI, VIII; " *Demandatam,*" Dec. 24, 1743, § 3.

7 Oct. 6, 1863 (*Coll.,* n. 1243).

8 S. C. P. F., April 11, 1894, ruled as per above text; the decrees on the Ruthenians offer nothing special.

9 Rit. Rom., tit. II, c. 1, n. 4.

10 S. O., April 6, 1741 (*Coll.,* n. 325).

11 S. C. P. F., Feb. 23, 1660 (*Coll.,* n. 139).

instead of baptismal water because the people whom the missionaries had been sent to baptize held the superstitious belief that the baptismal water was the cause of their children's death.[12]

Water for baptismal purposes must be blessed not only on Holy Saturday, but also on the Vigil of Pentecost, and the custom, no matter how inveterate, of blessing water on Holy Saturday only has been condemned as an *abuse*.[13]

Should it happen that the Holy Oils do not arrive in time for the blessing on Holy Saturday, they may be privately and separately poured into the blessed water when they are received.[14] If for some reason the Holy Oils can not be blessed or obtained in any year, the Holy Oils blessed the previous year may be used for the blessing of the baptismal font; in that case the baptismal water thus blessed with the old Oils should not be poured into the *sacrarium* when the new Oils arrive.[15] The following decision may be quoted as useful: A bishop requested that the priests of his diocese be permitted to use the Holy Oils blessed the year before, because their presence was needed in their parishes at the time when the Holy Oils were ready for delivery. The S. Congregation answered that each pastor should send a priest or cleric (if possible *in sacris*) to fetch the Holy Oils, and if this should prove impossible, the pastor or another priest in his name might bless the baptismal font without the Holy Oils, which should be poured into the water privately and separately afterwards. If it became nec-

12 S. O., May 14, 1851 (*Coll.*, n. 1060).

13 S. Rit. C., Dec. 7, 1844; April 13, 1874 (*Dec. Auth.*, nn. 2878, 3331).

14 S. Rit. C., April 12, 1755, ad 3 (*Dec. Auth.*, n. 2436). If the new oils arrive in time, these, not the old ones, must be used; S. Rit. C., April 19, 1890 (*Dec. Auth.*, n. 3724).

15 S. Rit. C., Sept. 23, 1837 (*Dec. Auth.*, n. 2773); the occasion of this *dubium* and its answer were the troublesome times in Spain; the ruling may be applied to Mexico.

essary meanwhile to administer Baptism, the old oils might be used for the solemn blessing of the water.[16]

§ 2. If the water in the baptismal font is so diminished that it appears to be insufficient for baptizing, ordinary water may be mixed with it again and again, but in steadily decreasing proportion.

§ 3. If the baptismal water becomes putrid (rotten) or runs out of the font, or disappears in some other way, the pastor shall cleanse the font and pour new water into it, which he shall bless with the proper rite as prescribed in the liturgical books. The formula for the blessing of baptismal water — which is permitted only in case of necessity [17] — will be found in the Roman Ritual.[18] We may add that, in case this blessing can not be performed, and no other baptismal water is available, natural water (not holy water) should be used for baptizing.[19]

METHOD OF BAPTIZING

CAN. 758

Licet baptismus conferri valide possit aut per infusionem, aut per immersionem, aut per aspersionem, primus tamen vel secundus modus, aut mixtus ex utroque, qui magis sit in usu, retineatur, secundum probatos diversarum Ecclesiarum rituales libros.

Baptism may be validly conferred by infusion, (pouring water over the head), by immersion, and by aspersion (or sprinkling). Where infusion, or immersion, or a combination of both methods is customary, the one most

---

16 S. Rit. C., Jan. 31, 1896 (*Dec. Auth.*, n. 3879).

17 S. O., Jan. 30, 1765 (*Coll.*, n. 459).

18 *Rit. Rom.*, tit. 2, c. 7 (ed. Pustet, 1913, p. 59 ff).

19 S. O., April 17, 1839; June 20, 1883 (*Coll.*, nn. 889, 1598).

commonly used should be retained, according to the approved rituals of the different churches.

These three methods or rites of baptizing are thus "canonized" by the Church, though immersion and aspersion are more ancient than infusion, which came into use only in the thirteenth century. The Greek Church still practices immersion and aspersion, whereas in the Latin Church infusion is more common.[20] The essential feature of all three methods is that the act of ablution be duly expressed, and hence, if possible, the water should flow.[21] This symbolism, however, may also be expressed by the use of a wet sponge or rag.[22]

A very doubtful, nay invalid manner was used by a certain pastor who was accustomed to baptize children by dipping his thumb into the baptismal water and anointing (!) the forehead of the child — *per modum unctionis* — with the thumb. The Holy Office declared that all who had been thus baptized should be rebaptized with water and the prescribed formula, but without other ceremonies, and that the bishop should take care to ascertain who of them had been promoted to sacred orders.[23]

PRIVATE BAPTISM

Can. 759

§ 1. In mortis periculo baptismum privatim conferre licet; et, si conferatur a ministro qui nec sacerdos sit nec diaconus, ea tantum ponantur, quae sunt ad baptismi validitatem necessaria; si a sacerdote vel dia-

---

[20] Benedict XIV, "*Etsi pastoralis*," May 26, 1742, § II, n. II; S. O., June 14, 1741 (*Coll.*, n. 326). *Infusio* should rather be called *effusio* or pouring on.

[21] S. O., Nov. 8, 1770; July 9, 1779 (*Coll.*, nn. 480, 536).

[22] S. O. Nov. 8, 1770; S. C. P. F., Jan. 21, 1789 (*Coll.*, nn. 480, 597).

[23] S. O., Dec. 14, 1898 (*Coll.*, n. 2028): "*Smus adprobarit.*"

cono, serventur quoque, si tempus adsit, caeremoniae quae baptismum sequuntur.

§ 2. Extra mortis periculum baptismum privatum loci Ordinarius permittere nequit, nisi agatur de haereticis qui in adulta aetate sub conditione baptizentur.

§ 3. Caeremoniae autem quae in baptismi collatione praetermissae quavis ratione fuerint, quamprimum in ecclesia suppleantur; nisi in casu de quo in § 2.

In *danger of death* Baptism may be privately administered. Two different cases are distinguished:

§ 1. If the Sacrament is conferred privately by one who is *neither a priest nor a deacon,* then no ceremonies or rites should be used, but only what strictly belongs to validity. In that case the person baptizing takes natural (not holy) water, pours it over the head of the one to be baptized,— whether once or three times does not matter [24]— and says: " I baptize thee in the name of the Father, and of the Son, and of the Holy Ghost." (2) If the person who baptizes privately, for instance, at the home of the person baptized, is a *priest or a deacon,* he must administer the Sacrament with the prescribed ceremonies and rites, unless there should be no time to apply all the ceremonies, or the parents would stubbornly oppose them, or the Holy Oils, chrism or salt could not conveniently be had. In these cases the priest or deacon would be permitted to omit the ceremonies.[25]   Otherwise there is a grave obligation to apply them even if Baptism is conferred privately.[26]

Hence § 2 rules that, outside the case of danger of death, the *Ordinary may not permit* private baptism to

24 *Rit. Rom.,* tit. II, c. 2, n. 28.
25 S. C. P. F., Aug. 30, 1775; Jan. 21, 1789, ad 1 (*Coll.,* nn. 510, 598).
26 S. O., Feb. 28, 1663; Nov. 8, 1770; Sept. 5, 1877 (*Coll.,* nn. 151, 480, 1480).

be conferred, except on non-Catholic adults who are baptized conditionally. This explains the serious obligation spoken of in the preceding section. The text does not limit the episcopal permission to individual cases, and hence Ordinaries may impart this faculty habitually.

§ 3. The ceremonies omitted for any reason in the administration of Baptism must as soon as possible be supplied in church, except in the case mentioned in can. 759, § 2. These supplementary ceremonies must be gone through in the church or oratory, to which the infant must be brought as soon as time and occasion are favorable.[27] It is hardly necessary to add that this is a grievous obligation, from which only the reason mentioned under § 2 excuses.[28] It is becoming that the ceremonies be supplied before sacramental confession, if this should be required.[29] When it is necessary to omit anything in private Baptism, all the ceremonies preceding the act of Baptism should be left out and no anointment with the Holy Oils (O. C.) performed,[30] because all these things must be supplied according to the form prescribed in the Ritual.[31]

CAN. 760

Cum baptismus sub conditione iteratur, caeremoniae, si quidem in priore baptismo omissae fuerunt, suppleantur, salvo praescripto can. 759, § 3; sin autem in priore baptismo adhibitae sunt, repeti in altero aut omitti possunt.

If Baptism is repeated *sub conditione*, the ceremonies

[27] S. C. P. F., Aug. 30, 1775; Nov. 28, 1785 (*Coll.*, nn. 570, 582).

[28] Benedict XIV, "*Inter omnigenas*," Feb. 2, 1744, § 19.

[29] S. C. P. F., July 19, 1838 (*Coll.*, n. 871).

[30] S. Rit. C., Sept. 23, 1820 (*Dec. Auth.*, n. 2607).

[31] *Rit. Rom.*, tit. II, c. 5 (ed. Pustet, 1913, p. 38 ff.).

must be supplied if they were omitted in the former Baptism, except in the case of adult non-Catholics (can. 759, § 2); but if the ceremonies were used in the first baptism, they may or may not be repeated in the second. A curious case was decided by the Holy Office.[32] In 1681 Scottish Protestants approached a priest with the request either to be rebaptized or at least to have the ceremonies repeated, because they were harassed by demons and felt relieved by conditional Baptism or the use of the customary baptismal ceremonies. The Holy Office allowed the practice, especially for non-Catholics, provided that conditional baptism was not administered for futile reasons. Concerning *parvuli* or infants of non-Catholics who are to be rebaptized conditionally, the Holy Office informed[33] the Bishop of Nottingham that such conditional baptism *in casu* should be administered secretly, but with the ceremonies prescribed in the Ritual.

As to adults, can. 759 § 2, says the ceremonies may be omitted or applied *ad libitum*. If applied, the ceremonies prescribed *pro adultorum baptisma* must be used,[34] unless, of course, where can. 755, § 2, may be made use of.

CHRISTIAN NAMES

CAN. 761

Curent parochi ut ei qui baptizatur, christianum imponatur nomen; quod si id consequi non poterunt, nomini a parentibus imposito addant nomen alicuius Sancti et in libro baptizatorum utrumque nomen perscribant.

32 S. O., Sept. 17, 1681 (*Coll.*, n. 225).

33 S. O., April 2, 1879 (*Coll.*, n. 1516).

34 S. Rit. C., Aug. 27, 1836 (*Dec Auth.*, n. 2743).

Pastors should see to it that a Christian name is given to all whom they baptize. If they can not obtain this, they shall add to the name given by the parents the name of some saint and enter both in the baptismal record.

The Church has always insisted [85] upon this pious custom, and priests must now obey the law and may no longer be accused of " cranky notions " when they do so. The name of his patron saint should remind the faithful Catholic of the example he is to imitate and of the protection he may expect through the intercession of the patron.[86]

Here we may describe the *manner of receiving non-Catholics into the Church*, according to the instruction given to the Bishop of Philadelphia, July 20, 1859:

1. When Baptism is to be conferred *absolutely*, no abjuration of heresy or absolution is required, because Baptism wipes out all sins.

2. When Baptism is to be administered *conditionally*, the *modus procedendi* is as follows:

   a) Abjuration of heresy or profession of faith;

   b) Conditional Baptism;

   c) Sacramental confession with conditional absolution.

The instruction adds the formula of abjuration and advises the clergy to comply with the wish of converts who desire to have the Catholic ceremonies supplied.[87]

---

[85] Clement XII, " *Compertum*," Aug. 24, 1734, ad II, dub.; Benedict XIV, " *Inter omnigenas*," Feb. 2, 1744, § 3. Pagan names are to be excluded entirely.

[86] S. C. Sacr., March 13, 1910, ad 9, n. 1 (*A. Ap. S.*, II, 195).

[87] *Coll. P. F.*, n. 1178.

CHAPTER IV

GODPARENTS OR SPONSORS

CAN. 762

§ 1. Ex vetustissimo Ecclesiae more nemo sollemniter baptizetur, nisi suum habeat, quatenus fieri possit, patrinum.

§ 2. Etiam in baptismo privato patrinus, si facile haberi queat, adhibeatur; si non interfuerit, adhibeatur in supplendis baptismi caeremoniis, sed hoc in casu nullam contrahit spiritualem cognationem.

That the custom of having sponsors at solemn baptism is very ancient is borne out by historical documents.[1] The name *sponsores* occurs in Tertullian's treatise on Baptism.[2] Other names, used especially in connection with spiritual relationship, were *compatres or commatres spirituales,*[3] and *patrini.* They were employed not only at the Baptism of grown persons, but also of children when infant baptism became more general in the fifth century, as may be seen from synodal acts. Monks and nuns were forbidden to act as godfathers and godmothers.[4] The reason for this prohibition is not far to seek. Their secluded life seemed to debar them from assuming the duties of sponsors, which are to instruct the godchildren and to exhort them to lead a Christian life, especially if the parents should die or neglect their

---

1 Cfr. Martène, *De Antiq. Eccl.
Ritibus,* l. I, c. 1, art. 16, n. 11.
2 Cap. 18 (Migne 1, col. 1221).

3 *Archiv für K.-R.,* 1906, 688 ff,
4 C. 104, Dist. 4, *de cons.*

obligations.[5] It must be added, however, that the authentic collections contain no text forbidding religious to become godparents. Our Code has a mitigated prohibition to that effect.

§ 1, then, enjoins the observance of the venerable custom of having godparents at solemn baptism, if possible.[6] If sponsors, as described in the Code, cannot be had, except with difficulty, Baptism may be conferred without them;[7] but if religious are present, they may and should be admitted as sponsors.[8]

§ 2. Also at *private* Baptism a sponsor should be employed if possible; if none was present, one should be called when the ceremonies are supplied; but in that case no spiritual relationship is contracted, and therefore relatives, too, may be admitted.[9]

SPONSORS AT CONDITIONAL BAPTISM

CAN. 763

§ 1. Cum baptismus iteratur sub conditione, idem patrinus, quatenus fieri possit, adhibeatur, qui in priore baptismo forte adfuit; extra hunc casum in baptismo conditionato patrinus non est necessarius.

§ 2. Iterato baptismo sub conditione, neque patrinus qui priori baptismo adfuit, neque qui posteriori, cognationem spiritualem contrahit, nisi idem patrinus in utroque baptismo adhibitus fuerit.

When Baptism is repeated *sub conditione*, if possible the same sponsor should be employed who was present

---

[5] S. Thomas, *S. Th.*, III, q. 68, a. 7; S. O., Dec. 9, 1745 (*Coll.*, n. 355).

[6] *Trid.*, sess. 24, c. 2, *de ref.*

[7] S. C. P. F., April 1, 1816, Louisville, Ky. (*Coll.*, n. 709).

[8] S. Rit. C., Feb. 15, 1887 (*Coll.*, n. 1667).

[9] S. C. P. F., Sept. 11, 1779 (*Coll.*, n. 537).

the first time; but if this is not possible — and it would not be possible if he had not the qualities negatively described in can. 765 — no sponsor is required for conditional Baptism. No spiritual relationship is contracted, unless the same qualified sponsor acts as such on both occasions.

NUMBER OF SPONSORS

CAN. 764

Patrinus unus tantum, licet diversi sexus a baptizando, vel ad summum unus et una adhibeantur.

There should be only one sponsor, but he may be of different sex than the one to be baptized; at most two may be employed, *viz.*, a man and a woman. This ruling[10] is evidently inspired by the desire to diminish spiritual relationship, which seems to have been the delight of older canonists and glossators.

REQUISITES OF LEGAL SPONSORSHIP

CAN. 765

Ut quis sit patrinus, oportet:
  1.° Sit baptizatus, rationis usum assecutus et intentionem habeat id munus gerendi;
  2.° Ad nullam pertineat haereticam aut schismaticam sectam, nec sententia condemnatoria vel declaratoria sit excommunicatus aut infamis infamia iuris aut exclusus ab actibus legitimis, nec sit clericus depositus vel degradatus;
  3.° Nec sit pater vel mater vel coniux baptizandi;

10 Cc. 100 f., Dist. 4, *de cons.;* c. 3, X, IV, 3; *Trid.,* sess. 24, c. 2, *de ref.*

4.° Ab ipso baptizando eiusve parentibus vel tutoribus aut, his deficientibus, a ministro sit designatus;

5.° Baptizandum in actu baptismi per se vel per procuratorem physice teneat aut tangat vel statim levet seu suscipiat de sacro fonte aut de manibus baptizantis.

We call the following legal requisites, because the term " valid " hardly covers them all:

(1) The sponsor must be baptized, have attained the age of discretion, and have the intention of taking the office of sponsor upon himself.

(2) He or she must belong to no heretical or schismatical sect, nor be excommunicated by either a condemnatory or a declaratory sentence, nor be infamous by law, nor be excluded from legal acts, nor be a deposed or degraded clergyman.

(3) He or she must be neither the father nor the mother nor the consort of the one to be baptized.

(4) He or she must be appointed either by the one to be baptized, or by the latter's parents or guardians, or, if these (three classes) be wanting, by the minister of the Sacrament.

(5) The sponsor must either personally or by proxy take upon himself the sponsorship by a physical act indicative of sponsorship according to custom.

Concerning n. 1, it is evident that sponsorship must be a human act, and as Christian Baptism is implied, it is required, besides, that the sponsor be himself initiated, *i. e.*, a member, like in any knighthood or society.

With regard to *heretics or schismatics* it has been the constant and uniform practice of the Church to refuse to admit as sponsors all persons who are not of the faith, since a sponsor assumes the duty of instructing his godchild in Christian doctrine.[11] It makes no difference whether such persons appear themselves or are represented by a Catholic proxy.[12] Neither is friendship, or blood relationship, or any other natural tie sufficient to break these rules.[13] From the fact that a notoriously censured Catholic may legally be a sponsor, it has been inferred that a non-Catholic might just as well be admitted. This conclusion is not justified [14] because of the implied office of teaching and of the position the Church has always maintained towards heresy and schism.

The code also draws a distinction between a condemned or declared *excommunicatus* and one notoriously excommunicated, as per can. 766, n. 2. By committing a crime to which the Code attaches the penalty of excommunication, one may be notoriously excommunicated, though no judge has declared him such or condemned him to that penalty.

What *legitimate acts* (not actions) are, is stated under can. 2256; one of them is precisely that of acting as sponsor.

No. 3 excludes *father and mother and consort* (husband or wife) of the one to be baptized from sponsorship. If any of these persons should act as sponsors, no spiritual relationship is contracted.[15]

No. 4 rules that *appointment* or designation is required for sponsorship. This must be made before Baptism. *Post factum* approval or ratification is insufficient, though

---

11 S. O., Oct. 14, 1676; Dec. 9, 1745; Jan. 1763; S. C. P. F., Sept. 8, 1869, n. 47 (*Coll.*, nn. 211, 355, 447, 1346); the admission of such persons is styled *abusus*.

12 S. O., June 30, July 7, 1864; Jan, 3. 1871 (*Coll.*, nn. 1257, 1362).

13 S. O., Oct. 14, 1676 (*Coll.*, n. 211).

14 S. O., May 3, 1893 (*Coll.*, n. 1831).

15 S. O., Sept. 15, 1869 (*Coll.*, n. 1347). This holds even if they have become sponsors by fraud or out of levity, and hence they neither lose the right to demand or the duty to render the *debitum coniugale*.

the parents may presume consent. The reason for this law is that the sponsor must have the formal intention and will to accept and perform the duties attached to sponsorship.[16]

No. 5 speaks of a *physical* act and enumerates four terms, which are used to signify sponsorship, *viz.: tenere, i. e.,* to hold the child in the act of Baptism, when the water is poured on the head; *tangere,* to touch the child on the arm or any part of the body whilst another holds it over the baptismal font; *levare,* which is derived from immersion, and means to lift or raise out of the water, lake or pond; *suscipere,* to receive from the baptismal font or the hands of the minister. Concerning *tenere,* to hold, a decision has been given to the effect that it is sufficient that the sponsor put his or her arm in that of the person who holds the child, or touch that person, *v. g.,* nurse or midwife, and accompany him or her to the baptismal font. It is not required that the sponsor personally offer the child for Baptism.[17] Whence it may be concluded that mediate physical contact is sufficient.

All the above-mentioned acts may be performed by *proxy.* The proxy must come in physical touch with the subject. Whilst there are decisions debarring non-Catholics from acting as sponsors, either personally or through a Catholic proctor, we can find no decision excluding them from acting as proctors for Catholic sponsors. However, as can. 2256, 2°, excludes them from legal acts, even those peculiar to a procurator, it would not be safe to employ them in Baptism. This does not mean, of course, that a non-Catholic may not act as a mere witness or nominal sponsor together with a Catholic sponsor.[18]

---

[16] S. O., Sept. 15, 1869 (*Coll.,* n. 1347); cfr. can. 1079.

[17] S. C. P. F., Jan. 21, 1856 (*Coll.,* n. 1119).

[18] The baptizing minister in such cases should gently insinuate that only the Catholic party is sponsor. S. O., Jan., 1763 (*Coll.,* n. 447).

CAN. 766

Ut autem quis licite patrinus admittatur, oportet:

1.° Decimum quartum suae aetatis annum attigerit, nisi aliud iusta de causa ministro videatur;

2.° Non sit propter notorium delictum excommunicatus vel exclusus ab actibus legitimis vel infamis infamia iuris, quin tamen sententia intercesserit, nec sit interdictus aut alias publice criminosus vel infamis infamia facti;

3.° Fidei rudimenta noverit;

4.° In nulla religione sit novitius vel professus, nisi necessitas urgeat et expressa habeatur venia Superioris saltem localis:

5.° In sacris ordinibus non sit constitutus, nisi accedat expressa Ordinarii proprii licentia.

That one may be *licitly* admitted to sponsorship, it is required:

1°. That the sponsor have *reached* (not completed) the *fourteenth year of age,* unless the minister, for a just cause, sees fit to admit a younger person. A just cause may be the moral or intellectual qualities of the person admitted; local or rather climatic conditions (in Southern countries maturity sets in sooner) ; family traditions, or particular circumstances.

2°. That the sponsor be not *excommunicated* for a notorious crime; or excluded from legal acts; or rendered infamous by law, without a sentence having been issued to that effect; or interdicted; or a public criminal; or infamous in fact. Evidently the Code wishes to debar from sponsorship all whose moral character and reputation do not guarantee fitness to raise a Catholic child, which, as sponsor, one would be expected to do in case of necessity. Besides, sponsorship is an honor and should not be conferred on unworthy persons. The former reason is alleged in an instruction of the Holy Office with regard to *Freemasons*. These, if their membership in the Order is notorious, are not to be admitted as sponsors.[19] The other points noted in the text must be interpreted according to Book V. Stress is to be laid on notoriety, as the text itself explains.

3°. That the sponsor know the *rudiments of faith*, which requirement is as stringent for sponsors as for adults who desire to be baptized (see can. 752).

4°. That the sponsor be neither a *novice* nor a *professed member* of any *religious institute*. However, in urgent cases, and with the express (not presumed) permission of at least the local superior, religious may be admitted to sponsorship.[20] An urgent case would be if Baptism would otherwise have to be conferred without sponsors.[21] In hospitals and other asylums Sisters are sometimes called upon to act as sponsors; they may do so with the permission of the superioress.

5°. That the sponsor be not a *cleric in higher orders*, for such may act as sponsors only with the express permission of the Ordinary. This includes subdeacons. An Ordinary, whether bishop or prelate regular, may grant himself permission, and therefore act as sponsor without consulting any one else.

19 S. O., July 5, 1878, *ad ordin. Brasil.* (*Coll.*, n. 1495).

20 Cfr. c. 8, C. 16, q. 1; c. 103 f., Dist. 4, *de cons.*

21 S. Rit. C., Feb. 15, 1887 (*Coll. P. F.*, n. 1667). Custom might also be alleged. Thus it is customary that the Abbot of Engelberg, Switzerland, acts as godfather to every firstborn boy in the village, and the S. Cong. did not wish to abolish this custom.

Can. 767

In dubio utrum quis valide vel licite admitti possit, necne, ad patrini munus, parochus, si tempus suppetat, consulat Ordinarium.

When in doubt as to whether any one may be legally or licitly admitted to sponsorship, the pastor should consult the Ordinary if time permits.

SPIRITUAL RELATIONSHIP

Can. 768

Ex baptismo spiritualem cognationem contrahunt tantum cum baptizato baptizans et patrinus.

Spiritual relationship is contracted only between the minister and the one baptized, and between the sponsor and his godchild. Of this more under can. 1079.

DUTIES OF SPONSORS

Can. 769

Patrinorum est, ex suscepto munere, spiritualem filium perpetuo sibi commendatum habere, atque in iis quae ad christianae vitae institutionem spectant, curare diligenter ut ille talem in tota vita se praebeat, qualem futurum sollemni caeremonia spoponderunt.

It is the duty of godparents, arising from sponsorship, to regard their spiritual children as their perpetual charges and to instruct them carefully in the obligations of the Christian life, in order that they may prove themselves such as they solemnly promised by their baptismal vows to be. The obligation exists even if the sponsors think they are not bound by it. It binds chiefly when the parents neglect their duty.[22]

22 S. O., Dec. 9, 1745 (*Coll.*, n. 355): "*Aliud est quod patrini. non curent, aliud quod non teneantur curare. Tenentur etiam hodie ad id praestandum, si carnales parentes id facere negligant, uti docet D. Thomas, III, q. 67, a. 8.*"

CHAPTER V

CAN. 770

Infantes quamprimum baptizentur; et parochi ac concionatores frequenter fideles de hac gravi eorum obligatione commoneant.

CAN. 771

Baptismus privatus, urgente necessitate, quovis tempore et loco administrandus est.

The first of these two canons confirms the old practice of having *infants baptized as soon as possible*. To admonish the faithful of their *grave obligation* to comply with this law is the office of pastors and preachers.

Private baptism, according to can. 771, in case of urgent necessity may be administered at *any time and in any place.*

The reason for the important law embodied in can. 770 is the necessity of Baptism for eternal salvation. Leo XIII justly called the practice of delaying Baptism a detestable and impious abuse.[1] An instruction of the Holy Office enjoined the Coptic missionaries to tell mothers that they are guilty of cruelty to their offspring if they delay Baptism for fear of temporal death while exposing them to eternal death.[2] The term *quamprimum,* as soon as possible, is assumed to signify three, or, at

[1] "*Gretae,*" July 22, 1899 (*Coll. P. F.,* n. 2060).   [2] S. O., June 14, 1741 (*Coll.,* n. 326).

85

most, eight days from the birth of the child.[3] An *urgens necessitas* would exist, *e. g.*, a) if the distance from church were great,[4] say more than three leagues; b) if the parents stubbornly objected to having the child brought to church. In these and similar cases private baptism without ceremonies and rites may be administered, but the latter must be supplied when the parents give their consent or the child can be brought to church.[5] When a child is so feeble that there is danger of death, the midwife may baptize him, provided the danger is quite positive.[6]

When Baptism, private or solemn, is administered *at home*, the faithful should be instructed that it is valid and not a mere ceremony.[7]

SOLEMN BAPTISM

CAN. 772

Etiam sollemnis baptismus qualibet die administrari potest; decet tamen adultorum baptismum, secundum antiquissimum Ecclesiae ritum, conferri, si fieri commode queat, in pervigilio Paschatis et Pentecostes, praecipue in metropolitanis aut cathedralibus ecclesiis.

Solemn Baptism, too, may be administered at any time; but it is becoming, if it can be done conveniently, that adults be baptized on the vigils of *Easter and Pentecost,* according to the ancient liturgies, especially in metropolitan and cathedral churches.

[3] S. C. P. F., Sept. 11, 1841 (*Coll.*, n. 939).

[4] S. C. P. F., Nov. 28, 1785 (*Coll.*, n. 582).

[5] S. C. P. F., Aug. 30, 1775 (*Coll.*, n. 510).

[6] S. C. P. F., Sept. 11, 1779; S. O., Jan. 11, 1899 (*Coll.*, nn. 537, 2033).

[7] This was the idea of the Nestorians; S. C. P. F., July 31, 1902 (*Coll.*, n. 2149).

The ancient custom was vindicated by Pope Siricius (384–398) and has been observed from time immemorial,[8] more especially with regard to grown persons, who were first received into the ranks of the catechumens and had to undergo a long trial and pass the *scrutinia* in Lent. On Holy Saturday they were mustered and marched into the baptistery, whilst the faithful in church attended the reading of the prophecies.[9] That the ceremony was impressive and an occasion of joy for the bishop goes without saying. The Church, in her truly conservative spirit, wishes to preserve the old tradition as much as modern circumstances permit. But, as the text says, according to the ancient ritual,[10] this custom should be observed only when *adults* are to be baptized, because it might be dangerous and fatiguing to delay Baptism or to attend such an extended ceremony for children.[11]

PLACE OF BAPTISM

CAN. 773

Proprius baptismi sollemnis administrandi locus est baptisterium in ecclesia vel oratorio publico.

The *proper place* for administering solemn baptism is the baptistery of a church or public oratory. The *sacristy* is *not* the proper place, unless there be a reasonable cause for using it. This cause must be submitted to the Ordinary.[12] A valid reason would be repair work going on in church, and, we believe, coldness of the

---

[8] Cfr. cc. 11, 15, Dist. 4, *de cons.*

[9] This is the origin of those prophecies being read in church.

[10] Tit. II, c. 1, n. 27; c. 3, nn. 4–6.

[11] The provincial Synod of Bene-

vento, 1693, held by the later Benedict XIII, allowed children to wait fourteen days; tit. 36, c. 8 (*Coll. Lac.*, I, 70).

[12] S. Rit. C., March 14, 1861, ad IX (*Dec. Auth.*, n. 3104).

church on a winter day when the whole church cannot be heated on account of a baptism occurring on a week-day.

Solemn Baptism may not be administered in the private oratories (for an exception see can. 776, § 1, 1°) of private persons.[18] Neither are semi-public oratories, for instance, Sisters' chapels or hospital oratories, the proper place to baptize, because the text plainly says "*public oratories.*"

Baptism may, by way of exception, be conferred at a special altar, on account of a particular devotion to the Saint to whom the altar is dedicated;[14] but this altar must be *in the church,* not in a private chapel or semi-public oratory.

A BAPTISMAL FONT IN EVERY PARISH CHURCH

CAN. 774

§ 1. Quaelibet paroecialis ecclesia, revocato ac re-probato quovis contrario statuto vel privilegio vel con-suetudine, baptismalem habeat fontem, salvo legitimo iure cumulativo aliis ecclesiis iam quaesito.

§ 2. Loci Ordinarius potest pro fidelium commodi-tate permittere vel iubere ut fons baptismalis ponatur etiam in alia ecclesia vel publico oratorio intra paroe-ciae fines.

The characteristic sign of a parish church has always been the baptismal font, though some canonists thought it was not essential to a parish church.[15]

---

18 C. un., Clem. III, 15; Bene-dict XIV, "*Magno cum,*" *June 2,* 1751, § 19; *Rit. Rom.,* tit. II, c. 1, nn. 28, 30; c. 3, n. 7.

14 S. Rit. C., Sept 1, 1888 (*Dec.*

Auth., n. 3695); with the approval of the Ordinary.

15 Cfr. S. C., EE. et RR., June 9, 1848 (Bizzarri, *Coll.,* p. 562 f.).

§ 1 of our canon revokes and reprobates every statute, custom or privilege which would prevent the *erection of a baptismal font in every parish church,* and commands that every parish church should have its own baptismal font.[16] This, of course, implies that the blessing of the baptismal water on the vigils of Easter and Pentecost must be performed in each and every parish church according to the Roman Ritual. The pastor is not allowed to put this ceremony off to another day.[17] From the above rule it follows that if a cathedral church is not a parish church, it is not entitled to a baptismal font,[18] unless, of course, the bishop should make use of § 2, can. 774. But the Ordinary is not empowered to erect in a cathedral church which is not a parish church a temporary baptismal font, or to allow a portable font and bless water without the mixture of the Holy Oils, for the two Saturdays mentioned.[19]

The meaning of the clause: " with due regard to the legitimate cumulative right acquired by another church " (*salvo legitimo iure cumulativo aliis ecclesiis iam quaesito*) may be illustrated by quoting a decision of the S. Rit. C. In the diocese of Spalato, Dalmatia, the baptismal font was blessed only in the cathedral, pro-cathedral, collegiate and in some principal parochial churches; the other churches got their baptismal water from the former. The S. Congregation decided that this custom was no longer to be tolerated, with due regard, however, to the special and determined rights of the mother churches. The churches which received their baptismal water from the others were most probably daughters or branches.[20]

---

16 S. C. C., Feb. 10, 1748, denied the right of having a baptismal font to a collegiate church (Richter, *Trid.*, p. 118, n. 12).

17 S. Rit. C., Jan. 13, 1899 (*Dec. Auth.*, n. 4005).

18 S. Rit. C., Aug. 31, 1872 (*Dec. Auth.*, n. 3272).

19 S. Rit. C., Jan. 13, 1899 (*Dec. Auth.*, n. 4005).

20 S. Rit. C., June 7, 1892 (*Dec. Auth.*, n. 3776).

What the special rights of the mother churches were is
not stated in the decision. They probably consisted in
a certain deference or respect which took the form of a
tithe or tribute, or perhaps mere precedence.[21] Sometimes, in such cases, express stipulations existed,
allowing the parishioners of the branch churches
to bring their children to the mother church for Baptism.[22]

In our country no such rights should be reserved because it would only cause confusion and curtail parochial
rights.

§ 2 rules that the local Ordinary may, for the convenience of the faithful, permit or command that another
baptismal font be placed in some other church or public
oratory within the boundaries of a parish. This new [23]
law gives the Ordinary the right of erecting baptismal
fonts in other than parish churches, e. g., public oratories
or chapels of ease, but not in semi-public or private
oratories. This will be very convenient for missionary
stations or missions attached to a quasi-mother church.
It seems logical that the blessing of the baptismal font
on the vigils of Easter and Pentecost should be performed in these churches or public oratories.[24] Yet the
wording *ponatur*, be placed, would seem to admit of another practice, *viz.:* that of receiving the baptismal water
from the parish church and putting it in the baptismal
font. We believe this practice could not be called unlawful.[25]

21 S. C. C., Aug. 3, Dec. 14, 1748
(Richter, *Trid.*, p. 118, n. 10).

22 S. C. C., June 22, 1720 (Richter. *l. c.*, n. 11).

23 S. C. C., Aug. 17, 1626; Sept.
22, 1742 (Richter, *Trid.*, n. 8)
would not permit this, but rather

recommends the erection of a new
parish.

24 S. Rit. C., June 7, 1892 (*Dec.
Auth.*, n. 3776) would seem to favor
this assumption.

25 S. C. P. F., Sept., 1779; Aug.
23, 1852 (*Coll.*, nn. 537, 1079).

Can. 775

Si ad ecclesiam paroecialem, aut ad aliam quae iure fontis gaudeat, baptizandus, propter locorum distantiam aliave adiuncta, sine gravi incommodo aut periculo, accedere aut transferri nequeat, baptismus sollemnis a parocho conferri potest et debet in proxima ecclesia aut oratorio publico intra paroeciae fines, licet haec baptismali fonte careant.

The Church to-day is even more condescending than formerly, and permits the administration of solemn Baptism in *any church or public oratory* situated within the parish boundaries, *even though it be destitute of a baptismal font.* However, there must be a reason for making use of this permission. A sufficient reason is if the one to be baptized, whether infant or adult, cannot, *without great inconvenience or danger,* be brought or go to a church, which has a baptismal font, whether it be a parish or some other church. In that case the *parish priest* may and should confer Baptism in the nearest church or public oratory within the parish boundaries. A serious *inconvenience* may arise from distance, or expense, or a contagious disease.

SOLEMN BAPTISM IN PRIVATE HOUSES

Can. 776

§ 1. In domibus autem privatis baptismus sollemnis administrari non debet, nisi hisce in adiunctis:

1.° Si baptizandi sint filii aut nepotes eorum qui supremum actu tenent populorum principatum vel ius habent succedendi in thronum, quoties isti id rite poposcerint;

2.° Si loci Ordinarius, pro suo prudenti arbitrio et

conscientia, iusta ac rationabili de causa, in casu aliquo extraordinario id concedendum censuerit.

§ 2. In memoratis casibus baptismus conferendus est in sacello domus aut saltem in alio decenti loco, et aqua baptismali de more benedicta.

§ 1. Solemn Baptism may not be administered in private houses except in the following circumstances—apart from cases of necessity [26]:

1°. If those to be baptized are the sons or grandsons of actual *rulers,* or of their prospective successors to the throne. If this privilege is desired, petition must be made for it either directly to the Ordinary, or to the parish priest, both of whom are entitled to perform the rite;

2°. If the local Ordinary, after prudent and conscientious deliberation, judges that there is a just and plausible cause for granting the permission in some extraordinary case. Such cases would be: if Catholics would demand to have their children baptized in the house of a *Catholic consul,* which may happen among foreigners; [27] if the distance from the church would be very considerable, say ten geographical miles.[28]   But solemn baptism may never be administered in the houses of non-Catholics, not even in case of necessity or danger of death.[29]

§ 2 enjoins the minister to confer baptism, in the cases mentioned under § 1, in the oratory or some other decent place, and with baptismal water, *i. e.,* water blessed on the vigils of Easter and Pentecost, or accord-

26 S. C. Sacr., Dec. 23, 1912 (*A. Ap. S.,* IV, 725).

27 S. O., Jan., 1763 (*Coll.,* n. 447). This may certainly be extended to the palaces of Catholic ambassadors who enjoy exterioriality and immunity, whilst the consuls are destitute of these privileges; cfr. Westlake, *International Law,* P. I, Peace, 1910, p. 288 f.

28 S. Rit. C., Feb. 10, 1871, ad III (*Dec. Auth.,* n. 3234).

29 S. O., Jan. 21, 1767 (*Coll.,* n. 465).

ing to the formula prescribed for supplementing it when the supply is exhausted; — except, of course, in urgent cases, which admit of the shortest possible form.[20]

[20] S. Rit. C., Jan. 17, 1914 (*A.* c. 1, n. 29; c. 7 (ed. Pustet, 1913, *Ap. S.,* VI, 32); *Rit. Rom.,* tit. II, p. 59).

CHAPTER VI

CAN. 777

§ 1. Parochi debent nomina baptizatorum, mentione facta de ministro, parentibus ac patrinis, de loco ac die collati baptismi, in baptismali libro sedulo et sine ulla mora referre.

§ 2. Ubi vero de illegitimis filiis agatur, matris nomen est inserendum, si publice eius maternitas constet, vel ipsa sponte sua scripto vel coram duobus testibus id petat; item nomen patris, dummodo ipse sponte sua a parocho vel scripto vel coram duobus testibus id requirat, vel ex publico authentico documento sit notus; in ceteris casibus inscribatur natus tanquam filius patris ignoti vel ignotorum parentum.

CAN. 778

Si baptismus nec a proprio parocho nec eo praesente administratus fuerit, minister de ipso collato quamprimum proprium ratione domicilii parochum baptizati certiorem reddat.

Parish priests must enter in the baptismal record the names of the baptized, the minister, the parents and godparents, the place and date of Baptism. This record must be made carefully and without delay.

In the case of an *illegitimate* child the *mother's name* must be put down if she is publicly known to be the

94

mother, or if, of her own accord, she demands it in writing or before two witnesses. The name of the father must be recorded only if he, of his own accord, demands it of the pastor either in writing or in the presence of two witnesses, or if he is known to be the child's father by an authentic public document. In all other cases the *one baptized* must be recorded as the offspring of an unknown father or unknown parents.

If the Baptism was not administered by the pastor, nor in his presence, the minister shall notify the pastor as soon as possible of the fact. It is hardly necessary to call attention to the *grave obligation* of keeping proper baptismal records, on which authentic testimonies depend.[1] Benedict XIV called upon the Ordinaries to examine the baptismal records at each canonical visit.[2] The Code enjoins recording *without delay* (*sine mora*), which means the same day the Baptism was conferred, unless the book were not at hand, as may happen with missionaries, who cannot carry the baptismal books from place to place. The term *sedulo* (diligently) includes whatever is necessary for clear, legible, and neat bookkeeping. The priest should if necessary, keep a separate record for children of another, (for instance, the Ruthenian) rite.[3]

PROOF OF BAPTISM

CAN. 779

Ad collatum baptismum comprobandum, si nemini fiat praeiudicium, satis est unus testis omni exceptione maior, vel ipsius baptizati iusiurandum, si ipse in adulta aetate baptismum receperit.

---

1 *Trid.*, sess. 24, c. 2, *de ref. mat.;* S. O., Dec. 9, 1745 (*Coll.*, n. 345). Instr. S. C. P. F., June 25, 1791 (*Coll.*, n. 605).

2 " *Firmandis*," Nov. 6, 1744, § 9.
3 S. C. P. F., Oct. 6, 1863, C. a. (*Coll.*, n. 1241): *in libro separato.*

If no prejudice is involved to a third person, one absolutely trustworthy witness is sufficient to prove that Baptism was conferred; the sworn statement of the one baptized is also admissible, if baptism was conferred on him as an adult. The reason why one witness suffices must be sought in the danger of incurring ecclesiastical penalties if one should baptize a child against the will of the parents. Hence no one is supposed to testify against himself, and therefore his testimony is admitted.[4] Thus the statement of a catechist, if he has a good reputation, would be sufficient.[5] We also think that a physician's or midwife's testimony may be admitted under the same condition.

The text says, *if no prejudice arises to a third person.* When a material advantage, for instance, a legacy, or a spiritual benefit (preferment) would be involved against the claim of another, two witnesses would be required. The statement of the baptized subject is admitted and affords full proof only if it is given under oath and the Baptism was conferred after the subject had attained the age of discretion (about the seventh year). No distinction is made between the testimonies of men and women.[6]

[4] Benedict XIV, "*Postremo mense,*" Feb. 28, 1747, n. 31; cc. 110, 112, 113, Dist. 4, *de cons;* Glossa ad c. 51, X, II, 20, *s. v.* "*nisi iuratus.*"

[5] S. C. P. F., Sept. 8, 1869 (*Coll.,* n. 1346).

[6] Benedict XIV, "*Postremo mense,*" nn. 35, 31, 55.

TITLE II

CONFIRMATION

CAN. 780

Sacramentum confirmationis conferri debet per manus impositionem cum unctione chrismatis in fronte et per verba in pontificalibus libris ab Ecclesia probatis praescripta.

CAN. 781

§ 1. Chrisma, in sacramento confirmationis adhibendum, debet esse ab Episcopo consecratum, etiamsi sacramentum a presbytero, ex iure vel ex apostolico indulto, ministretur.

§ 2. Unctio autem ne fiat aliquo instrumento, sed ipsa ministri manu capiti confirmandi rite imposita.

The Sacrament of Confirmation must be administered by laying on hands, and anointing the forehead with chrism, and pronouncing the words prescribed in the pontifical books approved by the Church.

The *chrism* to be used in the administration of this Sacrament must be blessed by a bishop, even though a priest may administer it, either by law or in virtue of an apostolic indult.

The *anointing* is not to be performed with an instrument, but with the minister's hand, placed upon the head of the subject to be confirmed.

The Sacrament of strength or of zeal is distinct from
Baptism, the indelible character of which it enlarges or
deepens. Confirmation confers a grace distinct from the
baptismal grace. It is pre-eminently the Sacrament of
the Holy Ghost.[1] Being essentially distinguished from
the Sacrament of Baptism, it requires a distinct matter
and form.

1. The *remote matter* is *chrism*, which is composed of
balsam and olive oil. The latter is essential for the
validity of the Sacrament. Balsam, too, must be said to
belong to the essence of the matter, at least according to
the Decree for the Armenians and the ancient Greek
Euchologia.[2] The validity of the matter is, however, not
affected by mingling other aromatics with the balsam.[3]
The blessing or *consecration* of the matter must be performed by a bishop. Whether a priest, with the permission of the Pope, could consecrate chrism is a specu-
lative question. The affirmative view is certainly ten-
able.[4] Licit administration requires that the consecration be performed by a *Catholic* bishop, and hence priests
are never allowed to receive chrism from a heretical or
schismatic bishop.[5] The *vicar-general*, although he may
be a bishop, cannot lawfully bless the chrism.[6] Lastly,
the chrism must be blessed the same year in which it is
used, counting from Holy Thursday to Holy Thursday.
It is not allowed to use chrism blessed the year before,
except in case of necessity.[7]

---

[1] Trid., sess. 7, c. 1, *de sacram.
in genere*; cc. 1, 2, *de confirm.*;
*Professio fidei Waldensibus prae-
scripta; Decretum pro Arm.* (Denzinger, nn. 370, 592); Pius X,
Syllabus, 1907, n. 44.

[2] Benedict XIV, " *Ex quo*," March
1, 1756, § 49; the testimonies of
the early Church see in M. O'Dwyer,
Confirmation, 1915, p. 49 ff.

[3] Benedict XIV, *l. c.*

[4] Benedict XIV, *De Syn. Dioec.*,
VIII, 1, 4.

[5] S. C. P. F., May 4, 1774 (*Coll.*,
n. 553).

[6] Benedict XIV, *De Syn. Dioec.*,
II, 8, 2–7.

[7] Benedict XIV, " *Anno vertente*,
June 19, 1750, § 5.

The *proximate matter of Confirmation is the anointing*. This is done by placing three or four fingers upon the forehead and using the thumb dipped in the holy chrism to anoint the same. The sign of the cross in the act of anointing is essential.[8]

§ 2, of can. 781 strictly forbids the use of any instrument (brush or cotton) in the act of Confirmation. The Holy Office has declared that the use of an instrument endangers the validity of the Sacrament and ordered secret and conditional repetition of Confirmation *in casu*.[9]

The *form* is that prescribed by the Roman Pontifical: " *Signo te signo crucis, et confirmo te chrismate salutis, in nomine Patris et Filii et Spiritus Sancti,*" the act of pronouncing the three Holy Names being accompanied by the triple sign of the cross.[10]

8 S. Rit. C., May 7, 1853, ad II (*Dec. Auth.*, n. 3012).
9 S. O., Jan. 14, 1885 (*Coll.*, n. 1630).

10 S. Rit. C., May 7, 1853 (*l. c.*). However the *triple* sign of the cross is not required for validity.

CHAPTER I

CAN. 782

§ 1. Ordinarius confirmationis minister est solus Episcopus.

§ 2. Extraordinarius minister est presbyter, cui vel iure communi vel peculiari Sedis Apostolicae indulto ea facultas concessa sit.

§ 3. Hac facultate ipso iure gaudent, praeter S. R. E. Cardinales ad normam can 239, § 1, n. 23, Abbas vel Praelatus *nullius*, Vicarius et Praefectus Apostolicus, qui tamen ea valide uti nequeunt, nisi intra fines sui territorii et durante munere tantum.

§ 4. Presbyter latini ritus cui, vi indulti, haec facultas competat, confirmationem valide confert solis fidelibus sui ritus, nisi in indulto aliud expresse cautum fuerit.

§ 5. Nefas est presbyteris ritus orientalis, qui facultate vel privilegio gaudent confirmationem una cum baptismo infantibus sui ritus conferendi, eandem ministrare infantibus latini ritus.

§ 1 and 2.— The ordinary minister of Confirmation is the bishop, but a priest may act as extraordinary minister if he has received this power either by law or by a special indult of the Apostolic See.

The *bishop and he alone* is the ordinary minister of Confirmation in the Latin Church. The Greek Church permits priests to confer Confirmation immediately after Baptism. St. Gregory the Great, upon the remonstrances of the Sardinians, allowed priests to confirm where no bishops were available; [1] but this concession was a unique one in the Occidental Church, whereas the Eastern Church with the permission, and we dare say, approval, of the Apostolic See, retained the custom mentioned.

Even a *heretical or schismatic* bishop can confirm validly. This at least we would infer from certain decisions of the Holy Office, though they mention only Confirmation conferred by a *schismatic priest;* for all of them seem to admit at least the conditional validity of Confirmation administered by such a priest. Only when there were among the *confirmandi* some who wished to be promoted to tonsure or sacred Orders, was the repetition of Confirmation imposed, "conditionally and secretly." [2]

The text adds that a *simple priest* may administer the Sacrament of Confirmation, provided he has *received that faculty* either by law or by a special indult of the Apostolic See. Who receive that faculty by *law* is stated in § 3. They are the *Cardinals* of the Holy Roman Church, according to the privileges enumerated under can. 239, § 1, n. 23. Cardinals, therefore, may administer Confirmation anywhere and to anyone, for no distinction is made in the text. The only obligation mentioned is that they record the fact in the book especially reserved for recording Confirmations (can. 798). Others who may administer the Sacrament of Confirmation by law are *abbots nullius or prelates nullius, vicars Apostolic* and *prefects Apostolic.* But these three kinds of ecclesiastics

---

1 Cfr. Reg. Greg. M., ed. Ewald-Hartmann, 1891, Vol. I, 241, 261 (Sept. 593, May 594).

2 S. O., July 5, 1853; March 16, 1872; April 2, 1879; Jan. 14, 1885 (*Coll. P. F.,* nn. 1095, 1381, 1515, 1630).

can make *valid use* of this faculty only *within the bound-aries of their own territory and during their term of office*. Hence, for instance, the Vicar-Apostolic of North Carolina may administer Confirmation validly only within his own territory. On the other hand, he may, within that territory also *confirm validly* such as are not his subjects by reason either of domicile or quasi-domicile, and may *licitly* confirm subjects of other dioceses if they show a letter of permission or other testimony from their own bishop or parish priest.[3] By a *special indult* the Guardian (O. F. M.) of the Holy Sepulchre at Jerusalem may confirm persons of the Latin Rite if no bishop of that rite residing in his own territory is at hand.[4]

The faculty to confirm is sometimes granted also to *missionaries* who preside over vast provinces. Thus it was given for China and Chile.[5] The condition is always added that they must use chrism blessed by a Catholic bishop.[6] In the instruction which they receive together with the faculty, it is also added that whenever they administer this Sacrament they must mention the special faculty in virtue of which they do so. But this is not required for the validity of the act.[7]

Vicars Apostolic have this faculty by law, yet their *pro-vicars*, during a vacancy, cannot confirm in virtue of their office, much less delegate other missionaries to administer Confirmation. Any attempt to do so would be invalid, and the Sacrament would have to be re-administered.[8] The very same decision, however, says that the

---

[3] S. C. EE. et RR., March 30, 1855 (Bizzarri, *Collectanea*, p. 637 f.); Dec. 11, 1897; can. 784.

[4] Benedict XIV, "*Cum ad*," Jan. 9, 1741; "*Demandatam*," Dec. 24, 1743, § 14.

[5] S. C. P. F., July 29, 1841; March 4, 1903 (*Coll.*, nn. 933, 2161).

[6] S. C. P. F., May 4, 1774 (*Coll.*, n. 503).

[7] S. C. P. F., Sept. 11, 1841 (*Coll.*, n. 940).

[8] S. C. P. F., Sept. 12, 1821 (*Coll.*, n. 766). This must, *a fortiori*, be applied to pro-prefects.

Pontiff may grant the faculty of delegating others.   The faculty of subdelegating a priest (*" benevisum sacerdotem "*) was given to the bishop of Concepcion, Chile.[9] A decision of the S. C. Propaganda, with the special approval of the Sovereign Pontiff granted the faculty of administering Confirmation to the *Superior internus,* or the *vicar general,* or the *Vicar Apostolic-elect* while not yet consecrated; this faculty included the power of subdelegating a priest of the vacant vicariate or diocese for giving Confirmation.[10]   Now a Vicar-Apostolic-elect, who has received his letters of appointment, according to can. 294, § 2, may administer Confirmation, and therefore no longer needs a special faculty for this purpose.

§ 4. *A priest of the Latin rite,* who enjoys this faculty by virtue of an indult, can administer Confirmation *validly only to the faithful of his own rite,* unless the indult expressly grants him larger powers.

§ 5. *Priests of the Oriental rite* who are entitled by virtue either of a faculty or of a privilege to confirm children of their own rite immediately after Baptism, may not lawfully confer Confirmation on children of the Latin rite.

§ 4 is taken from an Instruction of the Propaganda, issued in 1774, and extended in 1888 by the Holy Office to all priests who have the Apostolic indult for administering Confirmation.   But nothing is said therein of the validity or invalidity of Confirmation administered by a Latin priest to a person of the Greek rite.   The S. Congregation desired information to be gathered with regard to the following points: To what Oriental rite the *confirmandi* belonged; by whom they were confirmed, whether by their own bishop or by priests of their own

9 S. O., March 4, 1903 (*Coll.,* n.2161).
10 July 29, 1841 (*Coll.,* n. 933).

nation; whether they asked for Confirmation of their own accord; whether they could conveniently receive the Sacrament from their own bishops; whether, finally, Confirmation was to be administered in a diocese where there resides an Oriental bishop who is the Ordinary of the *confirmandus*.[11] Our text briefly declares that Confirmation can not be validly administered by a priest of the Latin rite to a Catholic, whether infant or adult, of an Oriental rite.

§ 5 *strictly forbids* Oriental priests to confirm infants of the Latin rite; that Confirmation thus unlawfully administered would be invalid, cannot be inferred either from the text itself or from the quotation given in Cardinal Gasparri's edition. On the contrary, the validity seems to be assured. *Nefas* is a strong term, but it cannot be stretched so as to involve invalidity.

Ruthenian priests of the Oriental rite would incur suspension *a divinis ipso facto*,[12] but this supposes only an illicit, not an invalid act. When the question was proposed to Rome, whether Oriental priests who are authorized to baptize babies of the Latin rite, may also administer Confirmation to the same, the answer was, *negative et ad mentem*. The mind of the Apostolic See was that the Oriental bishops should restrain their priests from such unlawful administration, which had been often and strictly forbidden by the Holy See. To the further question whether Confirmation thus administered should be conditionally repeated, the answer was, *non expedire*, except in the case of those who are to be promoted to tonsure or sacred orders, and then only conditionally and secretly.[13] Whether the priests of the *Greek-Ruthenian*

---

11 S. C. P. F., May 4, 1774 (*Coll.*, n. 503).

12 S. C. P. F., July 5, 1886 ad 1 (*Coll.*, n. 1660).

13 S. O., Jan. 14, 1885 (*Coll.*, n. 1630).

rite residing in the *United States* can validly administer Confirmation to the faithful of their own rite, seems doubtful. The decree *" Ea semper "* of Pius X [14] expressly denies the validity of such a Confirmation. The decree of Aug. 17, 1914, does not touch this subject, nor is there any such clause to be found in the decree of Aug. 18, 1913, for the Ruthenian Bishop in Canada. Hence we hesitate to deny the validity, as the later decree contains nothing to the effect. [15] The *Greek priests of Italy* were " expressly forbidden " (*expresse interdictum*) to administer Confirmation even to the infants of their own rite, as this power was reserved to the bishops of the Latin rite, under whose jurisdiction they lived. [16]

This, then, is the canonical status of the minister of Confirmation. The underlying theological question is a rather vexed one and would demand a more elaborate investigation. For the question would have to be solved: Does the power of conferring Confirmation emanate from the power of Holy Orders, or from jurisdiction? What does the priest receive by delegation? Is it a new power of Order, or is it power of jurisdiction? It cannot be an extension of the priestly character, making it episcopal for the time, because the episcopal character is conferred by ordination, not by a mere papal letter. [17] Benedict XIV, who devoted much study to this controversy, [18] supposes tacit or express reservation or limitation of the power of confirming made by the Apostolic See in favor of bishops, and continues: Although to confirm is an act of the episcopal order, the validity of which does not depend on the will of the Pontiff, yet to delegate to a

---

[14] June 14, 1907, art. 4.

[15] *Am. Eccl. Rev.*, Vol. 37, 516 ff.; Vol. 51, 586 ff.; Vol. 49, 593 ff.

[16] Benedict XIV, *" Etsi pastoralis,"* May 26, 1742, § III, 1.

[17] O'Dwyer, *l. c.*, p. 65 f.

[18] Cfr. *De Syn. Dioec.*, l. VII, 8, 7; IDEM, *" Ex tuis precibus,"* Nov. 16, 1748, § 9 to Abbot Engelbert of Kempten, who received the faculty of confirming his own subjects and those of the abbey church.

simple priest the power of performing such an act belongs to jurisdiction rather than to order. The jurisdiction of the bishop is subject to the Supreme Pontiff in such a manner that the latter may, by his authority and command, limit or take it away for a just reason. This, he says, is clearly the opinion of St. Thomas, who says that, as far as the real body of Christ (viz., the Holy Eucharist) is concerned, priests have equal power with bishops, whereas in regard to His mystic body bishops are superior to priests; and since the plenitude of power resides in the Supreme Pontiff, he may confer a power belonging to a higher rank on clergymen of inferior rank.[19] It would be difficult to assign the time when such a reservation of power was made concerning the Greek priests. With regard to the Latin clergy Benedict XIV could point to the letter of Innocent I (401–417) to Decentius of Gubbio. But as Gregory I reversed that general prohibition, it seems more natural to assume that the limitation or withdrawal of this restriction [20] was first introduced by custom and only at a later time determined by positive law for the Western Church, while in the Eastern Church, where children were confirmed immediately after baptism, no limitation was made, except in regard to subjects of the Latin rite. If it be asked, What does the delegation by the Pope to a simple priest of the power of conferring Confirmation imply? we answer: Not the conferring of a special dignity,[21] but merely an extension of the power, or faculty, or authority [22] of confirming. This delegation, however, is

19 Lib. IV, Dist. 7, q. 3, art. 1, gla. 3; *Summa Theol.*, III, q. 72, art. 11.

20 O'Dwyer, *l. c.*, p. 172.

21 Thus Lehmkuhl, *Theol. Moral.*, II, n. 99. But this is hard to understand, because dignity results primarily from jurisdiction, and therefore the highest dignity is that of the Pope, in whom resides the plenitude of power, which chiefly indicates and signifies jurisdiction.

22 All these terms occur in the documents.

limited either *territorially*, as for vicars-Apostolic, prefects Apostolic, prelates *nullius*, or *personally* as regards Latin priests with respect to persons of the Oriental Rite. If a curious reader would ask: Whence the difference? we should answer: The powers given to bishops and priests up to the beginning of the third century were not precisely determined, as the example of the *chorepiscopi* shows. The final answer, of course, must be sought in the theory of St. Thomas, that the power of confirming concerns the mystic rather than the real body of Christ, in other words, is directly connected with jurisdiction and rests fundamentally on the power of the priesthood. To us no other solution seems acceptable, especially in consideration of the fact that Rome has granted to bishops the faculty of subdelegating or delegating any priest they choose to administer Confirmation.

THE BISHOP'S POWER

CAN. 783

§ 1. Episcopus in sua dioecesi hoc sacramentum etiam extraneis legitime ministrat, nisi obstet expressa proprii eorum Ordinarii prohibitio.

§ 2. In aliena dioecesi indiget licentia Ordinarii loci saltem rationabiliter praesumpta, nisi agatur de propriis subditis quibus confirmationem conferat privatim ac sine baculo et mitra.

§ 1. A bishop may lawfully administer the sacrament of Confirmation in his own diocese, even to such as are not his subjects, unless their Ordinary has issued a special prohibition to the contrary.

§ 2. To confirm in a strange diocese he needs the at least reasonably presumed permission of the local Ordinary, unless he confirms his own subjects, in which case he is not allowed to use the pastoral staff or mitre.

Staff and mitre are the insignia of pontifical jurisdiction which no bishop may employ in another bishop's diocese without the other's permission.[23] The Vicar-Capitular must ask a bishop to confer Confirmation. This would offer an occasion for a presumed permission, *viz.*, if the administrator would call on a bishop to confer orders on the clerics of a vacant diocese, the bishop thus called for ordination could also licitly confirm. Absence and sickness would also be presumed reasons. If, however, a bishop would publicly declare that he would confirm only his own subjects to the exclusion of strangers in or outside his diocese, Confirmation bestowed on such non-subjects who presented themselves stealthily would be invalid.[24]

It may be added that a metropolitan is not entitled to administer Confirmation in the dioceses of his suffragan bishops without their special permission.[25]

Can. 784

Presbytero quoque licet, si apostolico locali privilegio sit munitus, in designato sibi territorio confirmare etiam extraneos, nisi id ipsorum Ordinarii expresse vetuerint.

A priest who has an Apostolic local privilege empowering him to administer Confirmation may licitly confirm subjects not his own in the territory assigned to him,

---

23 S. Rit. C., April 14, 1877 (*Dec. Auth.*, n. 3416); S. C. C., Aug. 2, 1596.

24 S. C. EE. et RR., Aug., 1682 (Ferraris, *Prompta Bibliotheca, s. v. "Confirmatio,"* art. II, n. 14),

because of lack of the necessary intention the S. Cong. decided negatively.

25 S. C. EE. et RR., April 18, 1599 (Ferraris, *l. c.*, art. II, n. 9).

provided the Ordinaries of the respective *confirmandi* have not expressly forbidden it. Hence, as already stated, such priests should procure testimonial letters from the Ordinaries whose subjects they confirm.[26] Note the words, " *locali privilegio.*" A local privilege is an indult given for a certain territory or district, whether large or small. Sometimes such a privilege is attached not to a territory, but to persons. Thus, for instance, an abbot received from Pope Benedict XIV the privilege to confer Confirmation on " the subjects of the aforesaid abbey and on the parishioners of the abbey-church." This was a personal privilege, restricted to the persons named and could not validly be extended to others who were not subject to the abbot.[27]

DUTY OF THE BISHOP

CAN. 785

§ 1. Episcopus obligatione tenetur sacramentum hoc subditis rite et rationabiliter petentibus conferendi, praesertim tempore visitationis dioecesis.

§ 2. Eadem obligatione tenetur presbyter, privilegio apostolico donatus, erga illos quorum in favorem est concessa facultas.

§ 3. Ordinarius, legitima causa impeditus aut potestate confirmandi carens, debet, quoad fieri possit, saltem intra quodlibet quinquennium providere ut suis subditis hoc sacramentum administretur.

§ 4. Si graviter neglexerit sacramentum confirmationis suis subditis per se vel per alium ministrare, servetur praescriptum can. 274, n. 4.

26 S. C. EE. et RR., March 30, 1855 (Bizzarri, *Collectanea*, p. 636 f.).

27 " *Suprema,*" April 26, 1749, § 3.

Every *bishop* is in duty bound to administer this Sacrament to those of his subjects who becomingly and reasonably ask for it, especially at the time of the canonical visitation. *Priests* who are endowed with an Apostolic privilege have the same duty towards those in whose favor the faculty was granted. This canon must be compared with Canons 786–788, which deal with the *subject* of Confirmation. Those ask for Confirmation "*rite et rationabiliter*" who are endowed with the qualities mentioned in said canons; for duty and right are correlative terms.

The question whether a bishop or priest who is empowered to administer Confirmation is bound in conscience to confirm such as suffer from a *contagious disease*, was answered by Benedict XIV, who says it would be difficult to prove such an obligation, since this sacrament is not absolutely necessary for salvation, and the example of St. Charles Borromeo was a heroic one, from which no strict obligation can be deduced. But he adds that if Confirmation were administered to such unfortunates, there would be no reason for using an instrument, brush, sponge or cotton, because the act is very short.[28]

The *time* for administering Confirmation is the canonical visitation, on which occasion the bishop is obliged to confirm.[29]

§ 3 says that an Ordinary who is lawfully prevented from, or does not enjoy the power of, administering Confirmation, should, as far as possible, take care that this Sacrament is conferred at least every *five years*. Should he, continues § 4, grievously neglect this duty of confirming his subjects, either personally or through another, the

---

28 *De Syn. Dioec.*, XIII, 19, nn. 6, 12.

29 S. C. C., July 18, 1699 (Richter, *Trid.*, p. 47, n. 3). Of course, if no one asks for Confirmation, or if Confirmation was administered a short time before, there would be no obligation.

metropolitan should see to it that this matter is attended to and inform the Holy See. *Legitimate causes* preventing a bishop from administering Confirmation within the term of five years, would be protracted illness, exile, and detention by higher superiors. The vicar-capitular has not the power to confirm, but should invite an outside bishop if this Sacrament has not been administered in the diocese for a long time.[30] If grievous neglect has crept into a suffragan's diocese, the *metropolitan* may compel or admonish the Ordinary of the same to comply with the law, but he may not administer Confirmation without the suffragan's permission because this case is not mentioned among those in which the metropolitan is authorized to supply the negligence of his suffragans.[31] However, if the canonical visitation would, upon request of the Holy See, be performed by the archbishop, we believe that Confirmation would also be mentioned in the *causa probata.*

[30] S. Rit. C., April, 1877 (*Dec. Auth.*, n. 3416).

[31] Barbosa, *De Officio et Potestate Episcopi*, P. I., tit. 4, nn. 12, 43; glossa ad c. 2, Clem. V, 7, s. v. "*Etiam celebrare.*"

CHAPTER II

Can. 786

Aquis baptismi non ablutus valide confirmari nequit; praeterea, ut quis licite et fructuose confirmetur, debet esse in statu gratiae constitutus et, si usu rationis polleat, sufficienter instructus.

Can. 787

Quanquam hoc sacramentum non est de necessitate medii ad salutem, nemini tamen licet, oblata occasione, illud negligere; imo parochi curent ut fideles ad illud opportuno tempore accedant.

Can. 788

Licet sacramenti confirmationis administratio convenienter in Ecclesia Latina differatur ad septimum circiter aetatis annum, nihilominus etiam antea conferri potest, si infans in mortis periculo sit constitutus, vel ministro id expedire ob iustas et graves causas videatur.

Can. 789

Confirmandi, si plures sint, adsint primae manuum impositioni seu extensicni, nec nisi expleto ritu discedant.

The first of these four canons embodies a deduction from can. 737, § 1, which calls Baptism the door to the other Sacraments. *One who is not yet baptized cannot be validly confirmed* because he is not yet initiated into the Christian mysteries or incorporated in the mystic body of Christ, which initiation or incorporation confers the right to receive the other Sacraments. Besides, in order to *receive this Sacrament licitly and profitably, one must be in the state of grace.* For though the indelible character is impressed even if one is not in the state of sanctifying grace, the sacramental grace, or, as a text of the *Decretum Gratiani* says, the sevenfold grace of the Holy Ghost with the plenitude of holiness and knowledge and strength does not descend in Confirmation if this Sacrament is received in the state of mortal sin.[1] Besides, *one who has attained the age of discretion must be sufficiently instructed* in the more important truths of faith as well as the nature and efficacy of Confirmation. The *confirmandus* should know the difference between Baptism and Confirmation, which resembles the difference between generation and growth and the distinction between enrolling in the army of Christ and training for active service.[2] Should it happen that an adult, especially an elderly person, has not even the intention of receiving strength for his soul through Confirmation, the Sacrament should not be administered.[3]

Can. 787 says that Confirmation is *relatively*, not *absolutely necessary* for salvation, and therefore must not be neglected. A canon of Gratian[4] declares that no one is a Christian unless he has been confirmed by the bishop

---

[1] C. 5, Dist. 5, *de cons.* Hence confession should precede Confirmation; cfr. *Pontificale Rom.*, tit. *De Confirmandis;* S. O., Dec. 11, 1850 (*Coll.*, n. 1054). As soon as the *obex* (state of grievous sin) is removed, the sacramental grace revives.

[2] Benedict XIV, "*Etsi minime*," Feb. 7, 1742, § 9; "*Eo quamvis tempore*, May 4, 1745, § 6.

[3] S. O., April 10, 1860 (*Coll.*, n. 1213).

[4] C. 6, Dist. 5, *de cons.*

with chrism. This is an exaggeration, but it indicates the danger to which, in the opinion of the early Church, one exposed himself by wilfully neglecting this great Sacrament. Those who were suspected of being imbued with the errors of Wiclif and Huss were asked whether they believed that one who spurned the Sacrament of Confirmation committed a grievous sin.[5] Our text says that, although this Sacrament is not absolutely necessary for salvation, no one may *lawfully neglect to receive it* if offered the opportunity.[6] For this reason *pastors* should take care that the faithful receive Confirmation at the proper time. An Instruction of the S. C. Propaganda enjoined the missionaries of Mesopotamia to instruct the Nestorians, bishops as well as priests, to receive this Sacrament.[7] Every pastor is in duty bound to teach the faithful under his care not only the necessity of this Sacrament, but also how to receive it worthily.

Can. 788 mentions the custom of the Latin Church, which differs from that of the Greek, to defer Confirmation to the age of discretion, *i. e.*, about the seventh year.[8] This *custom*, the text says, is quite proper, but the Sacrament may be administered at an earlier age if the child is in danger of death or the minister judges that there are other just and weighty reasons. Such reasons would be, *e. g.*, great distance preventing one from reaching a place within the time limit of five years,— surely a rare thing.[9]

It may not be amiss to add what Lehmkuhl says,[10] that

---

[5] Prop. 19 (Denzinger, n. 563).

[6] Benedict XIV, " *Etsi pastoralis*," May 26, 1742, § III, 4: " *Gravis peccati reatu teneri*."

[7] Instr., July 31, 1902 (*Coll.*, n. 2149).

[8] Benedict XIV, ' *Eo quamvis*

tempore," May 4, 1745, § 6: " *Allatae sunt*," July 26, 1755, § 22.

[9] S. O., Dec. 11, 1850, n. 12 (*Coll.*, n. 1054); S. C. C., March 12, April 23, 1774 (Richter, *Trid.*, p. 47, n. 1).

[10] *Theol. Moral.*, II, n. 100.

if the bishop would be obliged to administer Confirmation to the dying, he would have to do so to all or none, else there would be partiality and scandal; and if he had to confer the Sacrament on all the sick, there would be a great burden thrown upon him.   An Oriental priest who enjoys the faculty of administering Confirmation together with Baptism may apply this faculty not only to his own people, but also to Catholics of another rite, provided the tacit privilege of administering both Sacraments is in vogue in that rite.[11]

Can. 789 provides that the *confirmandi*, if there are a number of them, should be *present at the first imposition* or extension of the hands, and not leave before the whole rite or ceremony is completed.[12] This is not, however, a condition affecting validity.[13]

[11] S. O., April 22, 1896 (*Coll.*, n. 1926).
[12] *Pontificale Rom.*, tit. *De Confirmandis.*
[13] S. O., April 17, 1872 (*Coll.*, n. 1383).

CHAPTER III

CAN. 790

Hoc sacramentum quovis tempore conferri potest; maxime autem decet illud administrari in hebdomada Pentecostes.

CAN. 791

Licet proprius confirmationis administrandae locus ecclesia sit, ex causa tamen quam minister iustam ac rationabilem iudicaverit, potest hoc sacramentum in quolibet alio decenti loco conferri.

CAN. 792

Episcopo ius est intra fines suae dioecesis confirmationem administrandi in locis quoque exemptis.

This Sacrament may be conferred at any time, but it is most fittingly administered in the week after Pentecost. Whilst the Cardinal Vicar of Rome or his *vicegerente* may administer this Sacrament on any day or at any time in the Lateran Basilica, the Cardinal Archpriest of the Vatican Basilica may do so only during the Octave of the Feast of SS. Peter and Paul in St. Peter's.[1] The text designates the Octave of Pentecost as the most appropriate season. This praiseworthy custom may be conveniently observed especially in cathedral churches.

1 Benedict XIV, "*Ad honorandum,*" March 27, 1752, § 11.

Can. 791. Although the *proper place* for administering confirmation is the *church*, it may also be conferred in any other decent place, provided the minister has a just and plausible reason for so doing. Hence Confirmation may be administered in any private or semi-public oratory, and even in private houses if they are neat and properly kept; also, during the time of an interdict, in an interdicted place.[2]

Can. 792. Every bishop has the right to administer Confirmation within the *boundaries of his diocese also in exempt places*. When certain exempt regulars, insisting on their privileges, contended that the bishop was not entitled to administer Confirmation in their (parochial or non-parochial) churches, the S. Congregation decided in favor of the bishop, and Benedict XIV fully ratified the respective decisions.[3]

When confirming the bishop may make use of throne and baldachino and pontifical regalia.

Exempt places here are monasteries, convents, academies, colleges, churches and chapels (such as are *pleno iure* incorporated) of exempt religious, or other exempt persons; but *not* the exempt territories of prelates or abbots *nullius,* because these prelates are entitled to administer Confirmation in their own districts.

[2] C. 43, X, V, 39; c. 19, 6°, V, 11.
[3] " *Firmandis,*" Nov. 6, 1744, § 6.

CHAPTER IV

CAN. 793

Ex vetustissimo Ecclesiae more, ut in baptismo, ita etiam in confirmatione adhibendus est patrinus, si haberi possit.

CAN. 794

§ 1. Patrinus unum tantum confirmandum aut duos praesentet, nisi aliud iusta de causa ministro videatur.

§ 2. Unus quoque pro singulis confirmandis sit patrinus.

A most ancient ecclesiastical custom demands that, as at Baptism, so also at Confirmation, a sponsor be employed if possible. He should not stand for more than one or two *confirmandi*, unless the minister deems it prudent to deviate from that rule for a just cause. Each *confirmandus* should have but one sponsor.

The custom of employing sponsors at Confirmation would be very venerable indeed if a certain text of Gratian[1] could be ascribed to Pope Hyginus (136–140). Doubtless the practice was universal at the beginning of the Middle Ages. Ancient also is the custom that one sponsor, either a man or a woman,[2] stands for each *confirmandus*. That at least one sponsor should be employed at Confirmation is a grave obligation, unless weighty and

---

1 C. 100, Dist. 4, *de cons.*   2 C. 100 f., *ibid.*

urgent reasons excuse.[3] But the Roman Court will not, — except for reasons of strict necessity (*praecisa neces- sitas*) — tolerate the custom that one man stands for all the *confirmandi*, and one woman for all the *confirm- andae*.

It is left to the minister of Confirmation to decide whether there is such a strict necessity.[4] If only Sisters are at hand, they may be employed as sponsors for the *confirmandae*.[5] Now-a-days when spiritual relationship is no longer contracted as an impediment to marriage, the necessity of using only one sponsor for a whole class of males and females respectively seems to have abated. On the other hand, the rule that each *confirmandus* should have but one sponsor must be obeyed.[6]

REQUISITES OF SPONSORSHIP

CAN. 795

Ut quis sit patrinus, oportet:

1.° Sit ipse quoque confirmatus, rationis usum as- secutus et intentionem habeat id munus gerendi;

2.° Nulli haereticae aut schismaticae sectae sit ad- scriptus, nec ulla ex poenis de quibus in can. 765, n. 2 per sententiam declaratoriam aut condemnatoriam notatus;

3.° Non sit pater, mater, coniux confirmandi;

4.° A confirmando eiusve parentibus vel tutoribus vel, hi si desint aut renuant, a ministro vel a parocho sit designatus;

---

[3] S. O., Dec. 11, 1850; Sept. 5, 1877; S. C. P. F., May 4, 1774 (*Coll.*, n. 1054, 1480, 503).

[4] S. O., Nov. 20, 1873 (*Coll.*, n. 1408); S. C. C., June 14, July 12, 1823 (Richter, *Trid.*, p. 47, n. 2).

[5] S. Rit. C., Feb. 15, 1887 (*Dec.*

Auth., n. 3670); these religious, however, should have the permission of their superiors and Ordinary. S. O., Sept. 3, 1871 (*Coll.*, n. 198).

[6] C. 3, 6° IV, 3; S. O., Nov. 26, 1873 (*Coll* n. 1408).

5.° Confirmandum in ipso confirmationis actu per se vel per procuratorem physice tangat.

To be able to serve as sponsor:

1.° One must be confirmed, have the use of reason and the intention to assume the office of sponsor.

2.° He or she must belong to no heretical or schismatic sect, nor be under any of the penalties mentioned in can. 765, n. 2.

3.° He or she must be neither the father nor the mother nor the consort of the one to be confirmed.

4.° He must be appointed sponsor either by the *confirmandus,* his parents or guardians, or, if these should fail or refuse to appoint a sponsor, he is to be designated by the minister or pastor.

5.° The sponsor must physically touch the *confirmandus* in the act of confirmation, either personally or by proxy.

It is unnecessary to dwell on these requisites, which are about the same as explained under can. 765. The *act* the sponsor is called upon to perform is sometimes called *ligare,* to bind,[7] because he was supposed to tie a band around the forehead of the *confirmandus* after he had been anointed with chrism. However the proper *act of sponsorship* is laying the right hand on the right shoulder of the *confirmandus.* It is not necessary to put one's foot upon that of the godchild.[8] The act may be done *by proxy,* says the text. Thus, if the bishop who confirms a child wishes to be at the same time his godfather, he must appoint another to represent him, not confirm

---

[7] Hence the verse: "*Ligans, ligatus, ligatique parentes,*" which expresses the relationship between the sponsor, the god-child, and the latter's parents.

[8] S. Rit. C., Sept. 20, 1749, ad 6 (*Dec. Auth.,* n. 2404).

him with one hand, and hold him with the other.[9] It
may be added that the custom of choosing the name of a
Saint other than the baptismal one at Confirmation is
permissible, but by no means necessary.[10]

REQUISITES OF LICIT SPONSORSHIP

CAN. 796

Ut quis licite ad patrini munus admittatur, oportet:

1.° Sit alius a patrino baptismi, nisi rationabilis
causa, iudicio ministri, aliud suadeat, aut statim post
baptismum legitime confirmatio conferatur;

2.° Sit eiusdem sexus ac confirmandus, nisi aliud
ministro in casibus particularibus ex rationabili causa
videatur;

3.° Serventur praeterea praescripta can. 766.

To be licitly admitted to sponsorship at Confirmation:

1.° One must be different from the baptismal sponsor,
unless there be a plausible reason to disregard this rule,
or Confirmation is legitimately administered immediately
after Baptism.

2.° The sponsor must be of the same sex as the one
to be confirmed, unless the minister has a good reason
to depart from this regulation in an individual case.

3.° The other rules mentioned in can. 766 must be
observed.

What was said under can. 766 will suffice on this subject. Let us cite one decision of the S. C. C. Certain
pastors having complained to the bishop that they had
vainly endeavored to eradicate the custom of having the

9 This seems to have been the custom in a certain diocese; S. Rit. C.,
June 14, 1873, ad III (*Dec. Auth.*,
n. 3305).

10 S. Rit. C., Sept. 20, 1749, ad 7
(*Dec. Auth.* n. 2404).

same sponsors at Baptism and Confirmation, the bishop thought it best to tolerate the same. But the S. Congregation decided that, though it may be tolerated, this custom should be gradually abolished.[11] A plausible reason for which a man might be permitted to act as sponsor for a girl would be a special blood relationship, a happy coincidence, or the desire of the bishop to act by proxy as sponsor for a girl or young lady.[12]

SPIRITUAL RELATIONSHIP

Cap. 797

Etiam ex valida confirmatione oritur inter confirmatum et patrinum cognatio spiritualis, ex qua patrinus obligatione tenetur confirmatum perpetuo sibi commendatum habendi eiusque christianam educationem curandi.

Validly conferred Confirmation entails a spiritual relationship between the confirmed person and the sponsor, in virtue of which the latter is obliged to take a special and perpetual interest in the welfare of his godchild and to see to it that he or she receives a Christian education. However, according to can. 1079, this spiritual relationship no longer constitutes a matrimonial impediment and is therefore restricted to the merely spiritual part of education in case the parents fail to do their duty. That godparents, if able, may and should assist their spiritual children in case of need is a dictate of natural reason.[18]

---

11 S. C. C., Feb. 16, 1884 (*Coll. P. F.*, n. 1612).

12 This seems implied in the decision of the S. Rit. C., June 14, 1873, ad III (*Dec. Auth.*, n. 3305).

18 " *Sibi commendatum habere* " signifies a kind of protectorship, which must be understood according to the rules of charity. It is true charity, such as preached by Christ and His Church, yet often neglected, and now-a-days almost unknown, or at least not practised.

CHAPTER V

RECORD

CAN. 798

Nomina ministri, confirmatorum, parentum et patrinorum, diem ac locum confirmationis parochus inscribat in peculiari libro, praeter adnotationem in libro baptizatorum de qua in can. 470, § 2.

CAN. 799

Si proprius confirmati parochus praesens non fuerit, de collata confirmatione minister vel per se ipse vel per alium quamprimum eundem certiorem faciat.

The *Rituale Romanum*[1] prescribes that a Confirmation record be kept in *every church* in which this Sacrament is administered. This book, according to our canon, must contain the names of the minister, of the persons confirmed and their parents and sponsors, as well as the date of Confirmation. All these entries must be made by the pastor in a book specially set apart for the recording of Confirmations. Besides, he must also enter every Confirmation in the baptismal record.

Can. 799 enacts that if the *parochus proprius* of the *confirmatus* was not present at the Confirmation, he

---

1 Tit. X, c. 2, prescribes five books: for Baptisms, Confirmations, Marriages, Census, and Deaths. For the form of entering Confirmations see c. 4 (ed. Pustet, 1913, p. 328 f.).

should be informed as soon as possible of the fact by the minister or by some other person.

CAN. 800

Ad collatam confirmationem probandam, modo nemini fiat praeiudicium, satis est unus testis omni exceptione maior, vel ipsius confirmati iusiurandum, nisi confirmatus fuerit in infantili aetate.

When no prejudice to others is involved, *one trustworthy witness* is sufficient to prove the fact of Confirmation. Thus the testimony of the official or authentic record kept in the diocesan archives would be entirely sufficient, as also the pastor's testimony, given under his signature and seal. Besides, says the text, the *sworn statement* of the one who was confirmed must be admitted as proof, unless he received the Sacrament before he reached the age of discretion.

TITLE III

THE HOLY EUCHARIST

CAN. 801

In sanctissima Eucharistia sub speciebus panis et vini ipsemet Christus Dominus continetur, offertur, sumitur.

In the most Holy Eucharist Christ the Lord Himself is contained, offered, and received, under the species of bread and wine. This is an article of faith and as such properly belongs to dogmatic theology. The Real Presence of Christ in the Eucharist has been the belief of the Catholic Church for nineteen hundred years, despite all calumnies, assaults, and blasphemies. The Code, according to the twofold aspect of this holy Sacrament, *in fieri* and *in facto esse,* treats of the Holy Eucharist as a Sacrifice and as a Sacrament instituted for the spiritual life of the faithful.

CHAPTER I

THE HOLY SACRIFICE OF THE MASS

The seven Sacraments are intended for all the faithful, and the ancient adage: *"Sacramenta propter homines"* holds true with regard to all, at least in general. But the membership of the Church is essentially distinguished into clergy and laity, and hence the Church that sanctifies is distinct from the one that is sanctified (*ecclesia sanctificans et sanctificata*). This fact is most conspicuous in the Holy Eucharist, particularly in the Sacrifice of the Mass, where the hieratic character of the priesthood appears most obviously. Hence the Code naturally treats first of

ARTICLE I

THE CELEBRANT OF THE MASS

CAN. 802

Potestatem offerendi Missae sacrificium habent soli sacerdotes.

Priests alone have the power of offering the Sacrifice of the Mass.

It is not necessary to enter into the controversy regarding the universal priesthood of all the faithful.[1] The distinction between clergy and laity rests on a firm biblical and traditional basis. Only those may offer up gifts and sacrifices who are called by God and validly or-

---

[1] I Pet. II, 9 is abused or wrongly interpreted.

dained,[2] and the fiction of an assembly of predestined or an invisible congregation has never had a place in the Church of Christ.[3] The phrase *soli sacerdotes* excludes the inferior clergy as well as laymen, who, should they attempt to say Mass sacrilegiously, would not only act invalidly, but also incur severe penalties.[4]

CONCELEBRATING FORBIDDEN

CAN. 803

Non licet pluribus sacerdotibus concelebrare, praeterquam in Missa ordinationis presbyterorum et in Missa consecrationis Episcoporum secundum Pontificale Romanum.

Concelebrating takes place if two or more priests consecrate the same bread and wine or, as at the consecration of bishops, two hosts and the same wine in one chalice. It is, therefore, *not a mere recital* of the same prayers in general, and of the formula of consecration in particular, but a distinct rite,[5] which was once common in both East and West and is still in vogue in the Orient in cities where there is but one church. All the priests gather around the bishop, with whom they recite the prayers of the Mass and receive the Holy Eucharist under both species.[6] In the Latin Church concelebration is allowed and prescribed only at the *ordination of priests and the consecration of bishops according to the Roman Pontifical.*[7] Under Innocent III (1198–1216) concelebration was cus-

2 Heb. V, 1.

3 Cf. Trid., sess. 22, De Sacrificio Missae, c. 1, 2; can. 2; sess. 23, De Ordine, c. 1.

4 The penalty is excommunication *speciali modo* reserved to the Holy See, Can. 2322.

5 Benedict XIV, *De Sacrificio Missae*, l. III, c. 16, n. 5.

6 *Ibid.*, n. 1; *Cath. Encycl.*, Vol. IV, 190, *s. v.* "Concelebration."

7 Tit. *De Ordinibus Conferendis;* tit. *De Ordinatione Presbyteri;* tit. *De Consecratione Electi in Episcopum.*

tomary on higher feasts, but now it is forbidden in the Latin Church (this canon does not concern the Oriental Rite) [8] except on the two occasions mentioned.

Benedict XIV gives some practical hints for newly ordained priests how to concelebrate with the bishop. He says that the Roman Pontifical prescribes that the bishop should recite the words of consecration " *slowly and in a rather loud voice* " so that the neomysts may follow, and adds that the latter should have the intention of consecrating the same bread and wine together with the bishop. This is sufficient, and they need not worry about the difficulties proposed by some authors. Those difficulties are absurd because the bishop is the main consecrator and the priests merely concur in the act as accessories; the form they employ is morally one with the form pronounced by the bishop, and consequently, even though they finish the words of consecration a little before or after the bishop, the consecration is valid.[9] The same Pontiff, who was a great canonist, also says that there is no reason for depriving a priest thus celebrating with his bishop of the right of accepting a stipend.[10]

THE CELEBRET

Can. 804

§ 1. Sacerdos extraneus ecclesiae in qua celebrare postulat, exhibens authenticas et adhuc validas litteras commendatitias sui Ordinarii, si sit saecularis, vel sui Superioris, si religosus, vel Sacrae Congregationis pro Ecclesia Orientali, si sit ritus orientalis, ad Missae celebrationem admittatur, nisi interim aliquid eum com-

8 Benedict XIV, " *Allatae sunt,*" July 26, 1755, § 38.

9 *De Sacrificio Missae*, l. III, c. 16, n. 7.

10 *Ibid.*, n. 10.

misisse constet, cur a Missae celebratione repelli debeat.

§ 2. Si iis litteris careat, sed rectori ecclesiae de eius probitate apprime constet, poterit admitti; si vero rectori sit ignotus, admitti adhuc potest semel vel bis, dummodo, ecclesiastica veste indutus, nihil ex celebratione ab ecclesia in qua litat, quovis titulo, percipiat, et nomen, officium suamque dioecesim in peculiari libro signet.

§ 3. Peculiares hac de re normae, salvis huius canonis praescriptis, ab Ordinario loci datae, servandae sunt ab omnibus, etiam religiosis exemptis, nisi agatur de admittendis ad celebrandum religiosis in ecclesia suae religionis.

The Council of Chalcedon, A. D. 451, forbade clergymen to minister in a strange district without letters of recommendation.[11] The Decretals demanded that the testimonies of five bishops should be asked of a clergyman who came from across the sea or was otherwise entirely unknown.[12] This is now reduced to what we call *celebret* or *pastor bonus* or *litterae commendatitiae*, which are given for the secular clergy by the Ordinary and for the religious by the religious superior. The *celebret* merely attests the bearer's rank in the hierarchy and his freedom from ecclesiastical censure. It must be *per se* demanded from any priest who wishes to celebrate in a church not his own (*extraneus ecclesiae*). If he belongs to the *Oriental rite,* he must show letters from the S. Congregation for the Oriental Church. This rule, we suppose, applies only when a priest of the Oriental rite wishes to say Mass in a church of a different rite and diocese, otherwise it would be difficult to understand

11 Cf. c. 7, Dist. 71.   12 C. 7, 1, X, I, 22.

why priests of the Oriental Rite are treated more rigorously than others. The S. C. Propaganda only demands letters given by the respective bishop, or vicar, or prefect Apostolic.[13] Priests who come from an Eastern province to our country need letters from the S. Congregation for the Oriental Church. This was already laid down in the canons on incardination.[14]

Concerning *Ruthenian Priests* in the U. S. and Canada it seems that the *celebret* given them by the respective Ordinary or Ruthenian bishop suffices; at least this may be concluded from art. II of the decree of the S. C. Propaganda, Aug. 17, 1914, which says that the Ruthenian bishop may not grant permission to say Mass or perform sacred functions to a strange priest who was neither called by him or sent by the S. Congregation. A priest who was properly admitted by the Ruthenian Bishop, therefore, is under his jurisdiction in everything and needs a *celebret* only from him. This interpretation is not opposed to § I of can. 304, because the Ruthenian bishop is under the immediate jurisdiction of the Holy See.[15]

Secular priests receive their *celebret* either from the diocesan chancery or the vicar-general.[16].

Religious, of whatever denomination, with simple and solemn profession, must obtain a *celebret* from their own superiors.[17]

13 April 20, 1873 (*Coll.*, n. 1400).

14 The documents concerning the Ruthenian Rite in the *Amer. Ecc. Rev.:* — Pius X, "*Ea semper,*" June 14, 1907 (Vol. 37, 513 ff.); Letter of the Apost. Delegate, Aug. 25, 1913 (Vol. 49, 473 f.); Decree of S. C. P. F., Aug. 18, 1913, for Canada (Vol. 49, 593 ff.); Decree of S. C. P. F., Aug. 17, 1914, for the U. S. (Vol. 51, 586 ff.)

15 S. C. P. F., Aug. 17, 1914, art. 2 (*Amer. Eccl. Rev.*, 51, 587).

16 Cf. Benedict XIV, *Inst.*, 34, § 1, where he says that even rural deans may issue such a document. This may be accepted if the Ordinary grants him such power, otherwise the text excludes deans.

17 Cf. Benedict XIV, "*Apostolicum Ministerium,*" May 30, 1753, § 6: "*Quam Grave,*" Aug. 2, 1757,

Members of societies without vows, or only the one or other vow, who are not religious in the proper sense, must have a *celebret* from the local Ordinary.

A *celebret* is *authentic* if it is signed and sealed by the Ordinary or religious superior. All such are presumed to be genuine until the contrary is proved.[18] How long they remain valid, *adhuc validae litterae,* is not stated in our text. However, *celebrets* are generally issued for one year, but the Ordinary or superior may lengthen or shorten the term. A canonical impediment may be contracted within three or six months.[19] Hence the clause: "*unless it has become known in the meantime* that the bearer *has committed an act which would render it necessary to debar him from saying Mass.*" Where this is the case, a priest should be refused permission to say Mass in spite of a *celebret*. Thus if the rector of the church where the priest desires to say Mass knows of a suspension or ecclesiastical penalty or irregularity incurred by that priest, he would have to refuse him permission. But he could not make use of knowledge acquired in confession.[20] This is expressed in the words, *commisisse constet*, which imply proof to be brought.

§ 2. If a priest *has no celebret,* either because he has forgotten or lost it, but is known to the rector of the Church where he wishes to say Mass as a priest in good standing, he may be permitted to say Mass. Even if a priest is unknown to the rector, he may be permitted to say Mass once or twice, provided he is *dressed in the ecclesiastical garb,* accepts nothing for saying Mass from the church in which he celebrates, and duly enters his

§ 12, which mentions only regulars, but *a fortiori* includes all other religious.

18 Can. 1813 f.

19 Can. 994, § 1.

20 S. O., Nov. 18, 1682, *prop. proscripta* (Denzinger, n. 1087).

name, office and diocese in the book kept for that purpose.

This is a reminder that the ecclesiastical dress should be worn when demanding permission to celebrate Mass. The ecclesiastical dress here primarily means the cassock, but it may also signify the ecclesiastical travelling suit, inclusive of the Roman collar. A cassock may be had in the sacristy of almost any church.

§ 3. Any *special diocesan statutes* concerning this matter, which are in keeping with the present law, *must be observed by all,* including exempt religious, unless they wish to say Mass in a church of their own institute. This section extends to all religious, properly so-called, the privilege of saying Mass in a church of their own order or congregation without being bound by diocesan rules, which was formerly a prerogative of exempt religious only.[21] But if a religious wishes to say Mass in a church in charge of secular priests, or of religious of a different order or congregation, he is bound not only by the general law of the Church, but also by the particular laws of the diocese.[22] It is evident that the religious superior of the church where the religious wishes to say Mass is entitled to demand the *celebret*.[23]

THE OBLIGATION OF SAYING MASS

CAN. 805

Sacerdotes omnes obligatione tenentur Sacrum litandi pluries per annum; curet autem Episcopus vel Superior religiosus ut iidem saltem singulis diebus dominicis aliisque festis de praecepto divinis operentur.

---

[21] S. C. C., July 27, 1626; S. C. P. F., July 28, 1626 (*Coll.,* n. 25).

[22] S. O., Aug. 11, 1649 (*Coll.,* n. 118); Benedict XIV, "*Quam grave,*" Aug. 2, 1757, § 12.

[23] S. O., *l. c.*

All priests are obliged ·to say Mass several times a
year. But the bishop as well as the religious superior
ought to see to it that the priests subject to their jurisdiction celebrate the Sacred Mysteries at least on all Sundays and holy-days of obligation.

Innocent III complains woefully of some prelates who
would not celebrate Holy Mass even four times a year.[24]
His complaint led canonists and theologians to speculate
how many Masses a priest would have to say every year
to avoid grievous sin; for no canonical penalty is mentioned in Pope Innocent's canon. Benedict XIV did not
settle the question, though as private author he held that
it would be more in conformity with the decrees of
Trent if priests said Mass on Sundays and holy-days of
obligation, and whenever the Holy Viaticum had to be
administered to a sick person.[25] The same Pontiff held
that a superior may command his subjects to say Mass,[26]
which no doubt is true if there be any outward reason
for giving such a command, for instance, Mass for the
community, or in time of calamity. But it would certainly exceed the power of a bishop or religious superior
to command his subjects to say Mass every day. No
canonist or theologian has ever defended such a universal
and constant obligation.

Note that our text speaks only of *priests as such*.
The case is different if the obligation of saying Mass
arises from reasons of office or benefice. But not even
pastors or beneficiaries can be obliged to say Mass every
day.[27]

---

[24] C. 9, X, III, 41. If we press
the words of St. Thomas, *Sent.*, IV,
dist. 13, qu. 1, art. 2; *Summa*, III,
q. 82, art. 10, three times: Christmas, Easter and Pentecost, would be
sufficient.

[25] *De Sacrificio Missae*, l. III, c.
1.

[26] *De Sacrificio Missae*, l. III, c.
1, n. 8. The Carthusians said Mass
only on Sundays. *Ib.*, l. III, c. 2,
n. 5.

[27] S. C. C., Sept. 18, 1683; Benedict XIV, *De Sacrificio Missae*, l.
III, c. 3, n. 7 f.

CAN. 806

§ 1. **Excepto die Nativitatis Domini et die Comme-morationis omnium fidelium defunctorum, quibus fa-cultas est ter offerendi Eucharisticum Sacrificium, non licet sacerdoti plures in die celebrare Missas, nisi ex apostolico indulto aut potestate facta a loci Ordinario.**

§ 2. **Hanc tamen facultatem impertiri nequit Ordi-narius, nisi cum, prudenti ipsius iudicio, propter penuriam sacerdotum die festo de praecepto notabilis fidelium pars Missae adstare non possit; non est autem in eius potestate plures quam duas Missas eidem sacer-doti permittere.**

With the exception of Christmas and all Souls' Day, on which every priest may, if he wishes, say three Masses, *no priest is allowed to say more than one Mass a day* unless a papal indult or faculty from the Ordinary permits him to do so.

The Ordinary cannot grant this faculty unless he prudently judges that there is such a lack of priests as to leave a considerable number of the faithful without Mass on a holyday of obligation.

No Ordinary can give permission to a priest to say more than two Masses on one day.

Alexander II (1061–73) gives the reasons for this prohibition. "It is no small thing," he says, "to say Mass, and happy is he who says one Mass worthily." To say several Masses a day for the sake of gain or to be flattered by the worldly, he adds, is to merit damnation.[28]

---

[28] C. 53, Dist. 1, *de cons.*: "*Qui vero pro pecuniis aut adula-tionibus saecularium una die prae-*sumunt plures Missas non aestimo evadere damnationem.*" Cfr. c. 12, X, III, 41.

The custom of saying three Masses on Christmas is very old, as St. Gregory's homily for that feastday proves, and was acknowledged as lawful by the Decretals, which also permit the celebration of more than one Mass in case of necessity.[29]

The custom of saying three Masses on All Souls' Day was observed in Valencia and Catalonia since the pontificate of Julius III (1550–55), and Benedict XIV extended the privilege to the entire Spanish Kingdom and to Portugal.[30] His successor in the see of Bologna and St. Peter's Chair, our Holy Father Benedict XV, has now granted the same privilege to all priests of the universal Church[31] and embodied it in the Code. Priests who say three Masses on All Souls' Day may receive a stipend for one of them, but one of the two others must be applied *pro defunctis* and the other according to the intention of the Sovereign Pontiff. A priest who sings or says the conventual Mass may afterwards say two other Masses.[32]

There is no obligation of saying three Masses on *Christmas Day*. A priest may say one or two according to his good pleasure.[33] But if he says only one or two Masses he should say the Mass which corresponds to the hour of the day, *viz.*, the midnight Mass, about midnight, the second, about daybreak, and the last, after dawn.[34] Those who have obtained a papal indult to say the Mass *de Beata* on account of poor eyesight are not allowed to

---

[29] C. 3, X, III, 41. The custom is ascribed to Pope Telesphorus (125–136?).

[30] Benedict XIV, *De Sacr. Missae*, l. III. c. 4, nn. 9 ff.; "*Quod expensis*," Aug. 26, 1748. The Greek liturgies do not mention three Masses; Benedict XIV, "*In superiori*," Dec. 29, 1755, § 2.

[31] Benedict XV, "*Incruentum*," Aug. 10, 1915; S. R. I. C., Aug. 11, 1915 (*A. Ap. S.*, VII, 401, 422).

[32] S. Rit. C., Aug. 11, 1888 (*Dec. Auth.*, n. 3692).

[33] S. Rit. C., June 19, 1875 (*Dec. Auth.*, n. 3355).

[34] S. Rit. C., June 19, 1875, Feb. 13, 1892, ad XXI. (*Dec. Auth.*, nn. 3354, 3767).

say three Masses on Christmas Day, but only one.[85]   The prayers prescribed by Leo XIII and Pius X to be recited after Low Masses need not be said after each of these three Masses, if the priest does not leave the altar.[36]

These, then, are the two occasions on which each priest is allowed to say several Masses.   The general rule is that only one Mass be said each day, unless a papal indult has been obtained or the Ordinary has given permission to binate.   A *papal indult* is required if the Ordinary is not entitled to grant the faculty of binating.   Thus a papal indult would be necessary for cloistered nuns who wish to have two Masses [37] and also for having two Masses said in a private Oratory, of which more anon.[88]

The *Ordinary* may grant — and this is now a power given by law, and not a mere faculty — permission to binate, if the conditions set forth in can. 806, § 2, are verified.   These are (a) lack of priests, (b) convenience of the people, (c) a holyday of obligation.

(1) The *penuria sacerdotum,* or lack of priests, must be such that there is no other priest who could conveniently say the second Mass.   There may perhaps be traveling priests,[89] but unknown or of uncertain standing or physical condition, in which case they must be looked upon as not present.   On the other hand, if a priest is present who is still fasting and able to say Mass, he may be compelled by the Ordinary to say Mass in order to prevent bination.   But in that case the pastor must furnish a stipend, and if he cannot do so, the people are

---

85 S. Rit. C., April 11, 1840; April 28, 1866; (*Dec. Auth.,* 2802, 3146).

86 S. Rit. C., April 30, 1889 (*Dec. Auth.,* n. 3705).

37 Cfr. Prümmer, O. P., *Manuale Theol. Moralis,* 1915, Vol. III, p. 200.

88 S. C. P. F., May 24, 1870, n. 6 (*Coll.,* n. 1352).

89 Such was the case in a parish of Barcelona, a summer resort, where *sacerdotes ambulantes* were to be found, but sometimes they would come late, and sometimes not at all. Wherefore the S. C. C. (July 23, 1892) reasonably did not count them. (*A. S. S.,* 25, 182 ff.)

obliged to supply the deficiency, and if they are too poor, the Ordinary must procure the means.[40] Where there are sufficient priests bination is not permitted, because the case of necessity [41] is not verified, and other priests, as Benedict XIV says,[42] are bound to the people by virtue of sacred orders.

(2) The *convenience* or *necessity* of the people. Convenience it is to be understood relatively to the place or number of the faithful who would be deprived of Mass. For bination is permitted for the benefit of those who assist at, not of those who say, Mass. The favor is conditioned by *distance* or insufficiency of room, or the convenience of the people. Thus if a priest has to attend two parishes or missions, which are about half a league or two miles apart from each other, this circumstance suffices to permit bination.[43] The *size of the church* is also to be considered. If the parish is large and the church building comparatively small, there is sufficient reason for binating.[44] The *convenience of the people,* which falls under the heading of necessity established by law, but is included in the power of the Ordinary, chiefly depends on the number of the faithful. Our text says, "*notabilis fidelium pars.*" What is "a considerable part of a congregation"? Benedict XIV once explained this term as meaning *plures,*[45] or several. But no general rule can be deduced from the various decisions of the Roman Congregations. Sometimes fifteen or twenty persons were considered insufficient to permit bination, whereas on other occasions it was left to the

40 Benedict XIV, "*Declarasti,*" Mar. 16, 1746; S. C. P. F., May 24, 1870 n. 9 (*Coll.*, n. 1352).
41 C. 3, X, III, 41.
42 "*Declarasti*"; S. C. C., May 10, 1897 (*Anal. Eccl.*, t. V, 452).
43 S. C. P. F., May 24, 1870, n. 14 f. (*Coll.*, n. 1352).
44 *Ib.*, n. 10; Benedict XIV, "*Declarasti.*"
45 "*Apostolicum ministerium,*" May 30, 1753, § 11.

." charity and conscience of the Prefect Apostolic " to grant the faculty of binating when only ten or fifteen servants (*servi*, slaves) were present. Hence no precise number can be laid down. But it is undoubtedly the mind of the Church that, on the one hand, there must be a real necessity and, on the other, the Ordinary should not be too scrupulous about granting the faculty, but provide for the spiritual welfare of the faithful, so that all may be enabled to comply easily with the precept of hearing Mass.[46] It follows that in large congregations with a small number of priests each may say two Masses on Sundays and holydays of obligation, in order to accommodate the people, some of whom have to stay at home until the others return from church, and so forth.

(3) The faculty of binating, being granted for reasons of necessity and convenience, *cannot be made use of except on Sundays and holydays of obligation.* Therefore bination on suppressed feasts is not permitted.[47] Nor can the Ordinary grant the faculty for merely devotional purposes, for instance, on the First Friday. The Holy Office has declined to permit bination two or three times a year to satisfy the pious desires of neophytes to receive Holy Communion, considering all the circumstances of time and person in Corea, a missionary country.[48] Such a permission would not lie within the power of the Ordinary, but would need an Apostolic indult.

Permission is never given to say more than two Masses.

The text says that the Ordinary grants the faculty, which signifies that he should grant it to all pastors or curates who may need it. Suppose a pastor or assistant has not received this faculty, and of two priests who are

---

[46] S. C. P. F., May 24, 1870, n. 18.

[47] *Ibid.,* n. 5.

[48] S. O., June 20, 1860, ad 2 (*Coll.,* n. 1194).

wont to say one Mass each on holydays of obligation, one is taken ill suddenly, and there is no time left to consult the Ordinary: may the priest who is well say two Masses? Yes, he not only may but should say both Masses,[49] and afterwards notify the Ordinary. But what if the priest has *broken the fast?* May he then, in order to avoid scandal, say a second Mass? *Negative,* says the Holy Office.[50]

In order to prevent as much as possible the danger of violating the fast, the S. C. Prop. has issued an instruction bearing on bination. One section concerns bination in different churches, while the other touches bination in the same church.

(a) After having consumed *(sorbeat)* the sacred blood, the celebrant places the chalice upon the corporal and covers it with the pall. Thereupon he recites the prayer, *" Quod ore sumpsimus."* Then he washes his fingers in a special bowl, meanwhile reciting the *" Corpus tuum."* After that he removes the pall from the chalice, covers it with the purificator, paten, pall and velum, and continues the Mass. After the last gospel he stands in the middle of the altar and uncovers the chalice in order to see whether a drop of the sacred Blood has gathered in the chalice.[51] If this is the case, he consumes it, then pours as much water into the chalice as there was wine, rinses the chalice, and pours the water into a special vessel, cleanses the chalice, covers it, and leaves the altar. The "ablution" may be preserved for the next day or

---

[49] S. C. C., Feb. 3, 1884 (*Coll. P. F.*, n. 1611). This decision was rendered in a case where bination took place in two parishes or congregations, but by analogy it may safely be applied to our case.

[50] S. O., Dec. 2, 1874 (*Coll.*, n. 1425). Concerning the stipends, see can. 824.

[51] The Instruction says: This must not be omitted, because the sacrifice morally continues, and as long as some species of wine is present, it must by divine precept be accepted.

absorbed in cotton and burned or poured into the *sacrarium.*

(b) If he says the *second Mass in the same church,* the priest, after having carefully sipped the sacred Blood in the first Mass, shall leave the chalice covered with the pall upon the altar and recite the "*Quod ore.*" Then he shall wash his fingers in a special bowl, say the "*Corpus tuum,*" and cover the chalice with the velum, leaving it on the corporal. After Mass he shall carry the chalice into the sacristy, if there is one,[52] place it in a closed cupboard, and leave it there until the second Mass. At the Offertory of the second Mass he shall not remove the chalice from the corporal at the oblation of the bread, nor clean it with the purificator, nor wipe off the drops of wine inside the chalice, but take care, in pouring the wine into the chalice, that no drops adhere to the inside of the chalice.

MORAL DISPOSITION OF THE PRIEST

CAN. 807

Sacerdos sibi conscius peccati mortalis, quantumvis se contritum existimet, sine praemissa sacramentali confessione Missam celebrare ne audeat; quod si, deficiente copia confessarii et urgente necessitate, elicito tamen perfectae contritionis actu, celebraverit, quamprimum confiteatur.

What this canon prescribes concerning the state of grace required in the celebrant is the ancient doctrine of the Church,[53] and the teaching of moralists.[54] The Code

---

[52] If there is no sacristy, the chalice may be left on the altar. This is generally done, and we believe may be continued even if there is a sacristy, if the church is safe, and no irreverence to be feared.

[53] C. 7, X, III, 41; *Trid.,* sess. 13, c. 7, *de Euch.*

[54] Cfr. Lehmkuhl, *Theol. Moral.,*

follows the same teaching when it further says if no *copia confessarii* is at hand and the celebration of Mass is urgent, the priest should make an act of perfect contrition and say Mass, then go to confession as soon as possible, *i. e.*, in about three days. The term *"quamprimum"* indicates not a mere counsel, but a precept,[55] provided, of course, there be a *copia confessarii*.

THE OBLIGATION OF FASTING BEFORE MASS

CAN. 808

Sacerdoti celebrare ne liceat, nisi ieiunio naturali a media nocte servato.

A priest is not allowed to celebrate Mass unless he has observed the natural fast from midnight on.

The *natural fast* before Mass was prescribed by the ancient Church,[56] and the African synods (not without reason, as some of St. Augustine's sermons testify), were very strict in enforcing this ecclesiastical law. The prohibition comprises the taking of anything that is swallowed in the form of nutritive and digestive food or drink, but not what enters the stomach by way of saliva or breathing.[57] Thus if a drop of water is mingled with the sputum when one cleanses his mouth or teeth, the law is not violated. Smoking, nay even chewing tobacco, if nothing is swallowed *per modum cibi voluntarii*, does not prevent one from saying Mass.[58] Pumping out the

II, n. 153; Marc, *Institutiones Morales Alphonsianae*, ed. 9, n. 1547 ff.; Prümmer, *Manuale Theol. Moralis*, 1915, III, n. 194.

[55] Propp. 38, 39 dam. ab Alex. VII, March 18, 1666 (Denzinger, n. 1009 f.).

[56] C. 49, Dist. 1, *de consec.;* c. 16, C. 7, q. 1.

[57] Cfr. Lehmkuhl, *l. c.*, II, n. 160; Prümmer, *l. c.*, III, n. 199.

[58] Benedict XIV, *De Sacrificio Missae*, Appendix IX, where the development of that custom is traced from being laid under excommunication until it was declared not unbecoming.

stomach, although some water may be absorbed at first but is again given up, would not interfere with saying Mass.[59]

As to the *time* note that *midnight* is the starting point. Can. 33, as explained in Vol. I, pp. 177 f., permits us to follow any time, local, mean, or legal, and even where the public clock or time assumed by local custom is generally followed, there is no obligation to abide by it.[60] When several clocks or watches show a difference, one may securely follow the rules of probabilism.[61]

APPLICATION OF THE MASS

CAN. 809

Integrum est Missam applicare pro quibusvis tum vivis, tum etiam defunctis purgatorio igne admissa expiantibus, salvo praescripto can. 2262, § 2, n. 2.

A priest may apply the Mass for the living as well as the dead who expiate their faults in purgatory, with the exception of those mentioned in can. 2262, § 2, n. 2. What the priest is here said to apply is the so-called *fructus specialis or ministerialis, i. e.,* the special fruit or benefit of the Mass offered in the name of Christ and of the Church for a determined end or person. Besides the general blessing which accrues to the Church and the world at large, and besides the personal benefit which the priest derives from the Holy Sacrifice of the Mass, there is a special fruit which he may apply *ad libitum.* It is like a special prayer, which is more efficacious than a general prayer, and receives a particular value from

---

[59] Prümmer, *l. c.,* n. 199.
[60] S. Poenit., June 18, 1873 (*A. S. S.,* V, 399); Nov. 29, 1882 (*Coll. P. F.,* n. 1580).
[61] Lehmkuhl, II, n. 159. There is no "havoc" to be feared, as a somewhat confused critic observed concerning our interpretation of can. 33, if we follow the sound rules of interpretation and probabilism.

the efficacy of the unbloody Sacrifice itself.[62] Now it has been the constant and perpetual teaching of the Church that the unbloody Sacrifice of the altar benefits not only men living in this world, but also alleviates the sufferings of the souls in purgatory.[63] This it does not only by the general intention of the Church, but still more efficaciously by the application of the *special fruit* of the Mass by the sacrificing priest.[64]

The Code says that this fruit, whether expiatory or impetratory, may be applied (1) to the *living*, with the restriction mentioned in can. 2262, where the consequences of excommunication are set forth, among which is privation of spiritual favors and graces. Said canon says that the priest may, if no scandal is given, say Mass privately for an excommunicated person; but if the latter is *vitandus*, only for his conversion.

The question naturally arises whether Mass may be applied to *non-Catholics*, either Protestants or schismatics. This question reduces itself to another, *viz.:* whether Protestants and schismatics are *vitandi* or not. It cannot be doubted that, if they are formal heretics who pertinaciously deny an article of faith, they are excommunicated, but [65] they would be *vitandi* only if nominally excommunicated by the Apostolic See, publicly denounced as excommunicated, and expressly designated as *vitandi*.[66] This is not the case with ordinary Protestants or schismatics, though the latter are dealt with more severely, to

62 Lehmkuhl, *l. c.*, II, n. 173.

63 *Trid.*, sess. 22, c. 2, *De Sacrif. Missae*, can. 3; sess. 25, *de Purgat.*; *Decretum Unionis Graec.*, July 6, 1439 (Denzinger, n. 588); Benedict XV, "*Incruentum*," Aug. 10, 1915 (*A. Ap. S.*, VII, 401):

64 Pius VI, "*Auctorem fidei*," Aug. 28, 1794, prop. 30 (Denzinger n. 1393); cfr. Pohle-Preuss *The Sacraments*, 1916, II, p. 392.

65 S. O., July 25, 1865 (*Coll.*, n. 1274).

66 Can. 2258; the only exception to this general rule is the case mentioned in can. 2343, when one maliciously lays hands on the person of the Roman Pontiff.

judge from a decision of the Holy Office,[67] which says, in reply to the question whether a priest may say Mass for, and receive a stipend from, a Greek schismatic, that this is not allowed unless it is manifest that the stipend is offered for his conversion. This decision is reversed by the Code, which clearly says that, unless he is a *vitandus*, Mass may be offered for him. Therefore, a priest may say Mass privately for any living non-Catholic as long as he does not give scandal, *e. g.*, by announcing the fact publicly. But he is not allowed to sing High Mass for any non-Catholic, except for actual rulers, in which case the welfare of the country is the main purpose of the solemnity.[68]

The next question is whether Mass may be offered for *infidels*, *i. e.*, unbaptized persons, such as Jews, Turks, etc. The answer is yes, because, on the one hand, they are not excommunicated, never having belonged to the Church, and, on the other, there is no positive prohibition rendering such application unlawful.[69] But the same decision of the Holy Office from which this statement is taken also admonishes priests to scrutinize the purpose for which infidels, especially Mohammedans, offer a Mass stipend. If their intention is evil, or superstitious, or erroneous, the priest should not accept the stipend unless he can correct their error or at least tell them that he will offer the Mass according to the will of God. There is no superstition if they ask for a Mass in order to be freed from sickness, or prison, or capital punishment.[70] Nor was it considered to be superstitious if Christian Chinese made the offering called Phan-huong-hoa, which is a

---

[67] S. O., April 19, 1837 (*Coll.*, n. 858).

[68] Cfr. Gasparri, *De Ssma Euch.*, 1897, n. 483; Aichner, *Compendium Iuris Eccl.*, § 51, 2.

[69] S. O., July 12, 1865; S. C. P. F., March 11, 1848 (*Coll.*, nn. 1274, 1028); Gasparri, *l. c.*, n. 486.

[70] S. C. P. F., March 11, 1848 (*Coll.*, n. 1028).

burnt offering for the dead made by a last will, because thereby the Christians intended to have Masses said for their deceased relatives.[71]   All superstitions or erroneous intentions must be discountenanced when non-Catholics offer a Mass stipend, because to let them go unchallenged would be tantamount to fostering or spreading superstition.[72]

(2) Concerning the *dead*, the general principle applies that with those with whom we have associated when living we may also associate when dead.[73]   Hence for those who have died in union with the Church any kind of Mass, low or high, private or public, may be applied. On the other hand all those to whom ecclesiastical burial is denied are also deprived of the funeral Mass *(Missa exequialis.)*.[74]   Therefore no funeral Mass may be said for such as die unbaptized, unless they were catechumens who without their fault died before they received Baptism.[75]   Heretics, too, and schismatics, as well as condemned Masons, are to be denied the funeral Mass. Neither are dead rulers or persons of royal blood who were not Catholics to have a funeral Mass.[76].   However the term funeral Mass must be interpreted strictly.   It does not include a private Mass not connected with the funeral services.   What if a relative offers a Mass stipend for the repose of a deceased non-Catholic?   May the priest accept it?   A decision of the Holy Office [77] would seem to forbid such acceptance, no

---

[71] S. C. P. F., Aug. 6, 1840 (*Coll.*, n. 910).

[72] S. O., July 12, 1865 (*Coll.*, n. 1274). It would be superstitious if one believed that the Mass is an infallible remedy for all kinds of troubles or a sure means of obtaining any grace or favor.

[73] C. 1, C. 24, q. 2; c. 12, X, III, 28.

[74] Can. 1239–1241.

[75] For living and dead catechumens or converts *in fieri*, therefore, Mass may be said; cfr. c. 2, X, III, 43; Gasparri, *l. c.*, n. 487.

[76] Gregory XVI, Feb. 16, 1842.

[77] S. O., April 7, 1875 (*Coll.*, n. 1440).

matter whether the application is publicly known or known only to the priest and the person who offers the stipend. Yet in spite of this decision some authors say the priest may accept the offering privately on condition that he expressly declares that he will say the Mass as far as he is allowed to do so and according to the will of God.[78] This seems a plausible theory if the non-Catholic in question was not a bigoted and prominent defender of his belief, and especially if he was kindly disposed towards the Catholic religion, or died with signs of repentance. For the above-named decision lays stress on "manifest heresy." Besides our Code (can. 1240) insists upon *notorious* heresy or schism, which rarely occurs in our country. As to dead *infidels* or non-baptized persons no decision is known to us that would either forbid or allow the application of a Mass for them. However, a funeral Mass is forbidden. Whether a private Mass is allowed must, we believe, be decided according to the rule laid down with regard to baptized non-Catholics.[79]

PREPARATION AND THANKSGIVING

CAN. 810

Sacerdos ne omittat ad Eucharistici Sacrificii oblationem sese piis precibus disponere, eoque expleto, gratias Deo pro tanto beneficio agere.

The priest should not omit to prepare himself for the

---

[78] Lehmkuhl, *l. c.*, n. 176; Gasparri, *l. c.*; n. 4091, says that the priest would be allowed to accept the offering, but would have to declare that the Mass would be applied for all the poor souls with the intention of succoring the particular person if it pleased God. Lehmkuhl, *l. c.*, excludes a "Black" Mass with a special oration *pro hoc defuncto acatholico*. A "Black" Mass *pro defunctis* could be said if the rubrics permitted.

[79] Thus Gasparri, *l. c.*, n. 489, but the decision which he quotes from S. C. P. F., April 18, 1757 (*Coll.*, n. 405; ad 5) only speaks of *schismatics*.

celebration of the Eucharistic Sacrifice by pious prayers and give thanks to God for this great grace after celebration.

It is understood that the celebration of the divine office, especially in choir, is a fitting preparation for Mass, because the liturgical office tends towards the Sacrifice as its center.

VESTMENTS FOR MASS

CAN. 811

§ 1. Sacerdos, Missam celebraturus, deferat vestem convenientem quae ad talos pertingat et sacra ornamenta a rubricis sui ritus praescripta.

§ 2. Abstineat autem a pileolo et annulo, nisi sit S. R. E. Cardinalis, Episcopus vel Abbas benedictus, aut nisi apostolicum indultum eorundem usum in Missa celebranda eidem permittat.

The priest, when saying Mass, shall wear the cassock *(soutane)* and the sacred vestments prescribed by his rite; but no ring or skullcap, unless he is a cardinal, a bishop, or a blessed abbot, or unless an Apostolic indult permits him to wear these insignia at Mass.

The rule laid down in § 1 is sufficiently known from the general and special rubrics. No departure from it is allowed without weighty reasons. Such a reason would be persecution. But even in times of persecution the Holy See would not be likely to grant a general permission to all the priests of the province or country involved, but only to some who might be expected to make a wise use of the privilege.[80] The term *sui ritus* implies that

---

[80] S. C. P. F., Nov. 30, 1828 for China *(Coll.,* n. 807). Bishops and Vicars Apostolic should wear the rochette, ring, and pectoral cross, unless there is a grave and urgent reason which excuses them.— S. C.

Latin priests must observe the rules of the Latin rite as to the various vestments and their color, and that Oriental priests must follow the practice of their rite.

§ 2 enumerates the *skullcap* and the *ring*, which by law may be used only by Cardinals, bishops and abbots. No others are allowed to wear these insignia, though there seems to have been a special temptation to wear the ring. Rome has never allowed Cathedral and Collegiate Canons to wear a ring at sacred functions, not even when an immemorable or inveterate custom could be claimed.[81] Neither is a Commendatory Prior or Abbot, or the Provost of a Collegiate Chapter entitled to wear a ring.[82] Nor does the title of doctor give a claim to it, although it confers the right of wearing a ring outside the sacred functions.[83] The height of ambition was reached by some pastors, especially archpriests *(arcipreti)*, of a Sicilian diocese, who claimed the right to pontificate or chant High Mass with ring and purple mantelletta and surrounded by four ministers in cope.[84] A papal indult was granted to the *Protonotaries Apostolic de numero participantium* to wear a ring and black skullcap at all sacred functions, and to *supernumerary Protonotaries Apostolic* to wear a black skullcap under the mitre at Pontifical Vespers, and the ring at all functions.[85] The Vicar-General and honorary Prothonotaries Apostolic are not allowed to wear either the ring or the skullcap at any function.[86] We may add that no

P. F., March 22, 1669 (*Coll.*, n. 178 ad 1); on vestments see Benedict XIV, *De Sacrif. Missae*, l. I, c. 7.

[81] S. Rit. C., Nov. 20, 1628; April 11, 1840; Aug. 20, 1870; March 9, 1844 (*Dec. Auth.*, nn. 483, 2805, 3218, 3821).

[82] S. Rit. C., April 12, 1704, ad 2; Aug. 4, 1657 (*Dec. Auth.*, nn. 2130, 1032).

[83] S. Rit. C., May 23, 1846; June 30, 1883 (*Dec. Auth.*, nn. 2907, 3580).

[84] S. Rit. C., July 28, 1876; Jan. 30, 1878 (*Dec. Auth.*, nn. 3408, 3442).

[85] Pius X, "*Inter multiplices*," Feb. 21, 1905, nn. 4, 9 (*Am. Eccl. Rev.*, 32, 614).

[86] *Ibid.*, nn. 27, 28, 31, 47–49 (*Am. Eccl. Rev.*, 32, 619 f.).

titular abbot is entitled to wear either ring or skullcap unless this privilege was especially granted to him, and that there is no obligation to wear a skullcap at sacred functions either for prelates [87] or for the others who are entitled to these insignia by privilege, unless perhaps for the reason of using the privilege. There is some significance in the ring, but very little in the skullcap.

NO ASSISTANT PRIEST ALLOWED AT MASS

CAN. 812

Nulli sacerdoti celebranti, praeter Episcopos aliosque praelatos usu pontificalium fruentes, licet, sola honoris aut sollemnitatis causa, habere presbyterum assistentem.

With the exception of bishops and prelates entitled to the use of pontificals, no priest is allowed to have an assistant priest in celebrating Mass merely for the sake of honor or solemnity.

The right of pontificating belongs by law to *Cardinals* outside of Rome. If they pontificate in cathedral churches, which they may do upon due notice to the Ordinary of the diocese, they may employ a *presbyter assistens.*[88] *Bishops* and *archbishops* are expressly mentioned as entitled to this privilege. Other prelates who enjoy it are *abbates regiminis,* after they have been blessed by the bishop, and abbots or prelates *nullius.*[89] The supernumerary Protonotaries Apostolic may also have a *presbyter assistens* if no bishop or prelate of higher rank than a bishop is present. *Protonotaries Apostolic ad instar* may employ an assistant priest only when they pontificate outside their church or in other

---

[87] All the texts only say *poterunt,* they may.

[88] Can. 239, § 1, 15.

[89] Can. 325; can. 625.

churches when no bishop or higher prelate is present.[90] *Canons* of Cathedral or Collegiate churches, although dignitaries, and provosts *are not* allowed to have a *presbyter assistens*.[91] Much less can the custom, even though immemorial, be tolerated that simple priests celebrate Mass with an assistant priest.[92] But what about the custom of employing a *presbyter assistens* at the *first Holy Mass* of a newly ordained priest? This question was placed before the Sacred Congregation, who answered: *posse tolerari*.[93] In itself this answer does not sound favorable, since it implies a mere negative toleration; yet we believe the Code does not mean to reprobate the custom, because a *presbyter assistens* is, on such an occasion, not employed for mere honor or pomp, but for the purpose of aiding the neopresbyter.

MASS WITHOUT A SERVER

CAN. 813

§ 1. Sacerdos Missam ne celebret sine ministro qui eidem inserviat et respondeat.

§ 2. Minister Missae inserviens ne sit mulier, nisi, deficiente viro, iusta de causa, eaque lege ut mulier ex longinquo respondeat nec ullo pacto ad altare accedat.

A priest shall not say Mass without a minister who serves and answers him. *Women* may not serve Mass unless no man is present and there is a just cause, and then they must answer from a distance and not approach the altar.

90 Pius X, "*Inter multiplices*," nn. 29, 47 (*Am. Eccl. Rev.*, 32, 619, 623).

91 S. Rit. C., Aug. 7, 1628; April, 1666; Sept. 10, 1701; Sept. 19, 1883 (*Dec. Auth.*, nn. 475, 1337, 2078, 3588).

92 S. Rit. C., July 28, 1876; Jan. 30, 1878 (*Dec. Auth.*, nn. 3408, 3442).

93 S. Rit. C., Dec. 1, 1882 (*Dec. Auth.*, n. 3564).

The obligation to have a server at Mass is *per se* grievous, as it is prescribed by the rubrics.[94] However, by reason of the faculties formerly granted to our Ordinaries and communicated by them to all their priests, we have become accustomed to say Mass without a server for reasons which really would not stand the canonical and moral test. Does custom even now excuse us from grievous transgression in this matter? Where normal conditions exist in a regularly established parish it would be difficult to excuse the old custom. But where missionary conditions still prevail we believe priests need not scruple to say Mass without a server, especially when there are some frequent communicants and the boys are in school or on vacation. For there can hardly be a doubt that the spiritual benefit is proportionately greater than the observance of a law which, if too strictly enforced, would diminish religious fervor. This is our view. For the rest, all authors [95] agree that Mass may be said without a server if the Viaticum has to be consecrated, or on holydays of obligation for the people as well as the priest, or if the server should leave after Mass is considerably advanced.[96] Attention may be called to the fact that in our country people are neither scandalized nor surprised to see a priest say Mass without a server.

As to *women*, Benedict XIV ruled that they shall not serve at the altar, but the sacred Congregation has since permitted girls in institutions or Sisters to answer the

---

94 C. 6, X, I,17; *Conc. Basil.*, sess. 21, c. 8; *Missale Rom., Ritus Servandus in Celebratione Missae;* Gasparri, *l. c.*, n. 645 ff. The server at low Mass should not open the missal, or mark the several parts of the prayers, as the S. Cong. has forbidden this. The prohibition also applies to prelates inferior to bishops when they say Mass privately; Gasparri, *l. c.*, n. 648.

95 Cfr. Lehmkuhl, II, n. 244.

96 "*Etsi pastoralis,*" May 26, 1742, § VI, n. XXI; "*Allatae sunt,*" July 26, 1755, § 29 (referring to a Greek custom).

priest from behind a railing *in case of necessity.*[97] It seems to us that it would be preferable, for reasons of mere devotion, to employ a woman server, than to say Mass without any server at all.[98] But the faculty granted in virtue of Form I, Art. 23, to say Mass without a minister can no longer be made use of.[99]

ARTICLE II

RITES AND CEREMONIES OF THE MASS

The Species

CAN. 814

Sacrosanctum Missae sacrificium offerri debet ex pane et vino, cui modicissima aqua miscenda est.

CAN. 815

§ 1. Panis debet esse mere triticeus et recenter confectus ita ut nullum sit periculum corruptionis.

§ 2. Vinum debet esse naturale de genimine vitis et non corruptum.

The Holy Sacrifice of the Mass must be offered in bread and wine, and to the latter must be mixed a few drops of water.

The *bread* must be of pure wheat and freshly baked, so that no corruption need be feared.

The *wine* must be natural wine made of the juice of the grape and uncorrupted.

Can. 814 embodies an article of faith.[1] The Armen-

---

[97] S. Rit. C., Aug. 27, 1836; March 18, 1899 (*Dec. Auth.*, nn. 2745, 4015).

[98] Lehmkubl, *l. c.*

[99] S. C. Consist., April 25, 1918

(see Vol. II, p. 587); Putzer, *Comment. in Facul. Ap.*, ed. 4, p. 277; *Am. Eccl. Rev.*, 55, 314.

[1] *Trid.*, sess. 22, can. 9, *de Sacrif. Missae.*

ians, who were more or less inclined to Monophysitism, stubbornly refused to mix a little water with their wine. The Church, on the other hand, was just as tenacious in upholding the Apostolic or divine tradition and refused to deviate from it, though she freely acknowledges that the water does not belong to the essence of the sacrifice *(de necessitate sacramenti)*.[2] Therefore converted Armenian priests must adopt the Catholic practice,[3] which is based on John 19, 34 and Apoc. 17, 1, 15, as the Council of Trent says.[4] Our text, following the rubrics of the Missal, says *modicissima aqua*, a very small quantity. This means about three to ten drops. If the water would exceed in quantity one-third of the wine, consecration would be doubtful.[5]

§ 1 of can. 815 requires *pure wheaten bread* for valid consecration. This excludes every other kind of grain, such as barley, rye, oats, maize (corn), rice or potato flour, as also an admixture of one or more of the aforesaid substances. The wheat used may be hard or soft, red or white, etc., just so it is really wheat. If spelt is considered a hard-grained variety of wheat, it is valid matter; but if it is taken as an intermediate product between wheat and barley, it is not valid. This depends much on local nomenclature.

The wheat must be *recently* baked into bread, as bread is usually made,[6] that is mixed with water, not milk, or wine, or oil, or spices. *Recenter confectus* signifies, not that the flour must be freshly ground, but that the bread must be recently baked, *i. e.*, it should not be older than

---

2 S. C. P. F., Jan. 30, 1635 (*Coll.*, n. 81).

3 S. O., Aug. 7, 1704 (*Coll.*, n. 267).

4 Sess. 22, c. 7, *de Sac. Missae*.

5 Prümmer, *l. c.*, III, n. 173.

6 S. O., June 23, 1852 (*Coll.*, n. 1076) permitted the custom of putting ground grain into water for several hours to solve it and then placing the mass on hot irons.

fourteen days.[7]   In summer as well as in moist weather
or damp places the danger of corruption is especially
great, and hence the frequent renewal of the bread under
such conditions is not only advisable, but imperative.   A
late decree of the S. C. of Sac. says that altar bread
should not be bought for two or three months ahead and
that hosts more than two or three months old cannot be
used for the Holy Sacrifice of the Mass and for Communion.[8]

As to the *form* of the bread, *round* hosts are used in
the Latin Church, whereas the Oriental Church employs
square hosts.[9]   The *size* of the host for Holy Mass and
exposition in the Ostensorium should be from two to
three and of the particles for distribution about one
inch.   The altar breads should be neither too thick nor
too thin.[10]

§ 2 describes the quality of the *wine*.   It must be natural wine made from grapes.   But no wild grapes may
be used,[11] whilst wine obtained from pressed grapes, if it
has the taste, smell and color of wine, is allowed.[12]   The
wine must be *fermented*, for this is a natural quality of
wine, but it should not contain more than 12 per cent. of
alcohol.   If wine is very weak, so that it would suffer
from transportation or be easily corrupted, an admixture with wine spirit (alcohol obtained from wine) is permissible.   But the mixture is to be made in such a way
that the alcoholic percentage of both the natural wine
and the wine alcohol does not exceed 12 per cent., and
when the wine is still young, after the first fermentation.[13]

7 S. Rit. C., Dec. 1826; Sept. 12,
1884 (*Dec. Auth.*, nn. 2650, 3610).
8 S. C. Sacr., Dec. 7, 1918 (*A.
Ap. S.*, XI, 8).
9 Benedict XIV, *De Sac. Missae*,
I, c. 6.

10 Prümmer, *l. c.*, III, n. 171.
11 S. C. P. F., 1819 (*Coll.*, n.
732); Gasparri, *l. c.*, nn. 811 ff.
12 S. O., July 22, 1706; May 7,
1879 (*Coll.*, nn. 270, 1518).
13 S. O., July 30, 1890 (*Coll.*, n.
1735).

Spanish wines, being very sweet and easily liable to corruption, especially in transit, may be mixed with wine alcohol to such an extent that the whole alcoholic percentage would amount to 17 or 18 per cent.[14] If the wine does not contain sugar enough to preserve it, it is permitted to evaporate or boil the grapes recently pressed (must) so as to obtain a wine of 14 or 16 per cent. of alcohol. But this process is allowed only if it does not prevent the natural fermentation of the wine.[15] Not easily tolerated, or tolerated only for very special reasons and with the express approval of the Sovereign Pontiff, is the following: Ten pounds of sugar cane are mixed with 100 pounds of wine grapes, and both fermented until about sixty-seven pounds are left.[16]

These and other decisions show how careful the Church has been in procuring genuine bread and wine for the Holy Sacrifice, and how strictly she enjoins on Ordinaries to use great care in selecting wheat and wine dealers to supply the needs of the clergy.[17] A new obligation seems to arise for hierarchy and clergy from extreme prohibition. (For can. 816 see Appendix, pp. 572 sqq. *infra*.)

Can. 817

Nefas est, urgente etiam extrema necessitate, alteram materiam sine altera, aut etiam utramque, extra Missae celebrationem, consecrare.

It is unlawful, even in case of extreme necessity, to consecrate one species without the other, or to consecrate both outside the Mass.

14 S. O., Aug. 5, 1896; May 22, 1901 (*Coll.*, nn. 1950, 2113).

15 S. O., May 22, 1901 (*Coll.*, n. 2113).

16 S. O., June 25, 1891 (*Coll.*, n 1757).

17 S. O., July 9, 1881; Aug. 30, 1901 (*Coll.*, nn. 1556, 2122).

The first of these clauses touches the very essence of the Mass, which most probably consists in the consecration of both species. However, theologians [18] generally admit, following the *Missale Romanum*,[19] that the consecration of one species would be valid without the consecration of the other. This might happen if a priest would grow seriously ill after the consecration of one species, or if, by mistake, he would consecrate water and no wine would be at hand, or danger of death would immediately follow the consecration of one species. Yet all these are merely physical accidents. Intentionally to consecrate only one species is never allowed, not even to provide the Viaticum, although such consecration would be valid.[20]

To consecrate *outside the Mass* would not only be a sacrilege, but probably also an attempt at invalid consecration. The priest would certainly not perform that action in the person of Christ, nor according to the intention of the Church, which is restricted to the celebration of the Mass.[21]

OBSERVANCE OF RUBRICS AND RITES

Can. 818

Reprobata quavis contraria consuetudine, sacerdos celebrans accurate ac devote servet rubricas suorum ritualium librorum, caveatque ne alias caeremonias aut preces proprio arbitrio adiungat.

---

18 Cfr. Noldin, *Summa Theol. Moralis*, 1912, *De Sacram.*, n. 102.
19 *De Defectibus*, c. IV, nn. 5, 8.
20 Noldin, *l. c.*, and n. 104.
21 Prümmer, *l. c.*, III, n. 176.

CAN. 819

Missae sacrificium celebrandum est lingua liturgica sui cuiusque ritus ab Ecclesia probati.

The priest, when celebrating Holy Mass, must accurately and devoutly observe the rubrics of the respective ritual books and avoid the arbitrary addition of other ceremonies and prayers. Every contrary custom is hereby reprobated.

There is a distinction between prescriptive and directive rubrics which should be retained.[22] The obligation imposed by *prescriptive* rubrics is greater and more serious than that which attaches to merely directive rubrics. The former concern the celebration of the Mass itself, whilst the latter refer to what immediately precedes or follows the celebration, for instance, how the priest should approach or leave the altar, etc. But even the prescriptive rubrics do not all oblige with equal strictness. They distinguish between the *ordinary* and the extraordinary parts of the Mass, the former being such as occur in every Mass (confession, orations, offertory, breaking of the host and the dropping of a particle into the chalice), whereas the latter occur only in a certain kind of Masses (Gloria, Tract, Credo, various commemorations, etc.). But the juridical obligation of saying everything according to the rubrics, whether in red or black, is undeniable.[23] The rubrics of the canon in particular must be carefully followed.

No addition is allowed even for the sake of devotion, and the prayers and ceremonies must not be curtailed [24]

22 Noldin, *l. c.*, n. 208 f. It would be unreasonable to reject this distinction, and lead to unnecessary scruples, or Jansenistic rigorism, or Pharisaism.

23 S. Rit. C., Nov. 12, 1605 (*Dec. Auth.*, n. 194).

24 *Ibid.*

or mutilated. Hence no arbitrary prayers, ejaculations or gestures are to be used.

These rules also bind, to their fullest extent, *all religious,* whether exempt or not. They are not allowed to insert in the canon the name of their superior, unless, of course, he is an abbot *nullius.*[25] Should they attempt any change or mutilation or addition, the Ordinary may proceed against them with ecclesiastical censures, against which no appeal or injunction or inhibition is permissible.[26]

The ceremonies and prayers of the Mass must be carried out according to the *respective ritual books.* Hither refers also *can. 819,* which rules that Mass must be celebrated in the *liturgical language* proper to each one's rite, as approved by the Church. The Roman Pontiffs, whilst permitting and upholding the Oriental rites, at the same time kept watch against schismatical tendencies. The reason is obvious: the *lex orandi* reflects the *lex credendi.* Therefore the Orientals, no less than the Latins, are obliged to use the liturgical books approved by Rome.[27]

The *liturgical language* is Latin for the whole Western Church, and wherever else it is in use, as, for instance, in parts of Servia.[28] The Oriental Rites differ in language. The Missal for the Latin Church was issued and approved by Pius V, in 1570, and the last revision, comprising the chant, was made in 1883 by authority of Leo XIII. As to the *monastic Missal,* enough has been said

25 *Ibid.*

26 Benedict XIV, "*Ad militantis,*" March 30, 1742, § 6; S. Rit. C., March 16, 1591; Aug. 19, 1651 (*Dec. Auth.,* n. 9, ad 19, n. 937, ad II). Why regulars should wear a hood (*caputium*) instead of a birretta is not quite intelligible.

27 Benedict XIV, "*Etsi pastoralis,*" May 26, 1742, § IX, n. XVIII; "*Demandatam,*" Dec. 24, 1743, § 11; "*Inter omnigenas,*" Feb. 2, 1744, § 18.

28 Benedict XIV, "*Inter omnigenas,*" § 18.

in Vol. III of this Commentary; we will only add that its general rubrics are identical with those used by the secular clergy. .

Every edition of the Missal must be approved by the S. Rituum Congregatio, or at least contain a declaration by the Ordinary that it conforms to the edition of 1883. Lately a few additions have been made as to the Gregorian Chant, especially with regard to the " Gloria " and " Ite Missa est," of which we now have fifteen varieties,— certainly not to the gain of uniformity.

No *mixture* of rites or change from one rite to another by the same priest is allowed. Thus the Greeks are not allowed to say Mass in the Latin Rite, even in a Latin Church, nor are Latin priests allowed to celebrate Mass in the Greek Rite,[29] for instance, on the antimensia of Ruthenian churches. An exception was made in favor of some Oriental colleges in Rome and of the Greek College under the direction of the Benedictines, who may say Mass either in the Latin or in the Greek Rite. But this singular provision, made for the benefit of the students of these colleges, not for the benefit of the priests to whom the college is entrusted, cannot be alleged as a precedent for violating the general rule of not mixing the various rites.[30]

A curious mixture, however, is noticeable in the provinces of Gorizia, Zara, and Zagrab, where the use of the *old Slavic* or *Glagolitic* language is permitted under certain conditions which have been established by the S. Rit. C. after a protracted and heated controversy.[31]

29 St. Pius V, "*Providentia*," Aug. 20, 1566; "*Quoprimum*," July 14, 1570, § 3; Benedict XIV, "*Imposito Nobis*," March 29, 1751, § 9.

30 Benedict XIV, "*Allatae sunt*," July 26, 1755, § 34 f.

31 S. Rit. C., Feb. 13, 1892; Aug.

5, 1898 (*Dec. Auth.*, nn. 3768, 3999); Aug. 14, 1900; March 14, 1902 (*Anal. Eccl.*, VIII, 417; X, 206; XV, 22). Some Chinese missionaries were allowed to say Mass *tecto capite*, but the custom was to be eliminated gradually; S. C. P. F.,

Finally it may be added that Mass must be celebrated in a *standing,* not *sitting,* posture. This rule, being merely ecclesiastical, does not bind the Pope, who may therefore sit when saying Mass. Any other priest would need a papal indult (S. C. Sacr.) to say Mass either partly or entirely in a sitting posture.[32] Of course, when the rubrics permit the minister to sit down, he may and should do so.

ARTICLE III

TIME AND PLACE OF CELEBRATING THE MASS

CAN. 820

Missae sacrificium omnibus diebus celebrari potest, exceptis iis qui proprio sacerdotis ritu excluduntur.

Holy Mass may be celebrated on all days except those on which the respective rite forbids the priest to say it.

In the Latin Church the general rubrics prescribe that no private Masses be celebrated during the three days preceding Easter. This is to be understood as follows: On *Maundy Thursday one solemn* Mass should be celebrated in all the churches where the Blessed Sacrament is preserved[33] and the liturgical functions are performed according to the *Memoriale Rituum* issued by Benedict XIII. In churches where, on account of a lack of clerics or servers, the sacred ceremonies cannot be duly held, the bishop may grant permission to the priests to say a low Mass for the convenience of the people. However, this Mass should be said before the solemn High Mass

July 31, 1673 (*Coll.*, n. 206). They were not, however, allowed to say Mass in the Chinese language; S. C. P. F., Jan. 7, 1755 (*Coll.*, n. 394).

32 Benedict XIV, "*Aestas,*" Oct. 11, 1757, nn. VII–XII.

33 S. Rit. C., March 28, 1775 (*Dec. Auth.* 2503).

in the cathedral or mother church begins. Besides, according to the decree,[34] this permission must be obtained anew every year. However, even setting aside the contrary custom, the bishop can undoubtedly issue a faculty to be valid for a number of years. In a large diocese the annual issuance of such faculties would cost time and money without any special benefit.

Religious communities, under a decree of the S. Congregation of Rites,[35] may have one Mass said in their chapels, even though the prescribed liturgical functions are not performed there on the three days preceding Easter. If they have no chapel of their own, they may hear a private Mass in a neighboring church, but the doors must be shut.[36] If a feast of obligation falls on Maundy Thursday, it must be transferred to the day following Low Sunday, but the obligation of hearing Mass and abstaining from servile work remains attached to the original day.[37]

On *Good Friday* only one *Missa Praesanctificatorum* may be celebrated, and priests who have two parishes to attend to are not allowed to binate on that day.[38]

On *Holy Saturday* only one solemn Mass may be cele-

---

[34] S. Rit. C., July 31, 1821 ad 1 (*Dec. Auth.,* n. 2616); "*petita quotannis venia*" is put in brackets.

[35] S. Rit. C., Aug. 31, 1839 (*Dec. Auth.,* n. 2799). This may be extended to seminaries and pious places which have their own chaplain and the right of preserving the Bl. Sacrament. S. Rit. C., June 28, 1821, ad 1 (*Dec. Auth.,* n. 2616); whether the *venia Episcopi,* as Gasparri (*l. c.,* n. 81) maintains, is required, is doubtful. Contrary custom would rather deny it.

[36] Doubtless this provision was added because of the parochial serv-

ice, with which the private service should not clash.

[37] S. Rit. C., Sept. 13, 1692 (*Dec. Auth.,* n. 1883). If the feast of the Annunciation falls on Good Friday or Holy Saturday, the whole feast with all the obligations is to be transferred to the Monday after Low Sunday; S. Rit. C., March 11, 1690. If a patron feast falls on that day, the obligation of abstaining from servile work remains for Good Friday, but the obligation of hearing Mass ceases; Gasparri, *l. c.,* n. 85 f.

[38] Benedict XIV, *De Sacrif. Missae,* l. III, c. 5, n. 5.

brated in churches in which the liturgical functions of Holy Week are performed. Private Masses are not easily allowed in any church on that day.[39] In small or *poor parishes* a low Mass may be said if custom permits. But neither a local nor personal indult permits private Masses to be said in churches which are not parish churches. Therefore a special indult is required for such, and the priest who says this Mass must omit every ceremony and commence with the Confessio without the Introitus. A bishop who ordains on that day in his private chapel must begin the Mass with the prophesies.[40] Priests of the *Oriental Rite* do not say Mass on days of strict fasting. Thus during Lent they celebrate only the *Missa Praesanctificatorum,* except on Saturdays, Sundays, and high feastdays, when they say Mass as usual.

THE HOUR FOR SAYING MASS

CAN. 821

§ 1. **Missae celebrandae initium ne fiat citius quam una hora ante auroram vel serius quam una hora post meridiem.**

§ 2. **In nocte Nativitatis Domini inchoari media nocte potest sola Missa conventualis vel paroecialis, non autem alia sine apostolico indulto.**

§ 3. **In omnibus tamen religiosis seu piis domibus oratorium habentibus cum facultate sanctissimam Eucharistiam habitualiter asservandi, nocte Nativitatis Domini, unus sacerdos tres rituales Missas vel, servatis servandis, unam tantum quae adstantibus omnibus ad praecepti quoque satisfactionem valeat, celebrare potest et sacram communionem petentibus ministrare.**

39 S. Rit. C., Feb. 12, 1690 (*Dec. Auth.,* n. 1822).
40 Gasparri, *l. c.,* n. 88 ff.

§ 1. Mass should not be commenced earlier than one hour before dawn, nor later than one hour after noon.

The starting-point is dawn, or daybreak *(aurora)*, which, of course, depends on the hour of sunrise. Dawn in our country lasts about one hour and a half.[41] Therefore a priest is allowed to begin Mass about two hours and a half before sunrise. This, we believe, should be early enough for all reasonable demands, especially since the legislator himself has now added one hour to the time allowed before by common law. We do not believe that exempt and other religious who claim the privilege, granted after the Council of Trent, of celebrating one hour before dawn and one hour after noon, will now be allowed to extend the same to two hours. For the legislator by extending the time has not extended the starting-point (dawn) for the privilege. The privilege granted before the Council of Trent appears somewhat doubtful and it is in the ordinary power of bishops to compel even exempt religious to abide by the rule fixing the hour for celebrating Mass.[42] But we would not doubt the right of anticipating the hour of celebrating Mass when necessary for administering the viaticum[43] for devotion's sake. Another case of necessity would undoubtedly be the obligation of hearing Mass for working people who would otherwise have to arise before five o'clock in winter. (In summer time the case of necessity would hardly be verified.) Still another case of necessity would arise for the priest from the precept of

---

[41] See the table of duration of dawn in Benedict XIV's *Inst.*, 13, and Gasparri's, *De Ssma Euch.*, Vol. I, p. 65. Dawn, on May 1, lasts here, at Conception, Mo., 42nd degree latitude, one hour and 45 min.; on Jan. 1, 1 hour and 39 min.; on Oct. 13, 1 hour and 31 min. See *infra*, Appendix.

[42] Benedict XIV, *Inst.*, 68, n. 11.

[43] "*Praeceptum sumendi viaticum praevalet legi ecclesiasticae de tempore celebrandi Missam.*"—S. C. P. F., Feb. 29, 1836 (*Coll.*, n. 846).

hearing Mass on a holyday, which otherwise could not be complied with by reason of a necessary journey.[44]

The bishop may permit Mass, especially on a solemn occasion, to be protracted until after two P. M.[45] But he is not empowered to forbid the saying of Mass before sunrise.[46] In countries where there is hardly any dawn, as in the polar regions, Mass may commence about the time people arise and go to work.[47]

§ 2. On Christmas night only the *conventual or parochial Mass may be commenced at midnight* to the exclusion of every other Mass not granted by special Apostolic indult.

§ 3. *In all religious or pious houses* which possess an oratory with the faculty of habitually keeping the Holy Eucharist, *one priest* may say one or three Masses according to the rubrics Christmas night. Those who assist thereat comply with the obligation of hearing Mass, and Holy Communion may be administered to such as desire it.

The moment at which Mass *may be begun* on Christmas is the hour of midnight, not before. Hence it would be an abuse to commence Mass so early that the priest would be at the gospel or elevation when the clock struck twelve.[48] There is no strict obligation *(inchoari potest)* to commence at midnight, for the service may be postponed if there is an impediment. But the rubrics require of those bound to say public office, like cathedral chapters, and most of the regulars, that they sing

[44] Noldin, *l. c.*, n. 204; Marc, *l. c.*, II, n. 1625.

[45] S. Rit. C., July 7, 1899 (*Dec. Auth.*, n. 4044).

[46] S. Rit. C., Jan. 10, 1597 (*Dec. Auth.*, n. 62).

[47] Cong. Specialis, Sept. 18, 1634. The reason why Mass is to be celebrated at daytime is because Christ, the brightness of eternal light, is offered up therein.—Benedict XIV, *Inst.*, 13, n. 2.

[48] S. Rit. C., May 11, 1878, ad XV; June 2, 1883, ad X (*Dec. Auth.*, nn. 3448, 3576).

Matins before the Mass and Lauds after it. This order may not be changed on that day.[49]

Our text clearly states that *only* the *conventual* or *parochial* Mass may be commenced at midnight. Hence neither canons, nor dignitaries, nor regulars of any kind or exemption, nor religious in general, may, in virtue of the common law, say three Masses immediately after midnight.[50] The priest who says the conventual or parish Mass at midnight must wait with the other two Masses until the rubrical time has arrived,[51] that is to say, till about five thirty A. M., when he may say the other two. It requires an *apostolic indult* to say the three Masses one immediately after the other, commencing at midnight. An indult, though a species of privilege, is not given by way of communication, and therefore no *communicatio privilegiorum* is permissible in this case. This is evident also from the fact that the custom of celebrating the three Christmas Masses at midnight has been condemned as an abuse which must be entirely eliminated.[52]

§ 3, then, grants by universal law a favor which formerly was given only by a special indult. Thus, for instance, the Ursulines, their pupils and lay sisters enjoyed this privilege of a Mass and Holy Communion at midnight,[53] where their rules approved by the Holy See prescribed this custom.[54] Pius X, the great promoter of devotion to the Blessed Sacrament, extended this favor to all religious institutes, pious houses and clerical sem-

[49] S. Rit. C., April 3, 1830 (*Dec. Auth.*, n. 2676).

[50] S. Rit. C., Nov. 22, 1681; March 23, 1686 (*Dec. Auth.*, nn. 1683, 1761).

[51] S. Rit. C., Nov. 14, 1676 (*Dec. Auth.*, n. 1584).

[52] S. Rit. C., Sept. 18, 1781 (*Dec. Auth.*, n. 2520).

[53] S. Rit. C., July 27, 1720 (*Dec. Auth.*, n. 2267).

[54] S. Rit. C., Aug. 7, 1871, ad IX (*Dec. Auth.*, n. 3254).

inaries.[55] Our text simply says: *"in all religious or pious houses."* What a *religious house* is may be seen from can. 488, 5°, where such a house is said to belong to a religious institute in general. From this it follows that all communities of religious may enjoy the right granted in this canon. A *pious house* is one where Christian charity is practiced under the supervision of ecclesiastical authority. Charity here comprises every species of good works, educational, corporeal works of mercy, etc. But it is essential that such a house be superintended by ecclesiastical authority.[56] To this class belong hospitals, asylums for the aged, orphans, and foundlings, clerical seminaries, and houses of religious societies of men and women (see can. 673). The latter cannot *strictly* be called religious houses, because not inhabited by religious in the canonical sense of the word, but in a wider sense they may safely be styled religious houses. A doubt may arise concerning hospitals conducted by religious but really superintended by lay or civil officials. However, if the religious form a community of their own, and have their own oratory, in which the Blessed Sacrament is kept, we would not exclude them from the benefit granted by this canon. A different status is that of our State asylums and penitentiaries. They are purely secular institutions, entirely managed by seculars, even though there be a temporary chapel where the Blessed Sacrament could hardly be kept. These, therefore, are not entitled to the favor here in question.

Our canon requires that in all such houses there be an *oratory endowed with the privilege of habitually keeping the Blessed Sacrament.* According to certain decrees of the Holy Office, of 1907 and 1908, it makes no differ-

---

[55] S. O., Aug. 1, 1907; Nov. 26, 1908 (*A. Ap. S.*, I, 146).

[56] Devoti, *Institut. Canonic.*, 1874, Vol. I, p. 560; cfr. can. 1489.

ence whether this oratory be public, semi-public, or private. If it is a private oratory, an apostolic indult is needed to keep the Blessed Sacrament, whilst for a semi-public or public oratory the permission of the Ordinary is sufficient, as shall be seen under can. 1265.

The text furthermore says that one priest (*unus sacerdos*) may say one or three Masses (*Missas rituales*). Hence if there are more than one, the others must say Mass later. The three Masses must be said *according to the rubrics, i. e.*, as they follow each other in the Missal, and not all three according to the formulary *pro Missa in Nocte*. But if a priest (for instance, an assistant at the cathedral who is also chaplain of a convent or hospital) says only one Mass, he is bound to observe what the law prescribes, *servatis servandis*. In other words, if he says but one Mass at midnight, he must say the other two Masses according to the rubrical time, *i. e.*, the second not earlier than about 5.15 or 5.30 A. M., and the third, *de die*, after that.

The last clause is an extension of the decrees of the Holy Office of 1907 and 1908, which require that the doors of the oratory be shut (*ianuis clausis*). Our canon contains no such clause, wherefore outsiders, for instance, friends and relatives, may be admitted and by assisting comply with the precept of hearing Mass on Christmas Day, and also, if they so desire, receive Holy Communion. This is plainly expressed in the words: *adstantibus omnibus*, all who assist. But this favor can not be extended to the *churches* of religious, whether exempt or not, for not only was it directly denied to them by decree of the Holy Office, Nov. 26, 1908,[57] but our

---

[57] "*An indultum oratoriis concessum extendi possit ad ecclesias religiosorum, quae publico fidelis po-* *puli usui inserviunt? Negative, salvo tamen religiosorum privilegio in media nocte Missam celebrandi.*"

text itself excludes such an extension, as it speaks only of religious or pious houses which have an oratory, not of churches. The reason obviously is not to create a prejudice against parish churches. However, the same decree allows, and the text of our canon does not forbid, religious to have a midnight Mass for themselves, *i. e.,* behind closed doors, at which the members may receive Holy Communion.

CAN. 822

§ 1. Missa celebranda est super altare consecratum et in ecclesia vel oratorio consecrato aut benedicto ad normam iuris.

§ 2. Privilegium *altaris portatilis* vel iure vel indulto Sedis tantum Apostolicae conceditur.

§ 3. Hoc privilegium ita intelligendum est, ut secumferat facultatem ubique celebrandi, honesto tamen ac decenti loco et super petram sacram, non autem in mari.

§ 4. Loci Ordinarius aut, si agatur de domo religionis exemptae, Superior maior, licentiam celebrandi extra ecclesiam et oratorium super petram sacram et decenti loco, nunquam autem in cubiculo, concedere potest iusta tantum ac rationabili de causa, in aliquo extraordinario casu et per modum actus.

§ 1. Mass must be celebrated upon a *consecrated altar* and in a consecrated or blessed church or oratory.

The Latin Church does not allow the unbloody Sacrifice to be offered except on an entirely consecrated altar, or at least on an altar stone consecrated according to the prescribed rules (see can. 1197 ff.). The Orientals use

a so-called *antimension* or linen cloth blessed by the
bishop, into the corners of which relics are sewed, and
which is spread over the altar table.[58]

The *general rule* for the Latin Church is that, *outside
the case of extreme necessity*, it is never allowed to say
Mass in a place which is not sacred (*in aedibus non sacris*),[59] or, as our text has it, outside a church or an oratory which is either consecrated or blessed. In private
and semi-public oratories, which are neither blessed nor
consecrated, Mass may be celebrated only if they fulfil
the necessary requirements, as stated in can. 1196. In
private houses, especially sick persons, it is allowed
to say Mass only if the viaticum can be neither secretly
nor publicly brought to the sick.[60]

The *altar stone* must contain sacred relics. If the
relics have been removed, the stone must be reconse-
crated. To consecrate altars without relics for saying
Mass requires a very special indult, such as was given to
vicars Apostolic in times of persecution.[61]

§ 2 and 3. The privilege of a *portable altar* is granted
either by law or by an indult of the Holy See. This
privilege carries with it the faculty of celebrating Mass
in any place, provided it be respectable and decent, and
upon an altar stone; only celebration at sea is excluded.
Before the Council of Trent bishops were empowered to
grant permission to have a private oratory for the purpose of having Mass said therein, but after the Council
this right, and consequently also the grant of a portable
altar, was reserved to the Apostolic See.[62] This change,

[58] Benedict XIV, "*Imposito Nobis*," March 29, 1751, § 4; ID., *De
Sacrif. Missae*, l. I, c. 2; cfr. cc.
1, 2, 11, Dist. 1, *de cons.*
[59] Benedict XIV, "*Inter omnigenas*," Feb. 2, 1774, § 22.
[60] S. C. P. F., Dec. 14, 1668;

April 30, 1753 (*Coll.*, nn. 172, 388).
[61] S. Rit. C., Oct. 6, 1837; Dec. 7,
1844; May 23, 1846 (*Dec. Auth.*,
nn. 2777, 2876, 2911); S. C. P. F.,
Jan. 14, 1802; May 14, 1681 (*Coll.*,
nn. 660, 223).
[62] Benedict XIV, "*Magno cum*

however, did not affect the private oratories in episcopal palaces, because the latter are not comprised under the name of private houses.[63] Therefore episcopal oratories, as well as those of Cardinals,[64] exist by law. If special privileges are asked for, the S. C. Sacr. is competent to grant them.[65]

It must be added that even *exempt religious* require a special privilege, ratified after the Council of Trent, to make use of a portable altar, and the Ordinary, in virtue of *Sess. XXII, decretum de observandis et evitandis in celebratione missae,* may proceed against them if they presume to celebrate upon a portable altar or keep such an altar in their rural houses.[66] All privileges granted to that effect before the Council of Trent, even by the Pope himself, must be regarded as revoked.[67] On the other hand, Cardinals as well as bishops may continue to use the portable altar even without the permission of the local Ordinary in whose diocese they may wish to say Mass.[68] The clause, *" non autem in mari "* does not apply to Cardinals and bishops,[69] but to all others, unless besides the indult of a portable altar they also have a special indult permitting them to celebrate Mass on shipboard.[70]

§ 4. The local Ordinary, or, in the case of an exempt religious house, the higher superior, may grant permis-

animi," June 2, 1751, § 11; ID.; *De Sacrif. Missae,* III, 6, 5 f.

[63] Benedict XIV, *Const. cit.,* § 2.

[64] Cfr. can. 239, § 1, 7°; can. 349, § 1, n. 1.

[65] *Normae Peculiares,* c. VII, art. 3, n. 11 (*A. Ap. S.,* I, 88).

[66] S. C. C., June 4, 1672, Aug. 29, 1761 (Richter, *Trid.,* p. 130, nn. 9 f.).

[67] S. C. C., March 23, 1907 (*Anal. Eccl.,* t. 15, 101 ff.).

[68] Benedict XIV, *De Sacrif. Missae,* l. III, 6; n. 5; cfr. c. 12, 6°, V, 7.

[69] Can. 239, § 1, n. 8; can. 349, § 1, n. 1.

[70] S. Rit. C., March 4, 1901, ad 4 (*Anal. Eccl.,* t. 9, 115): *" Si capella navium locum fixum habeat in navi, uti publica pro navigantibus habenda est; secus neque publica est neque privata, sed habetur ut altare portatile;"* ad V, ibid.

sion to say Mass outside a church or oratory, upon a consecrated altar stone, provided the place is decent (no
bed room) and the permission is granted for a just and
reasonable cause, for extraordinary cases only, and not
habitually.

This canon contains part of the faculty formerly
granted to our American bishops.[71] Two Ordinaries are
named in § 4: the local Ordinary and the Ordinary of
exempt religious. To begin with the latter, note that the
major superior of exempt religious can give the permission in question only with regard to a *house* of his
own religious institute. Hence he cannot permit his subjects to say Mass in a strange place not owned by the
religious, for instance, on a missionary trip.[72] In this
case the competent Ordinary would be the Ordinary in
whose diocese the religious wishes to say Mass. But if
the house belongs to, and is occupied by, religious of the
same order, the legitimate superiors, *i. e.*, the general, the
provincial and all those who represent the former, may
grant the permission in question.

The *local Ordinary* is the one commissioned to watch
over his diocese, and is responsible for abuses which may
creep into it. He may grant the permission in question
under the following conditions:

(1) That Mass be said upon an *altar stone* which contains sacred relics and is validly consecrated and prepared.[73]

(2) That the place in which Mass is to be said is
decent or respectable. Decency must be gauged not by
adornment merely, but by the respect and reverence due
to the august Sacrifice. It is forbidden to say Mass in

---

71 Form I, art. 6; cfr. Putzer,
Comm., p. 277 ff.
72 S. C. P. F., Nov. 18, 1765
(*Coll.*, n. 461).

73 S. C. P. F., Feb. 29, 1836
(*Coll.*, n. 846).

the churches of heretics and schismatics (see can. 823, § 1), and it would be improper to offer the holy Sacrifice in the private houses of unbelievers or non-Catholics. Theatres and Masonic temples could hardly be styled respectable places for saying Mass, although the former might be used in case of extreme necessity. The open air would be a decent place.

(3) That no permission be given to say *Mass* in *bedrooms* (*in cubiculis*). Hence it would be better, in case of necessity, to choose the living or sitting room for saying Mass. However the S. C. Prop. has given permission to say Mass in the sleeping room of a sick person (*in cubiculo infirmi*) if there is no other way of administering the Viaticum.[74] But then the minister should see to it that there are no indecent or superstitious emblems or pictures in the room.[75]

(4) That the permission be granted for a *just and reasonable cause*. As stated above, the Blessed Sacrament may never be exposed to irreverence, nor should the faithful be scandalized. A just reason would be if an epidemic raged in the town or city which would necessitate the closing of the churches; if there were no Catholic church or public oratory in the town or city,[76] or if the precept of receiving Easter communion could not otherwise be complied with; or if the administration of the Viaticum required it.[77] War and social disturbances would be an additional reason for granting the permission.

(5) This permission, however, is *not* to be understood as an *habitual faculty* or a right to be used by the priest *ad libitum*, but only, as the text says, "*in casu extraor-*

---

[74] S. C. P. F., April 30, 1753 (*Coll.*, n. 388).

[75] S. C. P. F., Sept. 6, 1821 (*Coll.*, n. 764).

[76] S. C. P. F., April 30, 1753, ad 2 et 4 (*Coll.*, n. 388).

[77] S. C. P. F., Sept. 5, 1821 (*Coll.*, n. 764).

dinario et per modum actus." This would seem to imply that a priest should ask for it every time he deemed it necessary. However, we believe the Ordinary can grant the permission to priests in such a way that they would not have to ask for it every time they needed it, provided, of course, the conditions set forth in this section be present.[78] Lastly, it may be noted that this permission may be granted so as to allow Mass to be said in private houses and on any day;[79] but the permission must be issued gratis.[80]

CAN. 823

§ 1. Non licet Missam celebrare in templo haereticorum vel schismaticorum, etsi olim rite consecrato aut benedicto.

§ 2. Deficiente altari proprii ritus, sacerdoti fas est ritu proprio celebrare in altari consecrato alius ritus catholici, non autem super Graecorum *antimensiis.*

§ 3. In altaribus papalibus nemo celebret sine apostolico indulto.

§ 1 forbids saying Mass in *churches of heretics and schismatics,* even though these may have once been duly consecrated or blessed.

That the church sometimes reconsecrates temples formerly belonging to heretics, is proved by historical examples dating back to the sixth century (Arians).[81] From this practice it follows that churches once consecrated and hallowed by Catholic services, when they have fallen into the hands of non-Catholics, are considered desecrated and therefore unfit for the celebration of the

---

[78] S. C. P. F., Feb. 29, 1836 (*Coll.,* n. 846).

[79] S. C. Sacr., March 22, 1915, ad 1 (*A. Ap. S.,* VII, 147).

[80] S. C. Sacr., Dec. 23, 1912, ad 1 (*A. Ap. S.,* IV, 725).

[81] Cfr. cc. 21, 22, Dist. 1, *de cons.;* Benedict XIV, "*Iam inde,*" May 12, 1756, § 3.

Sublime Mystery. The decisions of the Roman Court are to the effect that rather than say Mass in a non-Catholic temple a priest should use a portable altar or celebrate the Holy Sacrifice in a private house.[82] However, the Holy Office once permitted the archbishops of Antivari to use a schismatic church, provided a separate Catholic altar was set up therein and one part of the church was reserved exclusively for Catholics.[83] But this was a case of necessity. Ordinarily priests should rather make use of portable altars. In another instance the Holy Office permitted the simultaneous use of a garrison chapel at Malacca for Catholic and non-Catholic services, but instructed the Vicar Apostolic to ask the government to build a separate chapel, or, if that could not be done, to build one himself from alms collected. It may be added that Clement XI permitted Catholic services to be held in so-called " simultaneous churches [84] in Switzerland.[85]

§ 2. A Latin priest may celebrate Mass on a consecrated altar of another rite, but not upon a Greek *antimension*. These antimensia being, as stated, not altar stones, but consecrated sheets of linen, do not come up to the requirements of the Latin Church.[86]

§ 3. On *papal altars* no one is allowed to say Mass without a special indult. Benedict XIV gives two reasons why an altar is called papal: either because it was consecrated by the Pope or because he said Mass upon

---

[82] S. C. P. F., May 21, 1627; Feb. 13, 1629; May 7, 1631 (*Coll.* nn. 34, 47, 69): neither chalices nor vestments of schismatics may be used.

[83] S. O., Dec. 1, 1757 (*Coll.*, n. 408).

[84] S. O., June 5, 1889 (*Coll.*, n. 1707).

[85] S. O., June 13, 1634 (*Coll.*, n. 75); Putzer, *l. c.*, p. 279. " Simultaneous " churches are those in which Catholics and Protestants hold service at different hours.

[86] Benedict XIV, " *Etsi pastoralis*," § VI, nn. VIII, XIX; S. O., June 7, 1726 (*Coll.*, n. 306).

it.[87]   Several altars in Rome are called papal, *viz.*, those
of the patriarchal basilicas of St. John Lateran, St. Peter,
St. Paul, and Santa Maria Maggiore.   There are also a
few papal altars outside Rome.   Benedict XIV sent one
to Lisbon [88] and on another occasion declared the high
altar on the side of the pontifical throne in the church of
St. Francis at Assisi a papal altar.[89]   From this we may
conclude that to the two reasons stated a third must
be added, *viz.*, a special distinction granted directly by
the Sovereign Pontiff.   The consequence is that no one,
not even a Cardinal or bishop, may say Mass on such an
altar without a papal indult.   This indult is generally affixed to the altar when another than the Pope says Mass
on it.   The reason for this rule lies in the dignity of
the consecrator or grantor of the privilege.[90]

ARTICLE IV

ALMS OR STIPENDS FOR MASSES

CAN. 824

§ 1. Secundum receptum et probatum Ecclesiae mo-
rem atque institutum, sacerdoti cuilibet Missam celebranti et applicanti licet eleemosynam seu stipendium
recipere.

§ 2. Quoties autem pluries in die celebrat, si unam
Missam ex titulo iustitiae applicet, sacerdos, praeterquam in die Nativitatis Domini, pro alia eleemosynam
recipere nequit, excepta aliqua retributione ex titulo
extrinseco.

§ 1 approves the time-honored custom which allows

87 " *Dilectus Filius*," Jan. 15,   89 " *Fidelis Dominus*," March 25,
1745, § 1 (S. Maria Maggiore).   1754.
88 " *In postremo*," Oct. 20, 1756,   90 Cfr. c. 97, Dist. 2, *de cons.*
§ 9.

every priest who says Mass to accept an alms or stipend for the same.

In the early days of Christianity the faithful were wont to offer bread and wine at each Mass which they attended. Money too was sometimes laid upon the altar, intended either for the poor members of the congregation or for the clergy in common. The practice of giving alms to a determined priest so that he might offer the special or ministerial fruit of the Holy Sacrifice either for the donor or his relatives and friends, began about the eighth century and became universal after the twelfth. There is no incongruity in applying the Mass for a special person or purpose. For, although the Holy Sacrifice, by reason of its main offerer and object, *viz.*, Christ, is of infinite value, yet the special fruit or effect is not infinite, and therefore one person may derive greater profit from it than the rest, and repeated oblations for a particular person or object will produce their effect more certainly and abundantly.[91] Nor is there any simony connected with receiving a Mass stipend. For, as St. Thomas says,[92] the priest does not receive the stipend as a price for the consecration of the Holy Eucharist, but as part of his support. Hence Wiclif and his followers misunderstood the nature of prayer for others when they called those who obliged themselves to pray for others simonists.[93] Mistaken also was the notion of the pseudo-council of Pistoja that the application of the priest did not produce a special effect in favor of those for whom it was made, and that the acceptance of stipends was a shameless abuse.[94] It cannot be denied, however, that abuses did creep in. Some avaricious priests either

---

[91] Benedict XIV, *De Sacrif. Missae*, l. III, c. 21, nn. 1–7.

[92] *Summa Theol.*, II–II, q. 2, art. 2.

[93] Cfr. prop. 25 (Denzinger, n. 501).

[94] Propp. 30, 54 (Denzinger, nn. 1393, 1417).

traded in Masses or said Mass several times a day for filthy lucre's sake.[95]   These abuses prompted the Church to enact, in the matter of stipends, severe laws, which are now embodied in the Code.   We add to § 1 only one comment, namely, that the text *requires that Mass be said and applied*.   Saying Mass, therefore, is not sufficient to justify a stipend, but application of its special fruits must be made at least before the consecration of the wine.   A *habitual intention* once made and not consciously retracted suffices.   It is also sufficient if one celebrates according to the intention of the superior who distributes Masses to his subjects.   If one has received a number of stipends and does not remember from whom or in what order they were given, it is sufficient that he say them with the intention to apply them in the order in which they were given.   If another has collected the stipends, it suffices that the one who says the Masses have the intention of saying them according to the order intended by the distributor.[96]

§ 2. A *binating* priest who is obliged to apply one Mass *ex titulo iustitiae, is not allowed to accept a stipend for the other*.   An exception to this rule is *Christmas Day*, on which a priest who says three Masses may accept three stipends.   A partial exception to the general rule is the privilege of accepting some compensation for the other Mass for a reason which is extrinsic to the nature of a Mass-stipend as such (*ex titulo extrinseco*).   Our parish priests and bishops are now obliged in *justice* to apply Holy Mass for the people *(pro populo)* on Sundays, holydays of obligation, and the suppressed holydays mentioned in can. 466 and 339 (see Vol. II of this Commentary).[97]   No pastor is allowed to accept a stipend

95 Benedict XIV, *l. c.*, n. 8.   97 Vol. II, p. 550. See also S. C.
96 Lehmkuhl, *l. c.*, II, n. 188 f.   C., July 13, 1918 (*A. Ap. S.*, XI,

on such days.   For the *titulus iustitiae* is strictly attached
to the obligation of saying Mass for the people.   The only
exception is for Christmas Day, when the pastor must apply only one Mass for his people, and may accept stipends
for the other two.[98]   On *All Souls' Day* he may receive a
stipend for one of the three Masses; and even if he says
only one, he is entitled to a stipend.[99]   For this day is not
one of the holy-days mentioned in canons 466 and 339.

Now what is an *extrinsic title* which permits a priest to
accept a remuneration for one Mass, whilst he is obliged
to offer another *ex titulo iustitiae?*   The general rule
may be stated thus: It must not be of the nature of a
stipend given for the application of the special fruits,
nor of the nature of a just claim which would oblige the
priest to apply them *ex iustitia*.   The Church has never,
except for very special reasons, allowed the acceptance
of two stipends on one day.   An extrinsic title, therefore, would exist if one had to walk a considerable distance to say a Mass for which he is not entitled to accept
anything, or if he had to fast for an unusually long time
to impart an extraordinary instruction to which he were
not otherwise obliged.[1]   Besides if bound merely by the
titulus caritatis, he would be allowed to say Mass to which
this title obliges him.   There is an authentic decision to
this effect.   A congregation of priests obliges its members
to say one Mass for every deceased member.   The question arose: May a priest of that society, when he bi-

46 ff.), S. C. Cons., Aug. 1, 1919
(*A. Ap. S.*, XI, 346 f.), has defi-
nitely settled this question. For the
decree quoted requires three things:
definite boundary lines, residence,
and endowment. And these conditions certainly obtain in many city,
and even in some country parishes.

[98] Benedict XIV, "*Quod expensis,*" Aug. 26, 1748; S. C. C., Sept.
25, 1858.
[99] Benedict XV, "*Incruentum,*"
Aug. 10, 1915 (*A. Ap. S.*, VII, 403).
[1] S. C. C., May 23, 1861; cfr.
Prümmer, *Theol. Moral.*, III, n.
288.

nates, apply the second Mass for a deceased member? The S. Congregation answered yes.[2] From this we may infer that the members of a purgatorial society of priests, on days on which they are allowed to binate, may apply one Mass for their people (or accept a stipend if they are not obliged to say Mass *pro populo*), and say the other for a deceased member of the society. For a purgatorial society is based upon the *titulus caritatis* no less than the above-mentioned congregation. We may further conclude that priests of a religious community who are compelled to binate, may apply one Mass for their deceased members, and the other either *pro populo* or for the donor of a stipend. Here again the *titulus caritatis* is obvious.

This extrinsic title, however, cannot be invoked for the two Masses which the priest says on All Souls' Day, one for all the deceased faithful and the other according to the intention of the Supreme Pontiff. Therefore, even if he has to say Mass at an inconvenient hour, or in a rural oratory, or on a cemetery, he is not allowed to accept anything for his labor or inconvenience. Furthermore, the stipend to which priests are entitled for one Mass must not exceed the usual or customary or synodal tax, though they are allowed to accept free offerings that are in no wise solicited. Besides, priests are forbidden to receive a stipend and apply the other two Masses which they may say on All Souls' Day for another person or purpose, reserving the two for the poor souls and according to the intention of the Holy Father for another day. The bishop may proceed against priests who fail to

2 S. C. C., Sept. 14, 1878 (*Coll. P. F.*, n. 1500); it is, of course, supposed, that the priest says one Mass *ex titulo iustitiae* or *stipendii*, otherwise no decision would have been required.

comply with these rulings with ecclesiastical censures, including suspension.[8]

The S. C. Propaganda sometimes, for particular reasons, granted permission to receive a stipend for both Masses a priest had to say.[4]   But this faculty was never given in virtue of the formularies formerly issued. nor is it to be expected now, except in very extraordinary circumstances.

CAN. 825

Nunquam licet:

1.° Missam applicare ad intentionem illius qui applicationem, oblata eleemosyna, petiturus est, sed nondum petiit, et eleemosynam postea datam retinere pro Missa antea applicata;

2.° Eleemosynam recipere pro Missa quae alio titulo debetur et applicatur;

3.ᶜ Duplicem eleemosynam pro eiusdem Missae applicatione accipere;

4.° Alteram recipere eleemosynam pro sola celebratione, alteram pro applicatione eiusdem Missae, nisi certo constet unam stipem oblatam esse pro celebratione sine applicatione.

It is forbidden:

1.° To apply a Mass for the *intention of one who may ask* for the application of a Mass and offer a stipend in future, but who has not yet asked for it, and to keep the stipend afterwards given for the Mass already said. This would be a sort of interpretative intention.   The priest, in this case, only surmises or supposes that he is to receive a stipend, but is certain neither as to the per-

---

[8] S. C. C., Oct. 15, 1915 (*A. Ap. S.*, VII, 480).

[4] S. C. P. F., Oct. 15, 1863; May 24, 1870 ad 18 (*Coll.*, nn. 1244, 1352).

son nor as to the stipend expected. This practice was strictly forbidden by the S. Congregation, though some theologians, especially in Spain, had defended it.[5]

It would not be contrary to law if one said Mass for the intention of a person who requested the favor but would offer the alms only after the Mass had been applied.

It is unlawful:

2.° To *receive a stipend for a Mass which is due and must be* applied for some other reason. Thus a pastor who is obliged to apply a Mass for his people, may not receive a stipend for the same, even though his salary is not sufficient to support him.[6] A canon or beneficiary who is bound to apply Mass for the benefactor or founder of the benefice or chaplaincy, is not allowed to receive a stipend other than the one that may accrue from the benefice or foundation.[7] For a conventual Mass, which is generally offered for the living and the dead benefactors of the community, no stipend may be accepted.[8]

It is furthermore forbidden:

3.° To *accept two stipends for the application of one and the same Mass.* Even after the Council of Trent, which branded the abuse of Mass stipends as akin to simony, there were theologians who thought it permissible to receive two stipends for one Mass. The reason they gave was that the fruit of the Mass which may be disposed of by the priest according to his own good pleasure, is of two kinds: satisfactory and impetratory. The former may be applied for a deceased person and the latter for a living sick person. Besides, they argued,

---

[5] Benedict XIV, *De Sacrif. Missae*, III, 22, 10.

[6] S. C. C., Aug. 30, 1698; Feb. 1716 (Richter, Trid., p. 134, n. 32).

[7] S. C. C., Nov., 1702; Sept. 18, 1603 (*ibid.*, nn. 33, 64).

[8] S. C. C. June 28, 1708; May 16, 1733 (*ibid.*, nn. 56, 58).

the priest may, as it were, give up his own personal fruit for the benefit of another and therefore receive a stipend for that as well as for the special or ministerial fruit.   Hence, they held, it is permissible to receive two stipends for one and the same Mass.   But neither the Holy Office nor the S. Congregation of the Council shared this opinion; on the contrary, they condemned the practice based upon it.[9]

It is unlawful, finally,

4.° *To receive one stipend for the celebration, and another for the application of the same Mass,* unless it is certain that one stipend has been offered for the celebration alone without the application.   Two decisions of the S. Congregation may illustrate this text.[10]   A pious testator had founded a benefice or chaplaincy with the *express clause* that the priest or beneficiary was not obliged to apply the Mass.   The S. Congregation decided that the fruit or interest of the benefice might be accepted and a stipend taken for the application of the same Mass.   In another case a founder had directed that a Mass be said by the chaplain on every Sunday and holy-day of obligation, without specifying on whose behalf it should be said or applied.   In that case, because nothing certain could be deduced from the will, the chaplain was instructed to apply for the benefit of the founder.   Perfectly legitimate is the acceptance of an offering for singing a High Mass in the place of a sick or absent pastor, who may not be able to sing that Mass on that day, but says nothing about its application, for instance, *pro populo.*   In that case the substitute may accept the offering for the singing

9 S. O., Sept. 24, 1665, prop. 8, 10 (Denzinger, nn. 979, 981); S. C. C., Dec. 13, 1859; Benedict XIV, *De Sacrif. Missae,* l. III, 22, 4 f.

10 S. C. C., July 13, 1630; March 18, 1668; Benedict XIV, *De Sacrif. Missae,* l. III, 22, 6 f.

of the High Mass and receive a stipend for the special intention. For it is evident that the offering is given for the special labor of singing High Mass and accommodating the absent pastor, who would be obliged to sing it himself if he were at home.[11]

VARIOUS KINDS OF MASS STIPENDS

CAN. 826

§ 1. Stipendia quae a fidelibus pro Missis offeruntur sive ex propria devotione, veluti ad manum, sive ex obligatione etiam perpetua a testatore propriis heredibus facta, *manualia* dicuntur.

§ 2. *Ad instar manualium* vocantur stipendia Missarum fundatarum, quae applicari non possunt in proprio loco, aut ab iis qui eas applicare deberent secundum tabulas fundationis, et ideo de iure aut Sanctae Sedis indulto aliis sacerdotibus tradendae sunt ut iisdem satisfiat.

§ 3. Alia stipendia quae ex fundationum reditibus percipiuntur, appellantur *fundata* seu *Missae fundatae.*

§ 1. Stipends offered, as it were, offhand by the faithful for Masses, either out of pure devotion, or in the form of an obligation, even perpetual, imposed upon his heirs by the testator, are called *manual.*

§ 2. *Quasi-manual* are stipends for foundation-masses, which for one reason or another cannot be said in the church in which, or by the priest by whom, they should be said according to the charter, and are therefore, either

---

11 This is also true of a low Mass, especially if one would have to travel a certain distance to say it for the required purpose, *e. g.,* to enable the faithful to comply with their duty on a Sunday or holy-day of obligation.

by law or by an Apostolic indult, to be handed over to other priests.

§ 3. Other stipends which are received from the interest of legacies, are called *foundations*. In order to understand the distinction between these three kinds of Masses we must proceed from the term *foundation*, which here means a legacy or testamentary bequest of goods or chattels, which,[12] by a legal fiction, bears the character of an artificial person or quasi-corporation. A foundation or pious legacy made for a good purpose is what we call a *pia causa* and possesses a juridical entity of its own. A foundation or founded Mass in the sense of our canon is a legacy made by a testator for the purpose of having a Mass said either at a certain place (altar, chapel, church) or by a certain priest. Such a legacy, to be valid, must be accepted by those to whom it is made, and made according to the rules prescribed by the Church. It may entail special conditions or qualifications which must be conscientiously carried out. A founded Mass, therefore, would be one to be said on a certain altar or in a certain church for all time. But if the testator had expressly stipulated only a certain altar or church, but no particular application, the Mass would not be a foundation, though it might be a benefice or chaplaincy. On the other hand, if the testator has not expressly excepted the application of the Mass, it is always to be presumed that the Mass is a founded Mass to be applied for the *legatarius*.[13] Sometimes the testator determines the priest who is to say the Mass, for instance, the chaplain attached to a certain church, or altar, or who says Mass at a specified hour (*primassarius*) or, more generally, the priests

---

[12] Blackstone-Cooley, *Com.*, Vol. II, 512.
[13] S. C. C., Jan. 11, 1710 *et*
pluries (Richter, *Trid.*, p. 137, n. 55); cfr. can. 1544 f.

assigned to a certain parish. If no special priest is mentioned, the choice is left to the heirs to determine.[14] Finally, it may happen that a testator leaves, say, $1000 for Masses to be said each year forever without further determination. In that case the executor has to see to it that the will is put into effect.[15] The final obligation rests on the heirs, who may relieve themselves of further responsibility by handing over the legacy to the Ordinary. In the last hypothesis no foundation would be created because no obligation is attached to any particular church or altar, nor are the celebration and application of the Masses imposed on a determined priest. Hence such Masses are really *manual stipends.* $1000, at 5% interest, would produce $50 *per annum* and entitle the testator to fifty Masses.

Quasi-manual Masses arise from founded Masses which are to be said either in a particular church or by a specially designated priest. If the testator has left it to the Ordinary to make a change concerning the place or priest, the latter may *de iure* order such a change and assign another altar or church and give the stipend to another priest. If the charter contains no clause as to the free choice of place or person, the Holy See (S. Cong. Conc.) must be asked. For the last will of the faithful is to be respected, especially with regard to Masses.[16]

A *manual stipend* may, therefore, be called an offhand stipend involving no obligation other than the application of the Mass. A *quasi-manual stipend,* on the other hand,

14 S. C. C., Jan. 15, 1639 and *passim* (Richter, *l. c.,* n. 59 f.).

15 Here it may not be amiss to draw attention to certain civil laws. Where these are not favorable to such legacies, it would be wise not to mention the specific purpose for which the sum is left, but leave it to the executor to specify and apply it. But the heirs are under grievous obligation of handing over the money.

16 Urban VIII, " *Cum alias,*" ad dub. 1 (Richter, *Trid.,* p. 146).

is a modified foundation, the obligation of which is limited as to place or person. A *foundation proper*, finally, is a legacy attached either to a certain place (altar, chapel, church) or to a certain priest by the will of the testator.

NO TRAFFICKING IN MASSES ALLOWED

CAN. 827

A stipe Missarum quaelibet etiam species negotiationis vel mercaturae omnino arceatur.

Every species of bartering or trafficking with Mass stipends must be strictly avoided.

The terms *negotiatio* and *mercatura* are nearly synonymous, except that the former, which may be translated by bartering or exchange of wares, has perhaps a more general meaning. Trafficking is a common term for buying and selling for the sake of gain. Even *negotiato* includes the notion of profit, at least in common parlance. To understand this canon fully, it must be viewed in the light of the following decisions.

1. *Collecting* of Mass stipends by booksellers and other merchants through public advertisements and promises of premiums is strictly forbidden, as is also the distribution of stipends in the form of books or merchandise, whether to the full amount of the stipends or retaining a profit, no matter whether this profit is given to pious institutions or kept by the agent, whether others have handed over these stipends to said merchants or whether they have collected them themselves. Stress is to be laid on the act of *collecting* and the number of Masses.[17]

2. It is also forbidden to *diminish Mass stipends;* thus

[17] S. C. C., July 25, 1874, n. 1–5 (*Coll. P. F.,* n. 1423).

from Masses to be said in a celebrated sanctuary nothing may be deducted for the adornment or decoration of the altars, etc.[18]

3. According to a decision of the S. C. C., it would *not* be trafficking if good books or magazines were given in place of stipends, or if other merchandise were given for the same *by ecclesiastics*.[19] However, a decree (*" Vigilanti "*) of May 25, 1893, prohibits accepting books from booksellers in lieu of Mass stipends. It is not without reason that Cardinal Gasparri in his notes omits all reference to this mitigated interpretation. In general, therefore, whatever savors of trade or bartering is forbidden, no matter what some theologians say who wrote before the Code. On the other hand, we hardly believe that a priest would be forbidden to give a book to a brother priest with the request: " Please say a Mass according to my intention." For there is no trafficking involved in such an agreement. The purpose of the legislator is to exclude trading in Masses.

CAN. 828

Tot celebrandae et applicandae sunt Missae, quot stipendia etiam exigua data et accepta fuerint.

The number of Masses to be said and applied must correspond with the number of stipends given and accepted, even though these be small.

This rule, given by Urban VIII and re-iterated by Innocent XII, is to be understood as follows:[20] If a priest receives, for instance, ten Mass intentions, but only five dollars, he is bound to say ten Masses, provided, of

---

18 S. C. C., May 25, 1893 (*Coll.*, n. 1832); this is only allowed by a special papal indult.

19 S. C. C., April 24, 1875; July 25, 1874 (*Coll. P. F.*, n. 1443, 1423).

20 Urban VIII, " *Cum alias* "; Innocent XII, "*Nuper*" (Richter, *Trid.*, p. 145 ff.).

course, as our text says, he has accepted the stipends. But it could not be said that he accepted the obligation if he received the five dollars without being aware of the smallness of the amount, or if the donor had deceived him or given him a counterfeit note. There is a contract between the one who offers the stipend and the priest who says the Mass.[21] This contract is of the nature of a tacit *do ut facias*. Now any contract that is not knowingly and willingly agreed to by both parties must be regarded as invalid, and a priest is not supposed to acquiesce in fraud or deceit. But if he accepts the five dollars with the promise that he will say ten Masses, he must abide by his promise, even though the amount is not the customary or synodal one. This rule affects all priests, regular as well as secular, individuals as well as communities, congregations and orders of religious.[22] Greek priests must offer the Holy Sacrifice according to the intention of those who make voluntary offerings (oblations), and if several persons make an offering, the priest must inform them of the preceding oblations, and, unless they all declare themselves satisfied with one Mass, he must offer as many Masses as there are oblations. Nor is it sufficient to put particles on the table according to the number of the offerers, or to make a simple commemoration for the different donors.[23]

21 S. O., Sept. 24, 1665, prop. 10 dam. (Denzinger, n. 981): "*Non est contra iustitiam, pro pluribus Sacrificiis stipendium accipere, et Sacrificium unum offerre. Neque etiam est contra fidelitatem, etiamsi promittam promissione, etiam iuramento firmata, dandi stipendium, quod pro nullo alio offeram.*"

22 Urban VIII, "*Cum alias,*" § 5.

23 Benedict XIV, "*Demandatam,*" Dec. 24, 1743, § 10; S. C. P. F., April 13 1807, n. XVI (*Coll., n.* 692).

CAN. 829

OBLIGATION NEVER CEASES

Licet sine culpa illius qui onere celebrandi gravatur, Missarum eleemosynae iam perceptae perierint, obligatio non cessat.

Even though the alms given for Masses have perished without the fault of the one who is obliged to say the Masses, the obligation does not cease.

This is merely a consequence of what was said in the preceding canon concerning the species of contract, which obliges as soon as it is entered upon. Hence if a priest has received money for some Masses and loses it, the loss is his *(res perit domino)* and he remains bound to say the Masses.

A reasonable doubt may arise about founded Masses, though there is a Roman decision which rather favors the existence of the obligation. Regulars were entrusted forever with a church to which the obligation of saying one Mass daily for the founders and benefactors was attached. Though it was not evident that this burden had been attached at the time of the foundation and there was no trace of annual revenues, the S. Congregation decided that the religious were bound to apply the Mass.[24] This is in keeping with can. 825, 4°, and therefore our present text probably also applies to foundations, unless the Holy See either modifies or abolishes the obligation.

[24] S. C. C., Jan. 28, 1708; Dec. 15, 1731 (Richter, *Trid.*, p. 137, n. 56).

CAN. 830

Si quis pecuniae summam obtulerit pro Missarum applicatione, non indicans earundem numerum, hic supputetur secundum eleemosynam loci in quo oblator morabatur, nisi aliam fuisse eius intentionem legitime praesumi debeat.

If one offers a sum of money for the application of Masses without determining the number, this is to be reckoned according to the amount usually given in the place where the donor lived, unless it may be lawfully presumed that he had a different intention.

This canon must be compared with canons 828 and 831. The former makes the number of Masses to be applied dependent upon the contract entered between the donor and the priest, whilst can. 831 rules that the Ordinary should determine what constitutes a stipend. Neither of these two canons applies to the hypothesis set up in can. 830. *In concreto,* this hypothesis is that a man hands a priest ten dollars for stipends without determining the number of Masses he wishes to have said. If he would say to the priest: " Please say *a* Mass," the remainder of the sum (nine dollars) might justly be taken as a personal gift, especially if the donor is known as a generous man, or if it would be around Christmas time or the priest's birthday, etc. But if the donor would say: " Please say *Masses* for my intention," then ten Masses would have to be said in our country, where the usual stipend is one dollar for a Mass.[25]

---

[25] Innocent XII, "*Nuper,*" § 15; S. C. C. Nov. 15, 1698; Benedict XIV, *Instit.,* 56, n. X.

CAN. 831

§ 1. Ordinarii loci est manualem Missarum stipem in sua dioecesi definire per decretum, quantum fieri potest, in dioecesana Synodo latum; nec sacerdoti licet ea maiorem exigere.

§ 2. Ubi desit Ordinarii decretum, servetur consuetudo dioecesis.

§ 3. Etiam religiosi, licet exempti, circa stipem manualem stare debent decreto Ordinarii loci aut dioecesis consuetudini.

§ 1. It belongs to the Ordinary of the diocese to fix, if possible by a synodal decree, the amount of a manual Mass stipend, and priests are not allowed to demand more.

§ 2. Where there is no episcopal decree on the subject, the diocesan custom must be observed.

§ 3. Religious, also, even though exempt, must abide by the episcopal decree or diocesan custom.

This text is so plain that it needs no explanation. We will therefore only add that the Ordinary may enact, and enforce his enactment with ecclesiastical censures, that the secular as well as regular clergy shall not accept *less* than what either the synodal decree or diocesan custom prescribes; but he may not forbid priests to accept *more* than is customary, if the faithful voluntarily offer more.[26] The Ordinary is *not* entitled to fix the stipend for founded Masses for exempt religious.[27]

---

[26] S. C. C., Jan. 16, 1649; Benedict XIV, *Instit.*, 56, n. XI.

[27] S. C. C., Jan 15, 1698; Benedict XIV, *De Sacrif. Missae*, l. III, 22, 9, in agreement with the superiors regular, fixed the sum at 60 scudi ($60). This sum, according to the present value of money, would be from $240 to $300.

Can. 832

Sacerdoti fas est oblatam ultro maiorem stipem pro Missae applicatione accipere; et, nisi loci Ordinarius prohibuerit, etiam minorem.

A priest is allowed to accept a stipend which is larger than the one determined by diocesan statute or by custom; and, unless the Ordinary has forbidden, he may also accept a lesser one. The prohibition to receive a stipend below the customary sum must be made antecedently, and it would not be just to punish a priest for doing so if no prohibition had been promulgated.

ADDITIONAL STIPULATIONS

Can. 833

Praesumitur oblatorem petiise solam Missae applicationem; si tamen oblator expresse aliquas circumstantias in Missae celebratione servandas determinaverit, sacerdos, eleemosynam acceptans, eius voluntati stare debet.

It is presumed that the one who offers a stipend asks only to have the Mass applied; but if he expressly determines certain circumstances to be observed in the celebration of the Mass, his wishes must be complied with.

This follows from the nature of the stipend as a contract. Any one who makes a contract is allowed to add stipulations *(modi contractus)*, provided, of course, they are not opposed to the substance of the contract or forbidden by law. The " circumstances " of which our canon speaks, may refer to time, day or feast, kind of Mass and altar, etc. Of the time within which Masses are to be said the next canon (834) treats. We will only observe that, if the petitioner asks to have the Mass said on a certain day, and the priest agrees to do so, this stipulation must be complied with.[28]

(a) Similarly, if a certain *day* or *feast* is stipulated, it must be strictly observed, or the stipend returned, unless the priest knows the mind of the donor.

(b) If the donor asks for a *certain Mass,* for instance, a votive Mass in honor of the Blessed Virgin, the priest should say that Mass, though not bound under grievous obligation to do so. If the priest is asked to say a Mass for the poor souls, he should say a " Black " Mass.

The question has been asked whether a priest would satisfy the obligation arising from a stipend for a Mass for the dead, if he said the Mass of the day, though he could and should say a " Black " Mass. The S. Congregation of Rites answered that if the rubrics permitted a votive Mass or *Missa de requiem,* the priest would not fulfill his obligation by saying the Mass of the day, because the will of the testator or giver, if reasonable, must be respected.[29] In a mitigated form the same answer was returned twenty years ago by the same Congregation. The question was:[30] " Does a priest who is given a stipend for a Mass to be said for one or several dead, or in honor of a holy mystery, or of the Blessed Virgin, or of a Saint, fulfill his obligation if he says and applies the Mass of the day, because the rubrics do not permit him to say the Mass especially asked for? The answer was:

28 Theologians (cfr. Prümmer, *l. c.,* III, n. 266) maintain that the obligation is a grave one if the donor insists on a special day, but only a *levis* if he asks for a certain day without insisting on it or for no special reason. Besides, if many Masses are offered, say to a monastery, without a specially urgent appeal, it may reasonably be supposed that the donors are satisfied to have the Masses said as soon as possible, even though they should prefer a certain day.

29 S. Rit. C., March 3, 1761, ad 7 (*Dec. Auth.,* n. 2461).

30 S. Rit. C., June 13, 1899, ad IV (*Dec. Auth.,* n. 4031).

Yes, but with the addition: " It would be more advisable
to comply, as far as possible, with the intention of the
giver by saying the ' Black ' or votive Mass." From this
decision we may gather that the priest should comply
with the manifest and expressed intention of the giver
but is not under a strict obligation to do so, unless a direct demand was made as to the kind of Mass to be said,
especially if it be a foundation. In our country, we believe, most people are satisfied if the priest says a " Black "
Mass, even though the intention was directed for the benefit of the living, and we do not quite understand why
some theologians [31] regard it as incongruous to say a
" Black " Mass for the living. Does not the act of charity done to the poor souls enhance, as it were, the fruits
of the Mass thus applied? Of course, if a Mass in honor
of a special Saint, *e. g.*, St. Anthony, were asked for,
based on the belief that this Saint is a particularly powerful intercessor with God, it would not be prudent to say
a " Black " Mass.

(c) If a *special altar* is asked for by the donor, this
wish should be conscientiously complied with, in as far
at least as canon 836 does not permit a deviation from
the rule.

Here the question of the *privileged altar*, which will be
more fully discussed under cans. 916–918, may be briefly
touched upon as far as it is connected with our present
subject. Generally speaking, privileged altars are intended for the dead, and therefore " Black " Masses
should, as a rule, be offered thereat. The rubrics forbid a *Missa de Requiem* on *duplex* days, unless it be a
cantata in die obitus, etc. Yet, says the S. Congregation,
if the Mass is *de facto* applied for the intention of the
giver or founder, the privilege is not lost, *i. e.*, the indul-

31 Thus Prümmer, *l. c.*, III, n. 268.

gence attached to such an altar is gained also by a *Missa de festo* or *die occurrenti* prescribed according to the rubrics. Neither does it matter whether the altar is thus privileged *in perpetuum, or ad tempus,* or *pro certis diebus,* if the Mass is said on the privileged days, and the Mass has to be said in the color of the day according to the rubrics.[82] Hence, to gain the indulgence attached to a privileged altar it is not necessary to say a " Black " or Ferial or Vigil Mass with the oration for the deceased, although this may be laudably done.[83]

(d) The donor may also stipulate that the Mass be said in a certain *church* or *chapel.* In that case the priest must say the Mass in the church or chapel appointed. A chaplain who is appointed to a certain chapel, must say Mass there, and if the founder has not expressly determined otherwise, he must also apply the Mass for the founder.[84] The rector of a church in which a Mass must be said by the last will of a testator, may not permit a priest to whom he has given the stipend to say the Mass in another church, or to subtract anything from the original alms.[85] If a Mass to be said in a certain church must be transferred to another church, some compensation for wine, altar bread, candles, and the use of vestments may be demanded.[86] From this it logically follows that a priest saying Mass in a strange church would not act against ecclesiastical law or natural courtesy if

---

[82] S. Rit. C., Aug. 5, 1662; Dec. 1, 1666; Aug. 13, 1669 (*Dec. Auth.,* nn. 1238, 1343, 1392).

[83] S. O. (sect. Indulg.), Feb. 20, 1913 (*A. Ap. S.,* V, 122); Benedict XIV, *Instit.,* 56, n. XV.

[84] S. C. C., Aug. 18, 1668; Jan. 11, 1710 (Richter, *Trid.,* p. 136 f. nn. 49, 55); Dec. 19, 1904, ad 3; especially is the chaplain not allowed to determine *ad libitum* the stipend to be given to another priest for saying Mass in that chapel (which would be against n. XV of the " *Ut debito,*" May 11, 1904).

[85] S. C. C., Dec. 19, 1904, ad 2 (*Linzer Q.-S.,* 1905, Vol. 58, p. 674).

[86] S. C. C., Jan. 15, 1639, *et pluries* (Richter, *Trid.,* p. 137, n. 62; Benedict XIV, *Instit.,* 56, n. XIII).

he would leave some compensation at least for the janitor and the altar boys.

Here we may add something concerning the thirty so-called *Gregorian Masses,* which, according to tradition, originated with St. Gregory the Great (590–604), who celebrated Mass for thirty consecutive days to redeem the soul of a monk who had died with some unlawfully retained property.   The custom is widespread to-day, but some have exaggerated notions as to the effects of these Masses.   We are concerned only with the law regarding them, which has lately been fixed as follows:

(a) The thirty Gregorian Masses must be celebrated on thirty consecutive days, without interruption;

(b) A priest cannot say, for instance, three Masses on Christmas Day as Gregorian Masses, and then on the 28th Dec. resume the celebration.

(c) Nor can he give the thirty Masses to different priests that they may be said in less than thirty days.

(d) It is not required that the same priest say all thirty Masses, or that he say a "Black" Mass on the days when the rubrics permit.[37]

Since the Gregorian Masses are a burden and a risk, it would not be against ecclesiastical law if the Ordinaries [38] would fix an "extra" tax for them. For religious the Ordinary in that case is the superior major, who, therefore, is entitled to make or authorize an additional charge for Gregorian Masses.

[37] S. O. (Sect. Indulg.), Dec. 12, 1912 (*A. Ap. S.,* V, 32 f.); the three last days of Holy Week do not interfere with the thirty *consecutive* days.

[38] This is done in some Eastern dioceses, where the charge is $45.

CAN. 834

§ 1. Missae pro quibus celebrandis tempus ab oblatore expresse praescriptum est, eo omnino tempore sunt celebrandae.

§ 2. Si oblator nullum tempus pro Missarum manualium celebratione expresse praescripserit:

1.° Missae pro urgenti causa oblatae quamprimum tempore utili sunt celebrandae;

2.° In aliis casibus Missae sunt celebrandae intra modicum tempus pro maiore vel minore Missarum numero.

§ 3. Quod si oblator arbitrio sacerdotis tempus celebrationis expresse reliquerit, sacerdos poterit tempore quo sibi magis placuerit, eas celebrare, firmo praescripto can. 835.

§ 1. If a term has been expressly fixed by the donor, the Masses must be said at the time required.

This obligation, as already observed, follows from the stipulation attached to the contract.[89]

§ 2. If no *time* has been expressly fixed for *manual stipends*, the following rules must be followed:

1°. *Urgent* Masses must be said *as soon as possible* within an equitable period. Thus if a Mass is ordered for a successful operation or child-birth, it is supposed to be said before or on the day of the event. However, the legislator says "*tempus utile*" (see can. 35), which here means, if the priest is not occupied with other intentions or obligations. Should he take sick or be lawfully prevented on the day on which he is obliged to say the

---

[89] S. C. C., June 23, Sept. 1, 1742, ad 9.

stipulated Mass, he would have to ask another priest to say the Mass in his stead,[40] provided he could find one who would be willing and able; if not, he may keep the stipend and say the Mass as soon as possible.

2°. If the Masses are not urgent, they must be said within a short time *(intra modicum tempus),* proportionate to the greater or smaller number of Masses. By *modicum tempus* was always understood *one month* from the date of the obligation in case of one Mass.[41]   A scale was proposed to the S. Congregation [42] for a greater number, as follows:

For	10	Masses,	1	month
"	20	"	2	months
"	40	"	3	"
"	60	"	4	"
"	80	"	5	"
"	100	"	6	"

The answer was: " It is left to the discretion of the priest, with due regard to the decree ' *Ut debita,'* of May 11, 1904, and to the rules of approved authors."   But it must be noted that the scale as proposed applied to stipends received from one person, not several.   Hence, if of 100 persons each would offer one Mass stipend, the six months' term would not apply, unless the intention of the donors to have them said within that time were evident.   Therefore, if the priest tells the person who offers a stipend that he cannot say the Mass within one month, or three months, and the person thus advised says: " All right, Father," he may accept the stipend.   An im-

40 S. C. C., Sept. 18, 1683; June 4, 1689 (Richter, *Trid.,* p. 138, n. 65 f.).

41 S. C. C., July 17, 1755; Benedict XIV, *Instit.,* 56, n. XIV; " *Ut* debita," May 11, 1904 (*Anal. Eccl.,* t. 12, 202).

42 S. C. C., Feb. 27, 1905 (*Anal. Eccl.,* t. 13, 124).

plicit stipulation to the same effect may be assumed if the faithful know that many Masses are said in a monastery or religious community and nevertheless send their stipends there. It may, we say, be presumed that they are satisfied to have the Masses said when it suits the community. If they are not " urgent " as to the time, *tempus utile* may be taken.

§ 3 renders this explanation clearer. If the donor *expressly leaves* the *time* for saying the Mass *to the discretion of the priest,* the latter may say it when most convenient for him, with due regard to can. 835.

CAN. 835

Nemini licet tot Missarum onera per se celebranda-rum recipere quibus intra annum satisfacere nequeat.

No one is allowed to receive more Masses to be celebrated by himself, than he can say within a year.

The phrase *" per se celebrandarum "* means that the *priest himself,* and not another, is supposed to say the Masses. Otherwise a priest may accept as many Masses as he wishes and dispose of them according to the rules laid down in can. 839 ff.

The phrase *" intra annum "* *(within a year)* also calls for an explanation. The starting point for *manual Masses* is the date on which the first Mass is received and accepted. Say this is the first of March, 1919, and suppose the donor (according to can. 834, § 3) has left it entirely to the discretion of the priest when to say the Mass. If he says it any time before March 1, 1920, he will have complied with the law. He may, before he has said the Mass accepted on March 1, 1919, accept others, and say them first. But if the donor has set no time for the Mass given on March 1, 1919, nor expressly left it to the discretion of the priest when to say it, the priest must say the Mass within a month, although he may receive other Masses before April 1, 1919, before having said the Mass accepted on March 1, 1919. For these Masses received in the meantime, say on the feast of St. Joseph, 1919, the same rules hold good.[43] It is well to instruct the faithful on this point and also to ask the giver in each instance whether he is willing to leave the time for saying the Mass to the priest.

POSTERS IN CHURCHES

Can. 836

In ecclesiis in quibus ob fidelium peculiarem devotionem Missarum eleemosynae ita affluunt, ut omnes Missae, celebrari ibidem debito tempore nequeant, moneantur fideles, per tabellam in loco patenti et obvio positam, Missas oblatas celebratum iri vel ibidem, cum commode poterit, vel alibi.

The churches here in question are mainly famous sanctuaries or shrines. When it proves impossible to say all Masses in such sanctuaries for which stipends are offered, in order that the expectations of the faithful may not be disappointed, they should be advised that the Masses will be said either in the church itself, if convenient, or else in some other church.[44] A public notice to this effect should be posted in a conspicuous and easily accessible place. If stipends are offered nevertheless, the ministers cannot be accused of " pious fraud."

Evidently this rule applies only to churches where the faithful make their offerings personally, not to communities to which stipends are sent.

---

43 Innocent XII, "Nuper," § 15 ad 1 (Richter, Trid., p. 146).   44 S. C. C., March 8, 1659; Benedict XIV, Instit., 56, n. XIV.

MASSES SENT AWAY

MASSES SENT AWAY

CAN. 837

Qui Missas per alios celebrandas habet, eas quamprimum distribuat, firmo praescripto can. 841; sed
tempus legitimum pro earundem celebratione incipit a
die quo sacerdos celebraturus easdem receperit, nisi
aliud constet.

Whoever has Masses to be said by others, should distribute them as soon as possible, with due regard to can.
841. But the lawful time for saying them commences on
the day on which the priest who is to say them has received them, unless the contrary is evident.

Here the *intentionarius* of religious communities and of
priests overloaded with Mass intentions is especially
aimed at. The second clause may be illustrated thus:
A religious in Rome receives from his home monastery
thirty Masses. Sent on Feb. 1, they arrive on March 1.
Ordinarily the religious would have time to say them
from March 1 to the middle of May. If, however, the
letter contains a clause urging him to say the Masses
as soon as possible, he would have to hurry up; but if the
letter says: "at your convenience," he could postpone
saying the thirty Masses and say them when he had no
other intentions.[45] A decision of the S. Congregation
advises that where there is a large number of intentions,
the Masses should be distributed among several priests,
so that they may be said more promptly.[46]

---

[45] "*Ut debito,*" n. 4. [46] S. C. C., Feb. 27, 1905, ad 4.

CAN. 838

Qui habent Missarum numerum de quibus sibi liceat libere disponere, possunt eas tribuere sacerdotibus sibi acceptis, dummodo probe sibi constet eos omni exceptione maiores vel testimonio proprii Ordinarii commendatos.

This canon is a corollary to the preceding one, for it describes the qualities of the priests to whom superfluous Masses, of which one may freely dispose, may be entrusted. Any priests may be freely chosen, provided they are absolutely reliable or recommended by the local Ordinary. It is not necessary, therefore, that they be known personally [47] *(facie ad faciem)* to those who distribute the Masses.

DURATION OF THE OBLIGATION OF A MASS STIPEND

CAN. 839

Qui Missas a fidelibus receptas aut quoquo modo suae fidei commissas aliis celebrandas tradiderint, obligatione tenentur usque dum acceptatae ab eisdem obligationis et recepti stipendii testimonium obtinuerint.

Whoever gives Masses received from the faithful or otherwise entrusted to his care to others is personally responsible for them until he is informed that the obligation has been accepted and the stipend received.

It is evident that the priests to whom Masses are sent according to this canon, must have the same qualities as those described in can. 838. The *obligation* for Masses

---

[47] " *Ut debita*," n. 5, says: " *personaliter sibi notis* "; but this is omitted in our text. However, even the wording of " *Ut debita* " did not absolutely require personal knowledge.

given to others does not cease until the other has *accepted* the obligation and *received the stipend*. The reason is evidently based upon the nature of the contract. For readiness to accept the obligation is only half efficacious, and does not become fully so until the object is delivered, which is done by actual transmission and reception of the price. It is further necessary to have reliable information with regard to both these essential conditions. This information may be given orally or in writing, but it must produce moral certainty. No Masses whatsoever are excepted from this law, not even those sent to the Ordinary or the Holy See. Therefore the old ruling of " *Ut debita*," 1904, n. 6, must be modified to the effect that the obligation remains until information is given either by the Ordinary or the Holy See if Masses are sent to either. Also the risk of losing the money must be borne by the sender. When a check or draft is sent, there is no loss to be feared except of time, and the cancelled check upon its return will serve as a receipt. Whether this would suffice for making sure of the acceptance of the obligation depends on the business capacity of the recipient and the custom of the country. In our country cashed and returned checks are acknowledged as legal receipts.

CAN. 840

§ 1. Qui Missarum stipes manuales ad alios transmittit, debet acceptas integre transmittere, nisi aut oblator expresse permittat aliquid retinere, aut certo constet excessum supra taxam dioecesanam datum fuisse intuitu personae.

§ 2. In Missis ad instar manualium, nisi obstet mens fundatoris, legitime retinetur excessus et satis est remittere solam eleemosynam manualem dioecesis in qua

Missa celebratur, si pinguis eleemosyna locum pro parte teneat dotis beneficii aut causae piae.

§ 1. He who sends manual stipends to others, *must transmit* them as he has received them, *i. e., in full,* unless the donor has expressly permitted him to retain part of the stipend, or unless it is evident that whatever exceeds the synodal or customary stipend was intended for the person of him to whom the stipend was given.

There are many strict prohibitions to this effect from the time of Urban VIII to our own, intended to keep " damnable lucre " out of the Church.[48] The decree " *Ut debita,*" of May 11, 1904, abolished all previous privileges or indults and demanded " a new and special concession of the Apostolic See," which cannot be communicated to others, for the superiors of famous sanctuaries who wish to retain a small percentage of the stipends for the upkeep and adornment of the church. If a Mass stipend for a certain place or sanctuary were $2, therefore, the priest who said the Mass must be given the two dollars in full.[49] However, the S. Cong. made an exception in favor of sanctuaries by adding: " *nisi de consensu oblatorum,*" that is, if the donors *expressly* (no *praesumpta* or *tacita licentia*) state that a small sum may be kept out of the usual stipend for the sustenance of the church, it would be allowed by law.[50]

Another reason for retaining a part of a Mass stipend would be if the amount exceeded the usual tax and was given *intuitu personae,* for personal reasons. In Holland the faithful often give their pastors stipends which are

---

[48] " *Alias,*" June 21, 1625, § 6: " *damnabile lucrum* "; S. O., Sept. 24, 1665, prop. dam. 9 (Denzinger, n. 980).

[49] S. C. C., Dec. 19, 1904, ad 3 (*Anal. Eccl.,* t. 13, p. 70). This

law also obliges the Oriental priests; S. C. P. F., Jan. 20, 1893 (*Coll., n.* 1823).

[50] S. C. C., " *Vigilanti,*" May 25, 1893 (*Coll. P. F.,* n. 1832).

almost equal to a salary. They do this partly to insure their support, and partly out of gratitude and affection. The pastors, when absent or sick, or for other reasons, have their chaplains or curates *(coadiutores)* say the Masses for the usual or synodal stipend and keep the surplus for themselves. The matter was brought to Rome, and the S. Poenitentiaria, in the name of Benedict XIV, decided that the practice was permissible.[51] Now a priest may receive a stipend of $5 from a friend, or as a present, and if he is certain that the *pingue stipendium* was given for merely personal motives, he may keep the $4 and give $1 to another priest to say the Mass, unless, of course, the donor had insisted that he himself say the Mass.

In another case solved by the S. Poenitentiaria [52] pastors were accustomed to exchange Mass intentions with their assistants or curates, who sang the *Missa cantata* in the pastor's place, but received no stipend. The pastor on his part did not say the Mass according to the intention of the assistant, but gave a manual stipend to a third priest, who said the Mass according to the intention of the assistant. The S. Congr. decided that such an exchange of intentions was allowed, provided the third priest was aware of the higher stipend and freely and of his own accord renounced it. The reason given was that there is no detestable trading in that case.

§ 2. The *excess or surplus of quasi-manual stipends* may be lawfully retained if the *pingue stipendium* takes the place of a partial endowment of an ecclesiastical pre-

51 S. Poenit., April 6, 1742 (*Coll. P. F.*, n. 336); Benedict XIV, " *Quanta cura*," June 30, 1741, enacted severe penalties against socalled trading and approved the decision of S. Poenit.   h

52 S. Poenit., Aug. 22, 1826 (*Coll. P. F.*, n. 789). This decision runs counter to the doctrine of St. Alphonsus.

bend or pious institution, unless the will of the founder
reads otherwise. In that case, then, if the beneficiary has
the Mass said by another priest, the former is bound only
to hand the customary or diocesan stipend to his substitute.

How can this ruling be made to square with § 1 of the
same canon? The answer is obvious. The surplus stipend is given as a sort of contribution to the necessary
support of the priest, who is employed for a certain benefice or chapel, and since the stipend itself is of the same
nature, there is no alienation involved either of the foundation or of the stipend. Besides, there is no trading,
because the priest receives the stipend to which he is entitled according to the diocesan custom. In Bavaria and
elsewhere, where the income of pastors is fixed by the
civil government by agreement with the ecclesiastical authority, the salary includes the stipends accruing from
foundation Masses, and from requiem and marriage
Masses, for which a larger stipend is paid than for ordinary Masses.

Since, however, the pastors are sometimes lawfully prevented from saying these Masses personally,
they give them to other priests, who say them for the
usual stipend, which is less than the one received by
the pastors, who retain a portion of the original stipend as part of their legitimate income. Rome has declared this practice lawful, because the money thus kept
is really a part of the salary.[53] The surplus may also
be retained in favor of the church to which a priest is
assigned.[54] If the founder, however, has set up a clause
forbidding such retention, it would be unlawful, as the

---

[53] S. C. C., Monacen., Feb. 28,
March 28, Aug. 22, 1874 (A. S. S.,
Vol. 8, 65 ff.).

[54] S. C. C., Jan. 21, 1898 (Anal.
Eccl., t. 15, 65).

will of the founder must be religiously respected.[55] This rule, we believe, may also be applied to our country, where quasi-manual stipends form part of the salary of priests, provided no contrary stipulation exists in the will of the founder.

CAN. 841

§ 1. Omnes et singuli administratores causarum piarum aut quoquo modo ad Missarum onera implenda obligati, sive ecclesiastici sive laici, sub exitum cuiuslibet anni, Missarum onera quibus nondum fuerit satisfactum, suis Ordinariis tradant secundum modum ab his definiendum.

§ 2. Hoc autem tempus ita est accipiendum ut in Missis ad instar manualium obligatio eas deponendi decurrat a fine illius anni intra quem onera impleri debuissent; in manualibus vero, post annum a die suscepti oneris, salva diversa offerentium voluntate.

§ 1. Administrators of pious institutions, and all, whether clergymen or laymen, who are in any way bound to have Mass obligations fulfilled, must at the end of each year send the Masses not yet said to their Ordinaries in some manner to be determined by the latter.

§ 2. The time for complying with this obligation runs, for quasi-manual stipends, from the end of the year during which the Masses should have been said, and for manual stipends from the day on which the obligation was accepted, with due regard to the intention of the donor.

Causae piae are *pious institutions* under the direction of the local Ordinary, which generally have a number of Masses either imposed by the will of founders or offered by the faithful. The administrator (or *syndicus*, as he

---

[55] S. C. C., Feb. 21, 1688 (Richter, *Trid.*, p. 138, n. 69); " *Ut de-* bita," May 11, 1904, n. 15; Feb. 23, 1907 (*Anal. cit.*, p. 64).

was formerly called) of each house is responsible for the Mass obligations being duly fulfilled. *Pia causa* in this context certainly includes the administration of any ecclesiastical institute with the sole exception of male religious, as can. 842 clearly implies. Hence it also comprehends religious houses of women who are not under the jurisdiction of a prelate regular. Besides *piae causae* here comprises also parishes, chaplaincies, rectories, in fact, any one, clergyman or layman, who has to see to the fulfillment of such obligations; also guardians or *executors* of last wills and the heirs upon whom devolves the duty of complying with pious obligations.

The Ordinary to whom the Masses not yet said must be sent, is the one in whose diocese the *pia causa* is located.

§ 2 defines the *date from which* the obligation commences. For *quasi-manual* Masses, which are attached either to a definite church or to a specified priest, the time runs from the end of the year within which the Masses were to be said. Suppose, *e. g.*, a quasi-manual Mass was to be said on St. Michael's Day, 1918. If this Mass was not said that year, it must be handed over to the Ordinary before the last day of Dec., 1918, because we now generally understand the civil year, which commences Jan. 1. However, if it were taken to mean the ecclesiastical year, the end of that year would be the Saturday before the first Sunday of Advent. If the document merely says: " So many Masses must be said each year," we should take the civil year. But if a date is stated, from which the obligation commences, the year is reckoned from that date.

If there is question of *purely manual stipends,* the obligation of sending them to the Ordinary commences on the first day after a full year has elapsed from the day when the obligation was assumed. For instance, a Mass was ordered on St. Michael's day, Sept. 29, 1918, but not said on that day, and hence the Mass must be sent to the Ordinary on Sept. 30, 1919. Only if the will of the donor has expressly left it to the discretion of the priest to prolong the term of one year, may he refrain from sending it to the Ordinary.

DUTY OF ORDINARIES AND RELIGIOUS SUPERIORS

CAN. 842

Ius et officium advigilandi ut onera Missarum adimpleantur in ecclesiis saecularium pertinet ad loci Ordinarium; in religiosorum ecclesiis, ad eorum Superiores.

The right and duty of watching over the fulfilment of Mass obligations belong to the Ordinary of the diocese with regard to the churches of secular priests, and to the superiors of religious with regard to *their* churches.

This canon repeats the ruling of Innocent XII, who gravely enjoined Ordinaries to see to it, at their canonical visitations and on other occasions, that all the regulations concerning Mass stipends are carried out without delay, cavil, or perverse interpretation.[56] However this duty extended only to churches where *secular priests* are employed — *in ecclesiis saecularium*. The legislator, by extending the exemption formerly belonging to exempt regulars exclusively, has made the *superiors of religious,* whether exempt or not, *responsible* in this matter. This had been the law ever since the times of Urban VIII and Innocent with regard to foundation Masses.[57] But the bishop of St. Pölten, in Lower Austria, thought he was

---

[56] "*Nuper,*" Dec. 23, 1697, § 24.
[57] Ib. § 25; S. C. C. Nov. 14, 1699; June 26, 1700.

entitled to inspect the books for manual stipends kept by the Franciscans of his diocese. The S. Congregation thought differently and told the bishop that he could not claim the right of inspecting the records of even manual Masses at the time of his canonical visitation. This decision touched the books kept in a parish church in charge of the Franciscans.[58]

The text says, *in ecclesiis religiosorum*. What churches are these? We believe that since the text draws no distinction between churches perpetually and temporarily entrusted to religious, the legislator intends to include both classes. But the religious must be such as defined by the Code, *viz.*, members of a congregation with the three religious vows. A doubt may arise as to communities of nuns or Sisters who are subject to the diocesan Ordinary but have a religious as chaplain. Who is the responsible person in that case? We believe a distinction will disperse the doubt. For the Masses which are sent to the religious community of Sisters, as such, and which cannot be said by the chaplain, the superioress is responsible, and ultimately the local Ordinary, because such congregations are subject to him. As to the Masses given to the chaplain, he must answer for them to his superior, because by the name of Ordinary, according to our text, is to be understood the superior of the religious; — *pro suis respectivis subditis*, as one decision declares.[59]

STIPEND-BOOKS

Can. 843

§ 1. Rectores ecclesiarum aliorumque piorum locorum sive saecularium sive religiosorum in quibus

---

[58] S. C. EE. et RR., May 11, 1904 (*Anal. Eccl.*, t. 12, p. 248).

[59] S. C. C., Feb. 27, 1905 (*Anal. Eccl.*, t. 15, 123).

eleemosynae Missarum recipi solent, peculiarem habeant librum in quo accurate notent Missarum receptarum numerum, intentionem, eleemosynam, celebrationem.

§ 2. Ordinarii tenentur obligatione singulis saltem annis huiusmodi libros sive per se sive per alios recognoscendi.

§ 1. Rectors of churches and other pious institutions, whether in charge of seculars or religious, where Mass stipends are wont to be received, shall keep a special book, in which the stipends are to be entered as to number, intention, amount, and date of celebration.

§ 2. The Ordinaries are obliged to inspect these books at least once a year, either personally or by a deputy.

The latter section, of course, affects mainly secular institutions, not exempt or other religious, as otherwise can. 842 would be meaningless; but the religious superiors, too, must inspect the books kept in or for the community.[60]

CAN. 844

§ 1. Ordinarii quoque locorum et Superiores religiosi, qui propriis subditis aliisve Missas celebrandas committunt, quas acceperint Missas cum suis eleemosynis cito in librum per ordinem referant curentque pro viribus ut quamprimum celebrentur.

§ 2. Imo omnes sacerdotes sive saeculares sive religiosi debent accurate adnotare quisque Missarum intentiones receperit, quibusve satisfecerit.

§ 1. Local Ordinaries and religious superiors who give Masses to their own subjects or to others, shall promptly enter the Masses they receive, together with the amount

60 Cfr. S. C. EE. et RR., May 11, 1904.

of the stipend, according to the order of time in which they were received, in a book, and see to it that they are said as soon as possible.

§ 2. All priests, secular as well as religious, shall keep an accurate account of the intentions received and the Masses said by them.

CHAPTER II

ARTICLE I

THE MINISTER OF HOLY COMMUNION

CAN. 845

§ 1. Minister ordinarius sacrae communionis est solus sacerdos.

§ 2. Extraordinarius est diaconus, de Ordinarii loci vel parochi licentia, gravi de causa concedenda, quae in casu necessitatis legitime praesumitur.

The ordinary minister of Holy Communion is the priest alone, the extraordinary minister may also be a deacon, if the local Ordinary or pastor grants him permission, which should be given for a grave reason, and is lawfully presumed in case of necessity.

Whereas *priests* by their ordination receive the power of consecrating and distributing the Holy Eucharist,[1] *deacons* only obtain the power of distributing the same. By custom rather than by divine law their power is made subordinate to the jurisdictional power of the Ordinary, in order to show forth the hierarchic order. Besides, since the pastor, who must be a priest, is the legitimate head of the flock assigned to him, it is becoming that the

---

1 C. 29, Dist. 2, *de cons.* (a text taken from the reform-synod of Paris, 829; cfr. Hefele, *Concil., Gesch.*, IV, 60, can. 45) relates with horror that women entered the sanctuary and distributed holy Communion.

deacon, who is his inferior, should depend on him for permission to exercise his power.

Lay men, and especially women, are expressly excluded from distributing Holy Communion, because they belong not to the *Ecclesia sanctificans,* but to the *Ecclesia sanctificanda.* That in extreme necessity laymen may give communion to themselves, may be admitted, since history reports examples of this practice.[2] *Deacons,* then (but not subdeacons),[3] may, with the permission of the Ordinary or pastor in whose diocese or parish they wish to distribute Holy Communion, perform that function. But the permission is not to be granted without a *grave cause.* Such a cause would exist if the pastor were lawfully prevented from giving Holy Communion to the people on a holyday of obligation, or if a large number of people had to be accommodated, making it impossible for the pastor to finish in time. We hardly believe permission should be granted for the sake of a few daily communicants, unless the parents of a newly ordained deacon should perhaps wish to receive Holy Communion at the hands of their son. In *case of necessity*[4] the permission may be presumed. Such a case would be the administration of the Viaticum, or of paschal Communion to such as have no opportunity to receive it on some other day.

When a deacon administers Holy Communion, he may proceed as follows: Dressed with the surplice and stole crossed on the right side, he recites the *Misereatur* and *Indulgentiam,* making the sign of the cross over himself or over the communicants (or, if he brings the Viaticum, over the sick person), distributes Holy Communion, re-

---

2 Noldin, *De Sacramentis,* ed. 10, n. 124.

3 They sometimes usurped that prerogative; cfr. Hefele, *l. c.,* p. 621.

4 S. Rit. C., Feb. 25, 1777 (*Dec. Auth.,* n. 2504): "*Extra casum necessitatis non licet diacono.*"

cites the " *O sacrum*," according to the season, then the *Dominus vobiscum*, and blesses the people (or the infirm) with the Blessed Sacrament. All this is allowed when the deacon has express or presumed permission.[5] If he is merely helping the pastor, he should abstain from reciting the prayers and blessing the people.

In case no other priest is present, a priest may administer Communion to himself, even for mere devotion; and the same holds good of a deacon.[6]

CAN. 846

§ 1. Quilibet sacerdos intra Missam et, si privatim celebrat, etiam proxime ante et statim post, sacram communionem ministrare potest, salvo praescripto can. 869.

§ 2. Etiam extra Missam quilibet sacerdos eadem facultate pollet ex licentia saltem praesumpta rectoris ecclesiae, si sit extraneus.

§ 1. Any priest may distribute Holy Communion *during* Mass, and, if he celebrates privately, also immediately *before and after Mass,* with due regard to the regulations for private Oratories laid down in can. 869.

§ 2. Even *outside of Mass* every priest enjoys the same right, provided he has at least the presumed permission of the rector of the church if he is a stranger.

§ 1 distinguishes between *two kinds* of Masses, of which one is called *private,* while the other is not determined. What, then, is a *private* Mass?

There are, as Benedict XIV says,[7] various meanings at-

5 S. Rit. C., Aug. 14, 1858 (*Dec. Auth.,* n. 3074).
6 Noldin, *l. c.,* n. 124.
7 *De Sacrif. Missae,* l. II, c. 22, n. 7.

tached to the term "private Mass." It may be a Mass said in a private place, or on a day not a feast-day, or because the fruit is applied to a private person, or because only a few persons are present, or because it is not said on the main altar or as a parochial or conventual Mass, or, finally, because the priest alone receives Holy Communion. There is a decision of the S. Congregation of Rites [8] which seems to throw some light on our subject. The question was asked whether priests duly vested for saying Mass could, for a reasonable cause, distribute Holy Communion before or after the *solemn* Mass, or at the *Missa cantata*, or the *conventual* Mass, as is permitted before and after the private Mass. The answer was, no. Hence a private Mass would be one said without solemnity or chant, not as a conventual Mass, but simply for the sake of devotion. But what about a *parochial* Mass? Here we believe a distinction should be drawn as follows: The parochial Mass, properly speaking, is the one said for the people,— the *Missa pro populo*, as it is now required on all holydays of obligation and some suppressed feasts. This is strictly the parochial Mass, because it is said for the people and, at least as a rule, in their presence. On other days the pastor is supposed to say private or merely devotional Masses, because there is no strictly juridical obligation of saying Mass on those days. We are aware [9] that some take the term "private Mass" simply in the sense of *Missa lecta*, even though it be a parish or conventual Mass. This may be true with regard to certain rubrical considerations, but in our case it certainly cannot be the underlying idea, as the decision

[8] S. Rit. C., Jan. 19, 1906 (*Anal. Eccl.*, t. 14, 104 f). A conventual Mass is one either sung or read by religious corporations.

[9] *Am. Eccl. Rev.*, 1916, Vol. 55, p. 429 f.

quoted proves. Hence *during*, but not immediately before or after, a solemn, or sung, or conventual, or strictly parochial Mass Holy Communion may be distributed, whilst a priest saying private Mass may also distribute it before, during, and after Mass.

Every priest is entitled to distribute Holy Communion even *in a church not his own*, provided he has the at least presumed permission of the rector of the church where he says Mass. The accessory follows the principal,[10] which in this case is the celebration of the Holy Sacrifice. This rule holds good also with regard to religious, although the Decretals [11] were rather severe in condemning religious who ventured to distribute the Holy Eucharist without the special permission of the pastor.

A permission may be presumed if no express prohibition has been issued by the local pastor.

If there is a public notice hung up in the sacristy regulating the hour for distributing Holy Communion, visiting priests should heed it, because it is intended to preserve order.

When Holy Communion is distributed at a "Black" Mass (which is not forbidden),[12] the priest may communicate the faithful during Mass with particles consecrated in another Mass, or before and after Mass if there is a plausible reason. However, before and after Mass the blessing is to be omitted.[13]

---

10 Reg. Juris, 42, in 6°.
11 C. 1, Clem. V, 7.
12 S. Rit. C., July 24, 1683 (*Dec. Auth.*, n. 1711).

13 S. Rit. C., July 23, 1868 (*Dec. Auth.*, n. 3177).

CAN. 847

Ad infirmos publice sacra communio deferatur, nisi iusta et rationabilis causa aliud suadeat.

CAN. 848

§ 1. Ius et officium sacram communionem publice ad infirmos etiam non paroecianos extra ecclesiam deferendi, pertinet ad parochum intra suum territorium.

§ 2. Ceteri sacerdotes id possunt in casu tantum necessitatis aut de licentia saltem praesumpta eiusdem parochi vel Ordinarii.

Holy Communion should be *brought to the sick publicly,* unless a just and reasonable cause advises otherwise.

The right and duty to bring Holy Communion publicly to the sick, even though they be not his parishioners, belongs to the *pastor* within the limits of his parish. *Other priests* may perform this function only in case of necessity or with the at least presumed permission of the pastor or Ordinary.

These two canons concern countries where it is still customary to bring Holy Communion to the sick publicly, *i. e.,* in procession, formed by the pastor and some faithful lay people, or by the pastor and his sexton or a cleric who carries a light or lantern.[14] Only in cases of necessity, when the *furor gentilium* or violence and great irreverence was to be feared, was secret communion permitted.[15] Special faculties were issued for countries in

14 Benedict XIV, "*Inter omnigenas,*" Feb. 22, 1744, § 21 f.; S. C. P. F., Sept. 11, 1779 (*Coll.,* n. 537). I, n. 1, 3–5; May 23, 1843; Sept. 12, 1857 (*Dec. Auth.,* nn. 3234, 2908, 3059).
15 S. Rit. C., Feb. 10, 1871, ad

which there was danger of sacrilegious irreverence. Now these faculties are no longer needed, as any reasonable cause suffices to dispense from what was formerly the general law. To decide whether such reasons exist, as they surely do in our country, belongs to the Ordinary, or the pastor, because the law fixes no limit. Our canon puts the right of bringing Holy Communion publicly to the sick among the parochial rights (cfr. can. 462, 3°), but this has reference *only to the public mode* of administering the Viaticum, not the private. What was said concerning religious under can. 514 must be here repeated.[16]

PRIVATE COMMUNION

CAN. 849

§ 1. Communionem privatim ad infirmos quilibet sacerdos deferre potest, de venia saltem praesumpta sacerdotis, cui custodia sanctissimi Sacramenti commissa est.

§ 2. Quando privatim sacra communio infirmis ministratur, reverentiae ac decentiae tanto sacramento debitae sedulo consulatur, servatis a Sede Apostolica praescriptis normis.

§ 1. Any priest may bring Holy Communion privately to the sick, provided he has the at least presumed permission of the priest who is the custodian of the Blessed Sacrament.

The custodian of a cathedral church properly is the chapter,[17] but generally the *custos* or dean of the chapter. In religious communities of men the custody is entrusted to the superior of the house, the *custos sacrae supellectilis*, or the parish priest, if a parish is attached to the house.

---

16 Cfr. C. 1, Clem. V, 7.   17 Can. 415, § 3, 1.°

The pastor is the custodian of the Blessed Sacrament in his parish; the chaplain, in religious communities of women and pious institutions.

§ 2. When Holy Communion is brought privately to the sick, care should be taken that due reverence and respect is rendered to the august Sacrament according to the rules prescribed by the Apostolic See.

One of the latest rules, taken from Benedict XIV's Constitution "*Inter omnigenas*," (Feb. 2, 1744) and re-enforced by the S. Congregation of the Sacraments,[18] is the following: Ordinaries may permit Communion to be brought to such as are sickly (*mala affectis valetudine*) and cannot leave their home, but would like to receive the Holy Eucharist for devotion's sake. But the priest must always wear the stole under his dress, or what we call coat; the pyxis must be placed in a burse appended by strings from the neck and carried on the breast. The priest shall never go alone, but be accompanied by at least one of the faithful. In case of necessity, we suppose, this last condition might be dispensed with, although it certainly is a very grave one, as appears from the aforesaid Constitution and other instructions.[19]

What we observed under can. 847 concerning the bringing of Holy Communion secretly is corroborated by this canon, and hence the faculty given in virtue of form 1, art. 24, is no longer needed.[20]

[18] Dec. 23, 1912 (*A. Ap. S.*, IV, 725).

[19] S. C. P. F., Sept. 20, 1739; Sept. 11, 1779; Feb. 25. 1859 (*Coll.*, nn. 324, 537, 1171); the stole was dispensed with on account of a long trip and the possible transparency through the light vestment.

[20] Cfr. Putzer, *Comm.*, p. 282 ff.

CAN. 850

Sacram communionem per modum Viatici sive publice sive privatim ad infirmos deferre, pertinet ad parochum ad normam can. 848, salvo praescripto can. 397, n. 3 et can. 514, §§ 1-3.

To bring Holy Communion as *Viaticum* to the sick, either publicly or privately, belongs to the *pastor* in accordance with can. 848, with due regard to can. 397, n. 3, and can. 514, §§ 1-3.

The right here established belongs to the *strictly parochial* rights, and must therefore be respected by all priests, assistants or curates, including religious, even if exempt or acting as missionaries.[21] This is also true if Tertiaries of the Order of St. Francis are sick in their own houses and wish to receive the Viaticum. A Franciscan may hear their confession, but the administration of the last Sacraments belongs to the pastor in whose parish they live.[22] Exempt from this rule are clerical religious and cloistered Sisters, as explained under can. 514.

Canons of the cathedral are obliged to administer the last rites to their bishop, according to canon 397, 3°. Canons who reside in a parish must receive the last rites at the hands of the pastor within whose jurisdiction they live, not from the canons or dignitaries of the chapters to which they belong, whether collegiate or cathedral.[23]

It may not be amiss to add that the Code mentions no punishment for trespassing upon the rights of the pastor

---

21 S. C. P. F., June 13, 1633 (*Coll.*, n. 73). Of course, if the express consent of the pastor is obtained, all those mentioned may administer the Viaticum.

22 S. Rit. C., June 20, 1609 (*Dec. Auth.*, n. 271).

23 S. Rit. C., Mar. 17, 1663, ad 4; Dec. 18, 1756 (*Dec. Auth.*, nn. 1255, 2441).

by religious, as was the case up to the date of its promulgation.[24]   But it may also be useful to state that, as the right of pastors is here set forth, obedience involves a duty. Hence the pastor should not wait until he is called to the sick, but lovingly and prudently seek them out and persuade them to receive the Sacraments.[25] He should not discriminate between poor and rich, between those of noble and those of low birth or station.[26] It is the duty of the Ordinary to see to it that this obligation is not neglected by the pastors under his jurisdiction. This is one point that may be investigated at the canonical visitation.[27]

Can. 851

§ 1. Sacerdos sacram communionem distribuat azymo pane vel fermentato, secundum proprium ritum.

§ 2. Ubi vero necessitas urgeat nec sacerdos diversi ritus adsit, licet sacerdoti orientali qui fermentato utitur, ministrare Eucharistiam in azymo, vicissim latino aut orientali qui utitur azymo, ministrare in fermentato; at suum quisque ritum ministrandi servare debet.

The priest shall distribute Holy Communion according to his rite, either in unleavened or in leavened bread. But in case of necessity, if no priest of the respective rite is present, a priest of the Oriental rite, who would otherwise use leavened bread, may administer the Holy Eucharist in unleavened bread, and, conversely, a priest of the Latin or Oriental rite, who would ordinarily use unleavened bread, may give Holy Communion in leav-

24 Pius IX, " Apostolicae Sedis," Oct. 12, 1869, II, 14.

25 S. C. P. F., Sept. 11, 1719 (Coll., n. 537).

26 Benedict XIV, Omnium sollici-tudinum," Sept. 12, 1744, § 14, ad dub. XII.

27 Ib., " Firmandis," Nov. 6, 1744, § 9.

ened bread; but each must observe the rubrics of his own rite.

Orientals generally use leavened bread for the Holy Eucharist, only the Armenians and Maronites are accustomed, ever since the fourth century, to consecrate and distribute unleavened bread.[28] The faithful, though they may gather in a church which serves both rites, must receive Holy Communion at the hands of the priest of their own rite, consequently in unleavened bread, if their rite so prescribes, or in leavened bread, if their rite prescribes that kind.[29] Pius X, who so ardently advocated frequent Communion, ruled in one of his Constitutions that, although unwarranted promiscuity of rite should be avoided, the faithful may, even for mere devotion's sake, receive Holy Communion according to any rite,[30] and consequently under the species of either leavened or unleavened bread. But the administering priest must say the prayers and observe the ceremonies according to his own language and rubrics.

COMMUNION UNDER THE SPECIES OF BREAD

CAN. 852

Sanctissima Eucharistia sub sola specie panis praebeatur.

Holy Communion may be administered under the species of bread only.

This brief canon recalls a long history of dissension and tragedy, especially in Bohemia, which the unhappy Hus attempted to separate from the centre of unity. He

---

[28] Benedict XIV, "*Allatae sunt,*" July 26, 1755, § 23.

[29] *Ibid.,* "*Etsi Pastoralis,*" May 26, 1742, § VI, n. XI.

[30] "*Tradita ab antiquis,*" Sept. 14, 1912 (*A. Ap. S.,* IV, 615 f.), II, III.

was not the originator of the demand for communion under both kinds, but his disciples carried the subversive principles of the master to their final consequences and adopted the chalice for the laity as a symbol of the Hussite union.[81] Against these heretics the Council of Constance, whose decision was approved by Martin V, maintained the ancient practice of the Church, which, as it says, was introduced in order to avoid the danger and scandals which so easily occur when Holy Communion is given under both species.[82] This text makes it evident that the *law* enacted in our canon is *ecclesiastical*, not divine, and, consequently, that the Church may tolerate a contrary custom, as she does among several (not all) Oriental rites.[83] But where the practice is connected with a heretical tendency, the Church must combat it. This tendency lies in the belief either that Christ is not received entirely under one species, or that the use of the chalice is required by divine law and hence the Church was mistaken in forbidding it. Where this error has taken root, the faithful must be carefully instructed and the use of the chalice gradually abolished.[84]

ARTICLE II

THE RECIPIENT OF HOLY COMMUNION

CAN. 853

Quilibet baptizatus qui iure non prohibetur, admitti potest et debet ad sacram communionem.

Every baptized person not forbidden by law may and must be admitted to Holy Communion.

[81] Cf. Funk, *Manual of Church History*, 1913, Vol. II, p. 35.

[82] Martin V, "*In eminentis*," Feb. 22, 1418 (Denz., n. 585).

[83] Benedict XIV, "*Allatae*," July 26, 1755, § 25.

[84] S. C. P. F., Dec. 6, 1777 (*Coll.*, n. 524).

Every baptized person is by divine right entitled to receive Holy Communion, because Baptism has bestowed this right upon him. The *obligation* to receive Holy Communion rests, not on its absolute necessity for salvation *(necessitate medii)*, but on the divine precept contained in the words of our Lord: "*Unless you eat the flesh of the Son of Man, you shall not have life in you.*"[35] This is a general law, which is based on the very end and organization of the Church. It has been modified in the course of centuries by special laws and regulations laid down by the Church for the welfare of the faithful and to safeguard the reverence and devotion due to this august Sacrament. The Church repels no one from the holy Table, even though his condition be humble, his mind weak, whether he lives in a palace or a sordid hut. All are called by Christ to His banquet,[36] and therefore the priests are in duty bound to offer every opportunity to the faithful for receiving Communion and to lay aside unreasonable and Jansenistic scruples. This does not mean that they should indiscriminately admit all, even public sinners, practical pagans, and unworthy Catholics who are a scandal to their community. Certain guiding rules[37] are set forth in the following canons.

COMMUNION OF CHILDREN

Can. 854

§ 1. Pueris, qui propter aetatis imbecillitatem nondum huius sacramenti cognitionem et gustum habent, Eucharistia ne ministretur.

§ 2. In periculo mortis, ut sanctissima Eucharistia

[35] John VI, 54.
[36] Alex. VII, "*Sacrosancti*," Jan. 18, 1658, in XII, XIII (*Coll. P. F.*, n. 129); of the same tenor is Clement IX, "*In excelsa*," Sept. 13, 1669.
[37] S. C. P. F., April 29, 1784 (*Coll.*, n. 569).

pueris ministrari possit ac debeat, satis est ut sciant Corpus Christi a communi cibo discernere illudque reverenter adorare.

§ 3. Extra mortis periculum plenior cognitio doctrinae christianae et accuratior praeparatio merito exigitur, ea scilicet, qua ipse fidei saltem mysteria necessaria necessitate medii ad salutem pro suo captu percipiant, et devote pro suae aetatis modulo ad sanctissimam Eucharistiam accedant.

§ 4. De sufficienti puerorum dispositione ad primam communionem iudicium esto sacerdoti a confessionibus eorumque parentibus aut iis qui loco parentum sunt.

§ 5. Parocho autem est officium advigilandi, etiam per examen, si opportunum prudenter iudicaverit, ne pueri ad sacram Synaxim accedant ante adeptum usum rationis vel sine sufficienti dispositione; itemque curandi ut usum rationis assecuti et sufficienter dispositi quamprimum hoc divino cibo reficiantur.

§ 1. To *children* who, by reason of their tender age, are unable to know and desire this Sacrament, *it should not be given*.

The dogmatic aspect of this canon is stated by the Council of Trent when it says that there is no obligation for children to receive Holy Communion,[88] because being regenerated in the laver of Baptism, and embodied in Christ, they have received the grace of adoption, which, at their age, they cannot lose.[89] The same Council refused to reprimand or forbid the custom of the Orientals to give Holy Communion to children under both species,[40] as

---

[88] Sess. 21, can. 4 de Communione.

[89] *Ibid.*, cap. 4.

[40] Among the Copts of Egypt the custom prevailed to administer holy communion even to children only eight days old, who would often vomit up the species of the sacred blood; S. O., June 14, 1741 (*Coll. P. F.*, n. 326).

long as belief in its necessity was not defended. But Benedict XIV forbade the Italian Greeks to follow that practice.[41] In the Latin Church the custom of administering Holy Communion to infant children never took root, and it is now universally forbidden. Our text is taken from the *Rituale Romanum*,[42] which has been the law for the Latin Church in the matter.

Our canon does not specify any age, but says, "*pueris qui cognitionem et gustum non habent.*" The limit, according to can. 83, § 3, is about the seventh year. But this limit is not to be taken in the strict sense, because the clause is modified by the apposition phrase: "*who have neither knowledge nor desire of the Holy Eucharist.*" Precocious children may have such a knowledge as well as desire, and may therefore be admitted to holy Communion. But no obligation to admit them before the seventh year can be read into the text, nor has such an obligation been established by the latest decrees.[43]

§ 2. Holy Communion *may and must be administered* to children who are in *danger of death* if they are able to distinguish the Holy Eucharist from common bread, and to adore it reverently. This means that they should be able to grasp at least the most necessary notion of that mystery, the real presence of Christ in the Holy Eucharist.[44] It has been officially styled a " detestable abuse " not to administer the Viaticum to children who have attained the age of reason.

§ 3. Apart from the danger of death, a fuller knowledge of Christian doctrine and a more careful preparation is justly demanded, so that they may know, as far

41 " *Etsi pastoralis,*" § II, n. VII; cf. IDEM, "*Allatae,*" July 26, 1755, § 24.

42 Tit. IV, c. 1, n. 11.

43 S. C. Sacr., Aug. 8, 1910 n. I (*A. Ap. S.,* II, 582).

44 S. O., April 10, 1861, ad 1 (*Coll.,* n. 1213).

as they are capable, at least the mysteries which are absolutely necessary for salvation (*necessitate medii*) and approach the Holy Eucharist devoutly, according to the capacity of their age. This sounds quite different from the propositions proscribed in 1687 and 1690, of which the former required a passive attitude without an act of virtue or personal effort, whilst the latter demanded an absolutely pure love of God without any alloy as a requisite for receiving Holy Communion.[45]

The mysteries that are necessary *necessitate medii* for salvation are the Blessed Trinity and the Incarnation, of which the latter is an indispensable preamble to the mystery of the Holy Eucharist.

The age at which the obligation of receiving Holy Communion begins is approximately the *seventh year*. A full and perfect knowledge of the catechism is not required.[46] Formerly children had to be fully instructed in all the questions of the Catechism before they were admitted to the Sacred Table, but Pius X changed that.

§ 4. It belongs to the *confessor* and to the parents or guardians to judge whether children are sufficiently prepared for first Holy Communion.

§ 5. But it is the *pastor's* office to see to it, even by an examination if he prudently deems it opportune, that children are not admitted to Holy Communion before they have attained the age of discretion or without sufficient preparation, and to take care that those who have attained the use of reason and are sufficiently prepared, are nourished with this divine food as soon as possible.

Benedict XIV instructed bishops to admonish pastors not to admit any one to Holy Communion who did not know the more important articles of faith and chapters

45 Prop. 32 (of Mich. Molinos); 46 S. C. Sac., Aug. 1910 (*A. Ap.* propos. 23 (Denz., nn. 1119, 1180). *S.*, II, 582, n. II & III).

of Christian doctrine and the strength and efficacy of the
Bl. Eucharist.[47]

CAN. 855

§ 1. Arcendi sunt ab Eucharistia publice indigni,
quales sunt excommunicati, interdicti manifestoque infames, nisi de eorum poenitentia et emendatione constet et publico scandalo prius satisfecerint.

§ 2. Occultos vero peccatores, si occulte petant et
eos non emendatos agnoverit, minister repellat; non
autem, si publice petant et sine scandalo ipsos praeterire nequeat.

§ 1. The Holy Eucharist may not be given to such as
are *publicly unworthy, e. g.,* the excommunicated, interdicted and notoriously infamous, unless they have given
signs of repentance and amendment and have repaired
the scandal publicly given.

The general rule, as laid down by Benedict XIV,[48] is
that *public and notorious sinners* must not be admitted
to Holy Communion, *no matter whether they demand it
publicly or secretly.* To give them the Body of Christ
would be to coöperate in a profanation of the Sacrament,
and such coöperation cannot be justified even on the plea
of saving the good name of the petitioner, because by the
publicity and notoriety of his crime he has lost the claim
to a good name.

---

[47] "*Etsi minime*," Feb. 7, 1742,
§ 9. There is, of course, room left
for speculation.

[48] "*Ex omnibus*," Oct. 16, 1756,
§ 3 f. The case concerned the

Constitution of Clement IX, "*Unigenitus*," Sept. 8, 1713, by which
101 propositions of Paschasius Quesnel were condemned and which had
aroused opposition.

The next question is: Who are *public and notorious sinners?* According to the same Pontiff sinners are public and notorious, (a) if they have been declared such by an ecclesiastical judge, or (b) if they have publicly confessed their crimes or, as we say, "pleaded guilty"; or (c) if they have committed in word or deed a crime that still lasts and is known to the public as not atoned for and therefore is a source of scandal. A sin is therefore *notorious* when it cannot be concealed, and *public*, like a matrimonial impediment, when it can be proved in court. All of which supposes, in our case, that the priest as well as the congregation, or at least the larger part thereof, are aware of the unworthiness of the one who wishes to receive Communion. If the priest knows nothing, or doubts the publicity or notoriety of the crime, it would certainly be safer to give the Holy Eucharist to one who publicly asks for it.[49]

The text adds: "*quales sunt excommunicati, interdicti manifestoque infames.*" *Excommunication* requires at least a declaratory sentence, and hence notoriety is easily acquired. By *interdicti* must here be understood those who are under a personal *interdict*, because this alone follows the person.[50] *Infamy* is attached to certain crimes, either *ipso facto*,[51] or by declaration of the ecclesiastical court. Our canon does not distinguish between *excommunicati vitandi* and *tolerati*, nor between infamy of fact and of law, nor between excommunication reserved to the Holy See (in whatever form) and excommunication re-

---

[49] Lehmkuhl, *l. c.*, II, n. 40.

[50] Cf. can. 2269, § 2.

[51] *Ipso facto infames* are those mentioned in can. 2320 (who desecrate the sacred species), in can. 2328 (who desecrate graves), in can. 2343 (who maliciously lay hands on the Pope), in can. 2351 (those who engage in duelling), in can. 2356 (polygamists), in can. 2357 (those condemned for unnatural crimes *contra sextum*). *Infames* formerly were the *histriones*, or public actors, who perverted young people; c. 95, Dist. 2, de cons.; also public usurers; cr. 3, 5, X, V, 19.

served to the Ordinary.[52] Hence all these categories are comprised by the term "*publice indigni.*"

But the legislator adds the clause: *unless it is known that they have repented and amended* and *repaired the public scandal they have given.* Both these conditions are required. The following rules [53] are generally set up for judging the external disposition — of the internal men can hardly form a judgment — of a penitent:

(1) If a public sinner has lived in proximate occasion of sin, he must abandon it before he can be admitted. This applies especially to concubinarians.

(2) If no proximate occasion is involved a confession made publicly, or seen by several persons who are ready to testify to the fact, suffices, provided no ecclesiastical sentence has been pronounced; for if sentence of excommunication or a verdict was publicly pronounced, or infamy publicly declared, mere confession is not sufficient, but the sentence must first be withdrawn by the authority who pronounced it. After proper rehabilitation the penitent may be admitted unless he has again given public scandal.

(3) If a public reparation is required, as it sometimes is from those who have contracted marriage before a non-Catholic minister, it must be made before the culprit is admitted to Holy Communion.

(4) In the case of those who have relapsed into a vicious crime, if confession was made and the scandal somewhat repaired, some time should elapse before they are admitted to Communion, so that there be some guarantee of genuine amendment.

Those who order their *bodies to be cremated after death,* though they are not members of a Masonic sect nor

---

[52] C. 9, C. 11, q. 3.
[53] Cf. Lehmkuhl, II, n. 41; Noldin, *l. c.,* n. 37.

have embraced its principles, must be admonished to retract the order, otherwise they cannot be given the last Sacraments. If admonition proves fruitless and no scandal is to be feared, they may be admitted to the Sacraments, provided they are in good faith.[54]

§ 2. *Occult sinners*, if they *ask secretly* and the priest knows they have not amended, should be refused the Bl. Sacrament; but not if they ask *publicly* and cannot be passed over without scandal.

This rule was made to spare the good name of such occult sinners as have not lost their reputation. *Occult* sinners are those whose unworthiness or crime is known only to a few persons and, we must add, which will not be proved in court within a short time.

All these, then, according to the general rule of the Church,[55] must be admitted to the Bl. Sacrament, if they ask for it publicly, *i. e.*, approach the Communion railing together with others. The same rule holds good if such a one asks for the Viaticum, but in that instance the priest should elicit an act of sincere contrition and demand the retraction of possible errors[56] before he administers the Viaticum.

Freemasons and others who *secretly* belong to a sect condemned by the Church, cannot be refused if they publicly approach the Holy Eucharist, but notorious members of a condemned sect may and should be repulsed.[57]

CAN. 856

Nemo quem conscientia peccati mortalis gravat, quantumcumque etiam se contritum existimet, sine

---

[54] S. O., July 27, 1892 (*Coll. P. F.*, n. 1802 ad 1).

[55] Benedict XIV, " *Ex omnibus*," § 9.

[56] *Ibid.* This may also be the case with secret Modernists.

[57] S. O., Aug. 1, 1855 (*Coll. P. F.*, n. 1116).

praemissa sacramentali confessione ad sacram communionem accedat; quod si urgeat necessitas ac copia confessarii illi desit, actum perfectae contritionis prius eliciat.

No one who is conscious of a mortal sin, no matter how sorry or contrite he may feel, is allowed to receive Holy Communion without having previously gone to confession. In case of urgent necessity, when no suitable confessor is at hand, such a one must make an act of perfect contrition before approaching the Sacred Table.

This canon we leave to moralists to explain, because it pertains to the court of consequence. We will only add that this law, no matter whether it be regarded as divine or ecclesiastical, is a grave one, as is apparent from the Council of Trent. *Copia confessarii* must be understood of any confessor with the necessary faculties who is not an accomplice of the penitent. Theologians say that the repugnance to, or impossibility of going to confession must be such as is not directly connected with the act itself. *Urgent necessity* of receiving Holy Communion exists when one has to fulfill the paschal obligation, and before contracting marriage.

COMMUNION MAY BE RECEIVED ONLY ONCE A DAY

CAN. 857

Nemini liceat sanctissimam Eucharistiam recipere, qui eam eadem die iam receperit, nisi in casibus de quibus in can. 858, § 1.

No one is allowed to receive Holy Communion on the day on which he has already received it; exception is made in case of the Holy Viaticum or irreverence to be avoided (see can. 858, § 1).

THE EUCHARISTIC FAST

Can. 858

§ 1. Qui a media nocte ieiunium naturale non servaverit, nequit ad sanctissimam Eucharistiam admitti, nisi mortis urgeat periculum, aut necessitas impediendi irreverentiam in sacramentum.

§ 2. Infirmi tamen qui iam a mense decumbunt sine certa spe ut cito convalescant, de prudenti confessarii consilio sanctissimam Eucharistiam sumere possunt semel aut bis in hebdomada, etsi aliquam medicinam vel aliquid per modum potus antea sumpserint.

§ 1. One who has not fasted since midnight cannot be admitted to Holy Communion, except he be in danger of death, or it be necessary to prevent irreverence towards the Blessed Sacrament.

This law is *ecclesiastical* only, but very ancient. It has always been rigorously enforced by the Church. The Pope alone has power to dispense from it.[58]

It does not, however, apply to those who are in probable danger of death, *i. e.*, suffering from a sickness which may prove fatal. Soldiers going into battle are not *per se* exempt from it. If wounded, of course, the law ceases for them too; but it does not cease for those who have to meet sentence of death, unless they are at the same time suffering from a serious disease.[59] The second reason which excuses from fasting and also from the law that Holy Communion may be received but once a day, is

---

[58] C. 54, Dist. 2, *de cons.*; Benedict XIV, "*Quadam*," March 24, 1756, § 3 (dispensing James III of England).

[59] July 5, 1854, ad 1 (*Coll.*, n. 1099); the quotation of Noldin (*l. c.*, n. 154), from S. C. P. F., July 21, 1841 (*Coll.*, n. 928) mentions the case of prisoners to whom Holy Communion must be given as Viaticum, but nothing is said of their being dispensed from the law of fasting.

the *necessity of preventing irreverence* towards the Blessed Sacrament. This would exist, *e. g.*, if the altar or church were on fire or about to collapse, leaving no time for removing the Bl. Sacrament to a place of safety; or if it would be impossible to secure it from profanation by invading barbarians, heretics or infidels.

Beyond these two cases a canonist cannot stretch the interpretation, although it is customary [60] to add another: *ad vitandum scandalum publicum.* This may be admitted as a matter of equity which inheres in every human law.

§ 2. The *sick who have been in bed for a month* and have no certain hope of speedy recovery, may, if the confessor prudently advises, receive the Holy Eucharist once or twice a week, even though they have taken medicine or something by way of a drink.

This privilege now applies to all the faithful without exception.[61] All that is required is the confessor's (not the pastor's) advice.

"*Per modum potus*" includes broth, coffee, or any liquid food mixed with something solid, as, for instance, wheat-meal (semolino) or ground toast (pangrattato), etc., provided the liquid form remains.[62] Whether an egg-nog would be allowed seems to be doubtful,[63] although in case of great weakness we should not hesitate to permit this mixture, as long as the liquid form prevails. We also submit the following considerations:

(1) The law of fasting before Holy Communion certainly is an ecclesiastical *positive* law which is complied

---

60 Noldin, *l. c.*, 153.

61 A decree of S. C. C., Dec. 7, 1906 (*Anal. Eccl.*, t. 14, 486 f.) permitted it once or twice a week for pious institutions; for the rest, once or twice a month.

62 S. O., Sept. 7, 1897 (*Coll.*, n. 1983).

63 Prümmer, *l. c.*, III, n. 203, would admit it; also Ballerini-Palmieri (*Opus Theol. Morale*, IV, 730).

with by those sick persons who can and do fast, say, three or five times a week. Consequently, they are entitled to receive Holy Communion without any restriction, provided they are disposed for, and desirous of, receiving it. In other words, they must strictly observe can. 858, § 1.

(2) § 2 of same canon undoubtedly is a favorable extension or mitigation of an otherwise strict law. And this modification allows sick persons *in casu* to receive Holy Communion once or twice a week even though they have taken medicine or something *per modum potus,* which a decree of S. C. C. (Dec. 7, 1906) explains as a beverage mixed with some bread (toast), egg or milk. This is a positive grant or permission which the lawgiver undoubtedly wishes to see made use of in order to foster the frequency of Holy Communion. However, there would be no grant or favor conveyed by § 2, can. 858, if the persons *in casu* would not be permitted to receive once or twice a week, supposing they had already received in compliance with § 1 of the same canon. Hence I conclude that § 2 grants something beyond and besides what is stated in § 1. Therefore if a sick person could receive five times with fasting, he or she would also be allowed to receive once or twice a week without fasting, and hence daily or almost daily. This view is in keeping with the mind of the lawgiver, who wishes to promote frequent Communion, and also with the old adage: *favores convenit ampliari.*

OBLIGATION OF RECEIVING COMMUNION

CAN. 859

§ 1. Omnis utriusque sexus fidelis, postquam ad annos discretionis, idest ad rationis usum, pervenerit, de-

bet semel in anno, saltem in Paschate, Eucharistiae
sacramentum recipere, nisi forte de consilio proprii
sacerdotis, ob aliquam rationabilem causam, ad tempus ab eius perceptione duxerit abstinendum.

§ 2. Paschalis communio fiat a dominica Palmarum
ad dominicam in albis; sed locorum Ordinariis fas est,
si ita personarum ac locorum adiuncta exigant, hoc
tempus etiam pro omnibus suis fidelibus anticipare,
non tamen ante quartam diem dominicam Quadrages-
imae, vel prorogare, non tamen ultra festum sanctissimae Trinitatis.

§ 3. Suadendum fidelibus ut huic praecepto satisfaciant in sua quisque paroecia; et qui in aliena paroecia satisfecerint, curent proprium parochum de adim-
pleto praecepto certiorem facere.

§ 4. Praeceptum paschalis communionis adhuc
urget, si quis illud praescripto tempore, quavis de
causa, non impleverit.

§ 1. *Every Catholic*, of either sex, who has reached the
age of discretion, *i. e.*, attained the use of reason, must
receive Holy Eucharist *once a year, at least during Easter
time*, unless his own priest should, for a reasonable cause,
advise him to abstain from it for a time.

The summary of the Decretals [64] says: "This is a
famous chapter and often to be quoted." It is famous
especially for the reason that some non-Catholic writers
use it to establish the date when auricular confession was
introduced into the Church. The initial words are taken
from a Decretal of the Fourth Lateran Council, which
was adopted as an ecclesiastical precept by the Council
of Trent.[65] The precept was made obligatory even for
missionary countries like China, as far as the annual

[64] C. 12, X, V, 38.   [65] Sess. 13, can. 9, *de Euch.*

obligation goes, though as to the time some liberty was naturally left to the missionaries.[66] The obligation commences as soon as *discretion has been attained, i. e.,* about the *seventh year of age.*[67]

The next clause, concerning the *confessor's counsel* to abstain for a time, may be understood in the sense of spiritual direction, or as a reparation for scandal given, or similar reasons. The penitent's *own priest,* according to the Decretal, means the parish priest, and this no doubt is also the meaning of our text, though we believe that if the penitent would tell the pastor about his confessor's counsel, the pastor should not further trouble himself or the penitent.

§ 2. The *time* for receiving the Paschal Communion extends from Palm Sunday to Low Sunday; but the local Ordinaries may prolong the time for all the faithful of their diocese from Laetare Sunday to Trinity Sunday, both inclusive, provided circumstances of persons and place demand such a prolongation.

Benedict XIV had extended the time for receiving the Paschal Communion for Servia[68] from the beginning of Lent to Pentecost and in our country it was by special faculties prolonged from Lent to Trinity Sunday. Hereafter the common law must be observed, which, however, permits the Ordinaries to extend the term as stated. Every such extension must be duly promulgated, and if the bishop extends the time, it also benefits religious, who may therefore distribute Holy Communion in their churches during that time.[69] If the Holy Eucharist is distributed during the solemn Mass on Holy Saturday, the

[66] S. O., March 23, 1656, Nov. 13, 1669; S. C. P. F., Sept. 12, 1645 (*Coll.,* nn. 126, 189, 114).

[67] S. C. Sac., Aug. 8, 1910, ad 1 (*A. Ap. S.,* II, 582).

[68] "*Inter omnigenas,*" Feb. 22, 1744, § 21.

[69] Benedict XIV, "*Magno cum animi,*" June 2, 1751, § 22.

faithful who receive it comply with this commandment.[70]

§ 3 says that it is *advisable* for the faithful (therefore, no longer [71] a strict command), to receive the Paschal Communion in their *own parish church*, and if they have received it in another church, to notify their pastor of the fact.

§ 4. The precept of receiving the Paschal Communion *obliges even after the lapse of the prescribed term*, and should therefore be complied with as soon as possible, and one may not wait until the next Easter time if he has neglected this duty.[72]

THE DUTY OF PARENTS AND OTHERS

CAN. 860

Obligatio praecepti communionis sumendae, quae impuberes gravat, in eos quoque ac praecipue recidit, qui ipsorum curam habere debent, idest in parentes, tutores, confessarium, institutores et parochum.

This canon reminds parents, guardians, confessors, directors of schools and pastors, of the obligation incumbent upon them to see to it that *impuberes* entrusted to their care comply with the precept of receiving Holy Communion at least once a year, during Easter time. Puberty, according to can. 81, § 2, commences for boys with the fourteenth, and for girls with the twelfth year, completed. After that age the obligation, if not morally, ceases at least juridically, for the classes of persons named in the text.[73]

70 S. Rit. C., March 22, 1806 (*Dec. Auth.*, n. 2561).

71 Cfr. Benedict XIV, "*Magno cum animi*," § 22.

72 Eugene IV, "*Fide digna*,"

July 8, 1440; Pruemmer, *l. c.*, III, n. 212.

73 S. C. Sac., Aug. 8, 1910, ad IV (*A. Ap. S.*, II, 582).

CAN. 861

Praecepto communionis recipiendae non satisfit per sacrilegam communionem.

The precept of receiving the Eucharist is not complied with by a sacrilegious Communion.

The contradictory proposition was condemned by Innocent XI.[74] One who has knowingly and willingly made a sacrilegious communion must, either before the lapse of the term, or as soon as possible after the expiration of the paschal time, receive Communion worthily.

CAN. 862

Expedit ut feria V maioris hebdomadae omnes clerici, etiam sacerdotes qui ea die a Sacro litando abstinent, sanctissimo Christi Corpore in Missa sollemni seu conventuali reficiantur.

It is *becoming* that, on Holy Thursday, all the clergy, even the priests who abstain from saying Mass on that day, receive Holy Communion at the solemn or conventual Mass.

Because, as a rule, there should be only one solemn Mass on Holy Thursday, many priests are free from the obligation of celebrating on that day. To perpetuate the memory of that Sacred Day, on which the Lord Himself distributed his Body and Blood, the Ordinaries are admonished to distribute Holy Communion to the clergy.[75] The S. Congregation has more than once declared that

---

[74] Prop. 55 dam., March 4, 1679 (Denz., n. 1072).

[75] *Caeremoniale Ep.*, l. II, c. 23, n. 6.

the bishop can compel dignitaries and canons and their substitutes, if they are not obliged to say Mass,[76] to receive Holy Communion from him or another celebrant.[77] However, our text cannot be construed as implying a strict obligation, as *"expedit"* does not signify a strict law in canonical language. The Ordinary shall, therefore, use persuasion rather than force. After all the clergy have received Holy Communion, the civil magistrates may be admitted before the rest of the people, and at the procession, march after the baldachino.[78]

CAN. 863

Excitentur fideles ut frequenter, etiam quotidie, pane Eucharistico reficiantur ad normas in decretis Apostolicae Sedis traditas; utque Missae adstantes non solum spirituali affectu, sed sacramentali etiam sanctissimae Eucharistiae perceptione, rite dispositi, communicent.

We are familiar with the rules concerning frequent Communion laid down by the saintly Pius X. The Church has never ceased [79] to exhort the faithful to frequent, nay even daily Communion, not only in spirit, but in reality, provided they were duly prepared. Jansenism, as is well known, was opposed to this practice, nor were the troublesome times of the French Revolution and the teaching of Wessenberg in Germany and the synod of

---

76 If a holy-day of obligation would fall on that day, several priests would have to say Mass; S. Rit. C., Sept. 27, 1716 (*Dec. Auth.*, n. 2240), and thus could not receive.

77 S. Rit. C., Sept. 19, 1654; Sept. 10, 1701; Dec. 22, 1770; Sept. 23,

1837 (*Dec. Auth.*, nn. 970, 2079, 2489, 2769).

78 S. Rit. C., Aug. 12, 1854 (*Dec. Auth.*, n. 3024).

79 S. C. C., Feb. 1679 (Denz., n. 1086).

Pistoja in Italy favorable to its growth. But finally a pacific victory was brought about by the efforts of Pius X.

Our text mentions the *norms laid down in the decrees issued by the Holy See*. These norms are especially the "*Sacra Tridentina Synodus*," of Dec. 20, 1905, the "*Editae saepe*," of May 26, 1910, and the "*Quam singulari*," of the S. Congregation of the Sacraments, of Aug. 8, 1910. The latter was ordered to be read annually in the vernacular, but the purpose of this provision seems to be attained by the promulgation of the Code, which embodies the main contents of the decree. We may therefore assume that the decree need no longer be read, though it would not be wrong to do so.

DUTY OF RECEIVING THE VIATICUM

CAN. 864

§ 1. In periculo mortis, quavis ex causa procedat, fideles sacrae communionis recipiendae praecepto tenentur.

§ 2. Etiamsi eadem die sacra communione fuerint refecti, valde tamen suadendum, ut in vitae discrimen adducti denuo communicent.

§ 3. Perdurante mortis periculo, sanctum viaticum, secundum prudens confessarii consilium, pluries, distinctis diebus, administrari et licet et decet.

§ 1. When there is *danger of death*, no matter from what cause it arises, the faithful are *obliged by the precept* of receiving Holy Communion.

This precept, though purely ecclesiastical, is a *grievous one*. It was insisted upon already by the Council of Nicaea.[80] Priests, therefore, should take care that

---

[80] C. 9, C. 26, q. 1.

the Holy Eucharist be always ready for sick calls.[81]
From *whatever cause* the danger may arise, says the text,
which means that not only intrinsic maladies or diseases
are to be considered but also extrinsic causes, such as a
sentence of death awaiting prisoners.[82]   Besides, though
the illness may last a long time, as is the case with consumptives, the Holy Viaticum should not be delayed, especially if they live at a distance.[83]

   § 2. Although these have already received Holy Communion on the same day, they should be strongly *advised*
to receive it again when the crisis sets in.

   The Code has hereby cut short the controversy [84] on the
necessity and admissibility of receiving Holy Communion
twice on the same day.   It is not only permissible, but
even advisable, when there is danger of death, though no
strict obligation is enforced.

   § 3. It is lawful and becoming to administer the Viaticum several times on different days as long as the danger
of death lasts, according to the prudent judgment of the
confessor.[85]   In that case the formula *" Corpus Domini "*
is used.

CAN. 865

   **Sanctum Viaticum infirmis ne nimium differatur; et
qui animarum curam gerunt, sedulo advigilent ut eo
infirmi plene sui compotes reficiantur.**

   The Holy Viaticum should not be too long deferred,
and those in charge of souls should take great care that
the sick receive it while fully conscious.

   This law has been time and again impressed upon

81 C. 93, Dist. 2, *de cons.*
82 S. C. P. F., July 21, 1841
(*Coll.*, n. 928), but in that case they
would have to fast.

83 S. C. P. F., Feb. 20, 1801
(*Coll.*, 657): *morbo etico.*
84 Cfr. Noldin, *l. c.*, n. 138.
85 *Rit. Rom.*, tit. IV, c. 4, n. 3.

bishops as well as pastors.[86] It is a matter for the Ordinary to investigate at the time of the canonical visitation.[87] The reason is not far to seek; the better the disposition of the recipient, the greater the effects of this holy Sacrament.

CAN. 866

RITE OF HOLY COMMUNION

§ 1. **Omnibus fidelibus cuiusvis ritus datur facultas ut, pietatis causa, sacramentum Eucharisticum quolibet ritu confectum suscipiant.**

§ 2. **Suadendum tamen ut suo quisque ritu fideles praecepto communionis paschalis satisfaciant.**

§ 3. **Sanctum Viaticum moribundis ritu proprio accipiendum est; sed, urgente necessitate, fas esto quolibet ritu illud accipere.**

Holy Communion, even for devotion's sake, may be distributed to the *faithful of any rite* in the species consecrated in any rite; but they should be advised to receive the *Paschal Communion* in their own rite. The Holy Viaticum should, except in case of necessity, be received by the dying in their own rite.

These are the rules laid down by Benedict XIV, Leo XIII, and Pius X,[88] who all wished to see the faithful receive Holy Communion as often as their devotion and spiritual welfare demand. The condition, of course, is that the rite be Catholic, not schismatic or heretical.[89]

86 Alexander VII, " *Sacrosancti,*" Jan. 18, 1658, § 2, n. XIII (*Coll. P. F.,* n. 129).

87 Benedict XIV, "*Firmandis,*" Nov. 6, 1744, § 9.

88 "*Etsi Pastoralis,*" May 26, 1742, § VI, n. XIII f.; "*Orientalium,*" Nov. 30, 1894, n. II; "*Tradita ab antiquis,*" Sept. 14, 1912, III–V.

89 S. C. P. F., Aug. 18, 1893 (*Coll.,* n. 1846).

ARTICLE III

TIME AND PLACE FOR DISTRIBUTING HOLY COMMUNION

Time

CAN. 867

§ 1. Omnibus diebus licet sanctissimam Eucharistiam distribuere.

§ 2. Feria tamen VI maioris hebdomadae solum licet sacrum Viaticum ad infirmos deferre.

§ 3. In Sabbato Sancto sacra communio nequit fidelibus ministrari nisi inter Missarum sollemnia vel continuo ac statim ab iis expletis.

§ 4. Sacra communio iis tantum horis distribuatur, quibus Missae sacrificium offerri potest, nisi aliud rationabilis causa suadeat.

§ 5. Sacrum tamen Viaticum quacunque diei aut noctis hora ministrari potest.

§ 1. The Holy Eucharist may be distributed *every day* of the year.

§ 2. But on *Good Friday* only the Viaticum may be administered to the sick.

§ 3. On *Holy Saturday* Holy Communion may be distributed only at the (solemn) Mass or immediately thereafter.

§ 4. Holy Communion may be distributed only *at hours when Mass may be said*, unless good reasons advise a deviation from this rule.

§ 5. But the *Holy Viaticum* may be administered *at any hour* of the day or night.

Although, says a well-known decree of the S. C. Concilii, frequent and even daily Communion has been recommended by the Holy Fathers, yet the Church has never appointed certain days of the week or month on which the faithful should abstain from, or receive, Holy Communion.   Much less is there any divine precept enjoining daily Communion.[90]   If the *Viaticum* is brought publicly to the sick on *Good Friday* the psalms must be recited in a very low voice, but the color of the stole is *white*. When it is brought quasi-privately, the people must be dismissed from church without the usual blessing, because the Blessed Sacrament should not be kept in the church [91] but in the sepulchre.

It is remarkable that Communion may now be distributed immediately after the conventual or solemn Mass [92] on *Holy Saturday*.   But the phrase " *continuo ac statim* " must be carefully noted, because it indicates that before the Mass, or after the priest has left the altar, no distribution of Holy Communion is allowed.   The faithful who receive Holy Communion on that day fulfill the paschal precept.

The *time* for receiving Holy Communion is during Mass, and the faithful should be exhorted to receive it when assisting at the Holy Sacrifice.   However, if they ask for it outside of Mass, they should not be refused, because they are supposed to ask reasonably.[93]   But Holy Communion is not to be distributed [94] before the time for Mass, as stated under can. 821, nor after that time, especially not until sunset, because abuses might easily creep in.

---

[90] Feb. 12, 1679 (*Coll. P. F.*, n. 219).

[91] S. Rit. C., May 15, 1745 (*Dec. Auth.*, n. 2383).

[92] S. Rit. C., March 22, 1806 (*Dec. Auth.*, n. 2561), did not yet allow that, but the decree of April 28, 1914, ad II (*A. Ap. S.*, VI, 196 f.) simply says: *et etiam expleta Missa*. Our text has two additions.

[93] Gasparri, *De SS. Euch.*, n. 1084.

[94] S. Rit. C., Sept. 7, 1816, ad 23 (*Dec. Auth.*, n. 2572); June 11, 1904, ad III (*Anal. Eccl.*, XII, 334).

Can. 868

Sacerdoti celebranti non licet Eucharistiam intra Missam distribuere fidelibus adeo distantibus ut ipse altare e conspectu amittat.

A priest saying Mass is not allowed to distribute Holy Communion during Mass to persons who are so far from the altar that he himself would *lose sight of the altar*.

The principle underlying this canon is that the priest must never lose sight of the altar for the reason that Holy Communion is an integral part of the Mass and some particles may remain unconsumed until the last ablution. Therefore the S. Congregation has decided more than once that a celebrating priest is not allowed to bring Communion during Mass to sick persons or others who are in a different though an adjoining room from the oratory where he says Mass.[95] This applies to pious institutions and private oratories. If all the particles have been distributed but some fragments remain on the paten, these should be placed in the pyxis which is kept in the tabernacle if no other priest says Mass in the same chapel.[96]

A practical conclusion from this law is that the Communion rails should be made so that the altar can be seen from every corner.

Place

Can. 869

Sacra communio distribui potest ubicunque Missam celebrare licet, etiam in oratorio privato, nisi loci Or-

---

[95] S. Rit. C., Dec. 19, 1829; Florentina, ad 1 (*Dec. Auth.*, n. 2672), Dec. 7, 1844 (n. 2883); May 11, 1878 (n. 3448).

[96] S. Rit. C., March 1860 (n. 3099).

dinarius, iustis de causis, in casibus particularibus id prohibuerit.

Holy Communion may be distributed wherever Mass may be said, even in private oratories, unless the local Ordinary should for just reasons forbid it in some particular case.

This text is based on a general decree of the Congregation of Rites permitting the distribution of Holy Communion to all the faithful who assist at Mass in a private Oratory.   But the decree expressly says: *with due regard to the rights of the pastor*,[97] and consequently these should never be curtailed or jeopardized, otherwise the Ordinary may forbid the distribution of Holy Communion.

[97] S. Rit. C., May 8, 1907 (*Anal. Eccl.*, t. 15, 403).

TITLE IV

CAN. 870

In poenitentiae sacramento, per iudicialem absolutionem a legitimo ministro impertitam, fideli rite disposito remittuntur peccata post baptismum commissa.

In the Sacrament of Penance, through a judicial absolution imparted by a legitimate minister, the sins committed after baptism are forgiven to every faithful Catholic who is properly disposed.

This is the true concept of the Sacrament of Penance based on Scripture and tradition. Penance is one of the seven Sacraments instituted by Christ. It follows Baptism and is therefore sometimes called the " second plank of salvation " or " laborious Baptism." It is effected by the *judicial absolution* of the priest, but not without the formal coöperation of the penitent, who must be properly disposed by having either contrition or attrition, as the theologians[1] say.

What most concerns the canonist is the *judicial absolution*.[2] The power of the keys, *i.e.*, to forgive and retain sins, is exercised by pronouncing the sentence of forgiveness or retention. This sentence is rendered by the judges of the society founded by Christ. The essence

1 Cfr. Palmieri, *De Poenitentia*, Romae 1879; Pohle-Preuss, *The Sacraments*, Vol. III, 3rd ed., 1919.

2 *Trid.*, sess. 14, c; 1-8; can. 1-4, 9, 12, 15, *de Poenit.*

of the judiciary power consists in authority to impose an obligation or to assert a right or law with regard to one who is subject to authority and a debtor to the law in a matter that falls under that law and authority. The penitent who accuses himself of guilt towards God, has contracted a twofold debt: the *reatus culpae* and the *reatus poenae:* guilt and punishment, and God alone can absolve him from either. He does not do so directly, but through certain human agents, who act by His authority and commission. These are true judges, and their power is a truly judiciary power which does not merely announce forgiveness, like a preacher of penance, but pronounces sentence of justification which is ratified by God.[3]

[3] *Trid.*, sess. 6, c. 14, can. 29, *de iustif.*

CHAPTER I

CAN. 871

Minister huius sacramenti est solus sacerdos.

CAN. 872

Praeter potestatem ordinis, ad validam peccatorum absolutionem requiritur in ministro potestas iurisdictionis, sive ordinaria sive delegata, in poenitentem.

The sole minister of this sacrament is the priest, who, to absolve validly, needs not only the power of order, but also the power of jurisdiction, either ordinary or delegated, over the penitent.

This again is a dogmatic truth, based on sources to which it is not necessary here to refer. Early documents amply prove that it was the *presbyteri*, both of the higher, i.e., episcopal and the lower, i.e., priestly rank, who exercised the power of the keys.[1] Peter Abélard wrongly limited the exercise of this power to the Apostles,[2] whereas Wiclif, Hus, and Luther unduly extended it to all Christians, including laymen.[3] The Church requires the priestly character as the fundamental condition or aptitude because of the hieratic element which is intimately connected with the jurisdictional

---

[1] Cfr *Trid.*, sess. 14, c. 1, de *poenit.*; sess. 23, c. 15, *de ref.*

[2] *Prop. dam. ab Innoc.* II., n. 12

(Denzinger, n. 321). Palmieri, l. c., p. 161 ff.

[3] Denzinger, nn. 565, 566, 637.

251

power. But since the exercise of this power is really a judiciary act, which pre-supposes jurisdiction, jurisdiction also is essentially required. The Code almost exclusively employs the term, *jurisdiction*,[4] *approbatio* being used, as it were, only by the way. Besides the term jurisdiction there occurs the noun *licentia*.[5]

1. *Jurisdiction* is here understood as the power of hearing confession or imparting judicial absolution *validly*, in the act of sacramental confession. This may, as the text says, like any other jurisdiction, be twofold, *viz.*, ordinary or delegated. It is *ordinary* if attached to the office one holds; *delegated* if given to the person by virtue of a special commission. It may be delegated either by a *local Ordinary* (can. 874, § 1), and in that case is limited to the territory of that Ordinary (can. 875, § 1) or by an *exempt religious superior*, and in that case is restricted to the person or subjects of the religious superior.[6]

2. *Licentia*, license or permission, is the formal approval required for *licitly* exercising the office of confessor. It is not necessarily the result of a doctrinal examination,[7] but may be a merely moral provision or concession made to render the act conformable to the requisites of obedience or subordination. And in this sense it may be identified with the former *approbatio*, inasmuch as this was considered to be an authentic judgment as to a priest's fitness for hearing confessions. The Code only mentions jurisdiction for validly, and license for licitly hearing confessions, but adds that the *jurisdiction* must concern the *penitent*, in other words, the con-

---

4 Cfr. Vol. II, p. 170 ff., of this Commentary.

5 Cfr. can. 881 f.; *approbatus*, as an adjective.

6 Not quite accurate, therefore, is what we read in Schmitt, S. J., *Supplementum ad Noldin*, 1918, p. 53: "*iurisdictio vero delegata est tantum territorialis.*"

7 Cfr. can. 877, § 1.

fessor must have power over the penitent, who therefore becomes, or is supposed to be, his subject. This power, as stated before, is acquired by reason of the office or by special commission. Thus according to can. 875, § 1, an exempt religious superior of the clerical order grants to the priests of his organization delegated jurisdiction over the professed members, novices and others mentioned in can. 514, § 1. The Bishop enjoys ordinary jurisdiction for his territory and may delegate priests, secular as well as religious, for hearing confessions in his diocese.

Here it may be proper to discuss the controversy concerning the exemption which has formed a favorite topic in theological circles since the time of Martin IV (1281–1285).[8] Boniface VIII endeavored to settle the dispute between the Ordinaries and the mendicant friars. His Decretal[9] says that even if the Ordinary has given any one permission to choose his confessor, the latter can not absolve from cases especially reserved by the Ordinary. But since the exempt regulars contended that they obtained jurisdiction immediately from the Pope through their superiors, for which contention they were able to quote a Constitution of Martin IV, the dispute was by no means ended. The Council of Trent finally enacted that no priest, whether secular or regular, could absolve any one except he had first been examined and approved by the Ordinary. Exception was made for those who held a parish benefice,[10] because no one could be promoted to such a benefice without an examination. The rule thenceforth was that secular as well as regular priests, who wished to hear confessions of secular persons or nuns not subject to regular prelates, were obliged to have the "approbation" of the Ordinary of

8 Cfr. Vol. III, p. 34 f., of this Commentary.

9 C. 2, 6°, V.

10 *Trid.*, sess. 23, c. 15, *de ref.*

the diocese.[11] Notwithstanding these plain rules, it happened in, Spain that persons sticking too closely to the "*Cruciata*," obtained special indults for choosing confessors not approved by the local Ordinaries. This abuse was done away with completely by Benedict XIV, following in the footsteps of his predecessors.[12] He, as well as Gregory XV and Clement X,[13] declared that a religious, even though approved for hearing confessions in his diocese by the local Ordinary, can not validly absolve in a strange diocese a penitent coming from the diocese for which he was approved. Some regulars, besides, claimed that a religious presented to the bishop but rejected in the examination, could validly hear the confessions of seculars and absolve from cases reserved to the bishop. This proposition was proscribed.[14] Parish priests, *i.e.*, priests who held a parish benefice, maintained that they could choose for their confessor any priest, even though he was not approved by the Ordinary. This proposition, too, was condemned.[15] Later it was asked of the S. Congregation whether a pastor, say of the diocese of St. Joseph, called in by a pastor of the diocese of Kansas City, may validly hear confessions without special jurisdiction from the bishop of Kansas City. The answer was: Yes, of his own subjects but not of others (*affirmative quoad subditos, negative quoad alios*).[16] This was the *status quaestionis* when the Code went into effect. These preliminary explanations will help the reader to understand the following canons.

11 S. C. C., June 7, 1755 (Richter, *Trid.*, p. 205, nn. 1, 4).

12 " *Apostolica indulta,*" Aug. 5, 1744.

18 Gregory XV, " *Inscrutabili,*" Feb. 5, 1622; Clement X, " *Superna,*" June 21, 1670, § 4.

14 *Prop. dam. ab Alex. VII*, n. 13,

Sept. 24, 1665 (Denzinger, n. 984).

15 *Prop. dam. ab Alex. VII*, n. 16, Sept. 24, 1665 (Denzinger, n. 987).

16 S. C. C. Nov. 19, 1707 (Richter, *Trid.*, p. 206, n. 3); Benedict XIV, *Instit.*, 86, n. 7.

ORDINARY JURISDICTION

CAN. 873

§ 1. Ordinaria iurisdictione ad confessiones excipiendas pro universa Ecclesia, praeter Romanum Pontificem, potiuntur S. R. E. Cardinales; pro suo quisque territorio Ordinarius loci, et parochus aliique qui loco parochi sunt.

§ 2. Hac eadem iurisdictione gaudent etiam canonicus poenitentiarius ecclesiae quoque collegiatae, ad normam can. 401, § 1, et Superiores religiosi exempti pro suis subditis, ad normam constitutionum.

§ 3. Haec iurisdictio cessat amissione officii, ad normam can. 183, § 1, et, post sententiam condemnatoriam vel declaratoriam, excommunicatione, suspensione ab officio, interdicto.

§ 1. Besides the Roman Pontiff, the Cardinals possess ordinary jurisdiction for hearing confessions *in the whole Church;* in the various dioceses the local Ordinaries, in their own districts the pastors, and those who take the place of pastors enjoy jurisdiction.

§ 2. The Penitentiary Canons of cathedral and collegiate Churches (can. 401, § 1) have the same jurisdiction; also *exempt religious* superiors with regard to their subjects, according to the constitutions of the respective institute.

1. The *Sovereign Pontiff* has the plenitude of the power of jurisdiction in and over the whole Church, and hence may hear confessions validly and licitly everywhere without notifying the local Ordinaries.

2. There can no longer be any doubt[17] that the

17 Formerly, unless they were *legati a latere*, cardinals did not, at least by law, enjoy this privilege.

Cardinals of the Holy Roman Church, too, may personally hear confessions everywhere; but theirs is a strictly personal privilege [18] that can not be communicated to others. Can. 239, § 1, 1° says that Cardinals may validly and licitly hear confessions throughout the whole world, of secular as well as religious persons, and absolve them from all sins and censures except those most specially reserved to the Apostolic See and those attached to the revealing of the secret of confession, called " secret of the Holy Office." [19]   From the general tenor of this canon it must be concluded that Cardinals may also absolve from cases reserved to, and by, the Ordinary.

3. The *Ordinary* enjoys ordinary jurisdiction *within his territory*, to which he is, as a rule, restricted.   However, he may validly absolve *his own subjects* everywhere (*ubique terrarum;* can. 881, § 2).[20]

4. The same law applies to *pastors* and those who *take their places*.   Pastors, therefore, enjoy ordinary jurisdiction in the court of conscience, for hearing confessions within the boundaries of their parishes, and for their *own subjects* also outside their parish limits, nay even outside the diocese.   This is in accordance with the Council of Trent and certain later decisions of the Apostolic See.[21]

What about our American *parish priests?*   We cannot

---

18 The S. C. Cons., April 25, 1918 (*A. Ap. S.,* X, 190) calls it a *personal* privilege, like those of Ordinaries, can. 349. Such personal privileges cannot be communicated *per modum facultatum;* cfr. S. Poenit., July 18, 1919 (*A. Ap. S.,* XI, 332).

19 The *secretum S. Officii* is a special secret to which all officials of the Holy Office and other persons placed under the same obligation are bound by an oath.

20 Cfr. Benedict XIV, "*Apostolicum ministerium,*" May 30, 1753, § 22.

21 *Trid.,* sess. 23, c. 15, *de ref.;* Benedict XIV, *Const. cit.;* S. C. C., Nov. 19, Dec. 3, 1707 (Richter, *Trid.,* p. 206, n. 3); Benedict XIV, *Instit.,* 86, n. 7; cfr. can. 881, § 2.

depart from what we have said in Vol. II of this Commentary on their legal status. They are and must be considered *parochi*, no matter whether they are removable or irremovable, because this quality is now accidental only, and not essential, to a pastor, as canon 454, § 2 clearly states. Consequently, by virtue of their appointment they obtain ordinary jurisdiction for hearing confessions and from the moment of taking possession of their parish,[22] may exercise this ordinary jurisdiction.

Who are a pastor's *subjects?* Those who have their domicile or quasi-domicile within the limits of his parish. The confessions of these, then, he may validly and licitly hear everywhere.[23]

The question again arises concerning our *linguistically distinguished parishes.* To these, we believe, the Constitution of Benedict XIV, "*Apostolicum ministerium,*" which was issued for England in 1753, may be applied. § 2 of this Constitution says that secular as well as regular priests may hear confessions in the whole city or town without discrimination. This, we say, is similar to our case, and therefore, for instance, the pastor of a German-speaking congregation may *validly* hear the confessions of any of his subjects in the same town or city by virtue of his appointment and also the confessions of those who come to him from another parish, or even from another diocese. Besides, with due reverence to the pastor of another parish,[24] or with his permission, he may also *licitly* hear confessions in the church of that parish. Lastly, § 2 of can. 881 may be applied also to pastors, who thus may hear their own subjects everywhere.

---

22 Can. 461; can. 1443.
23 See Can. 811, § 2.
24 Benedict XIV, *Const. cit.*, §

22: "*debitis tamen officiis cum ipsius rectore antea persolutis.*"

5. *"Aliique qui loco parochi sunt."* Who are these " others who take the place of a pastor "? They are the *oeconomi* and *coadiutores* who act as substitutes for disabled or absent pastors, as described in can. 473–475. Our so-called assistants or curates cannot be numbered among this class and therefore do not enjoy ordinary jurisdiction.

6. The *Canonicus Poenitentiarius* can absolve all, even strangers in the diocese, from sins and censures reserved to the bishop; he may absolve the subjects of his diocese outside his own territory. This power is granted to the canon penitentiary not only of the cathedral but also of a collegiate church.[25] Innocent III had ordained [26] that the bishops should choose helpers in the discharge of their pastoral office, especially for hearing confessions in cathedral and conventual churches. From this it follows that by their very appointment these canons enjoy ordinary jurisdiction according to what has been stated above.

7. *Exempt religious superiors,* finally, enjoy ordinary jurisdiction over their own subjects, according to the form of their constitutions. It was always understood that exempt religious superiors obtained their jurisdiction over their own subjects from the Sovereign Pontiff. This follows from the very notion of exemption. *Exempt superiors* are the superiors of all religious institutes which are exempt either by reason of their institution or by a special indult. As can. 875, § 2 clearly states, the privilege applies only to exempt institutes of *clerics*.

[25] Can. 401, § 1.
[26] C. 15, X, I, 31. The diocesan or collegiate chapter has no right to oppose the appointment of a

Canon Poenit. (S. C. EE. et RR., Sept. 19, 1846; Bizzarri, *Collectanea,* p. 548 f.).

The *superiors* here mentioned are those who are called *maiores*, hence the generals or provincials of exempt orders or congregations and their vicars, who hold a position similar to the provincial.[27] The text adds: *ad normam constitutionum,* in accord with the respective constitutions.

The abbots [28] of single and autonomous monasteries are real superiors in the sense of our text; such also are the *conventual priors* [29] of independent monasteries or convents, whereas the *priores claustrales* cannot claim ordinary jurisdiction, unless a special clause in the constitutions either denies that power to conventual priors or gives it to cloistral priors. Attention may here be drawn to can. 518, § 2, concerning the hearing of confessions of subjects.[30]

§ 3. *Ordinary jurisdiction for hearing confession ceases* when the office to which it is attached, is lost, as laid down in can. 183, and after a declaratory or condemnatory sentence of excommunication, suspension from office or interdict. Ordinary jurisdiction also ceases at the moment one's resignation is accepted, when privation or removal is duly intimated, when the term of office expires,[31] and after one has been declared to have incurred, or has been condemned to, excommunication,[32] or personal interdict,[33] or suspension from office.[34]

---

[27] Can. 488, n. 8.

[28] The Abbot President of the Swiss-American Congregation, *according to its Constitution,* may hear the confessions of all its members, otherwise the Abbot President would not be entitled to do so, nor is the Abbot Primate.

[29] Concerning the Priors of the Augustinians see S. C. EE. *et* RR.,

June 3, 1864 (Bizzarri, *l. c.,* p. 720); they are real conventual priors and therefore *superiores maiores.*

[30] Clement VIII, "*Sanctissimus,*" May 26, 1593; S. C. C., Sept. 21, 1624 (Bizzarri, *l. c.,* p. 246).

[31] Can. 183.

[32] Can. 2261, § 3.

[33] Can. 2275, n. 2.

[34] Can. 2284.

DELEGATED JURISDICTION

CAN. 874

§ 1. Iurisdictonem delegatam ad recipiendas confessiones quorumlibet sive saecularium sive religiosorum confert sacerdotibus tum saecularibus tum religiosis etiam exemptis Ordinarius loci in quo confessiones excipiuntur; sacerdotes autem religiosi eadem ne utantur sine licentia saltem praesumpta sui Superioris, firmo tamen praescripto can. 519.

§ 2. Locorum Ordinarii iurisdictionem ad audiendas confessiones habitualiter ne concedant religiosis qui a proprio Superiore non praesentantur; iis vero qui a proprio Superiore praesentantur, sine gravi causa eam ne denegent, firmo tamen praescripto can. 877.

§ 1. Delegated jurisdiction is conferred by the *local Ordinary in whose diocese the confessions are to be heard,* on priests, secular as well as religious, even exempt religious, for hearing confessions of both secular and religious persons; but priests of religious institutes, though thus endowed with delegated jurisdiction, in addition thereto need the permission of their superiors, in order to absolve licitly, with due regard always to can. 519. Here the recipients of *delegated jurisdiction* are mentioned as far as certain classes of penitents are concerned, namely:

(a) *Secular persons, i.e.,* such as have not entered the religious state by taking the three vows; hence also members of societies who live in common without vows;[35] secular clergymen, even priests of any clerical rank of the secular order.[36]

35 Cfr. can. 673, § 1.
36 Gregory XV, "*Inscrutabili,*"   Feb. 5, 1622, § 1; Clement X, "*Superna,*" June 21, 1670, § 1.

(b) *Religious of the male sex*, no matter whether exempt or not. All these may be validly and licitly absolved by any priest who has been endowed with delegated jurisdiction by the Ordinary.

Here a doubt may occur as to *pastors*, who have ordinary power, but are not specially mentioned in can. 519. This doubt seems unfounded because in said canon approval only is mentioned, and pastors are certainly supposed to be approved by the Ordinary, and, besides, the validity could certainly not be doubted.

The *ministers* who receive jurisdiction from the Ordinary are *priests, secular* as well as *religious*, including those who are exempt. Concerning the latter, especially the mendicants, there was a controversy, which is now decided. *Religious*, therefore, no matter of what order, congregation, institute or society, even though otherwise exempt from the law, need delegated jurisdiction to hear the confessions of secular persons, including priests.[37] No exception is made for any kind of regulars or religious, even at the time of missions or on the occasion of a jubilee — unless, of course, the Bull of the Jubilee decided differently.[38] All must have delegated jurisdiction from the local Ordinary.

Now the *local Ordinary* is the one in whose diocese the confessions are heard. Hence it is not sufficient that a religious obtains what we call the faculties for the diocese in which the religious house is located, to validly hear

[37] Cfr. the Constitutions quoted in the preceeding note, and S. C. EE. et RR., Zagabrien., Dec. 14, 1674 (Bizzarri, *Collectanea*, p. 271 ff.). Can. 514, § 1 is, of course, to be consulted, as seen under can. 875, § 1.

[38] S. C. C., Dec. 4, 1683 (Richter, *Trid.*, p. 206, n. 2); the confessions heard by regulars at the time of a jubilee were invalid, and the penitents who had a doubt about the validity of their confession, or knew of the lack of jurisdiction of such confessors, had to repeat the confession, in order to gain the indulgence; those in good faith were not to be disturbed.

the confessions of secular persons in another diocese. These faculties do not overlap. Hence if a religious whose house is located in the diocese of St. Joseph wishes to hear confessions in any part of the Des Moines diocese, he has to obtain the respective faculty from the Ordinary of Des Moines. This jurisdiction is needed even in the case of a penitent who has an apostolic indult permitting him to choose any confessor he pleases.[39] The same holds good concerning any secular priest who needs delegated jurisdiction.

In connection with this the question may arise: What about the *pastors* of a *diocese,* who according to can. 873, § 1, enjoy ordinary jurisdiction for their parishes, if they wish to hear confessions in another parish of the same or another diocese? Their jurisdiction as pastors is certainly limited to their own territory (*pro suo quisque territorio*). Consequently, in order to hear confessions validly outside their parishes they need delegated jurisdiction from the Ordinary of the diocese in which they wish to hear confessions, unless there is question of their own subjects, whose confessions they may hear anywhere.[40]

Another question: May the *pastor grant delegated jurisdiction* to another priest, secular or religious, to hear confessions within his district, without asking the local Ordinary? It would seem that canon 199, § 1, should be applied here, which says that those who enjoy ordinary jurisdiction may delegate it to others. But our text as well as certain decisions of the Holy See [41] plainly state that pastors cannot grant to other priests delegated jurisdiction to hear confessions in their parishes.

[39] Benedict XIV, "*Apostolica indulta,*" Aug. 5, 1744, §§ 3, 5.
[40] Can. 881, § 2.

[41] S. C. C., Nov. 19, Dec. 3, 1707 (Richter, p. 206, n. 3); Benedict XIV, *Institut.,* 86, n. VII. Hence

The last clause of § 1, says that *religious need at least the presumed permission of their respective superiors.* Religious, before being presented to the Ordinary for approval, are usually examined as to their qualification for that office by their superiors or a board of professors.[42] If a religious thus examined is approved by the Ordinary and continues to hear confessions without objection on the part of his superior, the permission may be presumed, even though it has not been asked for every single instance. Thus, also, permission may be presumed if one is sent to help another on a Sunday.

Note that this *permission in nowise affects the validity of confession* as long as the jurisdiction delegated by the Ordinary is not withdrawn. The Dominicans have a statute which says that their superiors should suspend from hearing confessions any religious found unfit for that office. If such a religious has obtained faculties from the Ordinary and continues to hear confessions, are the latter valid? They are, even though the absolution is given by a suspended religious against the will of his superiors. Such a religious, of course, acts illicitly, but the absolution he gives is valid because of the jurisdiction received from the diocesan Ordinary.[48]

§ 2 is the logical consequence of what has thus far been stated. The local Ordinaries shall not grant *jurisdiction* to hear confessions *habitually* to religious who are not presented by their own superiors. On the other hand they shall not, except for grave reasons, refuse faculties to such as are presented by their superiors, with due regard, however, to canon 877.

---

the pastor cannot delegate his assistants or curates; such delegation must be given by the Ordinary.

42 This is the practice in every well-regulated community; Bizzarri, *Collectanea*, p. 753.

48 S. C. EE. *et* RR., March 2, 1866 (Bizzarri, *l. c.*, p. 755). This religious incurred no irregularity; *ibid.*

This is a reminiscence of the medieval quarrel between the secular and the regular clergy, especially the Mendicants, which Boniface VIII and John XXII endeavored to settle.[44] The term *presented*, occurring in their Decretals, meant that the general or the provincial should present themselves personally or by deputy before the prelates (*i.e.*, Ordinaries, in order to obtain their *licentia, gratia et beneplacitum*, and then choose a sufficient number from among their members as confessors, who again must be presented to said Ordinaries for the "*licentia, gratia et beneplacitum.*" If the latter was refused, the Pope gave the power of hearing confessions "*ex plenitudine potestatis.*" It is not difficult to perceive that the Ordinaries and pastors were not satisfied with this solution. Hence the Council of Trent [45] and later papal Constitutions [46] demanded faculties properly so-called, but at the same time warned the bishops against unreasonable refusal. Now-a-days a recommendation from the religious superior may suffice, provided can. 877 is complied with. However, if the bishop insists upon personal presentation, he does not exceed the limits of his power.[47]

A *serious reason for refusing faculties* would be lack of knowledge, moral deficiency, or want of pastoral prudence.

[44] C 2, X, Clem. III, 7 (Boniface VIII, "*Dudum*"); c. un. Extrav. Comm., II, 1 (John XXII, "*Frequentes*") c. 2, Extrav Comm., III, 6 (Boniface VIII, "*Super cathedram*").

[45] *Trid.*, sess. 23, c. 15.

[46] Gregory XV, "*Inscrutabili*," 1622; Clement X, "*Superna*," 1670; Benedict XIV, "*Apostolica indulta*," 1744 (explaining the extent of the "*Cruciata*"); S. C. EE. et RR., April 11, 1698.

[47] S. C. C., June 4, 1755 (Richter, *Trid.*, p. 206, n. 4).

CONFESSORS OF EXEMPT RELIGIOUS

CAN. 875

§ 1. In religione clericali exempta ad recipiendas confessiones professorum, novitiorum aliorumve de quibus in can. 514, § 1, jurisdictionem delegatam confert quoque proprius eorundem Superior, ad normam constitutionum; cui fas est eam concedere etiam sacerdotibus e clero saeculari aut alius religionis.

§ 2. In religione laicali exempta, Superior proponit confessarium, qui tamen iurisdictionem obtinere debet ab Ordinario loci, in quo religiosa domus reperitur.

In *exempt religious* institutes of clerics delegated jurisdiction for hearing the confessions of the professed members, novices, and other persons mentioned in can. 514, § 1, may be gîven by their *own superior* according to the constitutions. This same Superior may also grant such jurisdiction to secular priests or priests of another religious institute.

The Council of Trent [48] did not change anything concerning the right of exempt religious to assign their own confessors. This right is part and parcel of the juridical institute of exemption. It was fully acknowledged by many constitutions and decisions of the Holy See.[49] But a dispute arose on the question whether, for instance, a Jesuit could validly absolve a Benedictine without faculties from the local Ordinary.[50] Our text clearly says that all that is needed is delegated jurisdiction from the exempt religious superior. Hence a religious of another religious institute, whether exempt or not, nay, even a

[48] Sess. 23, c. 15, *de ref.*
[49] Clement VIII, " *Sanctissimus,*" May 23, 1593; " *Romani Pontificis,*" Nov. 23, 1599; Clement X, " *Su-* *perna,*" June 21, 1670; S. C. C., Sept. 21, 1624 (Bizzarri, *Collectanea,* p. 246 f.).
[50] Cfr. Bizzarri, *l. c.,* p. 723, note.

secular priest, may validly absolve a religious whose exempt religious superior has granted to that religious or secular priest delegated jurisdiction. Therefore no jurisdiction from the local Ordinary is required. By *"proprius eorundem superior"* is to be understood not only the general or provincial, but also the conventual prior, unless the constitutions of the resp. institute rule otherwise.[51] What has been said under can. 514, § 1, is, we believe, amply sufficient.[52]

But this rule applies only to exempt *clerical* institutes, because § 2 rules that in exempt *lay* institutes the superior *proposes the confessor,* who must obtain *jurisdiction* — not only permission — *from the Ordinary* in whose diocese the religious house is located. This is a new canon, although quite old in effect, according to thé general principle: *Nemo dat quod non habet,* and superiors of lay institutes, although exempt, never, at least *de iure,* enjoyed jurisdiction in matters of confession. We may add that the superior has a strict right to present whom he pleases, and consequently the Ordinary *must* give the faculties if the presented candidate is fit.

CONFESSORS OF FEMALE RELIGIOUS

CAN. 876

§ 1. Revocata qualibet contraria particulari lege seu privilegio, sacerdotes tum saeculares tum religiosi, cuiusvis gradus aut officii, ad confessiones quarumcunque religiosarum ac novitiarum valide et licite recipiendas peculiari iurisdictione indigent, salvo praescripto can. 239, § 1, n. 1, 522, 523.

---

[51] S. C. EE. *et* RR., June 3, 1864 (Bizzarri, *l. c.,* p. 720 ff.).

[52] Cfr. Vol. III of this Commentary, pp. 141 f.

§ 2. Hanc iurisdictionem confert loci Ordinarius, ubi religiosarum domus sita est, ad normam can. 525.

§ 1. Secular as well as religious priests, of whatever rank or office, need a *special jurisdiction* for validly and licitly hearing the confessions of *female religious and their novices.* Only the Cardinals are exempt from this general law. Can. 522 and 523 mention some modifications of this general law which no contrary particular law or privilege can nullify or alter.

§ 2. This jurisdiction is granted by the *Ordinary in whose diocese the religious house is located,* according to can. 525.

This law, though not explicitly enunciated by the Council of Trent, was enacted by Gregory XV and reasserted in later papal constitutions. Wherefore, though the second order of nuns or *moniales* was subject to the jurisdiction of the prelate regular of the first order, yet the confessors appointed by that prelate were first to be examined or at least found fit and then to be given a special approbation.[53] The Constitution of Clement X, "*Superna*," further ordains that a confessor assigned to one convent of Sisters cannot validly hear confessions of the Sisters of another convent and that extraordinary confessors appointed for single monasteries and for single extraordinary occasions, need jurisdiction every time they are appointed for hearing confessions. This is still the rule [54] if the Ordinary, in granting faculties, does not explicitly state that the confessor appointed may hear the confessions of *all moniales on all occasions.* We may also add that the said constitutions mention only *moniales*, and therefore female religious with simple vows

---

[53] Gregory XV, "*Inscrutabili*," Feb. 5, 1622; Clement X, "*Superna*," June 21, 1670.   [54] Cfr. S. C. C., June 5, Aug. 2, 1755 (Richter, *Trid.*, p. 413, n. 10).

were not considered as falling under this law. The Code, which is now everywhere law, simply says *religiosarum ac novitiarum,* and consequently all *religious* who go by that name, and all their novices, can validly confess only to a priest endowed with special jurisdiction by the local Ordinary. This ruling must not, however, be extended to the other persons mentioned in can. 514, namely, pupils, servants, sick persons, and guests. For hearing the confessions of these no special jurisdiction is needed. The Code further establishes that *rank or office* exempts no priest from the duty of obtaining special jurisdiction. Therefore, with the exception of *Cardinals,* no other dignitaries may claim any privileges in this regard. Of course, the local Ordinary who imparts the special jurisdiction may himself hear the confessions of Sisters. This is also true of all others who go by the name of Ordinary,[55] such as prelates *nullius,* vicars general, administrators, vicars and prefects Apostolic, but no prelate regular as such.

Lastly, attention is drawn to the beginning of the canon: "*revocata qualibet contraria particulari lege seu privilegio.*" Such a particular law existed in Spain,[56] in virtue of a brief of Urban VIII, but has now ceased. We know of no privilege or special law granted after the aforesaid Constitution of Gregory XV; if any has been granted it is now void.

Concerning the *exceptions* mentioned in the present canon, these refer to Sisters who for conscience sake wish to go to a confessor approved by the Ordinary for hearing women's confessions in a church or semipublic oratory, and to sick Sisters, who may call in any confessor approved for women.[57]

---

[55] Can. 198, § 1.
[56] Benedict XIV, *De Syn., Dioec.,* IX, 15, 9.

[57] Can. 522 f.; see this Commentary, Vol. III, p. 162 f.

What does "special jurisdiction" mean? Simply that the Ordinary, in granting faculties, must expressly state: "*Etiam ad confessiones audiendas religiosarum ac novitiarum.*" Of course, if he appoints a priest as confessor for Sisters, he is supposed to grant this special jurisdiction, even though, by mistake, this is not expressly [58] stated in the written or oral appointment.

§ 2 refers to can. 525, which says that the local Ordinary appoints the confessors,[59] ordinary as well as extraordinary, for Sisters either immediately subject to the Apostolic See or to the Ordinary himself. The prelate regular may present a priest to the local Ordinary, who then imparts to him jurisdiction for such nuns as are subject to the regulars of the respective institute.

In the *Irish Ecclesiastical Record* of 1919 (March and May, pp. 239 ff., pp. 414 ff.; cfr also *American Eccl. Review*, Oct. 1919, pp. 446 f.), there was a controversy over the wording: "*ad suae conscientiae tranquillitatem,*" "for the peace of her conscience." The question was: Does this term imply a *conditio sine qua non* of valid confession, or is it simply a clause which does not affect the validity of confession? When we wrote on can. 522, we held it was no condition in the proper sense of the word, but a motive cause which prompted the legislator to do away with unnecessary and conscience-torturing restrictions. Nor have we been converted to the contrary view after having read the answers — we suppose by Dr. Kinane — to "Inquirer."

Here are our reasons: If we solved that "*ad*" into a dependent clause, this clause would read: *ut consulatur conscientiae tranquillitati.* Evidently here the motive is

---

[58] This is not contrary to can. 879, § 1, because the very appointment as such of a confessor includes jurisdiction.

[59] Cfr. this Commentary, Vol. III, p. 166 f.

expressed by the *ut finalis*. This, even if taken as a *causa finalis*, not merely *impulsiva*, cannot be construed as a *conditio sine qua non*. For, *finis legis non cadit sub lege*, unless it is expressed in the law itself (see can. 11). Take, for instance, the well-known Constitution of Martin V, "*Ad evitanda*," where the *finis legis* is clearly expressed. A similar phrase ("*ad consulendum conscientiae*") occurs in the decree "*Ne temere*," art. VII. Here the phrase is taken to mean a reason for admitting the extraordinary form of contracting marriage, the nonexistence of which reason would invalidate a marriage informally contracted. But it would need a strong proof to read a *conditio sine qua non* even into this phrase, notwithstanding the assertion of Vermeersch, quoted by Kinane. Vermeersch speaks of a strict obligation, but this may be only moral, as the preceding words seem to insinuate. The main point in said decree is the "imminent danger of death," which generally causes unrest or disturbance of mind which is made the *conditio in directo* for contracting marriage before any priest and two witnesses. Not even in that case would the priest have been obliged to ask the person "in imminent danger of death" whether or not he or she wished to appease his or her conscience. There, too, the "*consulendum conscientiae*" is the impulsive or, if you wish, the motive cause for this permission, but not the *conditio sine qua non*, this being the imminent danger of death. The Code (can. 1098) has happily omitted the clause.

The preposition *ad* has several meanings in law texts. It may signify nearness or approach to something, and also a final cause, or even a condition, but as a rule it has this latter meaning only when a contract or stipulation is involved; for instance, I promise you something *ad ar-*

bitrium boni viri, i. e., iudicis.[59a] What is conscience?
" Conscientia nihil aliud est quam sensus animae cogno-
scentis bonum et malum et quid intrinsecus latens in
mente, quod probari non potest directo." [59b] Now the
conscience is something hidden in the mind, and cannot
easily be proved in the external court. Can this be made
a *conditio sine qua non* of the validity of confession?
We hardly believe. Yet in the opinion of the learned
professor who answered " Inquirer " in the *I. E. R.,* this
would happen in our case. He reads three conditions
into can. 522: The religious must make her confession:
(1) for the peace of her conscience, (2) to a confessor
approved by the local Ordinary to hear the confessions of
women, (3) in a church or oratory, even a semipublic
oratory (March No., p. 239 f.). Then (May No., p.
418) he adds: " If it is stated that a certain act is invalid, when a number of conditions are fulfilled [we suppose there is a printing mistake, otherwise the sentence
is unintelligible, therefore either in the first clause we
must read *valid,* or put a negative in the second, *not fulfilled*], it is clearly implied that the defect of any of
these conditions involves the invalidity of the act."
Again: " The canon itself puts the three [conditions]
upon the same footing." The former statement is true
only if all the conditions are to be taken conjunctively,
but must be rejected if the conditions may be taken disjunctively (for instance, in can. 966), so that only the
one or the other condition is required for the validity of
an act. This is expressed by *aut* or *vel.*

But is it true that all three conditions are put upon the
same footing? And first is it really true that the phrase
ad conscientiae quietem involves a condition? As seen

59a Barbosa, *Tractatus Varii, Dic-*
tiones Usu Frequentes, n. VI, ed.
Lugd. 1660, p. 644.

59b Barbosa, *Axiomata,* 52, l. c.,
p. 34.

above it *may* signify a condition, but does so as a rule
only in onerous contracts.   That it has this signification
in can. 522, needs stronger proofs than those so far advanced.   But suppose it were a condition.   In that case
the peace of conscience would be on a level with the other
two conditions, which certainly affect the validity of the
confession.   Hence the religious herself would be made
co-arbiter of the validity of confession, or at least she
would administer the material for valid confession, not
only by her confession and contrition, but also by her
" peace of conscience."   This would be a new kind of
theology.

But let us not drift into ridicule.   We believe that
Benedict XIV, in his Constitution, *Pastoralis Curae*, of
Aug. 5, 1748, has solved the question quite clearly.   There
amongst other things he mentions a case quite similar to
ours.   Some nuns or sisters had asked for a special confessor, not only in case of sickness or aversion against
the ordinary confessor, but for their greater peace of
mind and further progress on the way of the Lord:
" *verum pro majori animi sui quiete atque ulteriori in
via Dei progressu.*"   The prelates regular refused to
accommodate the sisters, but Benedict XIV leaned to
a more lenient and charitable treatment.   He says:
" *Persuasum enim habebimus, adeoque habemus, non
solum integrae Communitati, sed singulis etiam Monialibus indulgendum esse in iis rebus, quae iuste et rationabiliter petuntur, maxime quum illae ad earum conscientiae
quietem, et securitatem conferre dignoscuntur.   Neque
sane huiusmodi postulationes aut temere exaudiri, aut
sine causa, reiici debere censemus; sed inquirendum in
primis esse de qualitatibus tum Monialis, quae Confessarium extra ordinem petit, tum Confessarii, qui ab ea
requiritur; ut utriusque diligenter inspectis, deliberari*

possit, an illius votis annuendum sit, an non. Si enim Monialis ex una parte nullum det adversae suspicioni locum, ex altera vero confessarius non modo legitimam Ordinarii approbationem, sed etiam commune probitatis testimonium pro se habeat, nullo modo probare possumus tam firmum huiusmodi Praelatorum in renuendo propositum; nec intelligimus, cur post Confessarium extraordinarium integrae Communitati, iuxta legem Concilii Tridentini, oblatum, nulla omnino Monialibus singulis spes relinquatur obtinendi peculiarem Confessarium, cuius consilio et opera, justis fortasse de causis, indigere se arbitrentur." If any one wishes to read a strict condition into this text, he may do so at his own pleasure, but he will certainly contradict the wording of the text, as well as the mind of the great Pontiff and canonist. The meaning is clear: in order not to torture the consciences of the poor sisters ("*pro animi quiete*," "*ad earum conscientiae quietem et securitatem*") the Pope gives them liberal and generous permission to call in another confessor, even if they have to apply to the S. Poenitentiaria. This is the motive cause, but not a condition in the proper sense of the word.

We finally draw attention to what we said in note 13, p. 156, Vol. III, of this Commentary. There is no need of inquiring into the reasons which prompted Pius X to unfetter the consciences of religious. The view advocated in the *I. E. R.* would re-enthrall them and throw a Jansenistic cloak about the generous law of the Code.

EXAMINATION OF CONFESSORS

CAN. 877

§ 1. Tum locorum Ordinarii iurisdictionem, tum Superiores religiosi iurisdictionem aut licentiam audiendarum confessionum ne concedant, nisi iis qui idonei per examen reperti fuerint, nisi agatur de sacerdote cuius theologicam doctrinam aliunde compertam habeant.

§ 2. Si post concessam iurisdictionem aut licentiam prudenter dubitent num probatus a se antea sacerdos pergat adhuc idoneus esse, eum ad novum doctrinae periculum adigant, etsi agatur de parocho aut canonico poenitentiario.

§ 1. The local Ordinaries shall not grant jurisdiction, nor the religious Superior jurisdiction or license for hearing confessions except to such as have been found fit upon *examination*. An exception may be made in favor of those whose theological competency is sufficiently known from other sources.

All the papal constitutions and decisions insist upon the *fitness* (*idoneitas*) of those who hear confessions. This includes two qualities, intellectual and moral. The *intellectual* consists in doctrinal knowledge, especially of the respective portions of Moral Theology [60] and Canon Law, and familiarity with the language in which confessions are to be heard.[61] The *moral* qualities required are prudence, probity of life, and zeal. Therefore the examiners should insist upon these qualities before they render their verdict to the Ordinary.[62]

Our Code admits a noteworthy mitigation in favor of those who are *known for their theological learning*. Thus now-a-days a teacher of Moral Theology or a synodal examiner may be exempted from this examination, also any one whose competency is well known to the bishop.

---

60 S. C. P. F., April 13, 1807, n. XII (*Coll.*, n. 692).

61 S. C. P. F., March 17, 1760; Aug. 2, 1762 (*Coll.*, nm. 427, 444):

this rule affects the secular as well as the religious clergy.

62 Benedict XIV, "*Apostolicum ministerium*," May 30, 1753. § 8.

§ 2. Should the Ordinary or religious Superior have a prudent doubt as to whether a priest once approved continues to be fit, they may submit him to a new doctrinal examination, no matter whether he be a pastor or canon penitentiary.

Here stress is laid on knowledge, and consequently the moral qualifications need not be re-examined because it might reflect on the priest's character.[63] The Ordinary is entitled to subject any confessor to an examination, even though he be a pastor or penitentiary canon. Also one, whose competence was assumed may be submitted to an examination after he has been given the faculties. The religious Superior may submit a religious to a new examination in case he has extra-sacramental knowledge of his doctrinal deficiency on some point.

LIMITED JURISDICTION

CAN. 878

§ 1. Iurisdictio delegata aut licentia audiendarum confessionum concedi potest certis quibusdam circumscripta finibus.

§ 2. Caveant tamen locorum Ordinarii ac religiosi Superiores ne iurisdictionem aut licentiam sine rationabili causa nimis coarctent.

Delegated jurisdiction, or the license for hearing confessions, may be limited, but local Ordinaries and religious Superiors should not restrict it unreasonably.

The first section is couched in general terms and *excludes no class of clergy* who need delegated jurisdiction. Therefore also exempt religious[64] who obtain delegated

---

[63] S. C. EE. *et* RR., May 29, 1760; April 11, 1698 (Bizzarri, *Collectanea*, pp. 546 f., 282).

[64] The regulars claimed exemption from all restrictions, but Alexander VII, Jan. 30, 1659 proscribed the

jurisdiction either from the local Ordinary or from their Superior may have their jurisdiction limited. But the reason for so doing should at least have the semblance of *justice*. The S. Congregations have more than once admonished Ordinaries not to vex religious with unnecessary restrictions.[65] Any limitations should be based on unfitness, as resulting from the examination, as the Constitution of Clement X, " *Superna*," plainly states.[66] Restrictions may be made as to persons, place and time. As to *persons* it may be that a priest may be too young to hear women's confessions, or may be suited for one class of persons but not for another, etc. The same reasons would also justify limitation as to *place*. As to *time*, the Constitution of Clement X distinguishes between priests who were found generally fit, and others who proved less or not quite fit in the examination. De Lugo says the bishop may have a reasonable suspicion that one approved forever might care little for further study or intellectual improvement, or the moral character of the candidate may not be fully known to him.[67] The Ordinary should not make the exercise of delegated jurisdiction dependent on the permission of the parish priest;[68] in fact, he should not lay down too many conditions.

proposition: "*Non possunt Episcopi limitare seu restringere approbationes, quas regularibus concedunt ad confessiones audiendas, neque ulla ex parte revocare.*" Cfr. Benedict XIV, *Instit.*, 86, n. IX.

65 S. C. EE. et RR., Sept. 13, 1641; Sept. 22, 1645 (Bizzarri, *l. c.*, p. 25 f.); S. C. P. F., Dec. 11, 1838, ad 5 (*Coll.*, n. 879).

66 See § 4, and Innocent XIII, *Apostolici ministerii*," May 23, 1723, §§ 16, 19.

67 Ballerini-Palmieri, *Opus Theol. Moral.*, V., p. 287.

68 S. Rit. C., May 13, 1719 (*Dec. Auth.*, n. 2264).

JURISDICTION EXPRESSLY TO BE GRANTED

CAN. 879

§ 1. Ad confessiones valide audiendas opus est iurisdictione scripto vel verbis expresse concessa.

§ 2. Pro concessione iurisdictionis nihil exigi potest.

For the valid hearing of confessions, jurisdiction must be *granted expressly* either in writing or by word of mouth; but *nothing is to be charged* for the grant. Tacitly granted jurisdiction is hereby entirely rejected. One would look in vain for the word "*expresse*" in the papal constitutions [69] quoted by Cardinal Gasparri, though its equivalent is certainly to be found there. What is *tacit jurisdiction?* It is one which an Ordinary or Superior knows to be exercised by his subjects, and to which he does not object, although he could easily do so. For instance, a bishop calls a missionary from another diocese to give a mission in a parish of his own territory. Thereby he was formerly supposed to have granted him the necessary faculties for hearing confession.[70] Such tacitly granted jurisdiction can no longer be held to be sufficient for validly hearing confessions. There must be an *express* grant. The Ordinary in calling a missionary must explicitly confer upon him delegated jurisdiction, and the pastor must expressly obtain the same for a missionary, unless the latter belongs to the diocese or has obtained faculties for the diocese in which he is to give the mission.

We said this express grant is required for *delegated* jurisdiction. The text does not contain this adjective;

69 Benedict XIV, "*Apostolica indulto*," Aug. 5, 1744, § 3, expressly mentions tacit approbation or jurisdiction as sufficient.

70 Noldin, *l. c.*, n. 347; Sabetti-Barrett, *Theol. Moral.*, ed. 1917, p. 706; *Am. Eccl. Rev.*, 1918, Vol. 58, p. 681.

but it is clearly implied, because ordinary jurisdiction is acquired by reason of the office to which it is attached.

Here it may not be amiss to answer the question whether jurisdiction for hearing confessions may be acquired *by custom*. The Decretals [71] absolutely deny the possibility of acquiring such jurisdiction at least directly, by custom, even though it be immemorable. Indirectly, as Pirhing says,[72] one could obtain ordinary jurisdiction by acquiring a parochial benefice. Now this way is precluded, since all provision must be made in writing.[73]

Different from the express or tacit grant of jurisdiction is a doubtful and probable jurisdiction. A *doubtful jurisdiction* would be if one would not remember the date when, or the time for which, it was granted, or doubt the material extent of the faculties. *Probable* would be the jurisdiction in reserved cases and censures as to whether the circumstances are really such as would render the sin a reserved one or one punished by censures. Our Code has solved this doubt in favor of validity in both cases.[74]

REVOCATION OF JURISDICTION OR LICENSE

CAN. 880

§ 1. Loci Ordinarius vel Superior religiosus iurisdictionem vel licentiam ad audiendas confessiones ne revocent aut suspendant, nisi gravem ob causam.

§ 2. At graves ob causas Ordinarius potest etiam parocho aut poenitentiario confessarii munus interdicere, salvo recursu in devolutivo ad Sedem Apostolicam.

71 C. 2, 6°, V. 10.
72 *Com.*, lib. V, tit. 38, n. 36.
73 Can. 159.

74 Can. 207, § 2; can. 209; Ballerini-Palmieri, *l. c.*, V, p. 319 ff.

§ 3. Non tamen licet Episcopo, inconsulta Sede Apostolica, si de domo formata agatur, omnibus alicuius religiosae domus confessariis una simul iurisdictionem adimere.

§ 1. Local Ordinaries *shall not revoke* or suspend jurisdiction or license for hearing confessions, *except for a grave* reason.

§ 2. But if there is such a reason, the local Ordinary may also forbid the pastor or canon penitentiary to exercise the office of confessor, with due regard, however, to the right of *appeal in devolutivo* to the Apostolic See.

§ 3. In the case of a *domus formata*, the bishop is not allowed, without having first consulted the Apostolic See, to take away jurisdiction from all confessors of a religious house at the same time.

Revoking the faculties or jurisdiction affects the validity of confessions, while the recall of the license only concerns licitness, but may reflect on the moral character and reputation of the confessor. Hence it is that a *grave reason* is required for the revocation of either. Such a reason is stated in a decree of 1615 and styled " a reason connected with confession." [75] This apposition is then further determined in the Constitution of Clement X, *"Superna,"*[76] which indeed speaks only of regulars, but may be said to cover our case, which includes both religious and secular clerics. It is stated there that if religious live scandalously or dishonorably, or if they have committed a crime which, according to the prudent judgment of the bishop, demands suspension from hearing confessions, these would be reasons justifying suspension from hearing confessions. For, adds said

75 S. C. EE. *et* RR., Nov. 20, 1615 (Bizzarri, *l. c.*, p. 21).   76 See §§ 5, 6.

Constitution, the principal quality of a minister of the Sacrament of Penance is probity of life and good conduct. The Code simply says: "a grave reason," and with this, says the "*Superna*," the conscience of the bishop is charged: *i.e.*, he must use common sense and act with due deliberation. A grave reason would also be disregard of a decree of interdict, or the discovery of irregularities at the canonical visitation.[77]

§ 2 applies the same law to *pastors* and *canonici poenitentiarii* of cathedral and collegiate churches who otherwise enjoy ordinary jurisdiction. Therefore these, too, may be suspended from the office of confessors, so that the confessions would no longer be valid, unless, of course, can. 209 would apply. But the text adds that they may have recourse to the Apostolic See *in devolutivo*, which signifies that the order must be obeyed until reversed by Rome.[78]

§ 3 repeats former enactments [79] concerning *confessors of religious communities*. The sources from which our text is taken mention the houses of exempt regulars and of *moniales*. There were many complaints against Ordinaries for suspending all the confessors of a convent, though formerly approved by them for *hearing the confessions of lay people*.[80] This, as one decree says, caused scandal and injury to souls. Hence the new law which has entered the Code. But our text apparently draws a distinction between *domus formatae* and *non formatae*, *i.e.*, houses in which at least six professed members live, four of whom are priests, and houses with less than this

77 S. C. EE. *et* RR., Nov. 20, 1615; Dec. 9, 1740 (Bizzarri, *l. c.*, pp. 21, 326, 350); S. C. P. F., Dec. 11, 1839, ad 4 (*Coll.*, n. 892).

78 Benedict XIV, "*Ad militantis*," March 30, 1742, §§ 15, 20.

79 Innocent X, "*Cum sicut accepimus*," May 14, 1648, § 4; Clement X, "*Superna*," § 6; S. C. EE. *et* RR., Nov. 20, 1615.

80 S. C. EE. *et* RR., Nov. 28, 1732 (Bizzarri, *l. c.*, p. 328).

number. The former documents simply say: *alicuius conventus*. But the Code implies that only in the case of a *domus formata* must the Holy See be consulted before the Ordinary can suspend all the priests of a community from hearing confessions. In smaller communities, which have not at least six members, four of whom are priests, all the priests may be suspended by the bishop from hearing the confessions of lay people or secular priests or non-exempt religious. From hearing the confessions of exempt religious the Ordinary cannot suspend exempt religious, since these receive delegated jurisdiction from their own superiors. If a bishop should attempt such suspension in the case mentioned (*domus formata*), it would be the Metropolitan's right and duty to remind him of can. 880, § 3.[81] On the other hand, the Ordinary may, for a grave reason, without asking or notifying the superior, remove or suspend a religious from hearing the confessions of female religious.[82] But if the female religious be subject to a religious exempt superior, the latter would be entitled to present another religious for approval or examination, in order to obtain jurisdiction.

It may strike the student as odd that the Code, in § 3, has chosen the term "*bishop*," whereas in the other two sections it uses the word "Ordinary." Was this done merely for the sake of change? We hardly believe so for reasons derived from a decision of the S. Congregation. The question was asked, whether the vicar capitular (diocesan administrator in our country) may suspend either secular or regular priests from hearing confessions. The answer was that there was no difficulty

---

81 *Ibid.*
82 S. C. EE. *et* RR., Dec. 9, 1740 Bizzari, *l. c.*, p. 350). Revoking or suspending faculties *without a reason* (also under § 1) would be valid, as clearly implied by "*Suprema.*"

as to secular priests, but the case was otherwise with regard to exempt religious once approved by the bishop either without limitation, or with the clause "*ad beneplacitum nostrum.*" To remove such is, according to the School, a personal right of the bishop which does not pass to the chapter or the vicar capitular,[88] and hence to proceed thus is not in the power of the administrator, nor, since it is a personal right, is it in the power of the vicar general except with a special mandate.

CONFESSORS OF VAGI AND PEREGRINI

CAN. 881

§ 1. **Omnes utriusque cleri sacerdotes ad audiendas confessiones approbati in aliquo loco, sive ordinaria sive delegata iurisdictione instructi, possunt etiam vagos ac peregrinos ex alia dioecesi vel paroecia ad sese accedentes, itemque catholicos cuiusque ritus orientalis, valide et licite absolvere.**

§ 2. **Qui ordinariam habent absolvendi potestatem, possunt subditos absolvere ubique terrarum.**

§ 1. Secular as well as religious priests who are approved for hearing confessions in some place, no matter whether their jurisdiction be ordinary or delegated, may validly and licitly absolve *vagi* and *peregrini* who come to them from another diocese or parish, and also Catholics of any Oriental Rite.

The Holy See, says an Instruction,[84] has always observed the rule that, in a matter so delicate as the Sacrament of Penance, the liberty of the faithful should not be impeded, but they should be free to confess to whom they prefer. Of course jurisdiction must always be

---

[88] S. C. EE. *et* RR., June 19, 1806 (Bizzarri, *l. c.*, p. 407 f.).

[84] S. C. P. F., June 2, 1835 (*Coll.*, n. 839).

supposed. Now the text says that *both* secular and religious priests may absolve *in casu,* whilst the Constitution of Clement X, "*Superna*" (§ 7) only mentions regulars who are approved for the place or diocese in which they hear confessions. Hence a confessor approved for the diocese of St. Joseph and hearing confessions in that diocese, may absolve such as come to him from the diocese of Kansas City. But what does "*approbati in aliquo loco*" mean? It can mean neither license nor something midway between license and jurisdiction. The text itself explains the phrase. Approval is here only a general term which includes both jurisdiction and permission (for religious especially, who need the latter in order to hear confessions licitly). Hence the addition without the copula *et:* "*sive ordinaria sive delegata iurisdictione instructi.*" Those who have ordinary jurisdiction are the bishops and pastors, each within his own territory, the bishop within the whole diocese, the pastor within his parochial district.[85] If the latter has received delegated jurisdiction for hearing confessions in the whole diocese, he may perform that office in any part of the diocese.

The *subjects* of this general rule are *vagi, peregrini,* and *Catholici ritus Orientalis. Vagi* are such as have neither domicile nor quasi-domicile in any place, diocese or parish. *Peregrini* are those who have a domicile or quasi-domicile, but for the time being live outside of it, in a strange place.[86] Oriental Catholics are those of an Oriental Rite differing from the Latin, though partaking of the Catholic communion. This threefold class of per-

---

85 S. C. C., quoted by Benedict XIV, *Institut.,* 86, n. 14: "*An provisus de parochiali per concursum, censendus sit approbatus idoneus minister ad audiendas confessiones in illa dioecesi, in qua illam parochialem obtinet?* RESP.: *Censeri dumtaxat in ea civitate, vel oppido, ubi sita est parochialis, non autem passim per totam dioecesim.*"

86 Can. 91.

sons, then, may be absolved by any priest who has either ordinary or delegated jurisdiction for the place in which he actually hears confessions. As to the difference of rite, there is no difficulty, because the Sacrament of Penance, as far as the formula of absolution is concerned, has little or nothing to do with the rite. Wherefore the S. Congregation [87] has more than once enjoined the bishops of the Oriental Rite not to forbid their subjects to go to confession to Latin priests. Neither is there any doubt as to *vagi*, because custom testifies to the fact that they may be absolved by any priest endowed with jurisdiction. Unless jurisdiction is granted in one way or another, absolution, which is given in the form of a judicial sentence, cannot be imparted validly. This calls for a brief observation concerning *peregrini*. We will not enter into the controversy which raged several years ago concerning this point,[88] but will only state what, according to the Code, seems to us the more probable and consistent view. All admit, with St. Alphonsus,[89] that the Pope may grant jurisdiction to any priest for absolving *peregrini* (strangers) and that, without either ordinary or delegated jurisdiction, no valid absolution may be imparted. The question is: Who grants the jurisdiction necessary for absolving a stranger:—the bishop of the stranger who has left his domicile or quasi-domicile, or the bishop in whose territory the stranger dwells at the moment? Concretely, if a stranger comes from the diocese of Kansas City to a priest in the diocese of St. Joseph, and asks to be absolved, which bishop grants jurisdiction, the

---

[87] S. C. P. F., June 2, 1835; Dec. 11, 1838; April 30, 1862, n. 2 (*Coll.*, nn. 839, 879, 1227). A general prohibition would render confession neither invalid nor illicit.

[88] Cfr. Ballerini-Palmieri, *Opus*

Theol. Moral., V. p. 305, nn. 613 ff.; Lehmkuhl, *l. c.*, II, n. 384; Noldin, *Zeitschrift für Kath. Theol.*, 1881, 453 f.; *De Sacramentis*, n. 349.

[89] *Theol. Moral.*, VI, n. 588.

bishop of Kansas City or the bishop of St. Joseph?
After reading the acute reasoning of Ballerini-Palmieri, it
seemed to us that they had gained the point, and certainly,
before the Code was promulgated, their position was
speculatively the stronger. But after pondering can. 881,
as compared with can. 879, § 1, this difficulty appeared:
How about express jurisdiction? Ballerini-Palmieri's
reasoning is based upon " tacit consent," " explicit or im-
plicit license or approbation." The *peregrinus* is supposed to have the tacit consent of his bishop which he
transfers to the confessor. However since tacit jurisdiction is now excluded, and since our text speaks of such
as are approved " *in* " some place or diocese, we cannot
help saying that the necessary jurisdiction must come
from the Ordinary of the diocese *in* which the confession
is heard. The difficulty arises from the fact that the
peregrinus is not *subject* to the Ordinary who is supposed
to grant jurisdiction over him. According to the Council
of Florence and that of Trent,[90] the confessor must have
either ordinary or delegated power over his penitent. It
is true that the jurisdiction cannot be claimed by reason
of domicile or quasi-domicile; yet it appears to us that the
old adage, " *Actor sequitur reum*,"[91] may to some extent
be applied here, for the penitent, being himself plaintiff
and defendant, may choose the *forum competens* and thus
submit himself to a judge otherwise competent, *i.e.*, any
priest who has jurisdiction. Therefore the Church, especially now-a-days when changes of domicile and wander-
ing are so frequent, has wisely left it to the penitent to
choose his own confessor, as long as the latter is qualified
according to general law of the Church.

90 Thus Ballerini-Palmeri, V, p. 306, n. 615; *Decret. pro Arm.* (Den- zinger, n. 594), *Trid.*, sess. 14, c. 7, *de poenit;* can. 872.

91 Cc. 5, 8, X, II, 2.

§ 2. *Those who possess ordinary jurisdiction for absolving may absolve their own subjects everywhere.* Therefore Ordinaries and pastors (but not curates, assistants, or rectors) may absolve their subjects by reason of their office, to which this power is attached. The Cardinals enjoy the same power by reason of a personal privilege, which, however, cannot be communicated to others, except on their own behalf and that of their *familiares.*[92]

Subjects of Ordinaries and pastors are those who have their domicile or quasti-domicile within the boundaries of the diocese or parish. These, then, may be absolved by their respective Ordinaries or pastors in any diocese or parish, no matter where they may meet.[93] The ordinary jurisdiction may therefore be called extra-territorial or personal.

ABSOLUTION IN DANGER OF DEATH

CAN. 882.

In periculo mortis omnes sacerdotes, licet ad confessiones non approbati, valide et licite absolvunt quoslibet poenitentes a quibusvis peccatis aut censuris, quantumvis reservatis et notoriis, etiamsi praesens sit sacerdos approbatus, salvo praescripto can. 884, 2252.

When there is danger of death, any priest, even though not otherwise approved for hearing confessions, may validly and licitly absolve any penitent from whatever sins and censures, including those which are reserved and notorious, even though an approved priest may be present. But the rules laid down in can. 884 and 2252 must be observed.

92 Can. 239, § 1, nn. 1, 2.
93 S. C. C., Nov. 19, Dec. 3, 1707 (Richter, *Trid*, p. 206, n. 3).

The penitential discipline,[94] which was rather severe in the first century, was gradually mitigated so as to open the gate of salvation to public penitents, who could receive the imposition of hands at least at the point of death. The last of the three customary impositions was indeed reserved to the bishop, but the priest was allowed to give it in the " last necessity,"[95] which certainly was the approaching end. The subsequent ages[96] witnessed further mitigations, until the present discipline was established by the Council of Trent,[97] which, *inter alia,* enacted the wholesome law that no censure or reserved sin can debar a dying penitent from receiving the benefit of absolution.

" How is the *periculum mortis* or danger of death to be understood?" was asked by a former bishop of Cincinnati, and the Holy Office[98] referred him to "approved authors." One of these authors tells us that danger of death exists, not only in a very serious sickness, but also when there is danger to life from an external cause, for instance, before a battle, upon setting forth on a perilous voyage, before a difficult childbirth, etc.[99] In such a circumstance, then, our canon may be applied, and any priest, even though he has neither ordinary nor delegated jurisdiction or permission, may validly and licitly absolve. The text goes still further by saying: *even though an approved priest may be present.* Hence any validly ordained priest, even though belonging to a heretical or schismatic sect, or apostatized or censured may, even in

94 Cfr. Pohle-Preuss, *The Sacraments* Vol. III, pp. 37 ff.; M. J. O'Donnell, *Penance in the Early Church,* 1907. Palmieri, *De Poenit.,* p. 159. justly distinguishes a threefold *manuum impositio;* at the beginning, during, and at the end of public penance, which latter signified absolution.

95 C. 14, C. 26, q. 6.

96 C. 1, Extrav. Comm., V, 7 (Boniface IX, " *Inter cunctas* ").

97 Sess. 14, C. 7, *de poenit.*

98 S. O., Sept. 13, 1859, ad 1 (*Coll. P. F.,* n. 1181).

99 Noldin, *De Sacram.,* n. 353.

presence of an approved confessor, validly absolve any one in danger of death, and if we connect that clause with the present, he may also do so licitly.[1] It is but just, however, to add another decision of the Holy Office, in answer to the question: "Whether it is permitted to demand absolution of a schismatic priest in danger of death if no Catholic priest is at hand," as follows: Yes, provided no scandal is given to the faithful, no danger of perversion threatens the sick person, and, finally, provided that it may be reasonably presumed that the schismatic minister will absolve according to the rite of the Church.[2] The validity is not affected, provided he pronounces the formula correctly, but the obligation here imposed should not be made light of.

Furthermore, the Code says: he may absolve from *all sins* and *censures*, although reserved and notorious, except in two cases: the *absolutio complicis*, of which can. 884 treats, and the obligation of recurring to the proper authority, if the penitent regains his health, as will be more fully explained under can. 2252. Observe that recourse to the Holy See, *i.e.*, the S. Poenitentiaria, must be had in case a sin has been forgiven which was *modo specialissimo* under censure reserved to the Holy See by either the law itself, or by the Holy See personally; and recourse must be had to the bishop if the law itself or the bishop has reserved a censure.

The time within which the application must be made is generally a month after the complete recovery of the penitent. It may be done either personally or through the confessor by mail,[3] of course, under fictitious names.

1 S. O., July 29, 1891 (*Coll. P. F.,* n. 1761) only mentions validity.
2 S. O., June 30, July 7, 1864, ad 6 (*Coll. cit.*, n. 1257).

3 Can. 2254, § 1; S. O., Aug. 19, 1891 (*Coll. P. F.*, n. 1764).

CAN. 883.

§ 1. Sacerdotes omnes maritimum iter arripientes, dummodo vel a proprio Ordinario, vel ab Ordinario portus in quo navim conscendunt, vel etiam ab Ordinario cuiusvis portus interiecti per quem in itinere transeunt, facultatem rite acceperint confessiones audiendi, possunt, toto itinere, quorumlibet fidelium secum navigantium confessiones in navi excipere, quamvis navis in itinere transeat vel etiam aliquandiu consistat variis in locis diversorum Ordinariorum iurisdictioni subiectis.

§ 2. Quoties vero navis in itinere consistat, possunt confessiones excipere tum fidelium qui quavis de causa ad navim accedant, tum eorum qui ipsis ad terram obiter appellentibus confiteri petant eosque valide ac licite absolvere etiam a casibus Ordinario loci reservatis.

§ 1. Any priest traveling on the ocean may hear the confessions of all Catholics who travel with him on board the same ship, although the vessel may on its trip pass, or even stop for some time at, various places subject to different Ordinaries. But in order to absolve these travelers validly and licitly the priest must have duly obtained the faculty either from his own Ordinary, or from the Ordinary of the place he sails from, or from the Ordinary of any port which the vessel passes.

This canon, as is natural, grew out of the recently increased travel. It is not surprising, therefore, that theologians as well as the Holy Office were at first in doubt as to which Ordinary should impart jurisdiction. It was first decided that the Ordinary of the diocese from which the ship sailed should grant the necessary faculty, but that it should last only until the vessel reached the next station where an Ordinary was located.[4] Later the faculty was extended over the whole trip, even though the vessel made several stops of some duration (*aliquandiu*).[5] Finally the Holy Office formulated the text which is our present § 1, but limited the faculty of hearing confessions to the ship itself.[6]

§ 2 is the final formulation as it was rendered by the Holy Office on December 13, 1906, but which has not entirely entered our Code. What the legislator has adopted into the text is the following: As often as the vessel stops on its trip, the priests endowed with faculties, as stated under § 1, may validly and licitly hear the confessions of such of the faithful as may for any reason visit the vessel, as well as the confessions of those who approach them for that purpose when they go on land for a short stop. In this latter case, they may absolve also from cases reserved to the Ordinary of the diocese where they stop. The omission in the Code of one clause inserted by the Holy Office is noteworthy. The Holy Office had made a condition in the case where a priest hears confessions on land and absolves from reserved cases, viz: "provided there be no, or only one, approved priest in that place and the Ordinary cannot easily be reached."[7] The legislator certainly knew of that ruling, and the fact that he omitted it purposely from the Code shows that he intended to free the priests in question from the condition named. It would, besides, be embarrassing for traveling priests, who perhaps do not even know the lan-

---

4 S. O., March 17, 1869 (*Coll. P. F.*, n. 1343).

5 S. O., April 9, 1900 (*ibid.*, n. 2082).

6 S. O., Aug. 23, 1905 (*ibid.*, n. 2244, note).

7 *Ibid.*

guage of the country, to have to ask about the presence of priests or the whereabouts of the Ordinary.

§ 1 states that the respective priests must have duly (*rite*) obtained the faculties. This implies that they were found worthy and fit, according to the enactment of the Council of Trent, to obtain the faculties.[8] Therefore Ordinaries are at liberty to subject them to an examination, unless, knowing them personally or from recommendation, they deem this measure superfluous. Now-a-days wireless telegraphy might prove a convenient means of obtaining faculties in case a priest has forgotten to do so, when leaving the port or diocese.

ABSOLUTIO COMPLICIS INVALIDA

CAN. 884.

Absolutio complicis in peccato turpi invalida est, praeterquam in mortis periculo; et etiam periculo mortis, extra casum necessitatis, est ex parte confessarii illicita ad norman constitutionum apostolicarum et nominatim constitutionis Benedicti XIV *Sacramentum Poenitentiae*, 1 Iun. 1741.

In the Constitution of Benedict XIV, "*Sacramentum Poenitentiae*," the *sin* from which an accomplice may not be absolved is called "*peccatum turpe atque inhonestum contra sextum decalogi praeceptum commissum.*" That it be such, it must be committed by both parties and constitute a certain, external, and grievous sin on both sides by reason of the internal and external act. The accomplice may be of either sex.[9]

If a confessor attempts to absolve his accomplice in

---

[8] S. O., Aug. 23, 1905 (*ibid.*).
[9] S. O., Sept. 13, 1859 (*Coll. P. F.*, n. 1181), which refers to *probatos auctores*, and especially to St. Alphonsus; cfr. Noldin, *De Sacramentis*, n. 384.

such a sin, his jurisdiction ceases: *nulla atque irrita omnino sit,* as if it were an absolution imparted by a priest who lacked jurisdiction and the faculty of absolving validly.   This invalidity, as stated by law in said Constitution, affects every person involved in such a crime, and comprises the whole act or matter of confession, not only the act of complicity.   Whether a confessor who would *bona fide* absolve his accomplice, either because he did not know the penitent, or was not aware of the law which deprives him of jurisdiction *in casu,* would absolve validly is a controverted point.[10]   The wording of the Constitution in our opinion rather favors the invalidity of such a confession, although the *excipere audeat* [11] seemingly supposes an act of presumption and voluntary disobedience, which, of course, in a case of ignorance or inadvertence the confessor could not be charged with.   If the accomplice should, by reason of forgetfulness or even purposely but *bona fide,* omit all mention of the complicity, the confession would be valid.[12]   If the penitent had already confessed the sin in question to another priest, and was absolved by him, the guilty confessor may afterwards validly and licitly absolve his accomplice, even though the latter should, among other sins, again confess the sin of complicity.[13]

When there is *danger of death,* the confessor may validly and licitly absolve his accomplice from the sin of

<hr>

10 Noldin, *l. c.,* n. 385.

11 The phrase *ausus fuerit* occurs in the clause which states the censure and commences with: *et nihilominus;* the absolution is not only invalid, but liable to censure. The censure would not, however, be incurred in the controverted case.

12 If the priest accomplice had either directly or indirectly induced his accomplice not to confess this

sin, excommunication would follow; cfr. can. 2367, § 2; S. Poenit., Feb. 19, 1896.

13 Noldin *l. c.,* n. 385, says in a note: "*Sunt tamen inter recentes praesertim D'Annibale (III, n. 32, 4 Scavini (III, n. 367) et Genicot (II, n. 352), qui confessario potestatem tribuunt etiam in peccatum complicitatis, postquam hoc semel directe iam remissum est.*"

complicity, if there is real *necessity, i.e.,* according to Benedict XIV,[14] *if no other priest,* whether with or without jurisdiction, *is to be had.* But the same Pontiff also foresaw the case of scandal or loss of reputation if another priest, *simplex sacerdos,* should have to be called. Hence he says: If another priest cannot be called without giving scandal or seriously impairing the reputation of the guilty priest, then the other priest may be considered as not present.

However, the guilty priest, continues the Pope, should not imagine danger of scandal and ill repute, but rather, if it should be necessary, endeavor, as much as lies in him, to prevent and remove by ordinary means the possibility of scandal, so that another priest can be called without causing a stir or surprise. Then is added the clause which our Code has adopted from said Constitution, *viz.:* Should the priest purposely neglect to employ the means for calling another priest, or put it off maliciously, so that really no urgent necessity would entitle the guilty priest to absolve his accomplice, *absolution* would indeed be *valid,* but grievously illicit, and the guilty priest would incur the censure inflicted by law. Thus far the Constitutions which concern our case. For the rest, we refer to can. 2367 and merely add that those who absolve an accomplice " *ex ignorantia crassa or supina* " incur the censure which the law has established.[15]

---

14 " *Apostolici muneris,*" Feb. 8, 1745. § 2–4: " *Tunc alium sacerdotem perinde haberi, censerique posse, ac si revera abesset, atque deficeret; ac proinde in eo rerum statu, non prohiberi socio criminis sacerdoti absolutionem poenitenti ab eo quoque crimine impertiri. Sciat autem complex ejusmodi sacerdos, et serio animadvertat, fore se re ipsa coram Deo, qui irrideri non* potest, reum gravis adversus praedictam nostram Constitut. inobedientiae, latisque in ea poenis obnoxium, si praedictae infamiae, aut scandali pericula sibi ultro ipse confingat, ubi non sunt."

15 S. O., Jan. 13, 1892 (*Coll. P. F.,* n. 1777). A very criminal yet curious proposition (n. 7) is that proscribed by Alexander VII, Sept. 24, 1665 (Denzinger, n. 978).

ADDITIONAL PRAYERS

CAN. 885.

Etsi preces, ab Ecclesia formulae absolutoriae adiunctae, ad ipsam absolutionem obtinendam non sint necessariae, nihilominus, nisi iusta de causa, ne omittantur.

The form of absolution is: "*Ego te absolvo a peccatis tuis*," and this is essential to the Sacrament.[16] However, there are some other prayers, *viz.*, the *Misereatur, Indulgentiam*, and the words which precede the formula: *Dominus*, etc., which, our text says, are joined to the formula of absolution by the Church, and though they are not required for absolution, yet should not be omitted without a just cause.

ABSOLUTION NOT TO BE REFUSED OR DEFERRED

CAN. 886.

Si confessarius dubitare nequeat de poenitentis dispositionibus et hic absolutionem petat, absolutio nec deneganda, nec differenda est.

If the confessor has no reason for doubting the proper disposition of the penitent, and the latter demands absolution, it is neither to be refused nor postponed.

This canon belongs mainly to Moral Theology, because it most intimately affects the conscience. Yet, it is astonishing how many wrong opinions, rejected by the Church, are connected with this subject. As usual, there are

[16] The word *ego* is not strictly essential to the formula of absolution, nor are the words *a peccatis tuis*; still less the *deinde*; but they should not be omitted; *nihil in-* *novetur*, said the S. Rit. C., March 11, 1837 (*Decreta Auth.*, n. 2764). The *Passio*, etc., is not prescribed, and may therefore be omitted. (Noldin, *l. c.*, n. 237).

excesses and defects. The former consist in demanding too much of the penitent. Thus Quesnel [17] called it wise, enlightened, and charitable to make penitents wait, to practice humility, to realize their state, to pray for the spirit of contrition and penance, and to make atonement before they are reconciled with God. The Synod of Pistoja [18] rejected attrition and demanded contrition for confession. The Jansenists required satisfaction before absolution could be imparted.[19] It would also be excessively rigorous to refuse absolution in time of sickness to such as were careless about receiving the Sacraments when they were in good health. No one who gives signs of repentance, should be refused absolution.[20]

A gross *defect* would be to give absolution to such as live in *proxima occasione peccandi* and make no effort to break the custom or remove the occasion, or such as are ignorant of the necessary mysteries of the Blessed Trinity and the Incarnation.[21] Concerning the necessary belief, a distinction between such articles of faith as are necessary *necessitate medii*, the two just mentioned, and such as are necessary *necessitate praecepti* must be made. Without belief in the former, absolution would simply be invalid.[22] If one is culpably ignorant of those articles of faith which are to be believed *necessitate praecepti*, he may be given absolution only if he is sorry for this culpable ignorance and accuses himself thereof, and also seriously promises to learn what he ought to know.[23]

17 *Prop. dam. a Clemente* XI, n. 87, "*Unigenitus*," Sept. 8, 1713 (Denzinger, n. 1302).

18 *Prop. dam. a Pio VI.*, n. 36, "*Auctorem fidei*" Aug. 28, 1794 (*ib.*, n. 1399).

19 *Prop. dam. ab Alex. VIII.*, n. 15 and 17, Dec. 7, 1690 (*ib.*, n. 1172 f).

20 S. O., May 9, 1821 (*Coll. P. F.*, n. 757).

21 *Prop. dam.*, n. 60–64, March 2, 1679 (Denzinger, nn. 1077 ff).

22 S. C. P. F., April 13, 1807, n. XXI (*Coll.*, n. 692).

23 Benedict XIV, "*Etsi minime*," Feb. 7, 1742, § 12.

As to Greeks who come to Latin priests for confession,—
the case was reported from Constantinople,[24] — it has
been decided that they must be asked not only whether
they believe what the Greek Fathers believed, but also
whether they maintain the faith of " old "[25] Rome, *i.e.*,
the Roman Pontiff.

As to *apostates* from the faith, they should not indiscriminately be refused absolution, but be absolved if they
show signs of sincere repentance. They must indeed
abjure their apostasy in the presence of the faithful to
whom they have given scandal, but it is not necessary that
they do so before infidels. They must, however, abstain
from every act and sign of infidelity or paganism, so that
the infidels gradually learn of the mental and moral
change that has come over the former apostate.[26]

With regard to *Freemasons* and kindred secret societies there are two decisions which concern the *Fenians*
of Ireland and of the U. S. These were declared to
belong to sects condemned by the Apostolic Constitutions
and their members cannot be absolved unless " they absolutely and positively abandon the society," otherwise
absolution is invalid.[27] In general the Holy Office [28] has
condemned all *societies* which plot against the ecclesiastical or civil government, no matter whether their members are bound by an oath of secrecy or not. Here
again the question about the *Knights Templars, Odd
Fellows, Sons of Temperance,* and *Knights of Pythias*
recurs, and we must repeat what we have said in our
Vol. III, namely, that these organizations are forbidden

24 S. C. P. F., Feb. 4, 1664, ad 2
(*Coll.*, n. 156).

25 The term is a counter-statement
of can. 3, Constant. I, and can.
28, Chalced.

26 S. C. P. F., 1629, Dec. 28,
1770 (*Coll.*, n. 481).

27 S. O., June 27, 1838; Jan. 12,
1870 (*Coll. P. F.*, nn. 868, 1350).

28 S. O., Aug. 5, 1840 (*ibid.*, n.
1350, note).

by the Church, but to exclude their members from absolution would be going too far,[29] since the Church has not pronounced them to be under censure. Here it may be well to report a reply given by the Holy Office to a Canadian bishop, who had asked whether or not Catholics who give their name to secret societies merely to avoid material loss, intending to remain good Catholics, could be absolved. The answer was that they may be admitted to the Sacraments, after previous absolution from censures, if necessary, provided that, (1) they separate themselves from the society; (2) they promise not to take any active part in the meetings or celebrations and not to pay the fees; (3) that they remove all occasion of scandal; (4) that they are ready to have their names cancelled from the list as soon as they can do so without serious loss.[30]

These then are the cases which refer more especially to the public discipline of the Church. As to the rules for the postponement of absolution and the treatment of *occasionarii* and *recidivi*, the reader must be referred to Moral and Pastoral Theology.[31]

WHOLESOME PENANCES

CAN. 887.

Pro qualitate et numero peccatorum et conditione poenitentis salutares et convenientes satisfactiones confessarius iniungat; quas poenitens volenti animo excipere atque ipse per se debet implere.

According to the quality and number of the sins com-

---

[29] Thus Schieler-Heuser, *Theory and Practice of the Confessional*, 1905, p. 335, note 126.

[30] S. O., March 7, 1883 (*Coll. P. F.*, n. 1593).

[31] Cfr. the Instruction of the S. C. P. F., of Oct. 3, 1736 (*Coll.*, n. 321); and Schieler-Heuser, *l. c.*, p. 407 ff.

mitted, and the condition of the penitent, the confessor should impose wholesome and proportionate penances, which the penitent must willingly accept and perform in person.

As the priest is under grave obligation to impose a penance or to demand satisfaction, the penitent is under the same obligation to accept and perform the penance personally, not by a substitute.[32] This obligation arises, not from the essence of Penance, but from the fact that satisfaction is an integral part of the Sacrament. For the significance or purpose of imposing a penance is not only to preserve the new life and to heal infirmity, but also to punish and destroy past sin.[33] From this it is evident why the penance is to be performed personally and that it is a really sacramental satisfaction or atonement for sins.[34]

At the same time the Code states that these penances should be *proportionate* to the sins committed and to the condition of the penitent, a point which is amply explained by the moralists.[35]

THE CONFESSOR A JUDGE AND PHYSICIAN

CAN. 888.

§ 1. Meminerit sacerdos in audiendis confessionibus se iudicis pariter et medici personam sustinere ac divinae iustitiae simul et misericordiae ministrum a Deo constitutum esse ut honori divino et animarum saluti consulat.

[32] *Trid.*, sess. 14, c. 8, *de poenit.*
[33] *Ibid.* and *prop. damn.*, Sept. 24, 1665, n. 15 (Denzinger, n. 986).
[34] *Prop. damn.* in the "*Auctorem fidei*," Aug. 28, 1794, n. 35 (Denzinger, n. 1328).

[35] Cfr. Sabetti-Barrett, *Theol. Moral*, 1916, p. 688 f.; Schieler-Heuser, *l. c.*, p. 256 ff.; and the Instructions of the S. C. P. F. of Oct. 3, 1736, and April 29, 1784 (*Coll.*, nn. 321, 569).

§ 2. Caveat omnino ne complicis nomen inquirat, ne curiosis aut inutilibus quaestionibus, maxime circa sextum Decalogi praeceptum, quemquam detineat, et praesertim ne iuniores de iis quae ignorant imprudenter interroget.

The confessor shall remember that he is a judge and physician appointed by God to administer divine justice as well as mercy, in order to provide for God's honor and the welfare of souls.

He shall be careful never to ask the name of an accomplice, nor to detain the penitent with inquisitive and useless questions, especially concerning the sixth commandment, and above all he shall not imprudently ask young people about things they are ignorant of.

Benedict XIV issued three Constitutions [86] to eradicate an evil which had taken root in Portugal, namely, the practice of some confessors to ask for the name of the accomplice and to refuse absolution if the penitent refused to reveal it. The Pontiff forbade this abuse under pain of suspension from the faculty of hearing confessions and other still severer penalties. Those who defended the proposition condemned by the Holy See were subject to excommunication *latae sententiae Romano Pontifici simpliciter reservatae.*[87] Though this penalty does not appear in our Code the grievous obligation and liability to punishment remain. It is not permitted to ask the name or residence of an accomplice, or to inquire into any circumstances that might indirectly lead to the manifestation of his or her name.[88]

---

[86] "*Suprema,*" July 7, 1745; "*Ubi primum,*" June 2, 1746; "*Ad eradicandum,*" Sept. 28, 1746.

[87] Pius IX, "*Apostolicae Sedis,*" Oct. 2, 1869, § II, 1.

[88] Cfr. c. 1, Dist. 6, de Poenit. (St. Aug.): c. 12, X, V, 38; Benedict XIV, "*Apostolica Constitutio,*" June 26, 1749, §§ 19, 20; *De Syn. Dioec.,* XI, 2, 18.

That the confessor should act as *judge and physician* is evident from the purpose of confession, which is not only to render a verdict, but also to apply the necessary means against the wounds inflicted by sin and against relapse.[39] Of course, the confessional should not be made a pulpit: the practice of preaching in it might deter people from going to confession.

THE SEAL OF THE CONFESSIONAL

Can. 889.

§ 1. **Sacramentale sigillum inviolabile est; quare caveat diligenter confessarius ne verbo aut signo aut alio quovis modo et quavis de causa prodat aliquatenus peccatorem.**

§ 2. **Obligatione servandi sacramentale sigillum tenentur quoque interpres aliique omnes ad quos notitia confessionis quoquo modo pervenerit.**

§ 1. The sacramental seal is inviolable, and hence the confessor shall be most careful not to betray the penitent by any word or sign or in any other way for any reason whatsoever.

§ 2. The obligation of keeping the sacramental seal binds also interpreters and all other persons who may in any way have acquired knowledge of confession.

As long as public confession, at least for public and heinous crimes, and consequently public penance were in vogue, the sacramental seal naturally was not often mentioned. But when, after the incident at Constantinople,[40] auricular confession became more frequent, nay common, the clergy had to be advised and enjoined to take

---

89 Cfr. Schieler-Heuser, *Theory and Practice*, pp. 435 ff.

40 Cfr. Pohle-Preuss, *The Sacraments*, III, p. 203 f.

heed lest they revealed anything that had been confessed in secret. St. Augustine demands of the priest that he, like a wise and perfect physician, first heal his own sores and then cure the wounds of others, and not make them known.[41] Leo the Great indicates the reason why auricular confession and the subsequent secrecy were commendable when he says men are more readily induced to confess their sins if their conscience is kept from the ears of the people.[42] A very remarkable text is that of the Decretals which says that what the priest knows from confession, he knows not as a (public) judge, but as God.[43] Hence under no pretext can the confessor be forced to reveal the crimes confessed to him.[44]

The seal of the confessional rests on natural, divine, and ecclesiastical law. The *natural law* dictates that an entrusted secret should never be revealed; it is privileged knowledge which even the civil courts respect in publicly acknowledged persons for the welfare of the community. The *divine law* demands that what is connected with a divine institution, such as confession, should be kept from profane ears, or, as the text above quoted says, that the secrets of God should not be revealed unless He gives permission to do so. But it would be absurd to assert that Christ permits such a revelation, because He knew that confession was a grievous burden, which would become intolerable if it impaired the penitent's good name. The divine precept of confessing even secret sins also demands absolute secrecy.

The *ecclesiastical law* inflicts the severest punishments on the transgressors of this divine command, subjecting

---

41 C. 7. C. 3, q. 7; cfr. *Reg. S. Bened.*, c. 46.
42 C. 89, Dist. 1, *de Poenit.*
43 C. 2, X, I, 31.
44 C. 13, X, V, 31.

those who directly violate the seal of confession to that form of excommunication which is most especially reserved to the Apostolic See.[45]

The seal is violated *directly* if a sin confessed in the confessional and the name of the penitent is revealed; *indirectly*, if from the confessor's way of acting or speaking there is danger that the sin of the penitent be made known or that confession itself becomes hateful. It would be an indirect violation if the priest would ask questions in such a loud voice that the bystanders could understand them, or if he would use gesticulations known to bystanders as indicative of certain sins.

The custom of giving certificates (*schedula confessionis*) to those of the faithful who are admitted to Holy Communion has been deservedly rebuked.[46] However, it is permissible to give a certificate which testifies to the fact that the bearer has received both the Sacrament of Penance and Holy Communion. Another custom was also reproved by the S. Congregation. Some missionaries were accustomed to put exactly as many particles on the *patena* as there had been persons absolved and admitted to Holy Communion. This they could not do except by using sacramental knowledge, and the practice was therefore rebuked as an abuse.[47]

From all that has been said it appears how careful the Church is in guarding the sacramental secret. No power on earth can compel the confessor to reveal anything he has heard in the confessional.

§ 2 obliges by virtue, not of the divine, but of the natural and ecclesiastical law, which latter threatens severe punishment against transgressors, *i.e.*, such as obtain and

---

45 Can. 2369.
46 S. C. P. F., Jan. 14, 1906 (*Coll.*, n. 683).
47 S. C. P. F., Feb. 29, 1836 (*Coll.*, n. 846).

make use of the *knowledge obtained in confession*. Thus, if a confessor directly or indirectly reveals anything out of confession, the hearers are bound to keep such knowledge to themselves. *Interpreters* are strictly bound to silence; bystanders who may perchance hear something said in confession are likewise obliged to secrecy.[48] Theologians and consultors are bound by the present law unless the one seeking advice frees them from this obligation. One who finds a list of sins drawn up for confession, is bound to keep it secret.[49] As to superiors, the following canon regulates their obligations.

USE OF KNOWLEDGE GAINED THROUGH CONFESSION FORBIDDEN

CAN. 890

§ 1. Omnino prohibitus est confessario usus scientiae ex confessione acquisitae cum gravamine poenitentis, excluso etiam quovis revelationis periculo.

§ 2. Tam Superiores pro tempore exsistentes, quam confessarii qui postea Superiores fuerint renuntiati, notitia quam de peccatis in confessione habuerint, ad exteriorem gubernationem nullo modo uti possunt.

§ 1. The confessor is strictly forbidden to make use of the knowledge gained from confession, if this use involves injury (*gravamen*) to the penitent, even though the seal of confession were not endangered.

Sacramental knowledge is, as it were, divine knowledge, and therefore must be kept as a divine secret. Hence, though a confessor knows one to be guilty of a crime, he is not allowed to rebuke him publicly or to excommunicate him, even if he is accused by others and apparently no

---

[48] S. C. P. F., Sept. 6, 1630 (*Coll.*, n. 61).

[49] Cfr. Noldin, *l. c.*, n. 425; Schieler-Heuser, *l. c.*, p. 466 ff.

violation of the seal would follow.[50] The sole reason
here given why the use of confessional knowledge is absolutely interdicted, is the damage or trouble (*gravamen*)
that may accrue to the penitent.[51] *Gravamen*, literally,
means heaviness; metaphorically trouble or complaint,
either in the spiritual or the material life.[52] Therefore
incautious remarks or personal references or intimations
must be avoided. Defamatory remarks about individuals or communities which are the result of hearing
confessions must be avoided. Even in his sermons the
priest must beware of describing details which might
point to a particular family or individual. All these are
gravamina, which cause aversion to confession.

How serious this obligation is may be illustrated by
the following case proposed by moralists.[53] If the confessor knows from confession that his life is at stake, he
may indeed make his escape if he can do so without endangering the seal of confession or damaging the penitent; but if he cannot escape without violating the seal or
causing a *gravamen* to the penitent, the confessor must
face his fate.

§ 2. *Superiors* who are actually such at the time, as
well as *confessors who afterwards become superiors*, are
not allowed to make use of confessional knowledge for
the *external government* of their subjects. This law was
given by Clement VIII, 1593, and ratified by Urban VIII,
from whom our text is almost verbally taken.[54]

Note that our canon speaks of *superiors generally*,
though the decree of Clement VIII was intended chiefly

---

[50] C. 2, X, I. 31.
[51] *Prop. damn. a S. O.*, Nov. 18,
1682 (Denzinger. n. 1087).
[52] S. C. P. F., Feb. 29. 1836
(*Coll.*, n. 846). The moralists are
rather reticent about the nature of
the *gravamen*.
[53] Cfr. Schieler-Heuser, *l. c.*, p.
482; Noldin, *l. c.*. n. 431.
[54] Cfr. Bizzarri, *Collectanea*, pp.
246 f.

for religious superiors. The Code therefore includes *all* superiors, whether they are already in office or to be afterwards elected. Hence bishops, religious superiors, directors of seminaries and colleges, vicars general, and also those who are employed by the Roman Congregations are included.

It is the use of *sacramental knowledge* that is forbidden. Thus a superior, whose knowledge is based solely on confession, cannot make use of it for purposes of *external government;* for instance, he cannot remove a minor official from office; he cannot remove a pastor who accused himself of a sin which would render him unfit for continuing as pastor; he cannot forbid him the sacraments, if publicly approached, even at the risk of sacrilege; he is not allowed to treat him unkindly or to withdraw from him his confidence or a post of trust; he may not change a previous arrangement after hearing confession, even though this arrangement had not yet been made public.

If a superior has reliable knowledge obtained outside the confessional, he may, of course, make use of it, provided that this extra-sacramental knowledge is the motive of his action.[55] If this were not the case, the superior could not, for instance, remove a priest from the office of confessor for occult crimes known to him outside of confession.[56]

[55] Thus the moralists in general.
[56] S. C. EE. *et* RR., July 2, 1627 (Bizzarri, *l. c.*, p. 24).

NOVICE-MASTERS AND DIRECTORS NOT TO HEAR CONFESSIONS

CAN 891

Magister novitiorum eiusque socius, Superior Seminarii collegiive sacramentales confessiones suorum alumnorum secum in eadem domo commorantium ne audiant, nisi alumni ex gravi et urgenti causa in casibus particularibus sponte id petant.

A logical consequence of § 2, can. 890 is that, as far as possible, every danger of using sacramental knowledge should be removed. A radical means is to forbid those directly concerned with disciplinary government to hear confessions. These are *masters of novices* and their *socii*, as well as the superiors or directors of *seminaries* and *colleges*. These, says can. 891, *should not hear the confessions of their subjects who live together with them in the same house,* unless the subjects themselves, for a grave and urgent reason, and in particular cases, ask them to hear their confessions. This demand must come freely and *spontaneously* and not be effected by insinuation or advice or threats or coaxing.

This enactment was first made for the superiors of the seminaries and colleges of Rome. It contained the phrase: " *excepto aliquo raro necessitatis, de quo eius conscientia oneratur."* This may explain the wording of our text: " in particular cases of urgent and grave necessity." [57] Thus the above mentioned superiors — novice masters are really the superiors of the novices — [58] are not allowed habitually to hear the confessions of their subjects, and the latter are not allowed to ask for it regularly.

[57] S. O., July 5, 1899 (*Coll. P. F.,* n. 2057).

[58] S. O., Dec. 20, 1899 (*Anal. Eccl.,* Vol. 8, 55).

The Holy Office, after (Aug. 23, 1899) extending the decree of July 5, 1899, to religious *congregations*,[59] declared officially (Dec. 20, 1899) that the religious *orders* might continue to be governed by the decree of Clement VIII, which ordained that the novices must confess to their novice-master, whereas the religious congregations were to obey the decree of July 5 and Aug. 23, 1899, which forbade that practice. The Code draws no distinction between orders and congregations, and consequently all religious communities must now abide by the law which forbids the novice-master to be the habitual confessor of the novices who live in the same house with him or his *socius*. A travelling novice stopping for a short time at a religious house, may choose the novice-master of that house for his confessor. A religious superior may be confessor of the students who live in the college if the latter is separated from his own dwelling place. But if the superior is at the same time the director of the seminary or college, can. 891 applies to him, even though he has his living-room in the convent, for as director he is supposed to live habitually with the students.

THE DUTY OF HEARING CONFESSIONS

CAN. 892

§ 1. Parochi aliique quibus cura animarum vi muneris est demandata, gravi iustitiae obligatione tenentur audiendi sive per se sive per alium confessiones fidelium sibi commissorum, quoties ii audiri rationabiliter petant.

§ 2. Urgente necessitate, omnes confessarii obliga-

---

[59] *Anal. Eccl.*, Vol. VII, 329.

tione tenentur ex caritate confessiones fidelium audiendi, et in mortis periculo omnes sacerdotes.

§ 1. Pastors and others entrusted with the care of
souls, by virtue of their office are strictly obliged in
justice to hear the confessions of the faithful committed
to their care as often as the latter reasonably demand to
be heard. This obligation, which is personal, may be
complied with through a substitute.

Here the legislator enjoins *pastors* in particular to perform the office of confessor, albeit not only pastors in the
strict sense of the word, but also quasi-pastors, and all to
whom the care of souls is entrusted (assistants, curates,
etc.), are bound by a strict and *grievous obligation* to hear
confessions. For their office has been given them for this
purpose, since all the faithful are obliged to confess their
sins at least once a year during the paschal time. There
is then a real obligation resting upon these priests to perform what charity, religion and their official character demand of them. And in performing this duty no discrimination is to be made between persons agreeable and
disagreeable or with reference to social, financial, or moral
conditions.[60]

The text says: " if *reasonably* demanded." The parish
priest, like everybody else, is entitled to reasonable treatment. Thus to keep order it is reasonable to set apart
certain hours for confession, provided, of course, they are
chosen with due regard to the circumstances of persons
and places. It is also reasonable to choose a heated
chapel, or even the school, if it has a confessional, for
hearing confessions in winter. Needless to add, a zeal-
ous pastor will never refuse to hear confessions even out-

[60] Clement XII, " *Compertum*," Aug. 24, 1734, §§ X, XII; Bene-dict XIV, " *Omnium sollicitudi-num*," Sept. 12, 1744, §§ 26, 33.

side the hours set by him in case of individual demand or necessity.[61] An orderly congregation and an orderly pastor will keep regular hours, and a reasonable·rule will preserve him from annoyance. The text further says: "*sive per se sive per alium.*" A pastor's obligation of hearing the confessions of his people is personal because attached to his office, which is generally bestowed for personal qualities (*intuitu personae*). Hence it is the pastor's duty to hear confessions unless he is lawfully prevented. For a legitimate reason, such as hard hearing, or pastoral business, or sickness, or a legitimate vacation, the pastor may send his assistants to fill his place. These *assistants*, too, are obliged, by virtue of the care of souls entrusted to them, to hear confessions, and their obligation also is grievous, unless they be employed solely for saying Mass, or the diocesan statutes, or their letters of appointment exempt them from the obligation of hearing confessions. In the latter case the assistant could not be forced by the pastor to hear confessions. Neither may beneficiaries, who are not obliged either by the rules of the foundation or by their benefice, be compelled to discharge the office of confessor.

The legislator has foreseen a case which may occur, and in § 2 adds a new regulation: "*In urgent cases all confessors* and in case of danger of death, *all priests*, are obliged *in charity* to hear confessions." An urgent case is one in which no time is to be lost, for instance, in epidemics, war, and also, perhaps, when there is a great *concursus populi* that could not have been foreseen, or if those bound in justice to hear confessions are suddenly and lawfully prevented. In such cases the duty of hear-

---

61 Of course, we do not mean that a pastor is obliged to hear every scrupulous person or *devotula* at any time. Pastors are obliged to hear confessions in case of contagious diseases; Benedict XIV, *De Syn. Dioec.*, XIII, 19, 6 f.

ing confessions obliges *omnes confessarii, i.e.,* all priests who possess the necessary jurisdiction. License may be presumed. As to religious, consult can. 608. Where there is *danger of death,* charity compels *all priests* to offer their services.

Exempt religious, at *home,* or in their regular residence, have to go to confession to the appointed confessors, with due regard to can. 519. When *travelling,* they formerly had to confess to their *socius,* provided they had one and he was *idoneus.* If they had no companion, or the *socius* was not *idoneus,* they could confess to any other priest, either secular or religious, even though the latter had no *approbatio Ordinarii,*[61a] *i.e.,* no jurisdiction in the sense of the Code. Can this practice be continued? The answer, we believe, should be as follows, *salvo meliore iudicio.* If this common doctrine is based *on law,* and not on mere privileges, the practice cannot be continued, because it is manifestly against the Code, which requires express jurisdiction in any case. If, however, the practice is based on *privileges,* it may be continued, because the Code has not done away with all the privileges granted to regulars; see can. 613. As far as we could gather from authors, the practice was based upon privileges. Of course, we suppose this one, too, would have to be submitted to the inspection and approbation of the S. C. of Religious.

[61a] See Ballerini-Palmieri, *l. c.,* p. 328 n. 640; Noldin *l. c.,* n. 360.

CHAPTER II

THE RESERVATION OF SINS

CAN. 893.

§ 1. Qui ordinario iure possunt audiendi confessiones potestatem concedere aut ferre censuras, possunt quoque, excepto Vicario Capitulari et Vicario Generali sine mandato speciali, nonnullos casus ad suum avocare iudicium, inferioribus absolvendi potestatem limitantes.

§ 2. Haec avocatio dicitur *reservatio* casuum.

§ 3. Quod attinet ad reservationem censurarum, servetur praescriptum can. 2246, 2247.

Those who possess ordinary power for granting faculties to hear confession or to inflict censures, are also empowered to call certain cases before their tribunal, thus restricting the power of absolving vested in their inferiors. However, vicars capitular and vicars general may not use this power of restricting without a special mandate. This *avocatio* or restriction of cases is called *reservation*. Concerning the reservation of censures, see can. 2246, 2247.

It is not a mere coincidence that reservation of certain, especially public and heinous, sins was not generally applied before the twelfth century, when the penitential discipline, which, according to our views, was rather severe from the seventh to the eleventh century, began to be systematized and organized. Public penance was of long duration and austere in character, especially for apostasy, homicide, and *moechia*. A special kind of penalty consisted in protracted pilgrimages to some well-known shrine.[62] Among these the tombs of SS. Peter and Paul in Rome were most frequently chosen. There was a reason for this choice. It not infrequently happened that the bishops, who at that time administered the public discipline of penance, were in doubt as to what kind of penance to impose for a specific crime which was not mentioned in the penitential books and imposed a pilgrimage to Rome with the express command that the penitent present himself before the Pope, in order to await his verdict. The Pope either sent the penitent back to his bishop to receive absolution after the penance imposed had been complied with, or reserved the penance and absolution to himself. This was the original *avocatio criminum graviorum* or *causarum maiorum*, of the existence of which there are testimonies in the early centuries. Thus St. Cyprian asked the " Apostolic Lord " what to do with the apostates of the persecution; Himerius of Tarragona and Exuperius of Toulouse wished to know of Innocent I how they should proceed against clerics who had violated the law of celibacy. Even Cerdo and the two other Gnostics who were excommunicated by their bishops sought absolution from the Roman Pontiff. Leo I and Gelasius I state it as a practice — which was acknowledged by the synod of Sardica, A. D. 341 — that the Apostolic See took cognizance of the "*maiora peccata*." Gregory I did so in the case of Hadrian, bishop of Thebes.[63] And if we go still further back, we find that

62 Wasserschleben, *Bussordnungen der Abendländ. Kirche,* p. 104; "*Qui moechator matris est, III annis poeniteat cum peregrinatione perenni.*" See also pp. 113. 186, 259, 265, 310. Hausmann, *Geschichte der päpstl. Reservatfälle,* 1868, pp. 35 ff. The practice commenced in Ireland and England.

63 Cfr. c. 17, C. 9, q. 3; c. 52, C. 16, q. 1.

the leniency of Pope Zephyrin (201–217) provoked the sarcasm and anger of Tertullian,[64] because it ran counter to the rigoristic tendency of a powerful party that had representatives even in Rome.

All this clearly shows that the Roman Pontiffs were conscious of their spiritual power. Excommunications inflicted *post factum* formed the first layer of reserved cases. From here it was but one step to the infliction of such penalties after the crime was committed and the determination of the penalty and the reservation of absolution for such who would commit such crimes. Here we have the origin of the distinction between a *censura lata a lege* and a *censura lata ab homine*. The crime furnished the guage for determining the penalty. If punished *ad libitum* by either pope or bishop after it had been committed, it was known as a penalty inflicted by the judge (*ab homine*); but if the judge merely applied a penalty already determined by law, it was a *censura* (generally) *a lege*.[65]

To return to the Middle Ages, we said that pilgrimages were frequently imposed as means of atonement for grievous crimes, and that they were most commonly made to Rome, the See of the Vicar of Christ. Such pilgrimages were at that time, *i.e.*, in the 10th and 11th centuries, considered the most efficacious and often the only means of bringing criminals, especially homicides, who then were rampant, to their senses. Disorder and lack of respect for authority grew to such an extent that in England, northeastern France, Germany, and Italy, crimes against the fifth and seventh commandments were frequently committed even against the lower and higher clergy. To counteract this lawlessness, many synods were held in the countries named, and the Second Lateran Council, in

---

[64] *De Pudicitia*, c. 5.   [65] Hausmann, *l. c.*, p. 22.

1139, summed up their enactments in the well-known decree which constitutes the *privilegium canonis*.[66] This is the first case of a reservation established by general law.[67] From the twelfth to the fourteenth century papal reserved cases were as yet few, but their number grew considerably after heresies became more wide-spread. A tentatively fixed number first appears in the so-called "*Bulla Coenae*" or "*Bulla in Coena Domini*," of which the written original dates from 1364, under Urban V. It mentions seven cases reserved to the Apostolic See. No adequate distinction between episcopal and papal cases can be discerned during this period. One rule indeed was strictly inculcated, *viz.*, that a simple priest, even if he were a pastor, could not impose penance for grievous sins, but had to refer all such cases to the bishop or, in more serious instances, to the Pope. After the "Babylonian Captivity" the catalogue contained in the "*Bulla Coenae*" was enlarged, first under Julius II (1503–1513), then under Paul III (1536), until Urban VIII, in 1627, put the final touches to it. It now contained twenty cases, and no change has been made in this solemn document since.[68]

Modern times required a different treatment, and this was applied by *Pius IX* in his Constitution "*Apostolicae Sedis*," of Oct. 12, 1869, which introduced the new penal code containing reserved censures. This, too, is now superseded by the Code. *Ad quid perditio haec?* one may ask. We will answer this question; for unless we touched upon it, at least briefly, the reservation of cases could not

[66] Can. 15; c. 29, C. 17, q. 4; see this Commentary, Vol. II, p. 58 f.

[67] Hausmann, *l. c.*, p. 66 ff.

[68] *Ibid.*, p. 88 ff. The Bull was called "*in Coena Domini*," because the list of grievous crimes was read on Maundy Thursday and those guilty of these sins were declared unworthy to receive Holy Communion.

be understood. Although the cases reserved to the Roman Pontiff in the first seven or eight centuries appear to have belonged to the external judiciary or executive power, yet the juridical basis for the court of conscience was not only acknowledged, but included, in the plenitude of the primacy. The very fact that cognizance could or should be taken of the criminal *causae maiores*[69] by the Supreme Pontiff pre-supposed that the right or power of absolving was believed to be vested in him. Besides, excommunication required a judiciary sentence, which, though mainly concerned with the external government of the Church, implied absolution in the true sense of the word, *i.e.*, for the court of conscience. And in the *forum internum*, too, there is a reservation of sins, properly so-called. That the two *fora*, like the two powers, papal and episcopal, were not always clearly distinguished, is easily understood.

After these preliminary remarks the text of our canon requires only a few observations.

1. The *persons who are vested with the power of reserving cases* are those who, *iure ordinario*, are entitled to grant the power of hearing confession or inflicting censures. These words emphasize an enactment of the Council of Trent,[70] which, after stating that it is conducive to morality that certain heinous sins should not be absolvable by every priest, but only by those of the highest authority, i.e., the Pope and the bishops, declares: " If any one saith that bishops have not the right of reserving cases to themselves, except as regards external polity, and therefore the reservation of cases does not hinder a priest from truly absolving from reserved cases, let him be anathema."[71] The right of the Pope and the bishops

69 Cfr. c. 52, C. 16, q. 1.   71 *Ibid.*, can. 11.
70 Sess. 14, c. 7, *de poenit.*

to reserve cases to themselves is based upon the judicial character of the Sacrament of Penance.[72] But this reason does not explain why simple priests, even though they be pastors,[73] cannot exercise this right. Therefore another element must be added: the jurisdiction of the primacy contains the plenitude of power, and the jurisdiction of the bishops, even though given immediately by God, depends on the will of the Sovereign Pontiff, who therefore may communicate it as and when he wills.[74] This is required by the unity of church government and the hierarchic order. Now the grant of faculties is part and parcel of that external forum which is ruled by those in power, and from this simple priests are excluded. By that we do not mean that reservation belongs solely to the external polity. For as the power of forgiving and retaining sins is an outgrowth of jurisdiction, so too, is reservation.

A third element is the need of determining which sins are heinous and extraordinarily grievous. This power certainly belongs to him who is the supreme judge in matters of faith and morals i.e., to the *magisterium ecclesiasticum*, from which simple priests, as such, are excluded.

Hence the power of reserving cases must be vindicated:

(1) to the *Pope*, because of the plenitude of his power over the whole Church and every part of it;

(2) to the *bishops*, each for his respective territory. As this prerogative belongs to them as Ordinaries, it might also be claimed by the *vicar-general*, were it not that positive law makes the valid and licit exercise of this power dependent upon the *special mandate* of the bishop.

Concerning the *vicar capitular* or administrator, our

---

[72] Cfr. Pohle-Preuss, *The Sacraments*, Vol. III, p. 129.

[73] Errors of those suspected of the heresy of Wiclif and Hus, n. 25 (Denzinger, n. 529).

[74] Palmieri, *De Poenitentia*, p. 179.

text says that he, too, needs a special mandate to exercise the power of reserving cases. But from whom? From the Apostolic See. At least this seems to be the most reasonable answer, as the chapter could not possibly grant that power. Benedict XIV says that though the power of granting indulgences flows from jurisdiction and not from the order, yet it is an extraordinary power attached to the episcopal dignity.[75] The same reasoning may be applied here by analogy, which in this instance is perfectly legitimate.

(3) Although this is true concerning vicars, it has been decided, and is expressly stated in can. 896, that *exempt religious superiors* enjoy the power of reserving cases among their own subjects. These superiors possess quasi-episcopal jurisdiction;[76] no other superiors are mentioned, nor may this power be extended to others, as the text says: " those who, *iure ordinario*, are entitled to grant faculties."

Febronius and his followers pretended that the right of reserving cases had *devolved* from the bishops to the Pope, and was based on mere custom, which might change with times and circumstances, and even be reasonably abolished.[77] However, this is not only perverting history, but is dogmatically wrong. The Pope's right of reserving cases existed before that of the bishops, who would surely not have applied for faculties to the Apostolic See had they not acknowledged a higher power in St. Peter. Of course, we do not mean to deny that the practice of reservation developed according to the exigencies of the times.

[75] *De Syn. Dioec.*, II, 9, 7; cfr. c. 12, X, V, 31.

[76] Clement VIII, " *Sanctissimus*," May 26, 1593; S. C. EE. *et* RR., Sept. 21, 1624 (Bizzarri, *Collec-*

tanea, p. 246); S. C. C., June 1584; April 1587 (Richter, *Trid.*, p. 85, n. 1); Benedict XIV, *De Syn. Dioec.*, V, 4, 2.

[77] *Prop. Synodi Pistorien. dam.*

ONLY ONE SIN PROPERLY RESERVED TO THE HOLY SEE

CAN. 894.

Unicum peccatum ratione sui reservatum Sanctae Sedi est falsa delatio, qua sacerdos innocens accusatur de crimine sollicitationis apud iudices ecclesiasticos.

Only one sin is, as such, reserved to the Holy See, to wit, falsely *accusing an innocent priest of the crime of solicitation* before the ecclesiastical court.

Solicitation here is understood as an external and grievously culpable provocation to a sin against the sixth commandment, perpetrated in the confessional, or in the act of confession, even though the confessor has no jurisdiction or does not impart absolution, and even though the provocation may not be effective. Solicitation may be made to a person of either sex.[78] If a person *not solicited* would thus accuse an *innocent priest* of solicitation in the ecclesiastical court, his crime would be reserved to the Holy See, even though no censure were attached to it.[79] Neither ignorance nor doubt as to the law of reservation or the fact of the grievousness of the sin of false accusation, excuses from this reservation, which is also incurred if the accusation to the ecclesiastical court is made by an intermediary.[80]

The *ecclesiastical court* is the Ordinary of the diocese or the Inquisitors, where these still perform their functions.[81] The accusation may also be made to the diocesan chancellor or to the rural dean, or, in the case of an assist-

in the "*Auctorem fidei*," Aug. 28, 1794, n. 47 f. (Denzinger, n. 1407 f).

[78] S. O., Feb. 11, 1661. It is not solicitation if a priest abuses knowledge gained in the confessional for soliciting a person afterwards; Lehmkuhl, II, n. 975 f.

[79] But there *is* a censure attached to it; see can. 2363.

[80] Benedict XIV, "*Sacramentum Poenitentiae*," June 1, 1741, § 3.

[81] *Ibid.* § 1.

ant, to the pastor; but if it is made orally to one of these, it should be put into writing and immediately forwarded to the Ordinary.[82] After accusation has been made in this formal way, the sin is committed and reserved.

Note that the accusation must concern a *priest*. Consequently, to accuse a cleric who heard confessions either in jest, or by mistake, or for the sake of practice, would not be a reserved case. It would be a reserved case, however, to falsely accuse a priest, even though he had no faculties for hearing confession. The intention of calumniating the priest need not be foremost in the accuser's mind,[83] but may be merely concomitant.

This law binds *all Catholics* and concerns all Catholic priests of whatever rite.[84]

This crime is *specially reserved to the Holy See*, and is never included in the faculties granted for absolving cases reserved to the Apostolic See.[85] Hence, to obtain absolution from this sin, even if the censure was not incurred or has been removed, application must be made to the S. Poenitentiaria, either personally or through the confessor. Fictitious names should be used in the petition.

RESERVATION TO BE MADE AT THE SYNOD

CAN. 895

Locorum Ordinarii peccata ne reservent, nisi, re in Synodo dioecesana discussa, vel extra Synodum auditis Capitulo cathedrali et aliquot ex prudentioribus ac probatioribus suae dioecesis animarum curatoribus,

82 Can. 1936.

83 Noldin, *l. c.*, n. 393, seems to over-emphasize the fact of calumny.

84 Benedict XIV, "*Etsi pastoralis*," May 26, 1742, § IX, n. V;

S. O., June 13, 1710; S. C. P. F., Aug. 6 1885, n. 2 (*Coll.*, nn. 279, 1640).

85 S. O., June 27, 1866 (*Coll. P. F.*, n. 1294).

vera reservationis necessitas aut utilitas comprobata fuerit.

Local Ordinaries should not reserve sins, unless the matter has been discussed at a diocesan synod, or consultation with the Cathedral Chapter and some of the more prudent and experienced directors of souls, has made evident the necessity or utility of a reservation.

Benedict XIV explains the reasons why reservations should be made at the *diocesan synod.* First, he says,[86] because a synod offers the best opportunity for discussion, since as a rule many worthy and experienced priests are present on that occasion. Secondly, in order that the pastors who enjoy jurisdiction may have no reason to complain of an undue restriction of their power. For they are supposed to be present at the synod and therefore have a chance to object or demand more solid reasons for an intended reservation. Lastly, because a reservation made at the synod is more in accord with a condition of stable and permanent law than one made by the bishop alone.

No doubt these reasons prompted the Holy Office to issue the decree of July 13, 1916, which furnished the text for our canon.[87] The best occasion, therefore, for establishing reserved cases is at a diocesan synod; but, as Benedict XIV adds, such a measure must be taken with great caution lest the sacramental seal be endangered.[88]

Another way of setting up such cases is after obtaining the *advice* (not consent) of the *cathedral chapter,* or, with us, of the diocesan *consultors.*[89] The bishop must call a meeting of these because the text says: *capitulum.* To this meeting he may also call other priests who have

86 *De Syn. Dioec.,* V, 4, 3.
87 *A. Ap. S.,* VII, 313.
88 *De Syn. Dioec.,* V, 4, 3.
89 Can. 427.

charge of souls. A decree of 1602 says that men distinguished by piety and learning should be called, in order to examine and discuss the matter thoroughly.[90] Our text reads: *animarum curatores,* a general term which is evidently used to exclude the idea that only pastors are to be invited. Assistants, confessors of religious, missionaries, etc., may be heard, provided they belong to the "more prudent and tried" class, and are or were actually engaged in the care of souls.

EXEMPT RELIGIOUS SUPERIORS

Can. 896

Inter Superiores religionis clericalis exemptae unus Superior generalis, et in monasteriis sui iuris Abbas, cum proprio cuiusque Consilio, peccata, ut supra, subditorum reservare possunt, firmo praescripto can. 518, § 1, 519.

Among the superiors of *exempt clerical institutes,* the superior general, and in autonomous monasteries the Abbot, with his counsellors, may reserve sins of their subjects, with due regard, however, to can. 518, § 1, and to can. 519.

Clement VIII and a decree of the S. C. of Bishops and Regulars had emphasized, not the power of exempt religious, for this follows from exemption itself, but the need of prudence and moderation in reserving cases, the number of which was reduced to eleven,[91] but is still more restricted by can. 897.

The superiors to whom can. 896 applies are those of

90 S. C. EE. *et* RR., Nov. 26, 1602 (Bizzarri, *Collectanea,* p. 13 f.).

91 Clement VIII, "*Sanctissimus,*"

May 26, 1593; S. C. EE. *et* RR., Sept. 21, 1624 (Bizzarri, *l. c.,* p. 246 f.).

exempt clerical orders or congregations. Superiors of exempt lay or of non-exempt clerical congregations do not enjoy the power of reserving cases. For the latter class the Ordinary may establish reservations, as also the Apostolic See when approving the Constitutions.

In centralized religious orders the *superior general* alone can reserve cases. In doing so, he must proceed like the bishop, *i.e.*, consult with his counsellors and, if he wishes, with others who are experienced in the direction of souls. It is true he is not bound by their advice, for the text of can. 895, to which our canon refers, does not require their consent. But it would be folly and a grievous transgression of a serious law in a serious matter not to obtain the advice of the counsellors.

The *abbot* of an *autonomous* monastery must proceed in the same manner. By the way it may be noted that neither the Abbot Primate of the Benedictine Order, nor the Abbot President of each congregation, has any power with regard to reserving cases. ·

Our canon, lastly, draws attention to can. 518, § 1, and can. 519. The former prescribes, in accordance with an enactment of Clement VIII, that a number of confessors shall be appointed in each house for absolving from reserved cases. Can. 519 grants to any priest approved by the Ordinary the right of absolving any religious from cases reserved by the religious superior.[92]

NUMBER AND QUALITY OF RESERVED CASES

CAN. 897

Casus reservandi sint pauci omnino, tres scilicet vel, ad summum, quatuor ex gravioribus tantum et atrocioribus criminibus externis specifice determinatis; ipsæ

92 Cfr. Vol. II, p. 152 ff. of this Commentary.

vero reservatio ne ultra in vigore maneat, quam necesse sit ad publicum aliquod inolitum vitium exstirpandum et collapsam forte christianam disciplinam instaurandam.

CAN. 898

Prorsus ab iis peccatis sibi reservandis omnes abstineant quae iam sint Sedi Apostolicae etiam ratione censurae reservata, et regulariter ab iis quoque quibus censura, etsi nemini reservata, a iure imposita sit.

The cases to be reserved shall be few, namely, three, or at most four, of the more grievous and atrocious external crimes, specifically determined. The reservation itself should not remain in force longer than is necessary to uproot some inveterate public crime and to restore Christian discipline.

But Ordinaries, and religious superiors as well, shall refrain from reserving sins already reserved to the Holy See by reason of the censures attached to them, and, as a rule, shall not reserve sins which the law has laid under censure, even though this censure be not reserved to any one in particular.

These two canons define the number and quality of the sins that may be reserved and the purpose of reservation, and declare which sins should not be made reserved cases.

1. The *number* is reduced to *four,* at the highest, beyond which neither Ordinaries nor exempt religious superiors may go. Rome had more than once on previous occasions declared that the number of reserved cases should be very small (*paucissimos*) and selected with great discrimination, lest reservation result in spiritual injury rather than benefit. It also enjoined that the con-

ditions of each province and the character of the people should be taken into consideration.[93]

2. The *quality* of the sins that may be reserved is described by four attributes: they must be particularly grievous, atrocious, external, and specified crimes. Although no definite rule can be formulated by which the *grievousness and hideousness* of a crime could be exactly determined, yet the habitual proclivity of a certain nation to a certain crime would be a sufficient reason for reserving that sin in order to break their obstinacy by making it difficult to obtain absolution.[94] Hence, as stated above, *local conditions* should be studied. No reservation should be attached to sins from which no absolution is given except under the condition of restitution, or to sins into which ordinary persons often fall. *"In peccatis etiam carnalibus reservandis multâ utantur circumspectione, propter periculum scandalorum in iis maxime personis, in quas ob accessum ad confessarios extraordinarios, vel frequentem reditum ad ordinarios, suspicionis aliquid cadere potest."* [95]

Broadly it may be stated that sins which are grievous by reason of their very nature or betray an atrocious character on account of the damage done to ecclesiastical discipline and the welfare of souls, may be reserved.

This is confirmed by the addition of the word *external*. For although, as some theologians say, internal sinful acts may in *summo iuris rigore* be reserved, yet it has never been Roman practice to reserve merely mental sins, for instance, internal heresy.[96] Note, however, that *external* is not the same as *notorious* or *public*. A sin may be

---

[93] S. C. EE. *et* RR., Jan. 6, 1601; Nov. 26, 1902 (Bizzarri, *l. c.*, p. 13 ff.).

[94] Benedict XIV, *De Syn. Dioec.* X, 5, 4.

[95] S. C. EE. *et* RR., Nov. 26, 1602 (Bizzarri, *l. c.*, p. 14).

[96] Benedict XIV, *l. c.*, V, 5, 5.

committed externally, yet be unknown to any one except the person who committed it. A *crime*, however, is always supposed to be external, for it is a *delictum publicum*, at least in the wider sense.

The Code requires that the crimes be *specified* or specifically determined. As sins are specified by their opposition to certain definite virtues or laws, and by the different objects comprised by the various virtues, so also should reservation be specific.[97] The quality and mode of a crime determine its specific nature and also the manner of reservation, whether or not under censure. Thus adultery, if it became rampant in a province, or diocese, or city, might become a matter for reservation; also incendiarism, burglary or bank-robbing.

The text says further that reservation should cease as soon as its purpose is attained. This is the case when an inveterate vice is extirpated and Christian discipline restored. Here the principle holds goods: Reservation, if uselessly protracted, might do more harm than good.

3. Canon 898 distinguishes between sins under censure reserved to the Holy See and sins under censure reserved to no one in particular. From reserving sins of the first kind, Ordinaries and religious superiors should *abstain entirely;* from reserving sins reserved under censure to no one they should refrain *as a rule.* This law rests on the *regula iuris* 54 in 6°: " *Qui prior est tempore, potior est iure,*" provided, of course, that all other things are equal.[98] As the common law is supposed to be prior to any particular law or jurisdiction, inferiors should cede power to the superior. But the cases reserved to no one suffer an exception, for the text says: as a rule (*regulariter*).

---

97 Marc, *Institut. Moral. Alphons.*, 1898, I, n. 324.

98 Reiffenstuel, *In Reg. Juris,* 54 in 60, n. 2.

" Frequency, scandal or another reason "[99] may advise reservation by the Ordinary besides the one imposed by common law, and in that case such a *double reservation* would be admissible.

It may be helpful to mention the cases which are reserved under censure.

I. Specialissimo modo reserved to the Apostolic See are:

1°. *Species consecratas desecrantes* (can. 2320);

2°. *Violentas manus iniicientes in Romanum Pontificem* (can. 2445);

3°. *Absolventes vel absolvere fingentes complicem* (can. 2367);

4°. *Directe violantes sigillum confessionis* (can. 2369).

II. Speciali modo reserved to the Apostolic See are:

1°. *Apostatae, haeretici, schismatici* (can. 2394);

2°. *Edentes, defendentes, legentes, retinentes, libros eorum, qui haeresim vel schisma propugnant* (can. 2318);

3°. *Laici celebrationem Missae vel confessionem simulantes* (can. 2322);

4°. *Violentas manus iniicientes in Cardinales, Legatos Ap. Sedis, vel Episcopos* (can. 2343);

5°. *Provocantes ad concilium generale* (can. 2332);

6°. *Recurrentes ad laicam potestatem ad litteras apostolicas impediendas vel acta quaelibet* (can. 2333);

7°. *Impedientes immunitatem ecclesiasticam* (can. 2334);

8°. *Violantes privilegium fori quoad praelatos superiores* (can. 2340);

9°. *Usurpantes vel detinentes bona ad Ecclesiam Romanam pertinentia* (can. 2345);

[99] S. C. EE. *et* RR., Nov. 26, 1602 (Bizzarri, *l. c.,* p. 14).

10°. *Falsarii litterarum apostolicarum* (can. 2360);

11°. *Falso denuntiantes sacerdotem innocentem de sollicitationis crimine* (can. 2363).

III. Simpliciter reserved to the Apostolic See are:

1°. *Quaestum facientes ex indulgentiis* (can. 2327);

2°. *Nomen dantes sectae massonicae etc.* (can. 2335);

3°. *Absolvere praesumentes ab excommunicatione Sedi Apostolicae specialissimo vel speciali modo reservata* (can. 2338, § I);

4°. *Impendentes auxilium vel favorem excommunicato vitando in delicto excommunicationis* (can. 2338, no. 2);

5°. *Violantes privilegium fori in praelatos episcopis inferiores* (can. 2341);

6°. *Clausuram papalem violantes et moniales exeuntes,* (can. 2342);

7°. *Duellum perpetrantes et cooperantes* (can. 2351);

8°. *Qui invalidum matrimonium attentant ex ordine clericorum vel religiosorum et personae cum ipsis contrahentes* (can. 2388).

IV. Nemini reservatae are the following excommunications:

1°. *Qui ausi fuerint mandare tradi sepulturae ecclesiasticae contra can. 1240 praescriptum* (can. 2339);

2°. *Alienantes absque beneplacito apostolico* (can. 2347);

5°. *Cogentes ad statum clericalem vel religiosum* (can. 2352).

V. Cases reserved to the Ordinary by law:

1°. Those mentioned under can. 2319 concerning marriage before a non-Catholic minister, etc.;

2°. *Conficientes falsas reliquias* (can. 2326);

3°. *Violentas manus iniicientes in clericos* (can. 2343, §
4);

4°. *Procurantes abortum, matre non exceptâ, effectu
secuto* (can. 2350);

5°. *Professi simpliciter matrimonium contrahentes et
personae contrahentes cum ipsis* (can. 2388);

6°. *Apostata religiosus, qui pertinet ad ordinem exemptum vel non exemptum, si pertinet ad religionem ex-
emptam, excommunicatio reservata est Superiori religioso
maiori (vel abbati monasterii sui iuris)* (can. 2385).

This conspectus shows who possesses the power of reserving and which cases should not be reserved, because
already reserved by law.   But those mentioned under IV
as *" nemini reservatae "* may, if frequency or scandal
should necessitate such a measure, be reserved also by the
Ordinary, as such.   The cases placed under that heading
are worthy of close inspection, especially at the time of
canonical visitation of religious institutes.

It may also be opportune to indicate some cases which
the Code does not expressly lay under censure, but in
regard to which it explicitly states that the Ordinary may
punish the transgressors " also by censure " (*etiam censura*).

1°. Those who trade in Mass stipends (can. 2324);

2°. Those who pertinaciously refuse to obey the legitimate injunctions of the Roman Pontiff or of the Ordinary (can. 2331);

3°. Those who have received legacies or bequests or
donations for pious or charitable purposes and refuse to
comply with the obligation of applying them to said purposes (can. 2348);

4°. Those who live in simultaneous bigamy (can. 2356).

In all these cases Ordinaries would act in conformity
with the Code if they reserved them to themselves, even

by previously promulgating the censure. Only one rule they should keep in view : the necessity or utility of reservation, and after the evil has been cured, they should remove the censure. A very opportune measure was taken by the bishops of Holland in their Lenten Pastoral for 1919. They forbade Catholics to join or remain in any socialist or anarchistic union or club, under penalty of refusal of absolution. The same penalty was threatened against those who regularly read anarchistic or socialist literature, or who professed subversive doctrines. This joint procedure was perfectly legitimate and may be justified on the basis of can. 2335.

If we may venture to suggest the cases which *exempt religious superiors* may eventually reserve, the following taken from the decree of Clement VIII, in a modified form, might be proposed :

1°. *Gravis transgressio voti paupertatis,* amounting to a sum which formerly was reserved to the S. Penitentiary, say, about $50.

2°. *Peccatum contra votum castitatis perpetratum cum religiosa femina, vel etiam repetita sodomia, vel concubinatus.*

3°. *Qui Romano Pontifici vel Superiori religioso aliquid legitime praecipienti vel prohibenti secundum regulam et constitutiones in materia gravi, e.g., missionis, scholae, officiorum, non obtemperant pertinaciter et cum scandalo aliorum sive extraneorum sive religiosorum.*

4°. *Falsificatio manus aut sigilli officialium monasterii aut conventus, aut litterarum vel actorum ecclesiasticorum tam publicorum quam privatorum.*

PROMULGATION AND ABSOLUTION OF RESERVED CASES

CAN. 899.

§ 1. Statutis semel reservationibus quas vere necessarias aut utiles iudicaverint, curent locorum Ordinarii ut ad subditorum notitiam, quo meliore eis videatur modo, eaedem deducantur, nec facultatem a reservatis absolvendi cuivis et passim impertiant.

§ 2. At huiusmodi absolvendi facultas ipso iure competit canonico poenitentiario ad normam can. 401, § 1, et habitualiter impertiatur saltem vicariis foraneis, addita, praesertim in locis dioecesis a sede episcopali remotioribus, facultate subdelegandi toties quoties confessarios sui districtus, si et quando pro urgentiore aliquo determinato casu ad eos recurrant.

§ 3. Ipso iure a casibus, quos quoquo modo sibi Ordinarii reservaverint, absolvere possunt tum parochi, aliive qui parochorum nomine in iure censentur, toto tempore ad praeceptum paschale adimplendum utili, tum singuli missionarii quo tempore missiones ad populum haberi contingat.

§ 1. Cases reserved for reasons of necessity or utility *should be brought to the knowledge of their subjects* by the Ordinaries, who should not grant indiscriminate faculties to absolve from them.

This rule was made by the Council of Trent [1] and insisted upon by the S. Congregation.[2] But a distinction must be made as to the manner in which the cases are reserved. If they are reserved at a diocesan synod, promulgation is supposed to be effected after the Ordinary has put his signature to the synodal acts, and no fur-

---

1 Sess. 14, c. 7, *de poenit.*
2 S. C. EE. *et* RR., Nov. 26, 1602 (Bizzarri, *l. c.*, p. 14).

ther publication is required, unless a clause to this effect appears in the synodal acts.[3] If the cases were reserved at a meeting of the consultors, they must be brought to the notice of the clergy[4] by an official circular letter, issued by the Ordinary or his chancellor.

The text furthermore says that *faculties for absolving from reserved cases should not be granted indiscriminately.* To do so would render reservation ludicrous and frustrate its purpose.

§ 2. The *Canonicus Poenitentiarius* has by law the faculty of absolving from the cases reserved to the bishop. This canon penitentiary may belong to a cathedral or to a collegiate church, both of whom enjoy the power of absolving by virtue of their office and of law, which is expressed in this canon as well as in can. 401, no. 1. Besides, the legislator wishes that the faculty of absolving from these reserved cases should be *habitually delegated* to the *rural deans*, who should also be given the power of *subdelegating toties quoties* confessors of their districts, especially in parishes distant from the episcopal see, whenever these confessors have recourse to the deans for individual and urgent cases.

Note well the difference between the faculties habitually given to the rural deans and the faculties given to confessors in distant parishes. The latter must be applied for in each single case, and can be granted only if the case is urgent. The application must be sent to the rural dean either in writing or orally; by telephone only if there is an absolute necessity and no violation of the sacramental seal need be feared. Any pastor or assistant, in fact, any confessor, may foresee the cases, and

---

3 See can. 362.

4 The clergy should, therefore, make these cases known to the people, for the term "*subditi*" comprises all the faithful.

hence apply for the faculty before going into the confessional. One thing is certain, *viz.*, that the faculty of absolving from cases reserved to the Ordinary should not be imparted habitually to all pastors, or curates, or assistants, but only in individual cases. Habitual faculties are to be given only to the rural deans.

The question may be asked: *Which are the reserved cases* from which the *Poenitentiarii* (by law) and the rural deans (in virtue of habitual faculties) may absolve? The answer is not as evident as one might wish, and it is therefore with some misgiving that we state our own view.

1°. It is certain that the cases are included which the Ordinary has reserved to himself, to wit, the three or four cases exclusive of the six mentioned in the preceeding canon under V.

2°. The *Canon Poenitentiarius* may absolve, not only from the three or four cases reserved by the Ordinary to himself, but also from the six cases mentioned under V. This we deduce from the wording of can. 401, § 1, where he is said to have jurisdiction by law to absolve from all sins and censures reserved to the bishop (*episcopo reservatis*) and from can. 899, § 2: "*ipso iure ordinario competit.*"

3°. The bishop may habitually delegate the *rural deans* to absolve, not only from the three or four cases he has reserved to himself, but also from the six cases mentioned under V as reserved to the Ordinary by law. For can. 2253 says clearly that the one to whom a censure is reserved by law, or his delegate, may absolve from the same.

4°. It matters not whether the Ordinary reserves his own cases under censure or not, or whether he reserves censures *nemini reservatae*.

§ 3 concerns pastors and all who, in law, go by the name of pastors, hence also *missionaries*. *Pastors* are defined in can. 451, where it is laid down that in law those, too, go by the *name of pastors* who govern *quasi-parishes* where the hierarchic order is not completely established or restored, and likewise *vicars of parishes* who are endowed with full parochial powers.[5] These are further determined in can. 471-473, *viz.*, the actual pastors of incorporated parishes, vicars *ad interim*, and administrators. Concerning temporary substitutes there might perhaps be a doubt. Yet if the last clause of can. 474 is not applicable, *i.e.*, if neither the Ordinary nor the pastor has excepted any parochial right, we believe that they may safely be called pastors under the law. But *assistants* or curates are not comprised here, because they do not go by the name of pastors in law.

Missionaries are those who give temporary missions to the people. Retreat masters are not included here, unless they give retreats to the whole parish or perhaps to a class or group of members, say, young men or women.

All these may absolve by law from *any case which the Ordinary has reserved to himself in any shape or form*, during the *whole time set for fulfilling the paschal duty.* *Missionaries* enjoy the same power, also by law, *during the time of a mission.* The *cases* are those which the Ordinary has reserved to himself, *i.e.*, the three or four which are reserved not to or by the Apostolic See, or by law to the Ordinary.[6] But it does not matter —*quoquo modo* — whether they are reserved as simply reserved cases, or under censure. *By law* signifies that no delegation or express concession is needed. Hence any missionary who has received express jurisdiction from the Ordinary for hearing confessions in the diocese or parish

---

[5] See our Commentary, Vol. II, p. 559 ff.
[6] S. O., July 13, 1916 (A. Ap. S., VIII, 314): "*Quaevis Ordinariorum reservatio ipso iure,*" etc.

where he is to give a mission, may absolve from the cases reserved by and to the Ordinary, even though this faculty is not mentioned in the general (but express) grant of faculties. Pastors, and all those who go by the name of pastors, may licitly and validly absolve from cases reserved to and by the Ordinary by the very fact that they hear confessions during the paschal season. If this season is extended by the Ordinary, *e.g.*, from Laetare to Trinity Sunday, they may during this whole period make use of the power granted by law without further application to the Ordinary. They may also absolve the same persons several times during this period, for the stress is on the time, not on the number of absolutions.

WHEN RESERVATIONS CEASE OR LOSE THEIR FORCE

CAN. 900

Quaevis reservatio omni vi caret:

1.° Cum confessionem peragunt sive aegroti qui domo egredi non valent, sive sponsi matrimonii ineundi causa;

2.° Quoties vel legitimus Superior petitam pro aliquo determinato casu absolvendi facultatem denegaverit, vel, prudenti confessarii iudicio, absolvendi facultas a legitimo Superiore peti nequeat sine gravi poenitentis incommodo aut sine periculo violationis sigilli sacramentalis;

3.° Extra territorium reservantis, etiamsi dumtaxat ad absolutionem obtinendam poenitens ex eo discesserit.

All reservations cease or lose their force:

1°. When those who go to confession are sick and cannot leave the house, or if they are about to be married;

2°. As often as the lawful superior refuses a faculty asked for in a particular case, or when, according to the prudent judgment of the confessor, the faculty cannot be asked of the lawful superior without great inconvenience to the penitent or without danger of violating the sacramental seal;

3°. Outside the territory of the one who has reserved the case, even though the penitent has repaired thither solely for the purpose of obtaining absolution.

" *Quaevis reservatio,*" says the Code, whereas the decree of the Holy Office from which the text is taken adds: " *quaevis Ordinariorum reservatio,*" which is certainly the meaning of this canon; we can hardly believe that *papal* reservations cease under the conditions mentioned, because papal reservations with one exception (see can. 894), all have censures attached, for the absolution of which canons 2253 f. must be consulted.

1. The *aegroti,* or sick persons, are not further described, and hence we may assume that any kind or degree of sickness suffices, provided only it detains the patient at home, even though it exists only in the imagination, as is sometimes the case with hysterical women. *Parties before marriage* are also benefited, but it must be *ineundi causa, i.e.,* for the purpose of marriage. We would not exclude the case of a marriage that has to be rectified as to its validity. The absolution from censure mentioned in can. 2319, § 1, n. 1, cannot be imparted because it is reserved to the Ordinary by law, not by himself.

2. The second number mentions *refusal of the lawful superior* to grant the faculty. Whether this refusal be reasonable or unreasonable, formal or informal, matters not for the purpose in question, for the confessor is the best judge whether the persons are deserving of absolution, and authority has been safeguarded by the petition.

Another reason which causes a reservation to cease is the *inconvenience* of the penitent. But this must be *great*. A little wait could not be called a great inconvenience for city folk. But if one living in the country would have to call again, this might be a great inconvenience. It might also be a great inconvenience to come again for a man or woman who is known as a rare church-goer; for in that case gossip might easily result.

The *danger of violating the seal of the confessional* is another reason for the cessation of a reservation. This would be present if the person who committed the reserved crime were known to the Ordinary, or if circumstances might point to his identity, or if he would be the only one to go to confession (and wanted to receive Holy Communion), while the confessor had to leave the confessional and go to the telephone. The confessor should prudently judge whether the seal is endangered in any case.

3. The last number applies the benefit of cessation even to the case formerly called *in fraudem legis*. A person who leaves the diocese where he knows that his case is reserved, and goes to another diocese where the case is not reserved, may be absolved validly and licitly. This is a change of legislation, as formerly such an absolution was invalid.[7] But *peregrini* are bound by the reservations of the place in which they confess (Com. Interpret. C. I. C., Aug. 17, 1919; see *Irish Eccles. Record*, XIV, 330).

[7] Clement X, "*Superna,*" June 21, 1670, § 7; S. C. C., Sept. 16, 1649 (Richter, *Trid.*, p. 85, n. 8).

CHAPTER III

THE SUBJECT OF PENANCE

MATTER AND INTEGRITY OF CONFESSION

CAN. 901.

Qui post baptismum mortalia perpetravit, quae nondum per claves Ecclesiae directe remissa sunt, debet omnia quorum post diligentem sui discussionem conscientiam habeat, confiteri et circumstantias in confessione explicare, quae speciem peccati mutent.

CAN. 902.

Peccata post baptismum commissa, sive mortalia directe potestate clavium iam remissa, sive venialia, sunt materia sufficiens, sed non necessaria sacramenti poenitentiae.

Whoever after Baptism has committed *mortal sins not yet directly forgiven* by the keys of the Church, must confess them and explain the circumstances which may change the species of sin. The accusation must be preceded by a careful examination of conscience. Necessary matter, therefore, are mortal sins not yet forgiven, whereas sins committed after Baptism, whether grievous but already directly forgiven by the power of the keys, or only venial, are sufficient matter for the Sacrament.

Like every other sacrament, Penance consists of matter and *form*. The latter, according to the teaching of the

337

Church,[1] is the act of absolution. As to the *matter*, there is a controversy in regard to the proper constituents, but it is safe[2] to say that the acts of the penitent, to wit, contrition, confession and satisfaction, are, as it were, the proximate matter of the sacrament, while the sins are the *materia remota* or *circa quam*.

Can. 901 states that *all mortal* sins committed after Baptism *must* be confessed. As Penance is applied by a judicial act, it follows that to the sacred tribunal must be submitted all those sins which constitute matter for juridical cognizance, in other words, all mortal sins, because these prevent man from attaining eternal salvation and make him an object of divine wrath. It was these sins which Christ intended when He instituted this sacrament and which He commanded to be directly submitted to the power of the keys. *Directly* to submit these sins to the power of keys means to accuse oneself of them before the appointed judge and to receive absolution from him by an exercise of jurisdiction.[3] *Indirectly* mortal sins may be forgiven concomitantly, as when a penitent omits a sin through inculpable ignorance, or forgetfulness, or inability, or when a confessor, for weighty reasons, imparts absolution though not empowered to do so.[4] No one mortal sin can be forgiven without the others.

Can. 901, then, requires that confession be integral, *i.e.*, comprise all mortal sins according to number and species. The *number* the penitent is obliged to state as far as he can recollect it, and if the exact number cannot be given, he should say " about," or " at least," or " more

---

1 *Decretum pro Arm.* (Denzinger, n. 594); *Trid.*, sess. 14, c. 3, *de poenit.*

2 Cfr. Pohle-Preuss, *The Sacraments*, Vol. III, p. 76 ff.

3 Palmieri, *De Poenitentia*, p. 99 ff; p. 359 ff.

4 Schieler-Heuser, *Theory and Practice*, p. 41.

or less."[5] Accuracy is also required in stating the
species,[6] for it is the species which determines the nature
of a sin, whether it is opposed to a special virtue, or to
specific objects of a virtue, or to a specific commandment.
Not only must the ultimate species (*infima species*) be
stated, but the *specific circumstances*, too, must be explained. These are such as alter the species of a sin, and
are attached to persons (*e.g.*, sacred persons), places or
objects. For instance, an act of violence done in church,
or a theft committed of sacred things.[7] The integrity of
confession may never be dispensed with, not even when
there is a great multitude of penitents, as may happen on
feast days.[8] If one is lawfully excused from making a
complete confession, for instance, on account of danger
of death, he is obliged to mention the sins omitted in his
next confession.[9] This, however, does not mean that a
penitent who has made a confession as completely as he
was able, is obliged to make another confession to supply
the number. Unnecessary and inculpable scruples are to
be discarded. In saying this we do not, of course, approve the Quietists' quaint and unqualified self-annihila-
tion which would render a soul advanced in sanctity the
purely passive and insensible instrument of even notably
immoral acts.[10]

Can. 902 states which acts constitute *sufficient* but not
necessary matter for confession. They are the mortal
sins already directly forgiven, and venial sins. This is
the doctrine of the Council of Trent.[11] Venial sins may

5 *Prop. Lutheri damn.*, n. 8
(Denzinger, n. 632); Schieler-
Heuser, *l. c.*, p. 163.

6 *Trid.*, sess. 14, c. 5, *de poenit.*

7 *Prop. damn.*, Sept. 24, 1665,
n. 24 sq.; *prop. damn.* March 4,
1679, n. 49 sq. (Denzinger, n. 995
f.; 1066 f.)

8 *Prop. damn.* March 4, 1679, n.
59 (Denzinger, n. 1076).

9 *Prop. damn.* Sept. 24, 1665, n.
11 (*ibid.*, n. 982).

10 *Prop. damn.* Nov. 20, 1687,
n. 47, 48, 60 (*ibid.*, n. 1134 f.;
1147).

11 Sess. 14, c. 5, *de poenit.*; cfr.
Pohle-Preuss, *l. c.*, p. 62.

be forgiven, but they cannot be retained, since they do not entail eternal damnation. On the other hand the custom of confessing them is praiseworthy, and there is no reason to fear that the Sacrament may be rendered contemptible by the confessing of venial sins, as the synod of Pistoja falsely asserted.[12]

CONFESSING THROUGH AN INTERPRETER

CAN. 903.

Qui aliter confiteri non possunt, non prohibentur, si velint, per interpretem confiteri, praecavendo abusus et scandala, firmo praescripto can. 889, § 2.

Those who are unable to confess otherwise, may, if they wish, confess through an interpreter, provided abuses and scandals are avoided, with due regard to can. 889, § 2.

The canon says, they *may*, but not, they are obliged to confess through an interpreter. For although confession is necessary by divine command, and, at least indirectly, *necessitate medii,* for salvation, yet there is a distinction between actual submission to the power of the keys and submission in desire (*in voto*). The latter means that one is ready to subject himself to confession if he can do so in the proper and ordinary way and an occasion offers.[13] However, confessing through an interpreter is an extraordinary and, considering human reluctance in matters of conscience, a very burdensome means. Therefore it cannot be held that God meant to impose such an obligation on men, especially since an act of contrition,— provided confession is not spurned for other reasons,— can effect justification.

12 *Prop. damn.,* " *Auctorem fidei,*"
Aug. 28, 1794, n. 30 (Denzinger, n. 1402).

13 Benedict XIV, *De Syn. Dioec.,* VII, 15, 8; VII, 16, 11.

The interpreter must observe the seal of confession. This is a grievous obligation.

By the way it may be stated that the term " interpreter " is to be understood strictly of a person, not of any other means, such as a letter, a telegram or a telephone message, etc.

OBLIGATION OF DENOUNCING SOLLICITATION

Can. 904.

Ad normam constitutionum apostolicarum et nominatim constitutionis Benedicti XIV *Sacramentum poenitentiae*, I Iun. 1741, debet poenitens sacerdotem, reum delicti sollicitationis in confessione, intra mensem denuntiare loci Ordinario, vel Sacrae Congregationi S. Officii; et confessarius debet, graviter onerata eius conscientia, de hoc onere poenitentem monere.

In accordance with the Apostolic constitutions, especially that of Benedict XIV, "*Sacramentum Poenitentiae*," June 1, 1741, a penitent is obliged to report, within a month, any priest guilty of solicitation in confession. The report must be made either to the local Ordinary or to the Holy Office, and every confessor has the strict obligation to admonish his penitent of this duty.

The obligation of reporting *priests* who solicit a penitent *ad turpia* in the act, or on occasion, or under pretext of confession, is a grievous one, as will be seen from the instructions of the Holy Office quoted below. First we will give a few decisions referring to our case. Alexander VII, on Sept. 24, 1665, condemned [14] the two following propositions:

Prop. 6: "Confessarius, qui in sacramentali Confes-

---

[14] See Denzinger, nn. 977 f.

sione tribuit poenitenti chartam postea legendam, in qua ad venerem incitat, non censetur sollicitasse in confessione, ac proinde non est denuntiandus."

Prop. 7: "*Modus evitandi obligationem denuntiandae sollicitationis est, si sollicitatus confiteatur cum sollicitante: hic potest ipsum absolvere absque onere denuntiandi."*

To the question proposed to the Holy Office, whether or not the expression, "*simulantes confessiones audire*" is to be understood conjointly of solicitation *and* confession, either real or feigned, the answer was: Either suffices. This must evidently be taken as bearing on confession. The same must be said of the answer given to the second question proposed on the same occasion: if a confessional (*i.e.,* confession-room) is also used as a parlor, and solicitation is made there, this would entail the obligation of denouncing the guilty priest.[15] This, we say, must also be considered as connected with confession. For the mere fact that the parlor also serves as a quasi-confessional would certainly not be sufficient to connect solicitation with confession.

The same S. Congregation has excused and exempted *women* from the obligation of denouncing if they live far from the seat of the Ordinary or the place where the denunciation should be made.[16] However the obligation revives[17] when the danger or impediments to the journey cease, and Ordinaries should, as far as possible, see to it that such impediments are removed.[18]

The *priest* who hears the confession of a person who

---

[15] S. O., April 28, 1700 (*Coll. P. F.*, n. 248). The so-called parlor was really the "confession-room," of a convent, such as cloistered nuns have in some countries.

[16] S. O., Jan. 22, 1727 (*Coll. cit.*, n. 308).

[17] S. O., May 20, 1842 (*ibid.*, n. 949).

[18] S. O., Feb. 20, 1866 (*ibid.*, n. 1282).

has been solicited must admonish him or her of the grave obligation of reporting the guilty priest within a *month* from the date when he or she learned or first realized the duty of denunciation. Should the penitent refuse to denounce the culprit, absolution must be denied after a repeated effort to induce him or her to comply with the obligation.

The *place* where denunciation is to be made is the Ordinariate or the Holy Office in Rome.[19] There is no intermediary instance or authority, and religious superiors are not allowed to interfere in this matter. The Ordinary, however, may delegate another priest to hear the case and to employ a third as notary. But no other persons are to be admitted as witnesses, except, of course, such as testify to the character of the priest and the person solicited. *Anonymous* denunciations are not to be accepted, and the obligation itself is personal, *i. e.*, incumbent on the person solicited.

The *interrogatory* to be made by the bishop or his delegate, follows below. The obligation of denouncing culpable priests of solicitation in the act of hearing or on the pretext or occasion of confession *binds all the faithful* of both sexes and of every rite, Latin and Oriental.[20]

INSTRUCTIO S. OFFICII (FEB. 20, 1866)

1. Personae sive mares sive feminae, quaecumque illae sint, ad turpia sollicitatae in Confessione vel occasione aut praetextu Confessionis, quemadmodum enucleate in memorata Constitutione praecipitur, rem ad Sanctam Sedem vel ad loci Ordinarium deferre debent.

2. Denunciare oportet quemcumque sacerdotem, etiam iuris-

---

19 The address is: Sant' Uffizio, Via del Sant' Uffizio 5, Roma, Italy.
20 Benedict XIV, "*Etsi pasto-* *ralis*," May 26, 1742, § IX, n. V; "*Apostolici muneris*," Feb. 8, 1745, § 2.

dictione carentem, vel etiam poenitentis sollicitationi consenti-
entem, quamvis statim dissentientem de turpi materia loqui,
illius complementum ad aliud tempus differentem, et non prae-
bentem absolutionem poenitenti.

3. Huiusmodi denunciationes a nemine absque culpa letali
omitti possunt. Qua de re poenitentes debent admoneri, neque
ab iis admonendis instruendisque eorum bona fides excusat.

4. Sacerdotes ad sacras audiendas confessiones constituti, qui
de hac obligatione poenitentes suos non admonent, debent puniri.

5. Poenitentes admoniti, et omnino renuentes, nequeunt absolvi;
qui vero ob iustam causam denunciationem differre debent,
eamque quo citius poterunt faciendam spondent serioque promit-
tunt, possunt absolvi.

6. Denunciationes anonymae contra sollicitantes ad turpia
nullam vim habent: denunciationes enim fieri debent in iudicio,
nempe coram Episcopo eiusve delegato cum interventu ecclesiastici viri, qui notarii partes teneat, et cum iuramento, et cum
expressione et subscriptione sui nominis; nec sufficit si fiat per
apochas vel per litteras sine nomine et cognomine auctoris.
Ceterum prohibetur, ne in recipiendis denunciationes praeter
iudicem et notarium, virum utrumque ecclesiasticum, speciali et
scripto exarata Episcopi deputatione munitum, testes intersint.
Cavendum quoque ne ex denunciantibus quaeratur, num sollicitationi consenserint: et convenientissimum foret, si de huiusmodi
consensu, quantumvis sponte manifestato, nihil notetur in tabulis.

7. Denunciationis onus est personale et ab ipsa persona sol-
licitata adimplendum. Verum si gravissimis difficultatibus im-
pediatur, quominus hoc perficere ipsa possit, tunc vel per se, vel
per epistolam, vel per aliam personam sibi benevisam suum
adeat Ordinarium, vel sanctam Sedem per sacram Poenitentiariam, vel etiam per hanc supremam Inquisitionem, expositis
omnibus circumstantiis, et deinde se gerat iuxta instructionem
quam erit acceptura. Si vero necessitas urgeat, se gerat iuxta
consilia et monita sui confessarii. Ast si nullo impedimento
detenta denunciationem omnino renuat, in hoc casu aliisque
supra memoratis, laudandus est confessarius, qui operam suam
poenitenti non denegaverit, et vel Ordinarium vel Sanctam Sedem
pro opportunis providentiis consuluerit, suppresso tamen poenitentis nomine.

8. Non infrequenter occurrit casus, ut confessarius aliusve
ecclesiasticus vir ab Episcopis (quorum utique haec potestas

est) deputetur ad denunciationes recipiendas in re ad sollicitationis crimen spectante absque interventu notarii. Huic instructioni folium adiicitur circa modum, quo hisce in casibus confici denunciatio debet.[21]

INSTRUCTIO S. OFFICII (JULY 20, 1890)

Modula Examinis Per Generalia Assumendi

Vigore epistolae Sacrae Supremae Congregationis datae sub die . . . (vel vigore decreti Illustrissimi ac Reverendissimi Domini Archiepiscopi Ordinarii) vocata personaliter comparuit coram Illustrissimo ac Reverendissimo Domino N. N. sistente in Cancellaria (vel in sacrario, aut in collocutorio monialium seu piae domus) in meique etc.

N. N. nubilis (vel uxorata) degens in hac civitate N. N., in paroecia N. N., filia (vel uxor) N. N., aetatis suae . . ., conditionis civilis (aut agricolae, aut famulatui addictae) cui delato iuramento veritatis dicendae, quod praestitit tactis SS. Dei Evangeliis, fuit Quest. An sciat vel imaginetur causam suae vocationis et praesentis examinis? — Ans. . . . Q. A quot annis usa sit accedere ad sacramentum Poenitentiae? — Ans. . . . Q. An semper apud unum eundemque confessarium sacramentum Poenitentiae receperit, vel apud plures sacerdotes: insuper an in una eademque, vel in pluribus ecclesiis? — Ans. . . . Q. An a singulis quibus confessa est sacerdotibus exceperit sanctas admonitiones, et opportuna praecepta, quae ipsam examinatam aedificarent, et a malo arcerent, et quatenus etc.— Ans. . . . Notandum: si responsio fuerit affirmativa, id est si dicat, se bene semper fuisse directam, tunc interrogatur sequenti modo: Q. An sciat vel meminerit aliquando dixisse vel audivisse, quod quidam confessarius non ita sancte et honeste sese gesserit erga poenitentes, quin murmurationes, seu verba contemptibilia contra ipsum confessarium prolata fuerint: ex. gr., quod ipsa examinata, ab uno vel a pluribus poenitentibus, atque ab uno abhinc anno, vel a quattuor aut tribus mensibus similia audierit? — Notandum: Si post hanc interrogationem et animadversionem examinata negare pergat, claudatur actus consueta forma, quae ad calcem huius instructionis prostat. At si quidquam circa aliquem confessarium, iuxta ea de quibus interrogatur, aperuerit, ulterius interrogabitur prout sequitur: Q. Ut exponat nomen,

---

21 *Coll. P. F.*, n. 1282.

cognomen, officium, aetatem confessarii, et locum seu sedem Confessionis; an sit presbyter saecularis vel Regularis, et quatenus etc.—*Ans.* . . . Q. Ut exponat seriatim, sincere et clare ea omnia, quae in sacramentali confessione vel antea vel postea vel occasione confessionis audierit a confessario praedicto minus honesta: vel an ab eodem aliquid cum ipsa inhoneste actum fuerit nutibus, tactibus seu opere, et quatenus, etc.— Notandum: hoc loco iudex solerte curabit ut referantur iisdem verbis, quibus confessarius usus fuerit, sermones turpes, seductiones, invitamenta conveniendi in aliquem locum ad malum finem, aliaque omnia, quae crimen sollicitationis constituunt, adhibita vernacula lingua in qua responsiones sedulo et iuxta veritatem exarabuntur; animum addat examinatae, si animadvertat, eam nimio timore aut verecundia a veritate patefacienda praepediri, eidem suadens omnia inviolabili secreto premenda esse. Denique exquiret tempus a quo sollicitationes inceperint, quamdiu perduraverint, quoties repetitae, quibus verbis et actibus malum finem redolentibus expressae fuerint. Cavebit diligenter ab exquirendo consensu ipsius examinatae in sollicitationem, et a quacumque interrogatione, quae desiderium prodat cognoscendi eiusdem peccata.— Q. An sciat vel dici audierit praedictum confessarium alias poenitentes sollicitasse ad turpia; et quatenus eas nominet (atque hic iubebit nomen, cognomen, et saltem indicia clariora, quibus aliae personae sollicitatae detegi possint).— Notandum: Si forte inducantur aliae personae sollicitatae, erit ipsius iudicis eas prudenter advocare, et singillatim examinare iuxta formam superius expositam.—*Ans.* . . . Q. De fama praedicti confessarii tam apud se quam apud alios? —*Ans.* . . . Q. An praedicta deposuerit ex iustitiae et veritatis amore, vel potius ex aliquo inimicitiae vel odii effectu, et quatenus, etc.— *Ans.* . . . Quibus habitis et acceptatis dimissa fuit iurata de silentio servando iterum tactis SS. Dei Evangeliis, eique perlecto suo examine in confirmationem praemissorum se subscripsit (si fuerit illiterata, dicatur) et cum scribere nesciret, fecit signum Crucis. (Subscriptio personae examinatae.)

Acta sunt haec per me N. N., cancellarium vel notarium ad hunc actum assumptum.[22]

22 *Ibid.*, n. 1732.

CONFESSIONS MAY BE MADE IN ANY RITE

CAN. 905

Cuivis fideli integrum est confessario legitime approbato etiam alius ritus cui maluerit, peccata sua confiteri.

All the faithful are free to confess their sins to any lawfully approved confessor whom they prefer, even though he belong to another rite.

It has always been the practice of the Church to allow the greatest possible liberty in such a delicate matter, and since the administration of this Sacrament involves no difference of rite, the choice of confessors is perfectly free,[23] and neither the higher nor the lower clergy are empowered to forbid their subjects to go to a confessor of another rite.[24] Neither are priests of the Latin Rite obliged to query penitents of an Oriental rite concerning their belief in such articles of faith as the Roman Pontiff, the *processio Spiritus Sancti,* the veneration of Saints, consecration in leavened bread, or purgatory, unless the confessor has a well-founded doubt concerning the penitent's orthodoxy.[25] The practice of obliging parishioners to make their *paschal confession* to their pastor or his substitute has been officially declared intolerable.[26]

[23] S. C. P. F., June 2, 1835 (*Coll.,* n. 839).
[24] S. C. P. F., Dec. 11, 1838 ad 3 f. (*Coll.,* n. 879).
[25] S. C. P. F., Jan. 22, 1688; April 16, 1862 (*Coll.,* n. 1227).
[26] S. C. P. F., Sept. 17, 1792 (*Coll.,* n. 610).

THE ANNUAL CONFESSION

CAN. 906.

Omnis utriusque sexus fidelis, postquam ad annos discretionis, idest ad usum rationis, pervenerit, tenetur omnia peccata sua saltem semel in anno confiteri.

All the faithful without distinction of sex, are obliged to confess all their sins once a year as soon as they have reached the age of discretion.

This text is taken from the famous Decretal which entered the eighth canon of the Council of Trent.[27] The duty has also been imposed on the missionary countries of China, India, etc., and missionaries of both the secular and the regular clergy are obliged to insist upon its fulfillment.[28] The obligation commences from the time the child begins to reason, *i. e.*, with us about the seventh year, sooner or later. Parents, confessors, directors or tutors. and pastors are under obligation to see to it that the children comply with this duty.[29]

Does the obligation bind even if no mortal sins have been committed? There is no strict obligation by divine law to confess any but mortal sins, yet the *positive law* of the Church obliges in this case. An analogy is easily found in the obligation of confession for gaining a plenary indulgence.[30]

Note that whereas Communion is prescribed for the paschal time, there is no period assigned for complying with the duty of annual confession and therefore the

[27] C. 12, X. V. 38; Sess. 14, can. 8, c. 5, *de poenit.*

[28] S. O., March 23, 1656; Nov. 13, 1669; S. C. P. F., Sept. 12, 1645; Sept. 21, 1840 (*Coll.*, nn. 126, 189, 114, 913).

[29] S. C. Sacr., Aug. 8, 1910, nn.

I, IV (*A. Ap. S.*, II, 582).

[30] Benedict XIV, "*Inter praeteritos*," Dec. 3, 1749. § 77. It appears to us that if the legislator had no strict obligation in view, he would have added the clause: *salvo praescripto can. 902.*

pastor is at liberty to choose for the first confession of the children some other time of the year.

SACRILEGIOUS CONFESSION

CAN. 907.

Praecepto confitendi peccata non satisfacit, qui confessionem facit sacrilegam vel voluntarie nullam.

He who makes a sacrilegious or wilfully invalid confession does not comply with the duty of confessing his sins. The contrary proposition was proscribed by the Holy Office [81] in 1665. One who has made a sacrilegious or voluntarily invalid confession has to go to confession again, worthily and validly, in order to comply with the law of the Church as embodied in can. 906.

[81] Cfr. *prop. damn.*, n. 14 (Denzinger n. 985).

CHAPTER IV

CAN. 908.

Sacramentalis confessionis proprius locus est ecclesia vel oratorium publicum aut semi-publicum.

The proper place for sacramental confession is the church, or a public or semi-public oratory.

This canon *excludes private oratories,* yet no rigid exclusion is intended, as is apparent from the text itself, which merely says: *proprius locus,* the proper place. This is also the intent of the Roman Ritual,[32] as Benedict XIV insinuates.[33] Hence any reasonable cause would justify hearing confession in a private oratory, for instance, if the family wished to prepare for Holy Communion.

CAN. 909

§ 1. Sedes confessionalis ad audiendas mulierum confessiones semper collocetur in loco patenti et conspicuo, et generatim in ecclesia vel oratorio publico aut semi-publico mulieribus destinato.

§2. Sedes confessionalis crate fixa ac tenuiter perforata inter poenitentem et confessarium sit instructa.

CAN. 910

§ 1. Feminarum confessiones extra sedem confessionalem ne audiantur, nisi ex causa infirmitatis aliave

---

32 *Rit. Rom.,* tit. III, c. 1, *de*   33 " *Magno cum,*" June 2, 1751,
Sacr. Poenit., n. 7.   § 20.

350

verae necessitatis et adhibitis cautelis quas Ordinarius loci opportunas iudicaverit.

§ 2. Confessiones virorum etiam in aedibus privatis excipere licet.

The confessional for hearing *women's* confessions must always be placed in an open and visible place, generally in the church or public or semi-public oratory assigned to women; it must have an immovable grate with small holes.

Women's confessions should *not be* heard *outside the confessional,* except in case of sickness or for other reasons of necessity, and under such precautions as the local Ordinary may deem opportune.

Men's confessions may be heard also in private homes. The assignment of a special place, or chapel, or room for hearing women's confessions is not customary in our country, nor have we seen it in vogue in other countries as a rule. It is different with Sisters, and especially cloistered nuns. These sometimes have special rooms, which are properly designated as confession-rooms, built within the enclosure, or at least in such a way that the nuns remain *intra septa,* whilst the confessor is outside. Such confession-rooms may be provided also for women who live in convents either as mere inmates or students (*conservatori, ritiri*). These rooms should serve as confessionals only, and are considered such for the Sisters as well as for the women or young ladies living in the convent.[34] Where no such special confession rooms are assigned for women, they must be heard in the church or oratory, where the confessor and penitent may be seen.

Women are not allowed to enter a convent of re-

[34] S. O., Nov. 25, 1874 (*Coll. P. F.,* n. 1424). If solicitation would take place in such a room, the ob-ligation of denouncing would certainly result.

ligious, where, for instance, only two or three priests dwell. If the chapel or oratory of these Fathers is located in the interior of the house, women may go by the public and direct way into the chapel, but no further, and there make their confessions. If there is no chapel attached to the hospice or residence of the missionaries, the confessional should be put in an open and accessible place, as near as possible to the gate or door. The Ordinary or local superior should assign the place and see to it that the rules are properly observed.[35]

The *confessional* itself should be furnished, if possible, with an iron grate [36] so fixed that it cannot be moved, and perforated with holes not bigger than the ring finger.[37] That a veil should be placed before it, is not prescribed. But the grate is of obligation everywhere, in all parts of the world. Where there is no stable oratory the women may cover their faces with a veil.[38]

Except in case of *sickness*, women's confessions shall not be heard outside the confessional. The term sickness includes old age, decrepitude, and deafness.[39] Whenever sick persons are heard outside the usual confessional, the door of the room should be left open, so that the confessor and the penitent can be seen from afar.[40] This may sometimes be impracticable in the case of hard-hearing penitents. For the rest, the precautions to be taken are left to the judgment of the Ordinary.

Here an additional remark may find a place. It con-

35 S. C. P. F., Aug. 26, 1780 (*Coll.*, n. 545).

36 *Ibid.*

37 S. C. EE. *et* RR., Sept. 22, 1645 (Bizzarri, *Coll.*, p. 26). This decision prescribes only a stole, but no surplice; and in case of sickness or necessity the regular habit without stole is sufficient.

38 S. C. P. F., March 17, 1785 (*Coll.*, n. 572).

39 S. C. P. F., Sept. 21, 1840 ad 8 (*Coll.*, n. 913).

40 S. C. P. F., April 13, 1807, n. XIII; Feb. 12, 1821 (*Coll.*, nn. 692, 754).

cerns can. 522, which allows female religious to go to any confessor approved by the local Ordinary for hearing women's confessions, and declares such a confession, made in any church or semi-public oratory, to be valid and licit. Does this also apply to the Sisters' own chapel? We answer, yes. Can. 522 speaks of *any* church or semi-public oratory, and revokes every contrary privilege. Besides, can. 519 should disperse all doubt as to the perfect liberty of religious in matters of conscience. If a religious, even though exempt, may go, in his own house, to any approved confessor, why should that liberty be denied to Sisters in their chapel? The decree of Feb. 3, 1913, cannot be urged against the decree of Aug. 5, 1913.[41]

41 Cfr. *A. Ap. S.*, V, 62, 431. The argument that the Code was prepared while that decree was published has no juridical value.

CHAPTER V

ART. I

GRANT OF INDULGENCES

CAN. 911

Omnes magni faciant indulgentias seu remissionem coram Deo poenae temporalis debitae pro peccatis, ad culpam quod attinet iam deletis, quam ecclesiastica auctoritas ex thesauro Ecclesiae concedit pro vivis per modum absolutionis, pro defunctis per modum suffragii.

An indulgence is a *remission* before God of *temporal punishment* due to sins, the guilt of which is already forgiven or wiped out. The source of indulgences is the treasury of the Churoh. They are granted by the ecclesiastical authority in favor of the living as well as of the dead, but to the former are applied by way of absolution, whilst the latter obtain their benefits only by way of suffrage. Indulgences should, therefore, be highly esteemed by all the faithful.

1. An indulgence is a remission of the *temporal punishments* which remain after the guilt (*culpa* or *reatus*) of sin has been taken away, either by sacramental absolution or by an act of perfect contrition.[1] It is a valid absolution, before God, from the punishments which a man

---

1 Cfr. Pohle-Preuss, *The Sacraments*, Vol. III, pp. 232 ff.

would have to expiate, either in this world by voluntary acts of penance, or in purgatory by involuntary suffering. It is, we say, valid before God as well as before the Church, although applied extra-sacramentally.

2. The *source and foundation* of indulgences is the inexhaustible *treasury of the Church*,[2] which consists of the sum-total of the superabundant merits of our Lord and His Saints, stored away for the benefit of the living as well as the dead, in as far as they are capable of receiving them.

3. The *authority* which dispenses these treasures is the Catholic Church, to whom God has entrusted the keys of His kingdom, acting through the Pope and the bishops, who possess the power of the keys.

4. The *beneficiaries* of this thesaurus are the living faithful and the souls in Purgatory, with this difference that the former are benefited in the form of a remission or grant from the treasury as well as by an act of jurisdiction (*per modum absolutionis*), whereas the *dead* can receive the grant of remission only through the intercession of the living (*per modum suffragii*) because they are, at least directly, beyond the jurisdiction of the Church.

5. Indulgences should *be greatly esteemed by all*. The reason is partly selfish,— but, then, " charity begins at home "— and partly of an objective doctrinal character, based on history. Self-love teaches us to choose the lesser evil, and indulgences are certainly an easier means of satisfying the justice of God than compulsory expiation. Besides, by making proper use of indulgences, we show our gratitude and esteem for the immense treasury of merits stored up in the Church. This certainly was the intention of all ages, whether we look to the intercession

---

[2] This notion was first systematically applied by Alexander of Hales (XIIIth cent.).

of the martyrs who offered *libelli pacis* to apostates who wished to be reconciled or whether we accompany public sinners on their pilgrimages, or the crusaders on their journey to the Holy Land. The idea remains the same: forgiveness, not of sins as such, but of the severe punishments meted out in the penitential books and by the ecclesiastical authorities. No doubt the ransom from penance as well as the works prescribed were liable to abuses and misconstruction, but the Church and her approved teachers always sought to enlighten the people and stem the mischief. Abuses attach themselves to the most sacred things. That they were connected with indulgences did not justify Wiclif in saying that "it is foolish to believe in the indulgences granted by the Pope and the bishops." [3]

WHO MAY GRANT INDULGENCES

CAN. 912.

Praeter Romanum Pontificem, cui totius spiritualis Ecclesiae thesauri a Christo Domino commissa est dispensatio, ii tantum possunt potestate ordinaria indulgentias elargiri, quibus id expresse a iure concessum est.

Besides the Roman Pontiff, to whom the stewardship of the whole spiritual treasury of the Church is entrusted by Christ our Lord, only those can by their ordinary power grant indulgences who are expressly authorized to do so by law.

Since the grant of indulgences is an act flowing from jurisdiction, not from the power of order,— because indulgences for the living are given in the form of absolution,— it follows that:

---

[3] *Prop. dam.,* n. 42 (Denzinger, n. 518).

1°. The *Pope* may grant indulgences for the whole Church, without any limit as to kind, place, and persons.

2°. *Archbishops* and *bishops*[4] may grant indulgences in their respective provinces and dioceses, the former of 100 days, the latter of fifty days. These indulgences are called local because they apply only to the territory over which these prelates have jurisdiction.

3°. *Cardinals*[5] may grant a two hundred days' indulgence, *toties quoties*, in any place, (titular church or institution) and to any person under their jurisdiction and protection.[6] Their power also is an ordinary one by law.

Besides these no other prelates by law enjoy the power of granting indulgences. Thus it has been decided that no *titular bishop,* who is at the same time auxiliary to another bishop, may grant an indulgence of forty days in the diocese in which he is auxiliary.[7]

Apostolic Delegates who have received faculties from the Pope for granting indulgences, should abstain from attaching such to devotional objects or acts of piety which have already been thus enriched by a bishop within his territory.[8]

Bishops and archbishops may attach the indulgence which the law empowers them to grant on the occasion of solemn functions, to images or statues, provided the material is such as prescribed by the Church. These indulgences of 50 or 100 days may be gained by the faithful who recite the prayers prescribed before said statues or images. But these prelates are not allowed to grant more than 50 or 100 days.[9]

---

[4] See can. 274, n. 2; can. 349, § 2, n. 2.

[5] Can. 239, § 1, n. 24.

[6] If they grant an indulgence of the same number of days outside the place of their jurisdiction or protection, this may be gained only by those present; *ibid.*

[7] S. C. Indulg., Jan. 12, 1878, ad 4 (*A. S. S.,* 11, 153 ff.).

[8] *Ibid.*

[9] S. C. Indulg., Jan. 24, 1846;

Can. 913.

Inferiores Romano Pontifice nequeunt:

1.° Facultatem concedendi indulgentias aliis committere, nisi id eis a Sede Apostolica expresse fuerit indultum;

2.° Indulgentias concedere defunctis applicabiles;

3.° Eidem rei seu actui pietatis vel sodalitio, cui iam a Sede Apostolica vel ab alio indulgentiae concessae sint, alias adiungere, nisi novae conditiones adimplendae praescribantur.

Prelates of inferior rank to the Pope:

1°. Cannot impart to others the faculty of granting indulgences, unless they have an express indult to that effect from the Apostolic See;

2°. Cannot grant indulgences applicable to the poor souls;

3°. Cannot attach additional indulgences to an object, or an act of piety, or a confraternity which have already been indulgenced by the Holy See or some other prelate, unless new conditions are prescribed.

The first clause of this canon is intended to prevent abuses. It renders control easier and the sources of abuses more readily discoverable.

No. 2 is based on the view that the supreme dispenser alone may exercise (indirect) power over those who are withdrawn from the proper jurisdiction of the Church.[10]

As to no. 3, two decisions will help to illustrate it.

Feb. 22, 1847 (Prinzivalli, *Resolutiones seu Decreta Authentica S. C. Indulg.*, Romae 1862, nn. 571, 583). The materials permitted are wood, ivory, iron, steel, stone, marble; excluded are lead, zinc, glass, gypsum, paper, pasteboard; cfr. Beringer, *Die Ablässe*, 10th ed., p. 302.

10 The question whether indulgences for the dead attain their purpose infallibly is controverted (cfr. Pohle-Preuss, *l. c.*, p. 201 f.); but acts of charity will certainly be rewarded.

Titius, a pious citizen of Marseilles, had an image of the Blessed Virgin, which had been enriched with an indulgence of forty days, granted to all who would recite certain prayers before it. As often as a bishop came to the city, Titius asked him to attach forty more days. They did it willingly, but the S. Congregation declared all these indulgences except the forty days granted by the local Ordinary invalid.[11]

The Ordinary may, however, attach additional indulgences to a pious object, such as beads or crosses, or to works of piety, for instance, the support of good literature, or to a sodality, over and above those already granted by the Holy See, provided he prescribes new conditions, *e.g.*, additional prayers or some other good work. The successor may, moreover, grant new indulgences to things or persons indulgenced by his predecessor, under the same condition, *viz.*, that new works or prayers be performed.[12] But no bishop can increase the extent of an indulgence by dividing the same act into different parts, for instance, attaching fifty days to every word of the Hail Mary.[13]

THE PAPAL BLESSING

CAN. 914.

Benedictionem papalem cum indulgentia plenaria, secundum praescriptam formulam, impertiri possunt Episcopi in sua quisque dioecesi bis in anno, hoc est die sollemni Paschatis Resurrectionis et alio die festo sollemni ab ipsis designando, etiamsi iidem Missae sollemni adstiterint tantum; Abbates autem vel Prae-

---

11 S. C. Indulg., Dec. 17, 1838 (Prinzivalli, *l. c.*, n. 480).

12 S. C. Indulg., Jan. 12, 1878, ad 1 *et* 3 (*A. S. S.*, 11, 153 f.).

13 *Ibid.*, ad 5 (*l. c.*).

lati *nullius,* Vicarii et Praefecti Apostolici, etsi episcopali dignitate careant, id possunt in suis territoriis
uno tantum ex sollemnioribus per annum diebus.

CAN. 915.

Regulares, qui privilegium habent impertiendi benedictionem papalem, non solum obligatione tenentur
servandi formulam praescriptam, sed hoc privilegio
uti nequeunt, nisi in suis ecclesiis et in ecclesiis monialium vel tertiariorum suo Ordini legitime aggrega-
torum; non autem eodem die et loco quo Episcopus
eam impertiat.

Every bishop may impart the papal blessing in his
own diocese with a plenary indulgence, according to the
formulary prescribed (in the *Pontificale Romanum*)
twice a year: once on the feast of Easter, and once on another day, which they themselves may designate, even
though they should only assist at the solemn Mass. The
same may be imparted, but only on one of the more
solemn feasts of the year, by abbots or prelates *nullius,* by
vicars Apostolic and prefects Apostolic, even though
they are not endowed with the episcopal dignity.

Regulars who have the privilege of imparting the papal
blessing, are not only obliged to use the formula prescribed, but may use the privilege only in their own
churches or in the churches of *moniales* and tertiaries
lawfully aggregated to their order, and are not allowed to
give the papal blessing on the same day and in the same
place on which the bishop imparts it.

Before the occupation of Rome, in 1870, the popes were
wont to bless the people solemnly on Maundy Thursday
and Easter (at St. Peter's), on the feast of the Ascension
(at the Lateran), and on that of the Assumption (at St.

Maria Maggiore). On these occasions the pope ascended the balcony and solemnly blessed the people gathered on the plaza before the basilica. Sometimes others were delegated to impart this blessing. Regulars obtained a special privilege or indult for this purpose under certain conditions imposed by Benedict XIV and Clement XIII.[14] A Constitution of Clement XIII gave to patriarchs, primates, archbishops, and bishops the faculty of imparting the papal blessing *twice a year*. *Coadjutor* bishops have this power (see can. 913) only if they obtained it expressly from the Apostolic See. Clement XIII expressly says: "as long as they rule over their respective churches," from which it is clear that *titular bishops* who do not actually govern a diocese are not entitled to impart the papal blessing.

The *days* on which the papal blessing may be imparted are Easter Sunday and some other *solemn feast day* to be designated by each prelate *ad libitum*. A solemn feast-day is one of obligation, which is certainly the intention of the grantor, because the blessing is given for the benefit of the people gathered in church on such holy days, as the Constitution of Clement XIII says.

The prescribed *formula* is that found in the *Pontificale Romanum*. None other is to be substituted.[15] Even if the people leave, or the custom exists of leaving after the Pontifical Mass, the Apostolic brief must be read in the Latin wording of the *Pontificale* and in the vernacular.[16] There is no excuse for curtailing this ceremony, for the reading of both texts takes only about three minutes. In

14 "*Exempla Praedecessorum*," March 29, 1748; "*Inexhaustum*," Sept. 3, 1762.

15 S. Rit. C., May 23, 1835 (*Dec. Auth.*, n. 2720).

16 S. Rit. C., Dec. 7, 1884 (*Dec. Auth.*, n. 2871). According to a decision of S. C. Indulg., June 30, 1840 (Prinzivalli, n. 501), all that is required for validity is that the indulgence be imparted by papal delegation. The formula see in *Pontificale Rom.*, P. III.

the mean while the people may pray for the Holy Father and the Church.

The S. Congregation has given permission to aged prelates to impart the papal blessing even when they have not themselves pontificated but merely assisted at Mass.[17] This is now the general law, and the privilege is not conditioned upon ill health. But a bishop can not grant this indulgence if he is entirely absent from the solemn Mass.

Inferior Prelates, as mentioned in the second clause of can. 914, are bound by the same conditions as bishops, but are, as the *"Inexhaustum"* of Clement XIII ruled, allowed to impart the papal blessing only once a year on a feastday.

Can. 915 mentions *regulars* who have obtained the privilege of imparting the papal blessing. Benedict XIV as well as Clement XIII desired their privileges to remain intact. The term *"regulars"* must be strictly interpreted, and not taken as synonymous with *exempt*. Not all regulars have obtained this privilege. We know that, for instance, Benedictine abbots have had to apply for it and obtained it *ad decennium*.

The regulars who have the privilege must observe the conditions set forth in our text, to wit:

1. They must use the prescribed *formula*. As there are several formulas, a distinction is necessary.

(a) Benedict XIV (*"Exemplis Praedecessorum,"* March 19, 1748) prescribed a special form of imparting the papal blessing for regulars,[18] which is still to be observed when the blessing is solemnly given. A reasonable doubt arises as to whether this form must be observed by prelates or abbots who pontificate and impart the papal blessing after a pontifical Mass or Vespers. While it is

---

17 S. Rit. C., Jan. 15, 1847 (*Dec. Auth.*, n. 2925).

18 Cfr. *Rituale Rom.*, tit. VIII, c. 32 (Ed. Pustet, 1913, p. 260 f.),

true that Benedict XIV prescribed the above-mentioned formula for all regular orders, "mendicant as well as non-mendicant, monastic as well as clerical," he says in the same Constitution that abbots may bless the people in the churches fully subject to them when they exercise pontifical functions. Hence it appears more reasonable to assume that they should make use of the form prescribed in the *Pontificale Romanum,* and not of the form prescribed for regulars by Benedict XIV. But this rule must strictly be observed: prelates with the right to pontificals may not use the form of the *Pontificale* if they do not pontificate themselves, but in that case must employ the form of the *Rituale Romanum,* as prescribed by Benedict XIV.

(b) When the *general absolution,* or the papal blessing with plenary indulgence, may be given according to a privilege obtained from the Holy See,[19] there are available *two different formulas*[20] prescribed by Leo XIII, "*Quo universi,*" July 7, 1882. The first begins with the words, "*Ne reminiscaris,*" the second with, "*Intret oratio.*" The latter, according to some decisions of the S. Congregation of Indulgences, should be applied in all religious congregations with simple vows which are *not* Tertiaries of a religious order, and *all secular* Tertiaries, for instance, of the Franciscans and Oblates of St. Benedict. The first-mentioned formula should be applied in all religious orders and such religious congregations with simple vows as are tertiaries of a religious order, for instance, Franciscan and Benedictine Sisters.[21]

2. Regulars may impart the papal blessing in their *own*

---

[19] O.S.B. may impart it five times a year: on Ash Wednesday and on the four vigils of Christmas, Pentecost, Assumption, and All Saints; S. C. Indulg., Jan. 10, 1906 (*Anal. Eccl.,* 14, 31).

[20] *Rit Rom.,* ed. Pustet, 1913, p. 134 f.

[21] S. C. Indulg., Dec. 18, 1885; Aug. 18, 1903; Nov. 11, 1903 (*A. S. S.,* 18, 413; 36, 498. We venture to say that it would be more

churches, i.e., such as are fully incorporated with the monastery or order; in churches of *moniales* who are under their jurisdiction, and, finally, in the churches of *Tertiaries* who are lawfully aggregated to their order. Tertiaries are *legitimately aggregated* as soon as the superior general has issued the decree of aggregation. (*Tertiaries* must here be understood of religious in the sense of can. 492, § 1). The papal blessing in the sense of general absolution with plenary indulgence may be imparted by any priest approved for hearing confessions, whether secular or religious, if the regularly appointed priest is absent for any reason.[22] Regular superiors may delegate a priest of their order who has no faculties for hearing confessions to impart the general absolution with plenary indulgence to secular Tertiaries in churches belonging to the regulars.[23] The one who imparts it to Tertiaries may also gain the indulgence,[24] provided, of course, he has complied with the prescribed conditions.

3. The *number* of times and the occasions on which regulars may impart the solemn papal blessing were determined by Leo XIII. In his "*Quo universi,*" 1882, he permitted regulars to give the blessing *twice* a year and emphasized that they must abstain from giving the solemn blessing on the same day on which and in the same town or city where, the Ordinary makes use of the same privilege. *In eodem loco* here means a town or city, not a parish. In a large city there may be many parishes, and if the bishop gives the papal blessing in one of them, the regulars are not allowed to give it in another.[25]

conformable to the Code if the first formula would be used by all religious, and the second by all secular Tertiaries, religious sodalities, and confraternities.

[22] S. O. (Sect. Indulg.), Dec. 15, 1910 (*A. Ap. S.,* II, 22).

[23] S. O. (Sect. Indulg.), May 28, 1914 (*A. Ap. S.,* VI, 347).

[24] See Beringer, *l. c.,* ed 13, p. 338.

[25] S. C. Indulg., May 20, 1896; Beringer, *l. c.,* p. 339.

To complete these comments it may be added that the bishop, too, who imparts the papal blessing gains the indulgence attached to it. Those who take part in the celebration from a window of a house situated on the place where the blessing is given may gain the indulgence attached to the same. But this blessing does not involve absolution from censures or penalties. The same is true of the general absolution.[26]

PRIVILEGED ALTARS

CAN. 916.

Episcopi, Abbates vel praelati *nullius*, Vicarii ac Praefecti Apostolici et Superiores maiores religionis clericalis exemptae, possunt designare et declarare unum altare privilegiatum quotidianum perpetuum, dummodo aliud non habeatur, in suis ecclesiis cathedralibus, abbatialibus, collegiatis, conventualibus, paroecialibus, quasi-paroecialibus, non autem in oratoriis publicis vel semi-publicis, nisi sint ecclesiae paroeciali unita seu eiusdem subsidiaria.

Bishops, abbots or prelates *nullius*, Apostolic vicars and prefects, and the major superiors of exempt clerical religious may designate and declare one altar daily privileged forever in their cathedral, abbatial, collegiate, conventual, parochial, and quasi-parochial churches, provided there be no privileged altar in said churches as yet. In public or semi-public oratories, unless they are united to a parish church or serve as its subsidiaries, no privileged altar may be assigned by the prelates mentioned.

No traces of papal concessions of a privileged altar

---

26 Clement XIII, " *Inexhaustum,*" Sept. 3, 1762. For the papal blessing in *articulo mortis* see *Rit. Rom.,* tit. V, c. 6 (ed. Pustet, p. 113).

can be found before the end of the XVth century. Severe
conditions were set up under Paul V (1605–1621) for
obtaining this privilege, which was only given to churches
where forty Masses could be celebrated daily. Succeeding popes, especially Benedict XIII and Clement XIII,
mitigated this rigor by granting the privilege to all patriarchal, metropolitan, cathedral, collegiate, abbatial and
parish churches.[27]

What is a privileged altar and what its purpose? The
S. Cong. of Indulgences has declared: " As far as the intention of the grantor and the power of the keys extend,
a *plenary indulgence* must be understood which in itself
would be sufficient to forthwith free the soul from the
pains of purgatory; but as far as the efficacy of the application is concerned, it is an indulgence the measure
of which must be left to the divine mercy and acceptance." [28]   In other words: the intention of the
Church, which can never be entirely frustrated, is to liber-
ate a determined soul from Purgatory, but whether this
is fully achieved, must be left to God. The practical
conclusion is that repeated Masses offered upon such an
altar guarantee surer acceptance, and repetition is not
superfluous.

The *prelates* who may assign such a privileged altar
are: bishops, prelates *nullius*, Apostolic vicars and prefects, and the major superiors of exempt clerical orders.
This classification is explained elsewhere as comprising all
prelates who enjoy ordinary jurisdiction.[29]   However, the
vicar-general is not included, and may therefore not
designate a privileged altar; for this privilege, says the

27 " *Omnium saluti*," Aug. 20,
1724; Decree of May 19, 1759
(Prinzivalli, n. 242).

28 S. C. Indulg., July 28, 1840
(Prinzivalli, n. 502).

29 S. C. Indulg., June 7, 1842
(Prinzivalli, n. 531).

S. Congregation, is given rather as a personal favor.[30]

The *churches* in which such privileged altars may be designated are cathedral, abbatial, collegiate, conventual, parish and quasi-parish churches. This is a complete enumeration.

If a cathedral church serves at the same time as a parish church, two privileged altars are not allowed.[31] Hence neither an abbey nor a collegiate church may have two privileged altars, at least by common law. *One is* the rule. If more are desired, a special indult should be asked for.

The text *excludes public and semi-public oratories,* except when such an oratory serves as *ecclesia filialis* of the principal or mother-church and parochial functions, such as funeral services, baptism, administration of the Holy Eucharist, are performed therein. The same rule applies to *subsidiary* chapels, for instance, during repairs of the parish church, and to chapels which may be called subsidiary *in perpetuum* on account of the distance from the parish proper;—provided always that parochial functions are held therein.[32] Purely semi-public oratories, such as we have in this country for religious communities, hospitals, or asylums, do not comply with the conditions laid down in our text.

What *qualifications* an altar must have to be declared privileged, is not determined in our text. We believe that the conditions formerly required still hold good. They are: (1) that the altar be *fixed or stable, i.e.,* irremovable, with an altar stone consecrated though not necessarily irremovable. It is not required that the altar be of marble

30 S. C. Indulg., May 24, 1843 (*ibid.*, n. 553).

31 S. Congr. Indulg., Sept. 18, 1776 (*ibid.*, n. 365).

32 S. C. Indulg., Jan. 30, 1760; Nov. 27, 1764 (Prinzivalli, nn. 246, 257).

or stone. (2) The second condition is that the altar be *not portable*. The privilege is attached not to the stone, but to the altar, and cannot therefore be transferred by changing the stone.[33]

CAN. 917.

§ 1. Die Commemorationis omnium fidelium defunctorum, omnes Missae gaudent privilegio ac si essent ad altare privilegiatum celebratae.

§ 2. Omnia altaria ecclesiae per eos dies quibus in ea peragitur supplicatio Quadraginta Horarum, sunt privilegiata.

On All Souls' Day all Masses enjoy the same privilege as if they were said on a privileged altar. All the altars of a chuch in which the *Forty Hours' Devotion* is held, are privileged during the days of this devotion.

Concerning the application on All Souls' Day a remark, although theological rather than canonical, may not be amiss. It appears that the Mass on that day can be applied for all the souls in purgatory. Yet it is the constant and common teaching of the Church that the application is made only *for one soul*, even when the Mass is said for the dead in general.[34] Hence, even if the privilege for a community or confraternity is worded in the plural: "*pro animabus presbyterorum, perinde suffragentur, ac si ad altare privilegiatum celebratae fuissent*,"[35] the benefit of the indulgence attached to the privileged altar is in fact applied only to one individual soul. Therefore, besides the intention for all the dead, it is

---

[33] Schneider, *Rescripta Auth. S. C. Indulg.*, 1885, n. 405; Beringer, *l. c.*, p. 462 f.

[34] S. C. Indulg., Feb. 29, 1864;

Dec. 19, 1885 (*A. S. S.*, 18, 340); Beringer, *l. c.*, ed. 13, p. 469 f.

[35] S. C. Indulg., July 16, 1765 (*Rescripta*, n. 228).

well, though not necessary, to make a special intention for a particular soul.

CAN. 918.

§ 1. Ut indicetur altare esse privilegiatum, nihil aliud inscribatur, nisi: *altare privilegiatum*, perpetuum vel ad tempus, quotidianum vel non, secundum concessionis verba.

§ 2. Pro Missis celebrandis in altari privilegiato nequit, sub obtentu privilegii, maior exigi Missae eleemosyna.

In order to indicate the fact that an altar is privileged nothing else is required but the inscription: *Altare privilegiatum*, whether perpetual or for a certain time, daily or not, according to the wording of the grant.

For Masses celebrated on a privileged altar no higher stipend may be charged because of the privilege.

The latter rule was made by the S. Congregation of Indulgences when, in extending the indulgence of the privileged altar to all Masses said on All Souls' Day,[36] it stated that only a synodal or usual stipend may be received. Our Code adds the words: " *sub obtentu privilegii*," which means that nothing more may be demanded on account of the altar being privileged, because this would be simony. If the privilege is personal, it is lost by asking more; if it is local, the indulgence is not gained.[37]

---

[36] S. C. Indulg., May 19, 1761 (Prinzivalli, n. 250).

[37] S. C. P. F., Aug. 13, 1774 (*Coll.*, n. 507).

PROMULGATION OF INDULGENCES

CAN. 919.

§ 1. Novae indulgentiae, ecclesiis etiam regularium concessae, quae Romae promulgatae non sint, ne pervulgentur, inconsulto ordinario loci.

§ 2. In edendis libris, libellis, etc., quibus concessiones indulgentiarum pro variis precibus aut piis operibus recensentur, servetur praescriptum can. 1388.

CAN. 920.

Qui a Summo Pontifice impetraverint indulgentiarum concessiones pro omnibus fidelibus, obligatione tenentur, sub poena nullitatis gratiae obtentae, authentica exemplaria earundem concessionum ad Sacram Poenitentiariam deferendi.

New indulgences not published at Rome, may not be promulgated without the consent of the local Ordinary. This law is binding also on regulars.

In publishing books, pamphlets, etc., which contain indulgences for various prayers and pious works, can. 1388 must be observed.

Those who have obtained from the Sovereign Pontiff indulgences intended for all the faithful are obliged under penalty of nullification of the favor granted, to send an authentic copy of the same to the Sacred Penitentiary.

In ancient times alms were collected for the crusades and buildings for charitable purposes. The collectors were often entrusted with the preaching or promulgation of indulgences. Abuses of a grievous nature crept in, and greed exploited the most sacred things. The Council of Trent [88] endeavored to remedy these abuses by making

---

[88] Sess. 21, c. 9, de ref.

the promulgation of indulgences dependent on the co-operation of the local Ordinaries and two canons. But simpletons — we have no other name for those who hunt up every indulgence and believe every scrap of paper which pretends to convey some extraordinary spiritual favor [39] — are still rampant, and hence the rules of the Code are timely.

New indulgences are those which have not yet been promulgated at Rome, and are therefore not registered in the office of the S. Congregation of Indulgences. Since the establishment of the official *Acta Apostolicae Sedis* (1909) it is easy to know what indulgences are authentically promulgated.

Indulgences are generally granted *in forma gratiosa*, and do not therefore, *per se*, require an executor. However, if the rescript contains a favor destined for the public welfare, such as an indulgence, it must be presented to the Ordinary for *recognition*. This does not mean that the indulgence could not validly be gained if the Ordinary would fail to recognize it, unless indeed there is attached an invalidating clause to that effect.[40] A pastor, therefore, who receives from Rome an indulgence for his parish, may not publish it before his Ordinary has been informed or advised.[41] Neither may regulars or religious communities promulgate indulgences which they have received without the consent of the local Ordinary. No exemption may be rightfully claimed from this law.[42] The Ordinary is the one in whose diocese the religious

---

[39] See, for instance, the facts reported by Beringer, *l. c.*, p. 118 f.: an indulgence of 80,000 years for one prayer!

[40] The invalidity is stated neither by the Council of Trent, nor by the Apostolic See (Beringer, *l. c.*, p. 112), nor by our text.

[41] S. O., July 8, 1846, ad 1, (*Coll. P. F.*, n. 1008).

[42] *Trid.*, sess. 21, c. 9, *de ref.*; S. C. C., June 21, 1760 (Richter, *Trid.*, p. 123, n. 3).

have their house or church and, according to can. 198, § 1, also the vicar-general, the administrator, a prelate *nullius,* an Apostolic vicar or prefect.

A strict prohibition to publish indulgences formerly bound *confraternities,*[43] to whom no spiritual favors or indulgences could be communicated without the formal recognition and knowledge of the Ordinary. Now, however, all that is required is that the Ordinary take cognizance of the indulgence — *praevia cognitione Ordinarii.*[44]

No recognition or cognizance by the Ordinary is required for promulgating indulgences granted by the Pope " *Urbi et orbi.*" To gain these it suffices that the faithful be certain that the grant has been made by the Pontiff.[45] Thus a religious superior, also of a female congregation, or a pastor, upon reading in the *Acta Ap. Sedis* of an indulgence granted " *Urbi et orbi,*" may apply it at once to his congregation.

Can. 920 embodies a law partly contained in a decree of Benedict XIV, Jan. 19, 1746, recalled to the knowledge of the bishops by Pius X, and finally by the present Pontiff. The respective documents ordain that *general concessions of indulgences* intended for all the faithful must be submitted to the S. Poenitentiaria. A *general indulgence* is one that can be gained by all the faithful everywhere and at any time (*universis catholici orbis christifidelibus*). A *particular indulgence* is one that can be gained either by belonging to a certain confraternity or by using a specified devotional object, or one granted to a certain person. Thus Pius X was wont to grant to

---

[43] Clement VIII, Dec. 7, 1604, § 7.

[44] S. C. Indulg., Jan. 8, 1861; (Beringer, *l. c.*, p. 539, 551).

[45] S. C. Indulg., July 1, 1839, ad 6 (Prinzivalli, n. 491).

priests orally the faculty of attaching the *toties quoties* indulgence to crucifixes. Such particular indulgences or faculties need not be reported to the above-named Sacred Congregation. Neither need indulgences granted to a certain diocese, or confraternity, or order, or religious congregation, if not intended for all the faithful, be referred to Rome. But all general indulgences must be reported. This rule was made to eradicate abuses and scruples which may arise from a publication made without the knowledge of the S. Congregation.[46]

The Code requires that *authentic* copies of the concessions granted be submitted to the S. C. This means that either the original grant, as issued by Rome, or in case this is impossible or impracticable, an authenticated copy be sent to Rome. Any ecclesiastical notary may make the copy. A photographic reprint would also be considered authentic. The texts of Pius X and Benedict XV only mention *documenta exhibenda,* but failure to send the document — which Pius X demanded to be done within six months from the date of issuance — would entail invalidity of the indulgence.

To return to can. 919, § 2, the following remarks concerning the *publishing of books, pamphlets,* or *leaflets,* or summaries of indulgences, may prove useful. The Code refers to can. 1388, which requires the *permission of the local Ordinary,* according to the well-known Constitution of Leo XIII, " *Officiorum ac munerum,*" Jan. 25, 1897, n. 17. But § 2 of can. 1388 also requires the *express permission of the Holy See* for the publication, in any language, of an authentic collection of prayers or good works

---

46 S. C. Indulg., April 14, 1856 (Prinzivalli, n. 556); Benedict XIV, Jan. 19, 1746; Pius X, "*Cum per Apostolicas,*" April 7, 1910 (*A. Ap. S.,* II, 225); Benedict XV, "*Quandoquidem,*" Sept. 16, 1915 (*A. Ap. S.,* VII, 457 f.).

to which the Apostolic See has attached indulgences, of a list of Apostolic indulgences, and of a summary of indulgences which have been previously collected but never approved, or are for the first time collected. Hence every new collection or new list (*elenchus*) or summary of indulgences which has not yet been approved by the S. C. Indulg., needs the express permission of the Holy See[47] and of the Ordinary. If an indulgence, or a list, or summary, or collection of indulgences which have been approved by the S. Congregation, or are taken from an Apostolic brief or rescript, is to be printed or published, the Ordinary may give permission to do so without submitting the same to the S. Congregation, unless a special prohibition has been issued.[48] Religious superiors may have a summary of the indulgences granted to confraternities established by their institute printed and circulated with the approval or *visum* of the Ordinary.[49]

PLENARY INDULGENCES

CAN. 921.

§ 1. Indulgentia plenaria concessa pro festis Domini Nostri Iesu Christi vel pro festis Beatae Mariae Virginis, intelligitur concessa dumtaxat pro festis quae in calendario universali reperiuntur.

§ 2. Concessa indulgentia plenaria vel partialis pro festis Apostolorum, intelligitur concessa dumtaxat pro eorum festo natali.

§ 3. Indulgentia plenaria concessa ut *quotidiana perpetua* vel *ad tempus* visitantibus aliquam ecclesiam vel publicum oratorium ita intelligenda est ut quacun-

---

47 S. C. Indic., Aug. 7, 1897 (*Coll. P. F.,* n. 1978).

48 S. C. Indulg., Jan. 22, 1858 (Prinzivalli, n. 674).

49 S. C. Indulg., Jan. 8, 1861 (Prinzivalli, n. 689); Beringer, *l. c.,* p. 116.

que die, sed semel tantum in anno, ab unoquoque fideli acquiri possit, nisi aliud in decreto expresse dicatur.

A *plenary indulgence* is the remission of the whole debt of temporal punishment due to sin. To gain it fully, one must be free from all affection for sin.

A *partial indulgence* is the remission of a part of the temporal punishment due to sin, and is gauged by the public penances or penitential canons of the early Church. In this sense a partial indulgence is indeed a remittance of penances imposed by the former penitential discipline and valid before the external forum of the Church, but it would be wrong to imagine that this is its only effect. Even a partial indulgence signifies and effects the remittance of temporal punishments due to sin before God or in the court of conscience. Consequently, an indulgence of seven years means a remission of the temporal punishments which were formerly imposed by the ecclesiastical authority, for instance, seven years of fasting twice a week on bread and water, but as effective of true remission.[50]

Canons 921 sqq. lay down certain rules for the understanding and gaining of indulgences granted for certain feasts, sacred places and objects, as well as with regard to the time of gaining them.

§ 1 of can. 921 says that if a plenary indulgence is granted for the feasts of our *Lord* or of the *Blessed Virgin*, it must be understood only of those feasts which are assigned in the general calendar of the Church, to wit: Christmas, the Circumcision (New Year's) the Epiphany, Easter Sunday, the Ascension, and Corpus Christi; or the feasts of the Immaculate Conception, the Purification, the Annunciation, the Nativity and the Assump-

50 Pohle-Preuss, *l. c.*, III, p. 238 f.

tion of the Bl. Virgin Mary.[51] Other feasts mentioned in private calendars, for instance those of religious, are not included in this grant.

§ 2 provides that an indulgence, whether plenary or partial, granted for the *feasts of the Apostles,* must be understood of the main or spiritual birthday feasts, not of other incidental feasts, therefore not of St. Peter's Chair or Chains, St. Paul's Conversion, etc.[52]

§ 3 declares that if a plenary indulgence is granted as daily forever or for a certain time (*quotidiana perpetua vel ad tempus*), this means that the faithful who visit the resp. church or public oratory may gain said plenary indulgence on *any day,*— weekday or Sunday,— *but only once a year,* unless the wording contains an extending clause. Therefore, if the grantor intends to grant an indulgence for every day, he must explicitly say so.[53]

THE TRANSFER OF FEASTS AND INDULGENCES

CAN. 922.

Indulgentiae adnexae festis vel sacris supplicationibus vel precibus novendialibus, septenariis, triduanis, quae ante aut post festum vel etiam eius octavario perdurante peraguntur, translatae intelliguntur in eum diem, quo festa huiusmodi legitime transferantur, si festum translatum habeat officium cum Missa sine sollemnitate et externa celebratione ac translatio fiat in perpetuum, vel si transferatur sive ad tempus sive in perpetuum sollemnitas et externa celebratio.

To understand this canon it had best be divided into three parts:

---

[51] S. C. Indulg., Sept. 18, 1862.
[52] *Ibid.,* Beringer, *l. c.,* p. 105.

[53] S. C. Indulg., March 15, 1852 (Prinzivalli, n. 624).

1. The indulgences here mentioned may be plenary or partial, and are granted for certain feasts, processions, or prayers recited during a certain time, three, seven or nine days. These processions or prayers (novenas, triduums or septenaries) may be performed either before or after the principal feast or during its Octave.

2. If a feast is legitimately transferred to another day, the indulgences, too, may be gained on that day. This is a general rule, established by the decree of Aug. 9, 1852.[54]

3. Here a distinction must be made as to *transfer and solemnity:* (a) If the feast has its office and Mass — although without solemnity and external celebration — *and* is transferred to another day *in perpetuum,* or forever, the indulgences are to be gained only on the day to which the feast is transferred. Thus, for instance, if the feast of a Saint is transferred forever to a day which would not otherwise be his *dies natalis,* the indulgence granted for his feast is also transferred.[55]

(b) If the feast is transferred as to its *solemnity and external celebration,* either accidentally, *i.e., ad tempus,* or forever, *in perpetuum,* the indulgence can be gained only on the feastday thus transferred.

A feast may be transferred *ad tempus* on account of a concurring feast. Example: On All Souls' Day a plenary indulgence *toties quoties* may be gained. However, it may happen that Nov. 2nd falls on a Sunday. In that case the indulgence can be gained on Monday, Nov. 3, because it is attached, not to Nov. 2nd, but to All Souls' Day.[56] Note that only a Sunday may interfere with the celebration of All Souls' Day, which is a first-class festi-

---

54 Prinzivalli, n. 627.

55 S. O., June 13, 1912, ad 1 (*A. Ap. S.*, VI, 624).

56 S. O. (Sect. Indulg.), Dec. 14, 1916 (*A. Ap. S.*, IX, 179).

val, and hence all particular feasts proper to certain places, churches, religious orders, and congregations, must make way for All Souls' Day and therefore be transferred to another day.[57]

A feast is transferred *in perpetuum* generally to a Sunday, for instance, the feast of SS. Peter and Paul, Epiphany (in France), etc. On that day, therefore, the *solemnity and external celebration* take place as if it were the proper day, even though the office and the Mass have been said on the latter. It may be asked: What does *external celebration* mean? It means the special prayers, solemn functions, and gathering of the faithful in church, exposition of the Saint's image or picture,[58] etc. The transfer of the indulgences takes place for religious orders or congregations no matter whether the transfer of the feast itself is made for the whole order or only for a province or house by reason of the diocesan or provincial directory.[59] And the members must follow the directory of their respective province. The faithful may gain the indulgences attached to a visit of a church of religious *either* on the day on which the diocese, *or* on the day on which the religious themselves celebrate the feast, but not on both.[60]

THE DAY FOR GAINING INDULGENCES

CAN. 923.

Ad lucrandam indulgentiam alicui diei affixam, si visitatio ecclesiae vel oratorii requiratur, haec fieri

---

[57] S. Rit. C., Feb. 28, 1917 (*A. Ap. S.*, IX, 186).

[58] Cfr. *Ephemerides Liturgicae*, 1892, p. 700, which says that it is immaterial whether all these or only parts occur.

[59] S. O. (Sect. Indulg.), June 13, 1912, ad 2 (*A. Ap. S.*, IV, 624).

[60] S. C. Indulg., Jan. 12, 1878; Beringer, *l. c.*, p. 111.

potest a meridie diei praecedentis usque ad mediam noctem quae statutum diem claudit.

To gain an indulgence which is attached to a certain day, if visiting a church or oratory is required, the visit may be made from noon of the preceding day until midnight of the day proper. This rule applies to all indulgences, plenary, partial, *toties quoties,* to such already granted or yet to be granted, no matter how the time or day may be designated.[61] Thus, for instance, the *toties quoties* indulgence granted for All Souls' Day may be gained from noon, Nov. 1st, to midnight, Nov. 2nd.

LOSS OF LOCAL AND REAL INDULGENCES

CAN. 924.

§ 1. Ad norman can. 75, indulgentiae adnexae alicui ecclesiae non cessant, si ecclesia funditus evertatur rursusque intra quinquaginta annos aedificetur in eodem vel fere eodem loco et sub eodem titulo.

§ 2. Indulgentiae coronis aliisve rebus adnexae tunc tantum cessant, cum coronae aliaeve res prorsus desinant esse vel vendantur.

§1. Indulgences attached to a church are not lost even if the church is entirely destroyed, provided it is rebuilt within the space of fifty years on the same or nearly the same place, and under the same title.

This is according to can. 75. If the new church would be built under the same title, for instance, Holy Rosary, on the same place where the old one stood, or not more than twenty or thirty paces distant therefrom, the indulgence would not be lost.[62] But if the new church, though

---

61 S. O. (Sect. Indulg.), Jan. 26, 1911 (*A. Ap. S.,* III, 64).

62 S. C. Indulg., March 29, 1886 (*A. S. S.,* 19, 93f.).

under the same title, would be built on the cemetery, the indulgence would be lost.[68] The same title must be attached to the whole building. Therefore it would not be sufficient to retain the indulgence if the new church were built on the same spot, but under a different title, even though a chapel or altar under the old title were erected in the new church.[64]

§ 2. Indulgences attached to rosaries (beads) and other objects are lost only if the beads or objects are destroyed or sold. If blessed crucifixes or crosses perish entirely, the indulgences attached to them are lost, but if only a small portion is destroyed or lost, this part may be renewed without losing the indulgences. If the cross is removed only temporarily, for a special reason, no new blessing is required.[65] If crosses or images of the XIV Stations are removed for a time and replaced, the indulgences are not lost. If the crosses of the XIV Stations, — not the images, which are not necessary for the indulgences,— are entirely destroyed or decayed, the indulgences are lost; if only a small portion is destroyed this may be repaired.[66] It is similar with beads. If the single beads are torn asunder but collected again and put on a new string, the indulgences are not lost, even though four or five new beads would have to be added.[67]

The *selling* of such articles entails entire loss of the indulgences, no matter whether a profit was made or not.[68] The Code says nothing of giving them away, and therefore we may conclude that, unless the article together with the indulgences is the exclusive property of any one

63 S. C. Indulg., Aug. 9, 1843, ad 2 (Prinzivalli, n. 557).

64 Beringer, l. c., p. 70.

65 S. C. Indulg., Jan. 30, 1839, ad 5 (Prinzivalli, n. 686).

66 S. C. Indulg., Sept. 20, 1839 (ibid., n. 694).

67 S. C. Indulg., Jan. 10, 1839 (ibid., 682).

68 S. C. Indulg., Dec. 14, 1722 (ibid., n. 50).

person, the indulgences are not lost if the article is given to another.[59]

ARTICLE II

THE GAINING OF INDULGENCES

CAN. 925.

§ 1. Ut quis capax sit sibi lucrandi indulgentias, debet esse baptizatus, non excommunicatus, in statu gratiae saltem in fine operum praescriptorum, subditus concedentis.

§ 2. Ut vero subiectum capax eas revera lucretur, debet habere intentionem saltem generalem eas acquirendi et opera iniuncta implere statuto tempore ac debito modo secundum concessionis tenorem.

To be capable of gaining an indulgence for onself one must be baptized, not excommunicated, in the state of grace at least when he complies with the last work prescribed, and a subject of the grantor. To really gain the indulgences the capable subject must have at least the general intention of gaining them and comply with the conditions prescribed at the time and in the manner prescribed in the grant.

The text distinguishes between the capability of gaining indulgences and the actual gaining of them. The only capable subject is a baptized Catholic who is not excommunicated, for a non-Catholic can hardly be styled *subditus concedentis*. That the *state of grace is necessary* appears from the nature of an indulgence as a remission of temporal punishment after the guilt of mortal sin has been wiped out. But the state of grace is required only

---

[59] Somewhat different Beringer, *l. c.*, p. 359, but he wrote before the Code was promulgated.

for the last act to be performed. Benedict XIV says that if one were not in the state of grace when making the visits of the churches prescribed for gaining the jubilee indulgence, but made a worthy confession and communion before he makes the last visit, he would gain the indulgence.[70] Of course, this is only the limit, not an example for imitation.

Another condition is that one must be a *subject* of the grantor. Therefore a bishop may grant indulgences only to his own diocesans, and a strange bishop could not, even with the consent of the local Ordinary, grant indulgences to one not of his diocese.[71]

For the *actual gaining* of indulgences the following conditions are required.

(a) One must have at least a general or *habitual intention* of gaining all indulgences which one may obtain. This lasts until formally revoked. But if Mass is said on a privileged altar, no special intention is required, nor even the general one of gaining the indulgence attached to that altar.[72]

(b) The prescribed works must be performed within *the time* prescribed, which, as said above, runs from noon to midnight. But if a special hour is stated, this must be observed.[73] Besides, the good works must be performed in the *manner* prescribed. Thus, as a rule, the prayer "*Sacrosanctae*" must be recited kneeling; yet if one is legitimately prevented, *e.g.*, by sickness or physical inability, from bending the knees, he may gain the indulgence walking or standing.[74] The indulgences attached to the

[70] "*Convocatis*," Nov. 25, 1749, n. XLVII; "*Inter praeteritos*," Dec. 3, 1749, § 75.

[71] S. C. Indulg., Dec. 17, 1838 (Prinzivalli, n. 480); Jan. 12, 1878, ad 2 (*A. S S.*, 11, 153 f.).

[72] S. C. Indulg., March 12, 1855 (Prinzivalli, n. 661).

[73] S. C. Indulg., March 7, 1771, ad 4 (*ibid.*, n. 511).

[74] S. C. Indulg., July 5, 1855; Jan. 7, 1856 (*ibid.*, nn. 652, 654).

Rosary and the Hail Mary may be gained by those who recite these prayers alternately.[75] If a member of a confraternity, sodality, or congregation, for reasons of sickness or imprisonment, cannot pay the prescribed visit to a church, he may gain the indulgence if he devoutly performs the other works described.[75] For the rest, the tenor of each rescript must be carefully inspected and its regulations observed.

CAN. 926.

Plenaria indulgentia ita concessa intelligitur ut si quis eam plenarie lucrari non possit, eam tamen partialiter lucretur pro dispositione quam habet.

A plenary indulgence is understood to be granted in such a way that if one cannot gain it in its entirety, one may gain it partially, in proportion to his disposition. See can. 921.

CAN. 927.

Nisi aliud ex concessionis tenore appareat, indulgentias ab Episcopo concessas lucrari possunt tum subditi extra territorium, tum peregrini, vagi omnesque exempti in territorio degentes.

Unless the tenor of the grant sounds differently, indulgences granted by the bishop may be gained by his subjects also when outside their own diocese. *Peregrini, vagi,* and all who live in a territory may gain the indulgences granted for that territory. This, of course, is to be understood of indulgences that are not merely local; for local indulgences cannot be gained outside the place to which they are attached.

[75] S. C. Indulg., March 1, 1820 (*ibid.*, n. 420).

[76] S. C. Indulg., Aug. 2, 1760 (*ibid.*, n. 248).

CAN. 928.

§ 1. Indulgentia plenaria, nisi aliud expresse cautum sit, acquiri potest semel tantum in die, etsi idem opus praescriptum pluries ponatur.

§ 2. Partialis indulgentia, nisi contrarium expresse notetur, saepius per diem, eodem opere repetito, potest lucrifieri.

Unless the contrary is expressly stated, a *plenary indulgence* may be gained only once a day, even though the same works are performed several times. But a partial indulgence may be gained as often as the works prescribed are repeated, unless the contrary is expressly stated.

The first clause is taken from a decree of the S. Congregation, which mentions a visit to a church or another good work to which a plenary indulgence is attached. This indulgence, says the decree, may be gained only once a day.[77] Whether several different plenary indulgences may be gained on the same day by performing different works prescribed, although only one confession and communion is made, is another question.[78] Our Code only mentions *idem opus*, the same work, and hence it would be possible to gain several plenary indulgences on one day.

[77] S. C. Indulg., March 7, 1678; Benedict XIV, " *Inter praeteritos*," Dec. 3, 1749, § 84.

[78] Beringer, *l. c.*, ed. 13, p. 107, affirms, and S. C. Indulg., Jan. 12, 1878, ad 3, (*Coll. P. P.*, n. 1486) favors the view.

VISIT OF A SEMI-PUBLIC ORATORY

CAN. 929.

Fideles utriusque sexus qui, perfectionis studio vel institutionis seu educationis aut etiam valetudinis causa in domibus ecclesia vel publico sacello carentibus, de consensu Ordinariorum constitutis, vitam communem agunt, itemque personae omnes ad illis ministrandum ibidem commorantes, quoties ad lucrandas indulgentias praescribatur visitatio alicuius ecclesiae non determinatae, vel indeterminati alicuius publici oratorii, visitare queunt propriae domus sacellum in quo obligationi audiendi Sacrum iure satisfacere possunt, dummodo cetera opera iniuncta rite praestiterint.

Up to the year 1909 practice and the law prescribed a visit to a public oratory, but several indults were granted enabling the inmates of religious institutes and seminaries to gain the indulgence in their own chapels.[79] Out of these indults developed the general grant,[80] given in the year 1909, which has entered our Code. The meaning of can. 929 is that:

(a) All the faithful of both sexes, who *lead a life in common,* either as religious or as inmates of an institution, a place of study, a hospital, or asylum for the aged or disabled, may gain an indulgence for which the visit of a public oratory is prescribed,

(b) By visiting the *semi-public oratory*[81] or chapel in the house in which they reside, if this house has no public oratory or church attached, provided the house has been

---

[79] Beringer, *l. c.,* p. 87.
[80] S. O., Jan. 14, 1909 (*A. Ap. S.,* I, 210).
[81] To visit a church or chapel, if one be physically or morally near it; Beringer, *l. c.,* p. 86 f.

established with the consent of the Ordinary and is considered a religious institute.

(c) The same indulgence may be gained in the same way by all who *wait on* or serve the members of such a house and reside therein,

(d) But this favor can be made use of only if the church or public oratory, the visit of which is prescribed for gaining the indulgence, is not determined or designated.   Hence, if the visit of a certain church or oratory, for instance, the parish church, or the church of a religious order, were expressly prescribed, the indulgence could not be gained in the manner described above.

(e) Finally, in order to gain the indulgence in the above-named semi-public oratory, the other works or conditions imposed must be complied with.

We may add that all who are *chronically or continually ill or prevented by some other physical obstacle* from visiting a church or public oratory, may gain the indulgence by contritely confessing their sins and, instead of receiving Holy Communion and visiting a public oratory, performing some other good works which the confessor may impose on them.[82]   This privilege was extended to all sick and aged persons who live in a community and under a rule — therefore also to religious societies which are not religious communities in the strict sense,— and who cannot make the prescribed visit. For these the confessor may prescribe other pious works.[83]

[82] S. C. Indulg., Sept. 18, 1862 (*Coll. P. F.*, n. 1231).

[83] S. C. Indulg., Jan. 16, 1886 (*Coll. P. F.*, n. 1649).

INDULGENCES APPLICABLE TO THE DEAD

CAN. 930.

Nemo indulgentias acquirens potest eas aliis in vita degentibus applicare; animabus autem in purgatorio detentis indulgentiae omnes a Romano Pontifice concessae, nisi aliud constet, applicabiles sunt.

No one who gains indulgences can apply them to other living persons, but he may apply all indulgences granted by the Roman Pontiff to the poor souls in Purgatory, unless a contrary provision has been made. The first part of this law is clearly intended to remove abuses. It has a dogmatical bearing, because the living gain indulgences by way of absolution, which is a strictly personal affair, whereas the *poor souls* receive the benefit of indulgences by way of suffrage and are in the state of grace. The text says that *all indulgences granted by the Roman Pontiff* are applicable to the souls in Purgatory. By decree of Sept. 30, 1852, the S. Congregation had declared that all indulgences contained in the so-called *Raccolta* could be applied to the poor souls.[84] This application must not be understood as if the living person first gains the indulgence for himself, and then transmits it to the poor souls, but in this sense, that he may gain it either for himself or for the dead.[85]

[84] Prinzivalli, n. 628.
[85] Beringer, *l. c.*, p. 73. The first genuine document of a papal grant of indulgences applicable to the poor souls is that of Callistus III, 1457; Beringer, p. 51 f.

CAN. 931.

§ 1. Ad quaslibet indulgentias lucrandas confessio forte requisita peragi potest intra octo dies qui immediate praecedunt diem cui indulgentia fuit affixa; communio autem in pervigilio eiusdem diei; utraque vero etiam intra subsequentem totam octavam.

§ 2. Pariter ad lucrandas indulgentias pro piis exercitiis in triduum, hebdomadam, etc., ductis concessas, confessio et communio fieri etiam potest intra octavam quae immediate sequitur exercitium expletum.

§ 3. Christifideles qui solent, nisi legitime impediantur, saltem bis in mense ad poenitentiae sacramentum accedere, aut sanctam communionem in statu gratiae et cum recta piaque mente recipere quotidie, quamvis semel aut iterum per hebdomadam ab eadem abstineant, possunt omnes indulgentias consequi, etiam sine actuali confessione quae ceteroquin ad eas lucrandas necessaria foret, exceptis indulgentiis sive iubilaei ordinarii et extraordinarii sive ad instar iubilaei.

§ 1. If *confession* is required for gaining an indulgence, it may be made within the eight days immediately preceding the day to which the indulgence is affixed; Communion may be received on the day before the feast; both confession and communion may be received during the *entire octave*. For instance, one may receive Holy Communion on the feast of All Saints, in order to gain the *toties quoties* indulgence of All Souls' Day. But if All Souls' should fall on a Monday and All Saints' on a Saturday, Holy Communion would have to be received on Sunday, for this is the day before the feast to

which the indulgence is affixed.[86] *Confession,* if prescribed as a condition for gaining the indulgence, must be
made sacramentally within eight days preceding the day
to which the indulgence is attached.[87] We mention sacramental confession because this is intended by the legislator as an *opus praescriptum.*[88] However, if the penitent
would have no sins at all, not even venial sins, to confess,
or if he would confess a venial sin for which the confessor would think it opportune not to impart absolution,
sacramental absolution would not be required for gaining
the indulgence.[89]

The Code adds that both confession and Communion
may be made *within the octave* following the feast day
proper. This is a new law, at least we could not find
any text corroborating this enactment. It can apply only
to feasts which have an octave, and hence we hardly
believe that the Portiuncula or All Souls' Day indulgence
could be gained by going to confession and Communion
during the eight days following Aug. 2nd or Nov. 2nd.
Yet we do not state this opinion without misgiving, especially because of

§ 2, which rules that indulgences granted for pious
exercises conducted during a triduum or a week may be
gained if the prescribed confession and Communion are
made during the octave immediately following the close
of these devotions. Of course in that case the visit of
the church or attendance at these pious exercises is
required during the time these devotions are held. But
confession and Communion would then be the last work
required for gaining the indulgence.

86 S. C. Indulg., Oct. 6, 1870
(*Coll. P. F.,* n. 1358).

87 S. O. (Sect. Indulg), April 23,
1914 (*A. Ap. S.,* VI, 308).

88 Benedict XIV, "*Inter praeteritos,*" Dec 3, 1749, § 77.

89 S. C. Indulg., Aug. 20, 1822,
ad 2 (Prinzivalli, n. 432).

§ 3 provides that those who are accustomed to go to confession at least twice a month, or to communicate daily in the state of grace and with an upright and holy intention, although they do not receive one or the other time a week, may without confession gain all the indulgences for which confession is prescribed as a necessary condition. From this favor are excluded indulgences of the ordinary and the extraordinary jubilee.[90]

Clement XIII had already granted indulgences to those who go to confession weekly. Pius X extended this privilege to daily or quasi-daily communicants.[91] Therefore in our text *two classes* are distinguished: (a) Those who go to confession twice a month — which means every two weeks [92] and (b) those who communicate daily or almost daily. For the latter no certain time for confession is prescribed, as they are presumed to be in the " state of grace." Monthly confession would be sufficient. But from this favor are excluded jubilee indulgences, for which the Sovereign Pontiff is entitled to impose confession as a special work.[93]

PRESCRIBED WORKS

CAN. 932.

Opere, cui praestando quis lege aut praecepto obligatur, nequit indulgentia lucrifieri, nisi in eiusdem concessione aliud expresse dicatur; qui tamen praestat

---

[90] An *ordinary jubilee* is one granted at stated periods. Boniface VIII decreed (c. 1, Extrav. Comm., V, 9) that such a one should be held every 100 years. Later one was celebrated every 33 years, and finally every 25 years, as decided by Paul II in 1470. An *extraordinary jubilee* is one held on special occasions, *e. g.*, the accession of a pope, or his golden sacerdotal jubilee.

[91] S. C. Indulg., Feb. 14, 1906 (*Coll. P. F.*, n. 2228).

[92] S. C. Indulg., Feb. 25, 1885 (*ibid.*, n. 1653).

[93] Benedict XIV, "*Inter praeteritos,*" Dec. 3, 1749, § 77 f.

opus sibi in sacramentalem poenitentiam iniunctum
et indulgentiis forte ditatum, potest simul et poenitentiae satisfacere et indulgentias lucrari.

Can. 933.

Uni eidemque rei vel loco plures ex variis titulis
adnecti possunt indulgentiae; sed uno eodemque
opere, cui ex variis titulis indulgentiae adnexae sint,
non possunt plures acquiri indulgentiae, nisi opus
requisitum sit confessio vel communio, aut nisi aliud
expresse cautum fuerit.

No indulgence can be gained by performing a good
work to which *one is obliged by law or precept,* unless
the grant expressly admits such duplication. Thus fasting in Lent cannot be taken as fasting for gaining an
indulgence. A priest cannot comply with the condition
of saying certain prayers for gaining an indulgence by
reciting the Breviary.[94] But religious may perform the
pious devotions which they are wont to perform, not as
strict obligation, but in virtue of their constitutions, with
the intention of gaining indulgences, which they thus
really gain,[95] provided it is not the Breviary or Holy
Office which they are bound to recite by common law
(can. 610).

Those, however, who perform a good work imposed as
a sacramental penance may thereby comply with the
penance and gain the indulgence, if said good work be indulgenced.

To one and the same object or place indulgences may
be attached on various titles, but by one and the same
good work, to which by reason of different titles indul-

94 S. C. Indulg., May 29, 1841, ad 2 (Prinzivalli, n. 511).
95 Beringer, *l. c.,* p. 81.

gences are attached, these various indulgences cannot be gained unless the work prescribed be confession or communion, or unless the rescript read otherwise. Thus if a plenary indulgence is attached to a church by reason of the patronal feast and for the Portiuncula indulgence, all these may be gained by one confession and Communion, unless confession is required for other reasons, *i.e.*, to put one into the state of grace. But the prayers or good works must be repeated for every indulgence.[96]

CAN. 934.

§ 1. Si ad lucrandas indulgentias oratio in genere ad mentem Summi Pontificis praescribatur, mentalis tantum oratio non sufficit; oratio autem vocalis poterit arbitrio fidelium deligi, nisi peculiaris aliqua assignetur.

§ 2. Si peculiaris oratio assignata fuerit, indulgentiae acquiri possunt quocunque idiomate oratio recitetur, dummodo de fidelitate versionis constet ex declaratione vel Sacrae Poenitentiariae vel unius ex Ordinariis loci ubi vulgaris est lingua in quam vertitur oratio; sed indulgentiae penitus cessant ob quamlibet additionem, detractionem, vel interpolationem.

§ 3. Ad indulgentiarum acquisitionem satis est orationem alternis cum socio recitare, aut mente eam prosequi, dum ab alio recitatur.

§ 1. If general prayers for the intention of the Sovereign Pontiff are prescribed for gaining an indulgence, *mental prayer is not sufficient;* vocal prayers may be chosen *ad libitum* by the faithful, unless some special oration is prescribed.[97] Mental prayer is praiseworthy, but to gain indulgences, vocal prayers are required, that

[96] S. C. Indulg., May 29, 1841; Jan. 12, 1878 (*Coll. P. F.*, nn. 1486 ad 3).

[97] Benedict XIV, "*Convocatis,*" Nov. 25, 1749, § LI.

is to say, the words must be uttered exteriorly, though they need not be audible. How many "Our Fathers" and "Hail Marys" should be recited the S. Congregation refused to decide.[98] Any prayer may be chosen, provided, of course, it be orthodox and approved by the Church. The general intention of the Holy Father is the exaltation of the Church, the propagation of the faith, the uprooting of heresies and schisms, the conversion of sinners, and peace and concord among the nations.

§ 2. If a special prayer is prescribed, the indulgence may be gained by reciting that prayer in any language, provided the accuracy of the translation is assured by a declaration of either the S. Poenitentiaria or the Ordinary of any diocese where the language is spoken. But all indulgences cease if any addition, subtraction or interpolation is made to the required prayers. Concerning the *quality* of the prayer it may be worth while to add a few remarks on the *Officium Parvum B. M. V.* A plenary indulgence may be gained by those who recite this office daily for one month; seven years and seven quadragenes (*i.e.*, 490 days of the old fast) for reciting it once a day. Formerly this office had to be said in Latin, but Leo XIII permitted it to be recited, privately, in the vernacular without losing the indulgence.[99]

For the *approval of translations* the diocesan ordinaries are competent. The text says: *unius ex Ordinariis*, one of the Ordinaries. Hence if the Ordinary of one diocese in our country approves an English translation of a prayer, it is sufficient for all dioceses where English is

---

[98] S. C. Indulg., May 29, 1841; Sept. 13, 1888 (*Coll. P. F.*, nn. 922, 1693).

[99] S. C. Indulg., April 30, 1852; Dec. 29, 1864; Sept. 13, 1888; Aug. 18, 1903 (*Coll. P. F.*, Vol. II, p. 699).

spoken, even across the sea. The Ordinary is the one in whose diocese the English translation is either printed or published.[1]

The last clause of § 2 speaks of *addition, diminution,* and *interpolation,* all of which processes are prohibited under penalty of depriving a prayer of its indulgences. Such an addition, for instance, is the repetition of the mysteries in saying the Holy Rosary.[2] No particular rescript can abolish this general law, unless it be granted *after* the promulgation of the Code.

§ 3. To gain an indulgence it is enough to recite the prescribed prayer alternately with a companion, or to follow it in one's mind while another recites it. Thus by reciting the Rosary or the Angelus in common or together with others the indulgences may be gained by all who participate in the recitation,[3] and even by those who follow the one who recites the prayers only mentally, not orally.

COMMUTATION OF PIOUS WORKS

CAN. 935

Pia opera ad lucrandas indulgentias iniuncta, confessarii possunt in alia commutare pro iis qui, legitimo detenti impedimento, eadem praestare nequeant.

Pious works imposed for gaining indulgences may be commuted by the confessor into other good works for those who are lawfully prevented from performing the good works prescribed.

---

1 Can. 1390.

2 There is absolutely no foundation for the assumption that a particular decision or indult given for any diocese or for a particular language, can be transferred to other dioceses and other languages.

If no other reason, at least the danger of exposing the faithful to losing the indulgence should stop this practice.

3 S. C. Indulg., 1820, ad 4 (Prinzivalli, n. 420).

Thus, as mentioned above, sick and aged persons who cannot visit a prescribed church may have that requirement changed into some other good work.[4] Christians in China and Siam, who were members of the Confraternity of the Holy Rosary, but unable to recite the beads in common, were permitted to have this work changed into other works of charity and religion.[5] A commutation may be granted by the confessor also outside the confessional,[6] but not beyond the limits set by the papal constitutions or rescripts.[7]

MUTES

CAN. 936

Muti lucrari possunt indulgentias adnexas publicis precibus, si una cum ceteris fidelibus in eodem loco orantibus mentem ac pios sensus ad Deum attollant; et si agatur de privatis orationibus, satis est ut eas mente recolant signisve effundant vel tantummodo oculis percurrant.

Mutes may gain the indulgences attached to the recital of *public prayers* if together with the other faithful they assist and raise their mind and senses to God; as to *private* prayers it is sufficient that they recollect them in their mind and follow them either by signs or with their eyes (if they are able to read).

They need not pronounce the prayers or move their lips; nor need they recur to the confessor in each case; the law grants them this facility for gaining indulgences.[8]

---

4 S. C. Indulg., Jan. 16, 1886, ad 2 (*Coll. P. F.*, n. 1649).

5 S. C. P. F., Sept. 19, 1773 (*Coll.*, n. 499).

6 S. C. P. F., Feb. 20, 1801 (*Coll.*, n. 657).

7 Benedict XIV, "*Inter praeteritos*," Dec. 3, 1749, § 52 f.

8 S. C. Indulg., Feb. 16, 1852; July 18, 1902 (*Coll. P. F.*, n. 2147).

TITLE V

EXTREME UNCTION

Can. 937

Extremae unction is sacramentum conferri debet per sacras unctiones, adhibito oleo olivarum rite benedicto, et per verba in ritualibus libris ab Ecclesia probatis praescripta.

The Sacrament of Extreme Unction must be administered by the sacred anointments, with duly blessed olive oil, and by pronouncing the words prescribed in the rituals approved by the Church.

This Sacrament, as the Council of Trent [1] defines, was instituted by our Lord and promulgated by St. James the Apostle in his Epistle, which Luther rejected as apocryphal. The *remote matter* is pure *olive oil,* to the exclusion of all other oils, such as that made from nuts, sesame, cottonseed. The *proximate matter* is the act of anointing the body. What parts of the body must be anointed, or how many anointings constitute the essence of the Sacrament, cannot be determined with certainty from the ancient rituals, as they show a great diversity. [2] However, since in case of necessity (can. 947), a single unction is admitted as valid, it would be presumptuous to demand more. Ordinarily, and outside the case of necessity, the separate anointment of the seats of the five

---

1 Sess. 14, c. 1: can. 1-3, *de extrema Unct.*

2 Cfr. Pohle-Preuss, *The Sacraments,* IV, p. 19; J. Kern, S. J., *Tract. de Sacr. Extr. Unct.,* 1907.

senses,— sight, hearing, smell, taste, and touch,— constitutes the proximate matter of Extreme Unction.[3] The form of the Sacrament consists in the *words* used at the anointings, as prescribed by the Roman Ritual.[4]

[3] *Decr. pro Arm.* (Denzinger n. 595).
[4] Tit. V, c. 1, n. 1.

CHAPTER I

CAN. 938

§ 1. Hoc sacramentum valide administrat omnis et solus sacerdos.

§ 2. Salvo praescripto can. 397, n. 3, 514, §§ 1–3, minister ordinarius est parochus loci, in quo degit infirmus; in casu autem necessitatis, vel de licentia saltem rationabiliter praesumpta eiusdem parochi vel Ordinarii loci, alius quilibet sacerdos hoc sacramentum ministrare potest.

CAN. 939

Minister ordinarius ex iustitia tenetur hoc sacramentum per se ipse vel per alium administrare, et in casu necessitatis ex caritate quilibet sacerdos.

Every priest, and no one but a priest, may validly administer this sacrament. This follows from James V, 14 f., and was expressly defined by the Council of Trent.[1] Since *every* priest may validly administer this sacrament, it follows that excommunicated, suspended, interdicted or degraded priests are not excluded, though such, of course, cannot confer it licitly, as it flows from the power of order, not of jurisdiction. And because *no one but a priest* may confer Extreme Unction, no inferior cleric, though otherwise of the highest rank, can validly admin-

[1] Sess. 14, c. 4, *de extr. Unct.*

ister it. Not even the Pope could grant this power to a cleric who is not endowed with the priestly character. The singular (*sacerdos*, priest) must not be understood as if several priests could not administer this sacrament conjointly, as is customary with the Greeks, among whom seven priests together confer this Sacrament. This custom has not been reproved by the Church, but the Greeks are held to believe that one priest is sufficient to administer Extreme Unction validly and licitly.[2]

The ordinary minister of Extreme Unction is the *priest of the parish* where the sick person resides. In case of necessity, however, any priest may administer this Sacrament.

Since the administration of Extreme Unction is strictly a *parochial right*, it is by law [3] reserved to the pastor, and assistant priests or curates must have the pastor's permission to exercise it. This permission may be given habitually. Besides, the diocesan statutes or letter of appointment [4] may determine whether assistants have the right. The *oeconomus*, or temporary administrator, of a parish enjoys full parochial rights and may therefore give permission to administer this Sacrament [5] to another priest. *Regulars* have been enjoined time and again [6] not to interfere with this right. Secular Tertiaries are not allowed to receive this Sacrament at the hands of the Friars Minor.[7] To canons of cathedral as well as collegiate chapters this Sacrament must be administered by the pastor in whose parish they have their domicile.[8] Ex-

2 Benedict XIV. "*Etsi pastoralis*," May 26, 1742, § V, n. III; "*Ex quo*," March 1, 1756, § 45.

3 See can. 462.

4 Can. 476, § 6.

5 Can. 473; S. C. C., Sept. 12, 1874 (*A. S. S.*, VIII, 129 f.).

6 C. 1, Clem. V, 7; S. C. C., June

7, 1698, etc.; Benedict XIV, *De Syn. Dioec.*, VIII, 4, 7; IX, 16, 2.

7 S. Rit. C., June 20, 1609 ad 1 (*Dec. Auth.*, n. 271).

8 S. Rit. C., March 17, 1663, ad 4; May 13, Dec. 18, 1756 (*Dec. Auth.*, nn. 1255, 2441).

empt from these rules is the Ordinary of the diocese, to whom the dignitaries or canons, according to rank and precedence, should administer Extreme Unction.[9] Besides can. 514 must here be applied, as explained elsewhere.[10]

The *ordinary minister*, says can. 939, is *obliged* in *justice* to administer Extreme Unction either himself or by a substitute. In case of necessity every priest is bound *by charity* to administer this Sacrament. This law was inculcated by Clement XII and Benedict XIV, who exhorted missionaries not to discriminate between rich and poor, as even pagan physicians do not disdain to minister to the lower classes (Pariahs).[11]

That great canonist and Pontiff, Benedict XIV, also discussed the question whether a pastor is obliged to administer Extreme Unction to such as are afflicted with a contagious or epidemic disease. After having quoted several authors, among them Suarez and Silvius, he concludes that sound theology answers in the affirmative, but adds that the pastor may send another priest and that all reasonable precautions should be taken to avoid contagion.[12]

9 Can. 397, n. 3.
10 Cfr. Vol. III, 141 ff., of this Commentary.

11 See the Constit. quoted by Gasparri *ad l. c.*
12 *De Syn Dioec.*, XIII, 19, 8-10.

CHAPTER II

CAN. 940

§ 1. Extrema unctio praeberi non potest nisi fideli, qui post adeptum usum rationis ob infirmitatem vel senium in periculo mortis versetur.

§ 2. In eadem infirmitate hoc sacramentum iterari non potest, nisi infirmus post susceptam unctionem convaluerit et in aliud vitae discrimen inciderit.

Extreme Unction may be administered only to faithful Catholics who have reached the age of discretion and are in danger of death on account of sickness or old age. The Sacrament may not be repeated in the same sickness, unless the patient has recovered after receiving Extreme Unction and his condition has again become critical.

The term *faithful Catholic* includes *neophytes, i.e.,* persons newly baptized, though concerning these, the Holy Office has decided that they may receive the Sacrament only if they are sufficiently instructed to receive it with profit and have the intention of receiving it for the benefit of their souls.[1]

The subject of Exreme Unction must have reached the *age of discretion, i.e.,* about the seventh year. It is the purpose of this Sacrament, as the form, *Indulgeat,* etc., indicates, to wipe out actual sins committed by the bodily

---

1 S. O., May 10, 1703 ad 8; April 10, 1801, ad 1; S. C. P. F., Sept. 26, 1821 (*Coll.*, nn. 256, 1213, 708).

senses, which could not be accomplished in infants.[2] The same rule applies to those who have been insane from childhood,[3] though if the disease was contracted after the age of discretion, Extreme Unction can be administered.

The person to whom Extreme Unction is administered, must be *sick or so old* that the danger of death is at least very probable. The Greeks were accustomed to administer this Sacrament also to the healthy, but the Church has never tolerated the custom.[4] Those who are not sick, though exposed to probable or certain danger of death (soldiers, condemned criminals, travellers engaged in a dangerous journey, etc.) cannot receive this Sacrament.[5] Neither may women at childbirth, unless some extraordinary and serious illness should accompany the labor pains.[6]

The text says *ob senium*, including those who are in danger of death on account of old age. Benedict XIV says that people of advanced age die easily, and old age leads to a dissolution of the bodily faculties.[7] But some signs of approaching dissolution, such as fainting or sinking spells, should appear before Extreme Unction is given. Old age is generally held to commence with the sixtieth year, which also frees from the obligation of fasting.

§ 2 forbids repetition of Extreme Unction in the same sickness. Benedict XIV, after an interesting historical investigation, says:[8] If the crisis is passed, but the pa-

---

2 S. Thom., *Com. in. Sent.*, IV, dist. 23, q. 3, art. 2; Benedict XIV, *De Syn. Dioec.*, VIII, 6, 1; S. C. Sacr., Aug. 8, 1910, n. VIII (*A. Ap. S.*, II, 583).

3 Benedict XIV, *l. c.*, VIII, 6, 3 f.

4 Benedict XIV, *"Etsi pastoralis,"* May 26, 1742, § V, n. II.

5 *Rit. Rom.*, tit. V, c. 1, n. 9.

6 Benedict XIV, *De Syn. Dioec.*, VIII, 5, 1.

7 *Ibid.*, n. 2.

8 *Ibid.*, VIII, 8, 3, where he mentions the fact that the monks of Hirsau used to anoint their sick brethren every three years.

tient has not entirely recovered, and suffers a serious relapse, Extreme Unction may be administered without hesitation.   If the pastor is in doubt whether the crisis is a new one, or a continuation of the former, he should incline to repeated administration, because this is more in conformity with the ancient practice of the Church. It is not necessary to await the last stage of danger, or even the critical moment, and consumptives, etc., may be anointed even if there is no immediate danger.   This rule applies especially in missionary countries, where priests are not always to be had.[9]

Can. 941

Quando dubitatur num infirmus usum rationis attigerit, num in periculo mortis reipsa versetur vel num mortuus sit, hoc sacramentum ministretur sub conditione.

When it is doubtful whether the sick person has attained the use of reason — not the age of discretion — or whether he or she is really in danger of death, or already dead, Extreme Unction should be conferred conditionally.

According to high medical authority death sometimes does not occur for an hour or more after a man has drawn his last breath, and hence Extreme Unction may be administered during the interval.

Can. 942

Hoc sacramentum non est conferendum illis qui impoenitentes in manifesto peccato mortali contumaciter perseverant; quod si hoc dubium fuerit, conferatur sub conditione.

9 S. C. P. F., Feb. 10, 1801 (*Coll.*, n. 651).

This Sacrament may not be administered to those who stubbornly and manifestly live in the state of grievous sin; in case of doubt, however, let it be administered conditionally.

This rule may cause some trouble, especially in the case of *Freemasons* and persons enrolled in a cremation society. All such persons should be admonished to retract the order they have given to have their bodies cremated. If they refuse, Extreme Unction cannot be administered. *When* and *how* the admonition is to be made, is a matter for pastoral prudence; above all, the danger of scandal must be removed.[10]

CAN. 943

Infirmis autem qui, cum suae mentis compotes essent, illud saltem implicite petierunt aut verisimiliter petiissent, etiamsi deinde sensus vel usum rationis amiserint, nihilominus absolute praebeatur.

To those who asked for Extreme Unction at least implicitly or interpretatively whilst in the full possession of their mental faculties, the Sacrament may be administered even though they lose their senses or the use of reason.

This agrees with the advice given to an American bishop who had asked which sacraments may or should be given to *consuetudinarii,* or *recidivi,* or such as are utterly careless of their spiritual welfare. The answer was: If they have given signs of repentance, Extreme Unction may be administered.[11] Broadly speaking, it may be said that, unless positive refusal lasting up to the moment of unconsciousness can reasonably be assumed, this Sacrament may be administered.

10 S. O., July 27, 1892, ad 1 (*Coll. P. P. F.,* n. 1808).

11 S. O., May 9, 1821 (*Coll. P. F.,* n. 757).

Can. 944

Quamvis hoc sacramentum per se non sit de necessitate medii ad salutem, nemini tamen licet illud negligere; et omni studio et diligentia curandum ut infirmi, dum sui plene compotes sunt, illud recipiant.

Although this Sacrament is not absolutely necessary as a means of salvation, yet no one may neglect it; and care and diligence should be taken that the sick receive it while fully conscious.

Although, according to the theologians,[12] it would not be a grievous sin not to receive Extreme Unction, every pastor is under grievous obligation to administer this Sacrament to those who ask for it.[13] Regulars or religious who are missionaries are obliged by a decision of the Holy Office to obey the same law.[14] The Nestorians, and Orientals in general, have been admonished not to be neglectful in the administration of this Sacrament.[15] Bishops should see to it that pastors perform their duty in this regard.[16]

12 Cfr. Noldin, *De Sacram.*, ed. 10, n. 461.

13 S. O., March 23, 1656; S. C. P. F., Sept. 12, 1645 (*Coll.*, nn. 126, 114).

14 S. O., Nov. 13, 1609 (*Coll. P. F.*, n. 189).

15 Benedict XIV, "*Ex quo*," March 1, 1756, §§ 44, 46; S. C. P. F., July 31, 1902, n. 7 (*Coll.*, n. 2149).

16 Benedict XIV, "*Firmandis*," Nov. 6, 1744, § 9.

CHAPTER III

OLIVE OIL BLESSED BY THE BISHOP

CAN. 945

Oleum olivarum, in sacramento extremae unctionis
adhibendum, debet esse ad hoc benedictum ab Episcopo, vel a presbytero qui facultatem illud benedicendi
a Sede Apostolica obtinuerit.

The olive oil to be used in the administration of Extreme Unction must be blessed for that purpose by the
bishop or by a priest who has obtained the necessary
faculty from the Apostolic See.

Concerning the necessity of using olive oil blessed
by a bishop different opinions were held, but it is safe
to say that this canon embodies an ancient practice,
mentioned by Innocent I as universal in the Western
Church.[1] In the Greek Church the priests themselves
bless the oil before administering this Sacrament.[2]

CAN. 946

Oleum infirmorum parochus loco nitido et decenter
ornato in vase argenteo vel stamneo diligenter custo-
diat, nec domi retineat nisi ad normam can. 735.

The " oil of the sick " must be preserved in a vessel of
silver or white metal (a composition of lead and silver),

---

[1] Innocent I, *Ep., ad Decent.*   [2] Benedict XIV, " *Etsi pastoralis,*"
Eugub., 25, (Denzinger, n. 60).   May 26, 1742, § IV, n. 1.

and in a neat and properly equipped place; — but it may not be kept at home, except in the case permitted by can. 735 (*q.v.*).

THE ANOINTINGS

Can. 947

§ 1. Unctiones verbis, ordine et modo in libris ritualibus praescripto, accurate peragantur; in casu autem necessitatis sufficit unica unctio in uno sensu seu rectius in fronte cum praescripta forma breviore, salva obligatione singulas unctiones supplendi, cessante periculo.

§ 2. Unctio renum semper omittatur.

§ 3. Unctio pedum ex qualibet rationabili causa omitti potest.

§ 4. Extra casum gravis necessitatis, unctiones ipsa ministri manu nulloque adhibito instrumento fiant.

The anointments must be accurately performed, as stated in the Roman Ritual, which prescribes the words, the order and the manner of anointing. In case of necessity one anointment on the forehead with the short formula is sufficient; but the obligation of supplying the other anointments remains when the danger is over. The anointment of the loins is always to be omitted. The anointment of the feet may be omitted for any reasonable cause. Except in case of grave necessity, the anointments must be made by direct touch, without instruments. The Ritual exactly prescribes the manner in which this Sacrament must be conferred. Its prescriptions should be strictly followed. An anointing performed simultaneously by several priests who would divide the sacred function in order to gain time would be valid, but allowed only in case of grave necessity,[3] for which, however, the Code provides more effectively by ordaining that, when there is grave danger, one anointment is sufficient. This must be made on the forehead, with the formula: *"Per istam sanctam unctionem indulgeat tibi Dominus quidquid deliquisti. Amen."*

A new and welcome regulation is the permission to *omit the anointment of the feet* for any reasonable motive, which we must leave to pastoral prudence and hygienics to determine.

Concerning the use of an " instrument," *e.g.*, a brush or a piece of cotton (*stylus, virgula*) or a little stick or twig, this may be allowed in contagious diseases, especially the bubonic plague,[5] but outside such cases of necessity, it is strictly forbidden.[6]

[3] Cfr. *Anal. Eccl.*, 1900, Vol. 8, p. 428 f.

[4] S. O., April 25, 1906 (*Coll. P. F.*, n. 2233).

[5] S. O., July 11, 1754; S. C. P. F., June 21, 1788. (*Coll.*, n. 596).

[6] S. Rit. C., May 9, 1857, ad II (*Dec. Auth.*, n. 3051).

TITLE VI

CAN. 948

Ordo ex Christi institutione clericos a laicis in Ecclesia distinguit ad fidelium regimen et cultus divini ministerium.

What was said in Vol. II of this Commentary on the hierarchic distinction between clergy and laity, and the degrees of the hierarchic order, may suffice to illustrate the present canon.[1] It is the hieratic element, the power of order established by Christ himself, which distinguishes the clergy from the laity or ordinary faithful. It is the clergy who govern the faithful and conduct the divine worship. To the clergy is entrusted the government and administration of the mystical and the real body of Christ, whereas the laity cannot validly perform any act of jurisdiction or order.[2] This power is conferred by the Sacrament called Orders. There are various degrees, but conjointly taken, they signify the Sacrament by which a layman is marked with the clerical character, which can never be effaced.

CAN. 949

In canonibus qui sequuntur, nomine ordinum *maiorum* vel *sacrorum* intelliguntur presbyteratus, diacon-

[1] Vol. II, p. 41 ff.
[2] *Trid.*, sess. 23, can. 3, *de Sacr.*

Ord.; cfr. *Professio Fidei Waldensibus proposita* (Denzinger, n. 370).

atus, subdiaconatus; *minorum* vero acolythatus, exorcistatus, lectoratus, ostiariatus.

In the following canons the term *higher* or *sacred orders* signifies the priesthood, the diaconate, and the subdiaconate; the term *minor orders* signifies the offices of acolythe, exorcist, lector and doorkeeper. Here we must again refer to Vol. II.

Subdeaconship, properly speaking, is a *major*, but cannot strictly be called *sacred* order because it is not a Sacrament in the true sense of the word.[3]

The *episcopate* is a Sacrament, but is not enumerated among the higher or sacred orders for the reason that ecclesiastical terminology[4] has drawn a line of distinction between the episcopate, which contains the fullness of the priesthood, and the inferior ranks. Hence the order of the episcopate is marked as an independent and superior dignity or office, a singular institution, for the reason, no doubt, that the bishops are the spiritual fathers of the clergy whom they ordain.

CAN. 950

In iure verba: *ordinare, ordo, ordinatio, sacra ordinatio,* comprehendunt, praeter consecrationem episcopalem, ordines enumeratos in can. 949 et ipsam primam tonsuram, nisi aliud ex natura rei vel ex contextu verborum eruatur.

Though the episcopate stands out prominently, it, too, is conferred by the Sacrament of Holy Orders, and order means a distinct degree of the hierarchic constitution, or of ecclesiastical power in general. In law, therefore, the

[3] Cfr. Pohle-Preuss, *The Sacraments*, IV, p. 107 f.; c. 11, Dist. 32.

[4] C. 4, Dist. 60: "*sacros autem ordines dicimus diaconatum et presbyteratum.*"

terms *"ordinare, ordo, ordinatio, sacra ordinatio"* comprise not only the orders mentioned in the preceding canon, but also the episcopate and the first tonsure, unless the nature of the thing itself or the context imply a different meaning.

The act by which one receives the *episcopate* is properly called *consecration,* but since this act requires the use of the same matter and form which constitute the substance of Holy Orders, it is evident that the general terms: to ordain, ordination, etc., include the episcopal order. The Code does not pretend to solve the controversy concerning the sacramental character of the episcopate or that regarding the essence of the Sacrament — whether it consists in the act of delivering the instruments or in the laying on of the hands, or in both. As to tonsure, we have elsewhere noted that it is not a Sacrament but merely a preparation for Holy Orders.[5]

5 Cfr. Vol. II, p. 43 f.; Layman, *Theol. Moralis,* l. V, tr. 9, c. 3, n. 3.

CHAPTER I

CAN. 951

Sacrae ordinationis minister ordinarius est Episcopus consecratus; extraordinarius, qui, licet charactere episcopali careat, a iure vel a Sede Apostolica per peculiare indultum potestatem acceperit aliquos ordines conferendi.

The ordinary minister of sacred ordination is every (validly) *consecrated* bishop, even though he be a schismatic or heretic.

This was defined in the Decree for the Armenians and again by the Council of Trent.[1] However, it must be added that although every validly consecrated bishop may ordain validly, yet he must make use of the proper form in the act of ordination, and have the intention of conferring the power attached to the Sacrament; or rather, let us say, the *ordinans* must not positively exclude the intention of the Church.   From this point of view the Anglican Orders were declared invalid by Leo XIII, in his " *Apostolicae curae*," of Sept. 13, 1896.[2]

In saying that the bishop is the ordinary minister of the Sacrament of Holy Orders, the Code implicitly admits an *extraordinary minister, i.e.,* one who, though lacking the episcopal character, has obtained the power of ordain-

---

[1] *Dec. pro Arm.*, Denzinger, n. 596; *Trid.*, sess. 23, c. 4; can. 7, *de Sac. Ord.*

[2] See *Cath. Encycl.*, I, 491 ff.

ing either by law, or by a special indult of the Apostolic See.

By law the following are extraordinary ministers of sacred ordination:

(a) The *Cardinals,* who have the privilege of conferring the *tonsure* and *minor orders,* provided the *promovendus* can show a dimissorial letter from his Ordinary. It is, of course, supposed that Cardinals are endowed with the priestly character; and if so, it matters nothing whether they are cardinal bishops, priests or deacons.[3]

(b) *Vicars Apostolic* and *Prefects Apostolic* may confer the tonsure and minor orders within their own territory and during their term of office, as per can. 957.

(c) *Abbates regiminis* may confer the tonsure and minor orders according to can. 964.

By a *special indult of the Apostolic See* a simple priest may obtain the faculty of bestowing tonsure and minor orders, though not, according to present practice, the subdeaconship or the diaconate.[4] Two things, however, are essential: (1) that the *ordinans* must be a priest, and (2) that a privilege or indult be obtained. If one who had received minor orders from a simple priest without faculties, were afterwards raised to sacred orders by a bishop, he would have to receive tonsure and minor orders again, but not the higher orders properly conferred by the bishop.[5]

---

[3] Cfr. c. 11, x, I, 14; can. 232, § 1; can. 239, § 1, n. 22.

[4] Concerning the Constitution of Innocent VIII, see Pohle-Preuss, *l. c.,* p. 124; *Anal. Eccl.,* 1901, p. 312 ff.

[5] Cfr. c. 2, Dist. 68; c. 11, x, I, 14; S. C. Ec. it RR., Dec. 22, 1578 (Bizzarri, *Collectanea,* p. 218 f).

PROMOTED BY THE POPE

CAN. 952

Nemini licet ordinatum a Romano Pontifice ad altiorem ordinem promovere sine Sedis Apostolicae facultate.

This is a celebrated text. Its original source is a rescript of Innocent III to the bishop of Modena. The facts were these: a cleric who had been ordained subdeacon by the Pope, was to be promoted to the diaconate by the bishop of Bologna, who had received an indult to that effect from Pope Innocent III.

Our canon says: *No one ordained by the Roman Pontiff may lawfully be promoted to a higher order without an Apostolic faculty.* This rule, however, holds only if the Pope in *person,* or another prelate by special command of the Pontiff, ordains a clergyman. Consequently, one ordained in Rome by the Cardinal Vicar does not enjoy this distinction.[6] On the other hand, it does not matter what order the Pope conferred, for the text says: "*Ordinatum a Romano Pontifice,*" and this term includes tonsure, according to can. 950. The episcopate also is comprised therein, but this is mentioned especially in can. 953.

MANDATUM DE CONSECRANDO

CAN. 953

Consecratio episcopalis reservatur Romano Pontifici ita ut nulli Episcopo liceat quemquam consecrare in Episcopum, nisi prius constet de pontificio mandato.

[6] Benedict XIV, "*In postremo,*" Oct. 20, 1756, § 3 f.

Episcopal consecration is reserved to the Roman Pontiff, and no bishop is allowed to consecrate anyone unless he is certain of the papal mandate.

Formerly, according to the Decretals,[7] the metropolitan had the right to consecrate suffragan bishops.[8] This right was, however, purely historic and could not prejudice the universal right of the Sovereign Pontiff, who at all times could, without usurpation, restrict or withdraw the faculty of metropolitans with regard to their suffragans. The change was brought about gradually in the form of a *mandate*. The *Pontificale Romanum*[9] prescribes that the consecrator must obtain a papal commission in the form of an Apostolic letter, if he resides outside the Curia, or an oral commission by the Roman Pontiff if he is a Cardinal,— we suppose *de curia*. Benedict XIV modified a former Constitution of Benedict XIII so as to permit the *consecrandus* to choose as his consecrator any bishop in union with the Holy See if the consecration was to take place outside the City of Rome. In Rome the *consecrandus* had to choose a cardinal endowed with the episcopal character, or one of the four titular patriarchs. As a reminder of the ancient discipline Benedict XIV ordered that if the metropolitan should chance to be in Rome at the time one of his suffragans was consecrated, the consecration should be performed by him.[10]

The canon then states: "*nisi prius constet de pontificio mandato.*" This mandate, as noted above, is given orally when the consecration is performed in Rome, but if it takes place outside the City, an *Apostolic letter* is required, which must be in the hands of the consecrator

---

7 Cc. 11, 32, x. I, 6; cfr. c. 3, Dist. 65.

8 Benedict XIV, *l. c.*, § 15.

9 *De consecratione electi in episcopum.*

10 "*In postremo*"; § 16.

before he is allowed to perform the function. Without such a mandate he acts unlawfully, though validly. It is not sufficient that the letters be expedited in Rome and unofficial notice be sent of the fact.[11] If, however, certain and authentic notice has been received that the letters have been expedited in Rome, the law is complied with.[12] But an official or authentic notice can come only from the Roman Court. Thus any message, sent by the Secretariate of State by telephone, telegraph, or (we presume) wireless, to the effect that the Apostolic letters were expedited, would create a certainty.[13] The *mandatum consecrationis* may be contained in the letters of promotion in the form of the clause: "*ut electus a quocunque maluerit catholico antistite, gratiam et communionem Apostolicae Sedis habente consecrationis munus accipere valeat.*" When this clause does not occur in the letter of promotion, or when the letter contains a clause to the contrary, a special papal mandate is required for the consecration.[14]

This law is technically perfect, as it has a *penal sanction* attached to it. Those who bestow or receive consecration without an Apostolic mandate incur *suspension ipso facto,* which lasts until the Apostolic See expressly dispenses therefrom.[15]

11 Alexander VII, "*Alias,*" Feb. 27, 1660.

12 S. C. P. F., Dec. 30, 1781 (*Coll.,* n. 551).

13 S. O., Aug. 24, 1892; Sec. Status, Dec. 10, 1891 (*Coll. P. F.,* nn. 1810, 1775).

14 Leo XIII, "*Trans Oceanum,*" April 18, 1897 (*Coll. P. F.,* n. 1965, ad 1).

15 Can. 2370.

CONSECRATORS

CAN. 954

Episcopus consecrator debet alios duos Episcopos adhibere, qui sibi in consecratione assistant, nisi hac super re a Sede Apostolica dispensatum fuerit.

Pseudo-Isidore has set up a fanciful reason why a bishop should not be consecrated by less than three bishops: — because, he says, James was consecrated bishop of Jerusalem by three Apostles, Peter, James the Elder and John.[16] The real reason for this ancient custom must be sought in the fact that the metropolitans were wont to consecrate their suffragans and the patriarchs the metropolitans, in the presence of the bishops of the same province. And as it was often impossible for all the bishops of a province to meet for the occasion, it grew to be the custom that at least three took part in every consecration.[17] Our canon prescribes that the *consecrator shall be assisted by two other bishops,* unless an Apostolic dispensation has been granted from this rule. This law does not affect the validity of a consecration,[18] but constitutes a grievous obligation to employ two co-consecrating bishops. Sometimes the Roman Court grants a dispensation permitting the employment of two dignities of the cathedral chapter, or simply two dignities, as assistants.[19] Thus Leo XIII permitted the bishops of *Latin America* to employ two dignitaries whenever two bishops were not readily available.[20] This indult is still

16 C. 2, Dist. 66.

17 C. 5, Dist. 51; c. 1, Dist. 64; c. 5, Dist. 65; Phillips, *K.-R.*, Vol. I, 1845, p. 362 f.

18 S. C. P. F., May 18, 1695 (*Coll.*, n. 239); somewhat surprising S. Rit. C., Dec. 17, 1642 (*Dec.*

Auth., n. 820): *convalidari posse;* but Benedict XIV, *De Syn. Dioec.,* XIII, 13, 7, plainly states the validity.

19 S. Rit. C., July 16, 1605 (*Dec. Auth.*, n. 186).

20 "*Trans Oceanum,*" ad 1.

in force for that country, as the Code clearly says: "*nisi Ap. Sedis dispensaverit.*" If the two assistants at a consecration are not bishops, they must touch the head of the *consecrandus* with both hands, and in all other respects, also, carefully observe the prescriptions of the *Pontificale Romanum.*[21]

THE EPISCOPUS PROPRIUS

CAN. 955

§ 1. Unusquisque a proprio Episcopo ordinetur aut cum legitimis eiusdem litteris dimissoriis.

§ 2. Episcopus proprius, iusta causa non impeditus, per se ipse suos subditos ordinet; sed subditum orientalis ritus, sine apostolico indulto, licite ordinare non potest.

It is a time-honored principle [22] in the Church that no bishop or metropolitan shall trench upon the rights or powers of another bishop or ordinary, especially in regard to the exercise of pontifical rights, such as ordination.[23] Since one becomes incorporated in the Church by Baptism, and Baptism in the first four centuries was conferred on adults by the bishop himself, it was but natural that the spiritual father had the first claim on persons thus regenerated. *Baptism* constituted the first title for the competency of the bishop, and the synods of Sardica (343) and Antioch (332) strictly forbade bishops to coax laymen or subjects of one diocese or province into another and to ordain them to the clericate, except after having obtained the consent of their proper bishop.[24]

21 S. Rit. C., June 9, 1853 (*Dec. Auth.*, n. 3014).

22 C. 1, Dist. 71 (*Conc. Sardic. x.*).

23 *Trid.*, sess. 6, c. 5 *de ref.*

24 Cfr. Dist. 71; Thomassinus, *Vetus et Nova Discipl. Eccl.*, P. II, l. 1, c. 1.

When infant Baptism came into vogue in the 10th century, it became necessary to examine the *origin* or birth of those who wished to enter the clerical ranks. Those who wished to be ordained in a strange country had to exhibit letters from the bishop of their own country. This practice was formally sanctioned by a decretal of Clement IV, who acknowledged as a further reason for competency *benefice*, by reason of which that Ordinary was competent who had bestowed a benefice upon the *ordinandus.*[25] The canonists and legists drew from the Roman law the title of domicile and introduced it into church discipline. Thus the *domicile* of the ordinand was legalized.[26] Three grounds of competency are therefore discernible in the Decretals: origin, domicile, and benefice. To these the Council of Trent added *familiaritas.*[27] The Code admits only origin and domicile.

It is almost superfluous to add that, as Clement IV had already decided that the *Pope* may grant permission to be ordained by any bishop, so he himself may ordain anyone anywhere.

Can. 955 in its § 1, lays down the general rule that *everyone should be ordained by his own bishop or at least with dimissorial letters from the latter.* These letters are nothing else but the (written) consent of the bishop permitting one of his subjects to be ordained by another bishop. The text plainly refers to the old practice and to the Council of Trent,[28] which complained that bishops *in partibus infidelium* had, like mercenaries, invaded the dioceses of others and ordained clerics indiscriminately without letters of recommendation. The result was that unfit and unworthy persons, nay even such as had been formally rejected by their own bishops,

[25] C. 1, 6°, I, 9.
[26] C. 3, 6°, I, 9.

[27] Sess. 23, c. 9, *de ref.*
[28] Sess. 14, c. 2, *de ref.*

were ordained. Therefore the Council required that no titular bishops should dare to ordain another bishop's subjects without his consent.

This prohibition was extended to all bishops in regard to those not subject to them.[29]

Dimissorial letters are required also for conferring the *tonsure*.[30] Vicars Apostolic are not exempt from this law.[31] One decision of the S. Congregation declares that patriarchs should not impede the exercise of the jurisdiction of their suffragans with regard to ordination.[32] From this it may be easily deduced that metropolitans are not entitled to interfere in this matter. Concerning the form of these letters, see can. 960.

§ 2 rules that the *episcopus proprius,* unless prevented by a just reason, *should himself ordain his subjects,* and that no bishop of the Latin rite may ordain a subject of an oriental Rite lawfully without an Apostolic indult.

The Council of Trent and a Constitution of Innocent XIII mention only one reason (sickness) which would justify the *ordinarius proprius* in not ordaining his own subjects.[33] Our Code, however, is more liberal, as it admits any *iusta causa.* Hence any lawful impediment, but not mere convenience or indolence, would justify an ordinary in granting dimissorial letters.

The second clause forbids Latin bishops to ordain any one belonging to an *Oriental rite* without an Apostolic indult.[34] The text mentions only Oriental rites. Are

---

[29] Sess. 23, cc. 3, 8, *de ref.*

[30] C. 4, 6°, I, 9; Innocent XII, "*Speculatores,*" Nov. 4, 1692, § 2; S. C. EE. et RR., April 8, 1859 (Bizzarri, *l. c.,* p. 662 ff).

[31] S. C. P. F., April 5, 1674; Jan. 17, 1793 (*Coll.,* nn. 207, 615).

[32] S. C. P. F., May 14, 1838 (*Coll.,* n. 866).

[33] *Trid.,* Sess. 23, c. 3, *de ref.;* Innocent XIII, "*Apostolici ministerii,*" Sept. 23, 1724, § 14.

[34] Benedict XIV, "*Etsi pastoralis,*" May 26, 1742, § VII, n. I, XVI, XXII; § IX, nn. XI, XIII.

Oriental bishops [35] allowed to ordain subjects of the Latin Rite? We hardly believe that this is the intention of the legislator, because he evidently wishes to prevent confusion and a mixing of rites.[36] Why, then, does the Code not include the Oriental bishops in this prohibition? Because it does not legislate for the Oriental, but for the Latin Church only.

What about the *Ruthenians of the U. S. and Canada?* The documents [37] relating to this subject contain no special regulation with regard to ordination. Hence the common law, as formerly and now understood, must be followed.

It is certain that Ruthenians who are neither baptized in, nor live according to their particular rite may not be considered as subject to the same, but are subject to the diocesan bishop of the Latin Rite. No layman of the Latin Rite, born of Latin parents, may transfer himself to, or be ordained in, the Oriental Rite. If a Ruthenian, however, although not baptized in the Ruthenian Rite, should wish to enter a Ruthenian seminary, we believe he may be admitted without an Apostolic dispensation. He would become a subject of the Ruthenian bishop, and no bishop of the Latin Rite could ordain him without an Apostolic indult.

CAN. 956

Episcopus proprius, quod attinet ad ordinationem saecularium, est tantum Episcopus dioecesis in qua promovendus habeat domicilium una cum origine aut

---

35 The Maronite and the Melchite Patriarchs of Antioch may grant dimissorials to their subjects to be ordained by a Latin bishop or a bishop of another Oriental Rite;

Conc. Montis Libani (*Coll. Lac.*, II, 240, 256).

36 Benedict XIV, "*Etsi pastoralis*," § VII, n. XX.

37 See *Am. Eccl. Rev.*, Vol. 51, pp. 580 ff., 710 ff.

simplex domicilium sine origine; sed in hoc altero casu promovendus debet animum in dioecesi perpetuo manendi iureiurando firmare, nisi agatur de promovendo ad ordines clerico qui dioecesi per primam tonsuram iam incardinatus est, vel de promovendo alumno, qui servitio alius dioecesis destinatur ad normam can. 969, § 2, vel de promovendo religioso professo.

The *bishop competent to ordain secular priests* is the one in whose diocese the ordinand (1) was born *and* has his domicile, or (2) has only a domicile, though not born there. In the latter case he must make oath as to his intention of remaining permanently in the diocese. Exceptions will be explained further down.

This canon embodies new legislation. The new elements are: neither pure origin nor mere domicile are titles *per se* sufficient, and benefice and familiar service are no longer considered.

1. *Origin and domicile.*

(a) *Origin* here signifies birthplace, or the diocese in which one was *born*.[38] The mere fact that one was born in a certain place, however, for instance, at a summer resort, hardly suffices to call that place his place of origin. One's birthplace, properly, is the natural and common domicile of one's parents, or, the place of their habitual residence. It is no longer necessary to distinguish between accidental and natural nativity,[39] if the domicile or quasi-domicile or permanent residence of the parents is certain.[40] This rule is doubtless better adapted to present conditions, as the population, especially of cities, is in a constant flux.

As to illegitimate or posthumous children, also of con-

38 C. 3, 6°, I, 9: "*oriundus.*" 40 See can. 90, § 1.
39 Cfr. Many, *De Sacro Ordinatione,* Paris, 1905, p. 84 ff.

verts, their *locus originis* follows the domicile or quasi-domicile of the mother; that of *vagi* and *expositi* is the place where they were actually born.[41]

(b) *Domicile* must here be understood of the true, not the quasi-domicile of the ordinand, for the clause concerning the oath excludes any other residence. But a *diocesan domicile* would certainly be sufficient in this case, because the Decretals [42] as well as the spirit of the law refer that domicile to the local or diocesan bishop. The same rule must be applied to the domicile or quasi-domicile of the parents of the ordinand.

The question may arise, whether one may have two domiciles in different dioceses, for instance, a summer and a winter domicile. The answer is, Yes, as the nature of domicile permits it. In such cases the bishops of both dioceses are competent to ordain and the choice is left to the ordinand.[43]

2. *Domicile alone*, without regard to origin, establishes the title of competency if the ordinand makes oath that he intends to remain permanently in the diocese whose bishop is to ordain him. This ruling goes back to Innocent XII.[44] The oath here prescribed may be made into the hands of the bishop himself, or of his delegate, or of the rector of a college or some other priest.

3. This *oath is not required* in three cases: (a) when the cleric to be ordained has already been incardinated in the diocese by the first tonsure; (b) when he is to be ordained *ad titulum servitii ecclesiae;* (c) when he is a religious with simple perpetual vows. The reason for *a* lies in the fact that incardination must be perpetual and absolute, and given with the required testimonials.[45]

41 *Ibid.*
42 Cc. 1, 3, 6°' I, 9.
43 Many *l. c.*, p. 97 f.
44 " *Speculatores,*" x. § 5.
45 S. C. C., July 20, 1898 (*Coll. P. F.*, n. 2011).

The reason for *b* must be sought in the oath which is required for being ordained on that title. And *c* is explained in can. 585, which says that by taking perpetual vows one loses membership in his own diocese.

The *episcopus proprius* of such as *have no domicile* is the Ordinary in whose diocese the ordination takes place, provided the ordinand first acquires the domicile by taking oath according to can. 956. (*Irish Eccl. Record*, 1919, XIV, 330). These are the only reasons by which the competency of the bishop is now determined, neither *beneficium* nor *familiaritas* being admitted.

VICARS AND PREFECTS APOSTOLIC, PRELATES NULLIUS

Can. 957

§ 1. Vicarius ac Praefectus Apostolicus, Abbas vel Praelatus *nullius,* si charactere episcopali polleant, Episcopo dioecesano aequiparantur quod pertinet ad ordinationem.

§ 2. Si episcopali charactere careant, possunt nihilominus in proprio territorio et durante tantum munere, conferre primam tonsuram et ordines minores tum propriis subditis saecularibus ad normam can. 956, tum aliis qui litteras dimissorias iure requisitas exhibeant; ordinatio extra hos fines ab eisdem peracta irrita est.

§ 1. *Apostolic Vicars and Prefects as well as abbots and prelates nullius,* if endowed with the episcopal character, are equal to diocesan bishops in matters of ordination.

§ 2. If they do not possess the episcopal character, they are nevertheless entitled to confer, within the boundaries of their district and whilst their office lasts, *tonsure and minor orders* on their own secular subjects, according to can. 956, and also on others who are provided with dimissorial letters as required by law. If they overstep the limits here drawn, any ordination performed by them is invalid.

This is a decidedly new and opportune law, which changes the discipline established by the Council of Trent.[46] Formerly the *episcopus vicinior* could confer orders on, or grant dismissorial letters to the secular subjects of a prelate *nullius*. The Vicar Apostolic could indeed confer orders on such as had the dimissorial letters from their ordinaries,[47] but this was no right, but merely a privilege granted for missionary countries only. Now the prelates mentioned, if they are *consecrated bishops,* may confer orders on all their subjects, secular as well as religious, though on the latter, if they are exempt, only upon receiving dimissorial letters from their superior. In ordaining seculars, however, these prelates are bound to observe can. 956, which defines competency. If these prelates *are not consecrated bishops,* they may confer *tonsure and minor orders,* (a) upon all their *secular* subjects, (b) upon others, religious as well as secular, who exhibit dimissorial letters either from the religious superiors or from the ordinaries of other dioceses or districts; but (c) only on condition that they adhere strictly to the limitations stated in this canon under *penalty of nullity.*

What are these limitations? There is no doubt as to the territory and duration of the term of office. Vicars Apostolic, Prefects Apostolic, and prelates *nullius,* who are not consecrated bishops, can validly confer tonsure and minor orders only within their own district and as long as their office lasts. But a doubt may arise

46 *Trid.,* Sess. 23, c. 10; Sess. 24,   47 Can. 964, n. 2.
c. 9 *de ref.*

concerning the *litterae dimissoriales* required by law: —
are they an essential condition for valid ordination of the
"others" (*alii*)? If these letters affect the validity of
ordination, the aforesaid prelates cannot validly ordain
a subject of another ordinary before they have received
these letters. The sources [48] which Card. Gasparri quotes
for can. 957, § 2 do not fully answer the question, either
negatively or affirmatively, because they do not expressly
mention the validity or invalidity of the ordination performed by prelates before having received the *litterae
dimissoriales*. Still we believe that the mind of the
legislator is to invalidate an ordination thus performed.
The same clause recurs in can. 964, n. 2, where the
validity of the tonsure and minor orders conferred by a
governing abbot is made dependent on three conditions,
although the contrary opinion prevailed at the Roman
Court at the time of Benedict XIV. Besides, the
dumtaxat of the S. C. P. F. is a rather strong indication
that invalidity was intended.[49] Of course, the legislator
who confers power can make the exercise thereof dependent on the fulfillment of certain conditions, especially
since tonsure and minor orders are not a Sacrament in
the proper sense.

Can. 958

§ 1. Litteras dimissorias pro saecularibus dare possunt, quandiu iurisdictionem in territorio retinent;

1°. Episcopus proprius, postquam possessionem
suae dioecesis legitime ceperit ad normam can. 334, § 3,
licet nondum consecratus;

2°. Vicarius Generalis, ex speciali tamen Episcopi
mandato;

48 C. 3, 6°, V, 7: "*nec licitum
esse abbatibus.*"

49 S. C. P. F., April 5, 1674, ad
1 (*Coll.*, n. 207).

3°. De Capituli consensu Vicarius Capitularis post annum a sede vacante; intra annum vero solis arctatis ratione beneficii recepti vel recipiendi, aut ratione certi alicuius officii, cui propter necessitatem dioecesis sine dilatione sit providendum;

4.° Vicarius ac Praefectus Apostolicus, Abbas vel Praelatus *nullius,* licet episcopali charactere careant, etiam ad ordines maiores.

§ 2. Vicarius Capitularis litteras dimissorias ne concedat iis qui ab Episcopo reiecti fuerunt.

§ 1. The following may, as long as they retain jurisdiction in their respective territory, grant *litterae dimissoriae* to their *secular* subjects:

1.° The *Episcopus proprius,* even though not yet consecrated, after having taken lawful possession of his diocese, *i.e.,* as soon as he himself or his proxy has exhibited the Apostolic letters of appointment to the diocesan chapter, or the diocesan consultors assembled *in corpore,* in the presence of the secretary of the chapter or the diocesan chancellor.[50]

2.° The *Vicar General,* but only by special command of or commission from the bishop. This command or commission may be given orally or in writing, either for one case or for several cases, during the bishop's absence, for instance, or sickness.

3.° The *Vicar Capitular* (our administrator) with the *consent* (not merely advice) of the Chapter (or the diocesan consultors) after the vacancy of the episcopal see has lasted one year. *Within the first year* of vacancy the Vicar Capitular may grant dimissorial letters only to *arctati,*[51] *i.e.,* such as have already received, or will re-

---

[50] Can. 334, § 3. The metropolitan may give these letters before having received the pallium, although he may not ordain to sacred orders before having received it.

[51] Cc. 1–4, 6°, I, 9; *Trid., Sess.* 7, c. 10, *de ref.*

ceive, within that year an ecclesiastical benefice (for instance, a canonicate) which requires ordination. *Arctati* are also called those who have received or are about to receive an office which, on account of the needs of the diocese, must be filled immediately. This may occur even now, especially after the late world war, in countries where there is a great want of priests or chaplains.[52] If the government — provided this right has been granted to it by the Holy See — has appointed a chaplain or nominated a pastor who is not yet a priest, the Vicar Capitular may give him the *dimissoriae*. The same is true if the deceased bishop has appointed one to an office requiring the priesthood.

4.° *Vicars Apostolic, Prefects Apostolic,* and *Abbots or prelates nullius,* even though they are not consecrated bishops, may now also grant dimissorial letters for sacred orders. This is but the logical consequence of can. 957. Formerly [53] prelates *nullius* could not grant dimissorial letters even for tonsure and minor orders, this right being reserved to the *episcopus vicinior.*

§ 2. The *Vicar Capitular* shall not grant dimissorial letters to such as were rejected by the deceased bishop. This enactment is similar to that of can. 44 concerning rescripts. The object is to protect the authority of the bishop and the unity of government, as well as to keep undesirable candidates out of the sanctuary.

CAN. 959

Qui potest litteras dimissorias ad ordines recipîendos dare, potest quoque eosdem ordines conferre per se ipse, si necessariam ordinis potestatem habeat.

---

[52] France, for instance, before the war, was short about 3,000 priests.

[53] *Trid.*, Sess. 24, c. 9, *de ref.*

Whoever is entitled to grant dimissorial letters for receiving orders may confer the same orders himself, provided he possesses the necessary power of order. Notice the subordination of the right of conferring orders to that of issuing dimissorial letters. We are allowed to invert the order: whoever may confer orders, may also grant *dimissoriae*. The granting of *dimissoriae* supposes the power of jurisdiction, but the conferring of orders supposes the power of orders for valid administration and jurisdiction for licit conferring, nay even for valid ordination, as far as inferior prelates are concerned. Hence it is that inferior prelates who lack the episcopal character are strictly limited to their territory and tenure of office, and must obtain *dimissoriae* if they wish to confer tonsure and minor orders on any subject not their own.

Can. 960

§ 1. Litterae dimissoriae ne concedantur, nisi habitis antea omnibus testimoniis, quae iure exiguntur ad normam can. 993–1000.

§ 2. Si post datas ab Ordinario litteras dimissorias nova testimonia necessaria sint ad normam can. 994, § 3, Episcopus alienus ne ordinet, antequam eadem receperit.

§ 3. Quod si promovendus tempus sufficiens ad contrahendum impedimentum ad normam mem. can. 994 transegerit in ipsa dioecesi Episcopi ordinantis, hic testimonia directe colligat.

§ 1. Dimissorial letters shall not be granted before *all the testimonial letters* required by law have been received, according to can. 993–1000. Note that, although the text mentions dimissorial *letters*, yet since the term signifies nothing else but permission given by a bishop to one of his subjects to have himself ordained by another bishop, it is evident that such consent may be given *orally*. Thus, for instance, if the " other " bishop should be present in the cathedral city, he may be asked by the *episcopus proprius* or the Vicar Capitular to confer orders. However, in order to avert fraud and procure greater certainty it is always safer to give the *dimissoriae* in writing.[54]

§ 2. If new testimonials are necessary after the dimissorial letters have been issued by the Ordinary, the other bishop shall not ordain the candidate before he has received them.

§ 3. If the candidate has lived in the diocese of the ordaining bishop long enough to contract a canonical impediment, the ordaining bishop shall himself gather the necessary informations. New testimonial letters are required if a candidate has lived in the same territory for six or three months after the first testimonials were issued and ordination has not yet taken place; for six or three months suffice to contract a canonical impediment. According to § 3, this residence may be taken up in the diocese whose bishop is to ordain the candidate provided with dimissorials from his own bishop. For instance, a candidate for ordination belonging to the diocese of St. Joseph, Missouri, has been a soldier in Camp Dodge, Iowa, for four months. The bishop of Des Moines, in whose diocese Camp Dodge is located, must gather the necessary information about his fitness, *directe, i.e.,* personally and from reliable sources. The fundamental signification of *directe* is reliability. Some elucidation of this point is afforded by the decree " *Redeuntibus,*" Oct. 25, 1918, concerning clerics who have returned from

---

[54] *Trid., Sess.* 14, c. 2, *de ref.*: " *expresso consensu aut litteris dimissoriis* "; cfr. Many, *l. c.,* p. 163.

military service.[55] Chapt. II of this decree reads: The Ordinaries of the places where clerics and seminarians have done service for a considerable time, *i.e.*, at least three months, are called upon most urgently to give all the necessary information to the ordinaries of said clerics and seminarians, but the latter ordinaries should supply this information by others gained from other sources and persons, and finally by a personal examination of the candidates. These, when duly asked by their bishops as to their conduct, are obliged to answer truthfully. *Directe,* however, in our canon, does not exclude the assumption that the Ordinary who wishes to ordain a candidate provided with dimissorial letters may conduct the inquiry through intermediary persons of ecclesiastical rank, for instance, the Vicar-General, or deans, or the diocesan chancellor. But it certainly requires that the bishop should examine the information carefully and, if necessary, summon the candidate before him for personal examination.

RECIPIENTS OF DIMISSORIAL LETTERS

CAN. 961

Litterae dimissoriae mitti possunt ab Episcopo proprio, etiam Cardinali Episcopo suburbicario, ad quemlibet Episcopum, communionem cum Sede Apostolica habentem, excepto tantum, citra apostolicum indultum, Episcopo ritus diversi a ritu promovendi.

CAN. 962

Quilibet Episcopus, acceptis legitimis litteris dimissoriis, alienum subditum licite ordinat, dummodo ipse

55 *A. Ap. S.,* Vol. X, 482 f.

de germana litterarum fide dubitare nullatenus possit,
salvo praescripto can. 994, § 3.

CAN. 963

Litterae dimissoriae possunt ab ipso concedente vel
ab eius successore limitari aut revocari, sed semel concessae non exstinguuntur resoluto iure dantis.

The first of these three canons repeats the old rule
that any bishop in communion with the Holy See may
accept dimissorial letters from the *episcopus proprius*
or a suburbicarian cardinal bishop, but not from a
bishop of a different rite. It is generally understood
that the *litterae dimissoriales* are granted in favor of the
ordinand, not of the ordaining bishop.[56] The privilege is
now extended to the six *suburbicarian* cardinal bishops,
who formerly could grant dimissorial letters only to the
Cardinal Vicar of Rome.[57] The *exception* is made manifestly in order to avoid confusion of rites; but *litterae
dimissoriae* may be sent to a bishop of a different rite if
an Apostolic indult has been obtained for the purpose.[58]

Can. 962 permits every bishop (in communion with the
Holy See), upon having received the lawful dimissorials,
to ordain a candidate not subject to his jurisdiction, provided he has no reason to doubt the genuineness of the
letters, and provided also he observe the ruling of can.
994, § 3, concerning additional testimonials. Authenticity
is beyond doubt if the signature and seal of the issuing
bishop are attached to the documents, though forgery is
never absolutely excluded.

Can. 963 rules that the dimissorial letters may be

---

[56] Many, *l. c.*, p. 163.

[57] Alexander VII, "*Apostolica
sollicitudo*," Aug. 7, 1662, § 2.

[58] Benedict XIV, "*Etsi pastoralis*," granted an indult to the
Calabrian bishops.

limited or revoked either by the grantor himself or by his successor, but do not expire, even if the grantor should lose his power.

A *limitation* may be made concerning the bishop, who may be personally designated in the letter, or concerning the time, which may be restricted to three or four months. There may also be limitation regarding examination (cfr. can. 997). Thus the letters may be worded: "If he is found fit after examination." If this is a real condition, clearly expressed as such in the letter, the dimissorial would become null if the candidate failed to pass the examination.

Revocation must be duly intimated either to the candidate to whom the letters were given, or to the bishop to whom they were addressed.

The last clause of canon 963 enacts that the dimissorials remain in force, even if the grantor loses the right of issuing them after they are issued. The reason is that dimissorial letters contain a favor, and every favor is valid *a die datae*.[59] Thus if a sick bishop had signed the *litterae dimissoriae*, and the candidate could not be ordained until after the bishop's death, the letters would be valid. Thus also, if the Vicar Capitular, according to can. 958, § 1, n. 3, had issued *litterae dimissoriae*, and the new bishop would take possession of the diocese in the meanwhile, the letters of the Vicar Capitular would remain effective. Lastly, not even a penal privation of office or a censure can render invalid dimissorial letters previously granted.

---

[59] S. C. EE. et RR., Nov. 21, 1600. (Bizzarri, *l. c.*, p. 232; Reg. iuris 16 in. 6°).

CAN. 964

Quod attinet ad ordinationem religiosorum:

1°. Abbas regularis de regimine, etsi sine territorio *nullius,* potest conferre primam tonsuram et ordines minores, dummodo promovendus sit ipsi subditus vi professionis saltem simplicis, ipse vero sit presbyter et benedictionem abbatialem legitime acceperit. Extra hos fines, ordinatio, ab eodem collata, revocato quolibet contrario privilegio, est irrita, nisi ordinans charactere episcopali polleat;

2°. Religiosi exempti a nullo Episcopo ordinari licite possunt sine litteris dimissoriis proprii Superioris maioris;

3°. Superiores professis votorum simplicium, de quibus in can. 574, litteras dimissorias concedere possunt dumtaxat ad primam tonsuram et ordines minores;

4°. Ordinatio ceterorum omnium alumnorum cuiusvis religionis regitur iure saecularium, revocato quolibet indulto Superioribus concesso dandi professis a votis temporariis litteras dimissorias ad ordines maiores.

As to the ordination of religious:

1.° A *governing abbot of regulars,* even though he be not an *abbot nullius,* may confer tonsure and minor orders on such as are subject to him by virtue of at least simple profession, provided the Abbot himself be a priest and have lawfully received the abbatial blessing. Outside these limits ordination is invalid unless the abbot possesses episcopal character, and all contrary privileges are hereby revoked.

This canon ends the controversy [60] concerning the validity of ordinations performed by an abbot, either *benedictus ab episcopo* or endowed with a special privilege, on a candidate not his subject. The relevant points of this section are:

(a) The abbot must be an *abbas regiminis,* that is to say, one actually governing, whether for life or for a certain number of years. Hence a *titular abbot* or a commendatory abbot, or an abbot who has entirely renounced his office, may neither validly nor licitly confer tonsure and minor orders.[61] An abbot who has a co-adjutor is still a governing abbot, and is therefore entitled to perform the aforesaid ordinations. Whether the *coadjutor* can validly confer them depends entirely on his letters of appointment from Rome.

(b) The abbot must be a *priest,* as the II Council of Nice and the Decretals clearly state,[62] otherwise the ordination is invalid.

(c) He must have been *lawfully blest, i.e.,* he must have received the abbatial benediction. The *Pontificale Romanum* prescribes that the *benedicendus* must be provided with an *Apostolic mandate* which commits the blessing to a bishop.

The bishop is the one in whose diocese the monastery is located, unless the mandate permits the abbot-elect to choose one according to his good pleasure. The *Pontificale* also prescribes that two abbots should assist the bishop in that function. By the way it may be added

---

60 This controversy was justified by conflicting decisions of the S. C. C. (Richter, *Trid.,* p. 198); cfr. Benedict XIV, *De Syn Dioec.,* II, 11, 13, Gasparri, *De S. Ordinatione,* n. 955 ff; Many, *l. c.,* p. 135 ff.

61 S. C. C., Sept. 20, 1788; S. O., July 15, 1903 (*A. S. S.,* 33, 167); S. C. EE. et RR., Sept. 20, 1697 (Bizzarri, *Coll.,* p. 282).

62 C. 1, Dist. 69; c. 11 x, I, 14; c. 3, 6°, I, 7.

that the abbatial blessing, though an imposing ceremony, is not a Sacrament,[63] but merely a sacramental.

(d) Those upon whom abbots may validly and licitly confer tonsure and minor orders are the *subditi vi professionis saltem simplicis, i.e.,* his own subjects by religious profession, which is always made into the hands, or at least in the name, of the governing abbot. This too is ancient doctrine.

When any one of these four conditions is wanting, the ordination is invalid. But if a religious who is a consecrated bishop, *e.g.,* a titular bishop, would ordain religious who are not his subjects, these orders would be validly conferred, since, as it seems, the episcopal order would supply the defect of jurisdiction.

2.° *Exempt religious* can not be *licitly* ordained by *any bishop* without dimissorial letters from their own higher superior. This ruling, too, was insisted upon by ancient synods and in many papal decrees,[64] from which sources it may be seen that exemption as well as the obedience due to the lawful superiors would render the conferring of orders by any bishop grievously *illicit*, though not invalid.

3.° Religious superiors may grant dimissorial letters, but only for *tonsure and minor orders,* to such of their subjects as have taken the *simple triennial vows*[65] that precede either solemn or perpetual vows.

Who are the *superiors* who may grant these dimissorial letters? The *superiores maiores* of orders of regulars, of exempt and non-exempt religious congregations whose members take triennial vows before they pronounce

---

[63] A pamphlet was published some twenty years ago in Rome in which it was asserted that the abbatial blessing imprints an indelible character.

[64] Cfr. c. 33, C. 16, g. 1 (Syn. Agde, 506); c. 1, Dist. 5 (Greg. I); c. 5, C. 18, g. 2 (Greg. I); c. 5, X, I, 11.

[65] See can. 574, § 1.

solemn or simple perpetual vows. This ruling marks a change in the former discipline,[66] for the superiors of religious congregations with merely simple vows did not enjoy the privilege of granting such letters to their subjects.

4.° The ordination of *all other members of religious institutes* is governed by the same laws as that of seculars, and every indult granted to superiors for issuing dimissorial letters to those of their members with temporary vows who wish to receive major orders is hereby revoked. This is a reminder of the "*Auctis Admodum,*" of Nov. 4, 1892, n. I and II. Formerly no religious who had not professed solemn or perpetual vows could be ordained to major orders. If an urgent case came up they were allowed to anticipate solemn or perpetual profession before the regular term had expired.

It may be asked who exactly are meant by "*ceterorum omnium alumnorum cuiusvis religionis*"? Only members of non-exempt congregations whose members are promoted to sacred orders: at least the revoking clause points to these. It is evident, then, that can. 964 must be understood as follows:

(1) *Governing abbots*, provided they are priests and duly blessed, may confer tonsure and minor orders on their own subjects only.

(2) Superiors of *exempt religious* institutes, whether regulars or otherwise exempt, must give dimissorial letters to their subjects, in order that a bishop may licitly ordain them. Such dimissorial letters must be given for tonsure and minor orders as well as for major orders, for n. 2 of our canon does not distinguish between the different orders. Therefore the religious exempt superiors, not

---

[66] S. C. EE. et RR., May 6, 1864 (Bizzarri, *l. c.*, p. 711); Feb. 9, 1894 (*A. S. S.*, 26, 619).

the local Ordinary, grant dimissorial letters for all *orders*, lower and higher.

(3) *All religious superiors* of orders as well as congregations, the constitutions of which prescribe perpetual vows, may grant dimissorial letters to their *temporarily professed* members, but only for *tonsure and minor orders*.

(4) Members of *religious institutes which are not exempt* need *litterae dimissoriae* from their *own bishop* if they wish to be promoted to *major orders*, beginning with subdeaconship. Hence with regard to sacred orders these members fall under can. 956, which determines the competency of the bishop. Every indult to the contrary must now be regarded as void.

(5) *Novices* of religious orders as well as congregations must observe the law binding seculars (can. 956).

(6) *Members of religious societies* must follow the same rule (can. 956).

Here it may be asked whether a governing abbot may address dimissorial letters to *another abbot*, who is entitled to confer tonsure and minor orders on his own subjects: for instance to the Abbot President or Abbot Primate. This was possible and actually done before the promulgation of the Code. But the practice can no longer be sustained, since the legislator emphasizes the invalidity of ordination performed on a non-subject. Notice well the subject is one *vi professionis*, not by a transient transference of jurisdiction. N. 3, can. 964, does not contradict this interpretation, because it permits the superiors only in general terms to grant dimissorial letters without specifying the prelate to whom they must be directed.[67]

67 S. Rit. C., Sept. 27, 1659, n. 19, referred to by Card. Gasparri, reads: " *Reliqua pontificalia extra loca ipsis Abbatibus subiecta, vel pro servitio alienae Ecclesiae, aut in subditos pariter alienos, etiam de licentia Ordinariorum, exercere non valeant: puta Campanarum benedic-*

THE BISHOP OF THE DIOCESE

CAN. 965

Episcopus ad quem Superior religiosus litteras dimissorias mittere debet, est Episcopus dioecesis, in qua sita est domus religiosa, ad cuius familiam pertinet ordinandus.

The bishop to whom the religious superior must direct the dimissorial letters, is the bishop in whose diocese the religious house of which the ordinand is a member, is situated.

It is not necessary to repeat the just complaints of Benedict XIV concerning some religious who apparently spent their night watches in profane things rather than in the study of the sacred canons, and boasted of privileges that existed only in their imagination.[68] The law, as stated in this canon, is an almost verbal repetition of an enactment made by Clement VIII, or, at his command, by the S. C. Concilii, on March 15, 1593. The privileges granted to the Camaldolese did not greatly help them because the S. Congregation insisted upon their adapting themselves to the actual practice,[69] as stated in the following canon.

CAN. 966

§ 1. Tunc tantum Superior religiosus ad alium Episcopum litteras dimissorias mittere potest, cum Episcopus dioecesanus licentiam dederit, aut sit diversi ritus, aut sit absens, aut non sit ordinationem habi-

tionem, Calicum, et similium, in quibus sacra adhibetur unctio, nec non Minorum Ordinum collationes."

68 " Impositi Nobis," Feb. 27,

1747, repeating the enactment of Clement VIII.

69 S. C. EE. et RR., July 13, 1730 (Bizzarri, l. c., p. 341 f).

turus proximo legitimo tempore ad normam can. 1006, § 2, vel denique cum dioecesis vacet nec eam regat qui charactere episcopali polleat.

§ 2. Necesse est ut singulis in casibus id Episcopo ordinaturo constet ex authentico Curiae episcopalis testimonio.

Only in the following cases may the religious superior direct the *litterae dimissoriae* to *another* than the diocesan *bishop:* (1) If the diocesan bishop has given permission; (2) or if he is of another Rite; (3) or if he is absent; (4) or if he does not hold ordinations at the time stated in can. 1006, § 2; (5) or if the diocese is vacant or ruled by one who lacks the episcopal character. However in every such case the facts must be attested to the ordaining bishop by an authentic document of the court of the bishop competent for ordination.

Notice that the text speaks disjunctively, which signifies that any one of the enumerated reasons may be advanced and is sufficient for the religious superior to direct the *dimissoriae* to another bishop. The first and second of the five reasons mentioned are newly formulated, though implied in former rules. Thus it is evident that if a bishop is prevented from ordaining, he may entrust another bishop with this function.[70] The *difference of rite* always was acknowledged as sufficient reason for choosing another bishop.[71]

The last three reasons were officially recognized by the Roman Court.[72] A bishop must be regarded as " absent " from his diocese also if during his absence he calls in another bishop to hold ordinations.[73] The competent

---

70 *Reg. iuris* 68, 72 in 6°.
71 Benedict XIV, " *Etsi pastora-lis*," May 26, 1742, § VII, n. XXII f.; § IX, n. XIII.
72 Benedict XIV, " *Impositi Nobis*," Feb. 27, 1747.
73 Many, *l. c.*, p. 382.

bishop is supposed *not to hold ordination at the next term set by law* if he does not ordain on one of the four Ember Days, on the Saturday before Passion Sunday, and on Holy Saturday.[74] For these are the regular days for general ordinations. Hence, even though the bishop would have an ordination on another than the six known *Sabbata*, the law would permit the religious superior to direct his subject to another bishop. On the other hand, the religious superior would not be allowed to address the *dimissoriae* to another bishop, if the diocesan ordinary held general ordinations on one of the six Saturdays, not in his episcopal city, but in another place of his diocese, or if he would have the ordinations held by another bishop, provided he himself were present in the diocese.[75]

The last reason mentioned in our canon is *vacancy of the episcopal see* whose occupant would be competent for ordaining religious. This rule was established by the practice of the Roman Court.[76] Vacancy is here taken in the strict sense of the word, as the modification evidently shows. Therefore a *sedes impedita* is no true vacancy, nor would suspension or excommunication of the bishop constitute vacancy. Besides, if the Vicar Capitular or the regular Administrator, or the Administrator Apostolic were a consecrated bishop, vacancy would not be verified *in casu*.

Finally, § 2 requires *authentic attestation* by the episcopal court to the effect that one of the five cases really exists. This document may be issued by the Vicar-General, or by the Chancellor of the diocese, or by the secre-

---

[74] Can. 1006, § 2. Although § 3 of the same canon permits the bishop to hold "general" ordinations on a Sunday or feast-day of obligation, yet our text, referring only to can. 1006, § 2, certainly intends the "six Saturdays" only, as it was understood generally.

[75] S. C. C., Aug. 18, 1888 (*A. S. S.*, Vol. 21, 359 ff); Feb. 11, 1708; Many, *l. c.*, p. 383.

[76] S. C. C., Tirascon., July 13, 1782.

tary of the bishop;[77] it must be given under the diocesan seal, signed by one of the aforesaid officials, and enclosed with the dimissorial letters from the religious superior.

CAN. 967

Caveant Superiores religiosi ne in fraudem Episcopi dioecesani subditum ordinandum ad aliam religiosam domum mittant, aut concessionem litterarum dimissoriarum de industria in id tempus differant, quo Episcopus vel abfuturus, vel nullas habiturus sit ordinationes.

This canon, adopting the words of the Constitution "*Impositi Nobis*," of Benedict XIV, cautions religious superiors against committing fraud by abusing the permission granted in the foregoing canon. It would be fraudulent if they sent a religious to another house purely for the purpose of avoiding the diocesan bishop. There would be no fraud if the religious would dwell in another religious house in another diocese for the sake of study, or health, or vacation. Fraud is also committed, as the text says, if the religious superior intentionally delays the issuance of dimissorial letters to a time when the bishop is absent from the diocese or will not hold general ordinations. Of course, fraud may not be presumed, but must be proved, which, generally speaking, is not an easy thing.[78]

The reader will have noticed that there is no clause revoking the privilege which some religious (for instance, the Society of Jesus) enjoy of having their candidates ordained by any bishop. Hence if this privilege was granted after the Council of Trent, and directly, not by communication, it still holds.[79]

[77] Benedict XIV, "*Impositi Nobis*," Feb. 27, 1747.

[78] Many, *l. c.*, p. 383 f.

[79] "*Impositi Nobis*."

What if the competent or diocesan bishop refuses to ordain a religious provided with *litterae dimissoriae* from his superior? In that case the superior is not allowed to send the ordinand to another bishop, for this is not mentioned in can. 966, and hence nothing is left but recourse to the Holy See (S. Cong. Relig.).

CHAPTER II

VALID AND LICIT ORDINATION

CAN. 968

§ 1. Sacram ordinationem valide recipit solus vir baptizatus; licite autem, qui ad normam sacrorum canonum debitis qualitatibus, iudicio proprii Ordinarii, praeditus sit, neque ulla detineatur irregularitate aliove impedimento.

§ 2. Qui irregularitate aliove impedimento detinentur, licet post ordinationem etiam sine propria culpa exorto, prohibentur receptos ordines exercere.

Only a baptized male can validly be ordained. In order to receive orders licitly, the candidate must, according to the judgment of the Ordinary, be endowed with the qualities required by the sacred canons and free from any irregularity or canonical impediment.

Those who have incurred an irregularity or other impediment, even after ordination and without their own fault, are not allowed to exercise the orders they have received.

§ 1 defines who are *capable* of receiving orders validly, and who may receive them licitly according to canon law. Two conditions are required for valid ordination, viz.: the male sex and Baptism. The following classes of persons are therefore *incapable of being validly ordained:*

444

(1) *Women*, who are debarred from the sanctuary by divine positive law, if not by the natural law, according to reason. This has been the constant teaching and practice of the Church from the time of St. Paul[1] up to our day. The tenets of the Pepuzians or Quintillians, of Marcus Magus, and of the Collyridians, who admitted women to the priesthood and its sacrificial functions, were condemned as heretical.[2] As to the institute of *deaconesses* and *widows*, it may be admitted that they formed a special ecclesiastical corporation, or class, endowed with quasi-clerical prerogatives. Their functions were similar to those of the deacons, whom they assisted with regard to the female catechumens, the poor, and the sick. At the same time authentic historical documents, especially can. 19 of the Council of Nicaea, prove that no hierarchic or liturgical character can be attributed to these deaconesses and widows, or, in the words of the aforesaid canon 19, that they were ranked with the laity since they received no orders.[3]

Concerning *hermaphrodites*, it must be said that complete hermaphrodites, whose sex cannot be determined, may not be validly ordained; whereas those with whom the male sex prevails may be ordained validly but not licitly.[4]

(2) Incapable of validly receiving orders are also men who *are not baptized*, because Baptism is the foundation of, and the gate to, all the other sacraments. This, too, is ancient and constant ecclesiastical law.[5]

---

[1] Cfr. I Cor. xiv, 34 f.; I Tim. ii, 11.

[2] Epiph., *Haeres.*, 49, n. 2 f.; 79; Irenaeus, *Adv. Haer.*, I, 13, 2; Gelasius I, Ep. 11 (Constant, *Epp. Rom. Pont. f.*, 1721, p. 85); Connick, *De Sacram. et Censuris*, disp. 20, n. 94.

[3] Wieland, "*Die Genetische Entwicklung der sog. Ordines Minores,*" in *Röm. Quartalschrift*, 1897 Suppl., p. 60 ff.

[4] Eschbach, *Disputationes Physiologico-Theologicae*, 1901, p. 53 f.

[5] C. 19, *Conc. Nic.* I., (= c. 52, C. 1, g. 1); cc. 1-3, X, III, 43.

Our text says *vir*, a man, which term, however, must not be pressed to the extent of assuming a full-grown man. For the ordination of *infants*, though illicit, is valid, as Benedict XIV says.[6] On the other hand, even an adult man, if physically *compelled* to receive orders, would not be ordained at all.[7] As to grave fear brought to bear upon an unwilling person, see can. 214.

The other class of persons mentioned in our canon are those who may receive orders validly, but *not lawfully*. They are either irregular or suffer from a canonical impediment. This is a new regulation, for thus far a distinction was made only between incapacity and irregularity. Now a strictly so-called canonical impediment is introduced, which is less than irregularity.

Irregularity is derived from the Latin *contra regulam*, and as a canonical term seems to occur first in a work of Peter of Blois (+ 1200).[8] It signifies general inhability established by law, for there is no irregularity except it be expressed in the law (can. 983). The *effect* of this inhability consists in forbidding one from being licitly ordained and from exercising the orders received. In this respect there is no distinction between irregularity and the simple canonical impediment, as § 2 of our canon plainly states. Where, then, *is* the difference between both? It must be sought in the higher degree of inhability and in the secondary effect attaching to irregularity. For irregularity, although *per se* no penalty,[9] yet may originate from guilt, which is followed by penalty constituted in law, for instance, in the case of homicide and others

---

6 " *Eo quamvis*," May 4, 1745, §§ 20, 28.

7 C. 3, X, III, 42.

8 *Speculum Iuris Canonici* (Hinschius, K.-R., I, 9, note 4).

9 Cfr. Layman, *Theol. Moral.*, l. I, tr. 5, P. 5, c. 1, n. 1. To deny every feature of penalty, as Philipps, K.-R., 1845, I, 418 ff., does, seems to us labor lost. We agree that the *poena* is not intended *in recto*, but *in obliquo* it is attached to the irregularities *ex delicto*, as the latter term implies.

mentioned in can. 985. One who is simply suffering from an impediment is not supposed to have incurred a guilt in the proper sense of the term, even though *infamia facti* might be imputable to him.   The consequence is that one who, while suffering from a simple canonical impediment, receives or exercises an order, should not be punished as severely as one afflicted with irregularity.[10]   Any other distinction between irregularity and the canonical impediment proper, is, we believe, difficult to establish.

It may be added that irregularity is generally distinguished into a *perpetual and a temporary* one, according to the duration or cessation of the impediment.

It may be *total* or *partial*.   Total irregularity incapacitates one for the reception and the exercise of all orders, whereas *partial* irregularity merely deprives one of the right of receiving or exercising a higher order.

The distinction between an irregularity from *defect* and from *guilt* will be explained under 983, where reference is made to the origin of irregularities.

NECESSITY AND UTILITY OF THE DIOCESE

CAN. 969

§ 1. Nemo ex saecularibus ordinetur, qui iudicio proprii Episcopi non sit necessarius vel utilis ecclesiis dioecesis.

§ 2. Non prohibetur tamen Episcopus proprium promovere subditum, qui in futurum, praevia legitima excardinatione et incardinatione, servitio alius dioecesis destinetur.

10 Cfr. can. 2374; Thesaurus-Giraldi, *De Poenis Ecclesiasticis, Romae*, 1831, p. 311 (P. II, c. 10). Irregularity does not create irregularity, but the penalty is *ferendae sententiae;* c. 1, Dist. 51: "*irregularis se faciens promoveri est deponendus.*"

True to the admonition of St. Paul " not to impose hands lightly upon any man," the Tridentine Council commanded Ordinaries to ordain only such, or as many, as would be useful to the diocese.[11] The same law is re-enacted in our canon, with the limitation that it concerns only the *secular clergy*. The bishop is to judge as to the number of priests needed or useful for his diocese. Why the *religious clergy* is *not* mentioned may be deduced from the fact that their support and conduct, being guaranteed by their constitutions, obviates the danger of their becoming a burden or a stumbling block to the diocese.

§ 2 permits the bishop to ordain any one of his subjects who may be destined for the future service of another diocese, supposing legitimate excardination and incardination.

This might happen if a diocese were well provided with priests. But the bishop, before ordaining one who is his own subject by reason of origin or domicile, must excardinate him and the bishop for whose diocese he is destined must incardinate him, according to can. III, § 2 (Com. Int. C. I. C., Aug. 17, 1919).

FORBIDDING ORDINATION EX INFORMATA CONSCIENTIA

CAN. 970

Proprius Episcopus vel Superior religiosus maior potest suis clericis ex quavis canonica causa, occulta quoque, etiam extraiudicialiter, ascensum ad ordines interdicere, salvo iure recursus ad Sanctam Sedem, vel etiam ad Moderatorem generalem, si agatur de religiosis quibus ascensum interdixerit Superior provincialis.

---

11 I Tim. v, 22; *Trid.*, Sess. 23, c. 16, *de ref.;* Pius X, " *Pieni l'ani- mo,"* July 28, 1906; S. C. P. F., Aug. 1827 (*Coll.*, n. 798).

A bishop or higher religious superior may, for any canonical, even though secret, reason, and without a formal trial, forbid his subjects to receive orders; but a subject thus interdicted retains the right of recourse to the Holy See, or in the case of religious who have been enjoined by their provincial, to the superior general.

This text is taken from the Decretals and the Council of Trent. Lucius III (1183) admonished religious that it is more becoming and safer for subjects to obey their superiors and remain in the lower ranks, than to strive after a higher rank to the scandal of their prelates.[12] The Council of Trent,[13] making these words its own, added that the prelate may forbid any one to receive a sacred order for any reason, even for a secret crime,[14] and without legal procedure. Our text simply says "*ascensum ad ordines interdicere,*" which manifestly includes all orders, also tonsure and minor orders. The bishop, therefore, may forbid a student of a clerical seminary to enter the clerical state, the religious superior may refuse to a religious subject tonsure and minor orders, and the ascent to higher orders. However, there must be a *canonical reason,* even though only an occult one. Why a reason is required is easily understood from the fact that the one thus treated may have recourse to the Holy See, which will in each case demand the reason. Besides, it would be unjust to repel from the sanctuary one whom God may have called. We hardly believe that the Holy See will now-a-days [15] ask the Metropolitan or nearest suffragan to demand of the bishop the reason

12 Cc. 5, 17, X, I, 11.

13 Sess. 24, c. 1, *de ref.*

14 The crimes mentioned in c. 17, X, I, 11 are: *adulterium, periurium, homicidium, falsum testimonium;* but with the exception of homicide the other crimes had to be notorious and proved, and penance had to precede.

15 S. C. C., April 21, 1668, quoted by Benedict XIV, *De Syn. Dioec.,* XII, 8, 4.

for refusing ordination, but will rather obtain that information directly from the bishop. But the rule still holds that the *prelate is not bound to state the reason* for his refusal to the candidate himself.[16] The latter may have *recourse* to the Holy See (S.C. Concilii), but the appeal does not suspend the effects of the prohibition.[17] If a religious has been excluded from the reception of orders by his provincial, recourse (not appeal) may be had to the superior general. If the latter should confirm the injunction, nothing is left for the religious but to have recourse to the S. Cong. Religiosorum.

Finally note may be taken of the *causa canonica,* which does not necessarily imply a crime, but may mean an irregularity, or a canonical impediment, or lack of canonical requisites. In order to form an objective and impartial judgment it is advisable to follow the rules laid down by Benedict XIV for discerning the qualities of candidates.[18] These rules provide for (1) Great vigilance over the conduct and character of the candidates; (2) properly and honestly conducted examinations which show the intellectual and moral capacity of the aspirant; (3) spiritual exercises or retreats; (4) observance of the interstices between the various orders.

The same Pontiff gives some hints to *confessors* and retreat masters with regard to *recidivi et consuetudinarii* preparing for orders. The confessor should ponder all the circumstances and probabilities and remember that he is a spiritual physician who should prescribe the proper remedies. After having implored the divine assistance, he should proceed firmly and justly and without human respect. He may tell the candidate whom he thinks unfit

---

16 S. C. C., March 21, 1643 (Richter, *Trid.,* p. 87, n. 1).

17 Benedict XIV, "*Ad militantis,*" March 30, 1742, § 23.

18 *De Syn. Dioec.,* XI, 2, 16 ff.

for the high vocation that there is no disgrace or shame attached to withdrawing from the course begun, that he had best take time for further deliberation, and that the salvation of his soul is a stronger motive than human respect.

THE CLERICAL STATE MUST BE EMBRACED FREELY

CAN. 971

Nefas est quemquam, quovis modo, ob quamlibet rationem, ad statum clericalem cogere, vel canonice idoneum ab eodem avertere.

It is criminal to compel anyone, in whatsoever manner or for whatsoever reason, to embrace the clerical state, or to turn away therefrom anyone canonically qualified.

This has always been the practice of the Church,[19] which even threatened with heavy penalties any minister who ordained one against his will. The Code inflicts *excommunication* (reserved to no one, however) for the same transgression.[20] Parents ought to know that they commit a grievous sin against their children, the Church, and society at large if they disobey this canon.

CLERICAL TRAINING IN SEMINARIES

CAN. 972

§ 1. Curandum ut ad sacros ordines adspirantes inde a teneris annis in Seminario recipiantur; sed omnes ibidem commorari tenentur saltem per integrum sacrae theologiae curriculum, nisi Ordinarius in casibus peculiaribus, gravi de causa, onerata eius conscientia, dispensaverit.

[19] Cc. 1, 2, 7, Dist. 74; c. 23, C. 25, c. 2.   [20] Can. 2352.

§ 2. Qui ad ordines adspirant et extra Seminarium legitime morantur, commendentur pio et idoneo sacerdoti, qui eis invigilet eosque ad pietatem informet.

Care should be taken that those who aspire to sacred orders be received into a seminary at an early age. All candidates for the sacred ministry are obliged to live in a seminary at least throughout the entire course of their theological studies, unless the Ordinary, for grave reasons and upon due deliberation, dispenses in individual cases.

Candidates for orders who lawfully dwell outside the seminary should be commended to a pious and worthy priest, who should watch over them and train them to piety.

In former times cathedral schools were conducted under the guidance of a *scholasticus*, and monastic schools were also open to such as aspired to the clerical state.[21] The Council of Trent [22] ruled that a seminary be established in every diocese, if possible. The Febronians and Josephinists tried to remodel the clerical seminaries after a pattern unacceptable to the Church. Equally unacceptable was the plan of certain university professors and rectors, who insisted that clerical students should attend the public State universities on the ground that it was necessary to raise the educational standard of the clergy.[23] Pius X centralized the many (about 300) diocesan seminaries of Italy into provincial seminaries.[24] This measure had become necessary to insure greater efficiency. All these, the so-called liberal no less than the conservation movements prove the importance of the clerical semi-

21 C. 1, C. 12, c. 2.

22 Sess. 23. c. 18, *de ref.*

23 H. Schell, *Der Katholizismus als Prinzip des Fortschrittes*, 1907, p. 28 ff.

24 Pius X, "*La Ristorazione,*" May 5, 1904; *Pio X, Suoi Atti e Suoi Intendimenti*, 1905, p. 13 f.

nary. Modern conditions require greater attention to this matter, as may be seen from an Instruction of the S.C. of Bishops and Regulars,[25] where the rules for frequenting non-ecclesiastical institutes are laid down. If at all possible, the young candidates should enter a Catholic college to be educated for the priesthood. As to frequenting secular universities, taking a post graduate course may be permitted after the philosophical and theological courses have been completed in a Catholic school. But no more clergymen are to be sent to secular universities than is necessary for the diocese. While they study at the university, they should dwell in a seminary, or, if this is impossible, live with an elderly priest or in a community. If the university is located outside the diocese, the Ordinary shall recommend his students to the Ordinary in whose diocese the university is, and the students must present themselves to, and obey the latter. Both Ordinaries should entrust the students to the care of a priest of approved virtue, learning, and knowledge of the young. This priest shall frequently inform the Ordinary of the conduct of the clerical students at the university, and the Ordinary himself shall demand frequent communications from the students. This regulation was inculcated anew and made universal by the *Motu proprio* of Pius X, " *Sacrorum Antistitum*," of Sept. 1, 1910, which especially warned the students against Modernism.[26] Our canon permits the Ordinary to make an occasional exception from the rule of taking the full theological course in a clerical seminary, but it does not exempt him from the obligation of entrusting such students to the

25 July 21, 1896 (*Coll. P. F.*, n. 1948); cfr. S. C. P. F., Oct. 18, 1883, IV, 1 (*Coll.*, n. 1606) recommended, especially for China, receiving youths from the 10th to 14th year of age, and have them pass a preparatory term of about two years.

26 *A. Ap. S.*, II, 658 f.

vigilance of a pious priest. This does not precisely mean that the student must live in the priest's house, although to do so would be highly commendable. He may, according to the said Instruction, live, *e. g.*, with his parents, provided only that a certain kind of spiritual guidance is proffered.

It may be added that the Ordinary has full power to demand compliance with these regulations, and no appeal therefrom is permissible.[27]

ARTICLE I

REQUISITES OF CANDIDATES FOR ORDINATION

CAN. 973

§ 1. Prima tonsura et ordines illis tantum conferendi sunt, qui propositum habeant ascendendi ad presbyteratum et quos merito coniicere liceat aliquando dignos futuros esse presbyteros.

§ 2. Ordinatus tamen qui superiores ordines recipere recuset, nec potest ab Episcopo ad eos recipiendos cogi, nec prohiberi a receptorum ordinum exercitio, nisi impedimento canonico detineatur aliave gravis, iudicio Episcopi, obsit causa.

§ 3. Episcopus sacros ordines nemini conferat quin ex positivis argumentis moraliter certus sit de eius canonica idoneitate; secus non solum gravissime peccat, sed etiam periculo sese committit alienis communicandi peccatis.

§ 1. Tonsure and inferior orders should be given only to such as have the intention to ascend to the priesthood and give reason to hope that they will one day be worthy priests.

27 Benedict XIV, " *Ad militantis,*" March 30, 1742, § 34.

§ 2. If, however, one who has been ordained (say to subdeaconship) refuses to receive higher orders, he cannot be compelled by the bishop to receive such higher orders, nor be forbidden the exercise of the orders he has received, unless a canonical impediment or some other grave cause, in the judgment of the bishop, should intervene.

§ 3. The bishop shall not confer sacred orders on any one unless he has positive proof, amounting to moral certainty, of the candidate's canonical fitness; otherwise he not only commits a grievous sin, but exposes himself to the danger of sharing in the guilt of another.

§ 1 is taken partly from the Council of Trent and subsequent papal constitutions.[28]

§ 2 forbids forcing one into an ecclesiastical rank which he perhaps thinks himself unworthy to hold. To prevent a cleric from exercising an order which he has duly and canonically received would be tantamount to declaring him irregular. A canonical impediment, *i. e.*, one strictly so-called, or an irregularity, must be proved in order to justify such a prohibition. The other *grave reason* for which one may be forbidden to exercise an order received, is a crime which, though as yet occult, is liable to be divulged.

The *moral certainty* mentioned in § 3, as to the proofs for the fitness of an aspirant to the sacred ministry may be gathered from information given by the director of the seminary and from the report of the synodal examiners. These suffice to exonerate the conscience of the Ordinary. It will not surprise the reader that the legislator here speaks in the tone of a severe preacher, if he remembers

28 *Trid.*, Sess. 23, c. 4, *de ref.*; Innocent XIII, "*Apostolici ministerii*," May 23, 1723, § 2; Benedict XIII, "*In supremo*," Sept. 23, 1724, § 2.

that a great canonist and a great pastor, Benedict XIV
and Pius X, in their first encyclical letters drew the attention of the bishops to this important matter. Benedict
XIV, among other things, says it is better to have few
priests, but righteous, fit and useful, than many who contribute nothing to the edification of the mystic body of
Christ.[29]   Pius X tells the bishops to carefully ponder the
fact that the faithful generally will be as good or as bad
as those whom they destine for the priesthood, and reminds them of St. Paul's warning not to be partakers of
other men's sins.[30]

CAN. 974

§ 1. Ut quis licite ordinari possit, requiruntur:

1°. Recepta sacra confirmatio;

2°. Mores ordini recipiendo congruentes;

3°. Aetas canonica;

4°. Debita scientia;

5°. Ordinum inferiorum susceptio;

6°. Interstitiorum observatio;

7°. Titulus canonicus, si agatur de ordinibus maioribus.

§ 2. Quod pertinet ad consecrationem episcopalem,
servetur praescriptum can. 331.

§ 1. That candidates *may be licitly ordained* the following conditions *are required*:

1.° They must have received the Sacrament of Confirmation;

2.° Their moral conduct must be conformable to the
order they wish to receive;

3.° They must have attained the canonical age;

---

29 " *Ubi primum*," Dec. 3, 1740,   30 " *E supremi*," Oct. 4, 1903
§ 1.   (*Anal. Eccl.*, XI, 378).

4.° They must have the necessary knowledge;

5.° They must have received the inferior orders;

6.° The canonical intervals must be observed;

7.° They must be in possession of a canonical title, if they wish to receive higher orders.

§ 2. As to episcopal consecration, can. 331 must be observed.

These points call for no comment here, as most of them will be explained in connection with the following canons.

THE CANONICAL AGE

CAN. 975

Subdiaconatus ne conferatur ante annum vicesimum primum completum; diaconatus ante vicesimum secundum completum; presbyteratus ante vicesimum quartum completum.

No one shall be ordained subdeacon before he has completed his twenty-first year; deaconship cannot be received before the twenty-second year is completed, and the priesthood cannot be received before the twenty-fourth year is completed.

For tonsure and minor orders no age is prescribed, but the following canon establishes a certain limit.

THE KNOWLEDGE REQUIRED

CAN. 976

§ 1. **Nemo sive saecularis sive religiosus ad primam tonsuram promoveatur ante inceptum cursum theologicum.**

§ 2. **Firmo praescripto can. 975, subdiaconatus ne conferatur, nisi exeunte tertio cursus theologici anno;**

diaconatus, nisi incepto quarto anno; presbyteratus, nisi post medietatem eiusdem quarti anni.

§ 3. Cursus theologicus peractus esse debet non privatim, sed in scholis ad id institutis secundum studiorum rationem can. 1365 determinatam.

§ 1. Neither seculars nor religious may receive the tonsure before they have *begun the course of theology.*

By the term *cursus theologicus* is to be understood theology proper, which presupposes a course in the classics and philosophy. It had been previously decided that the theological course would not be legally acknowledged unless preceded by a collegiate and philosophical course.[31] Consequently, although hermeneutics or an Oriental language may be taught in the two year's philosophical course, these would have to be considered as secondary or accessory branches which follow the principal branch, *i. e.,* philosophy. Note that *religious* are expressly included in this law and no exception is made for religious who only make a promise, not strictly so-called vows, as, for instance, the Eudists.[32] The consequence for religious is that their clerics cannot be ordained before they have begun their theological course. Beginning, however, may lawfully be taken even for the first month of the theological course.

§ 2. With due regard to the ruling concerning age (can. 975), *subdeaconship* may be conferred only towards the end of the *third year* of the theological course, *deaconship* only after the beginning of the *fourth year,* and the *priesthood* only in the second term of the *fourth year* of theology.

The school year should last at least nine months, and

31 S. C. Rel., Sept. 7, 1909, ad IV (*A. Ap. S.,* I, 702); can. 1365, § 2. 32 S. C. Rel., May 31, 1910 (*A. Ap. S.,* II, 449 f).

these must be reckoned according to the calendar. The feasts of Pentecost or Trinity cannot be taken as the end of the school year because they are movable. If the school starts about Sept. 10, it should last until June 10 of the following year and close with a final examination.[33]

Post medietatem signifies the second term, or semester, during the whole of which the priesthood may be received. But ordination to the priesthood does not dispense a candidate from completing his course. Therefore, one who is ordained on Holy Saturday must continue his studies until the end of the school year and then pass the examination (*cum examine finali feliciter emenso*).[34]

§ 3. The theological course must be taken, not privately, but in a school conducted according to can. 1365. A *private course* made outside a properly instituted school, even under the direction of a professor, is not legal, nor may the Ordinary accept it as sufficient for the *litterae testimoniales*.[35] However, the same S. Congregation has also declared that private studies may be permitted in rare individual cases, but only for the secondary branches. Which branches of a priest's education are primary, and which secondary, the Code does not state, but we may deduce from can. 1365, § 2, that dogmatic and moral theology are the main branches, whereas holy Scripture, Church history, Canon Law, liturgy, sacred eloquence and ecclesiastical music may be considered accessory. A more satisfactory division may be derived from a decision given in 1912. There dogmatic and moral theology, Scripture, Church history, and Canon Law are styled main branches, whilst Biblical Greek, Hebrew, homiletics, Patrology, liturgy, archaeology, ecclesiastical art, and the

---

[33] S. C. Consist., March 24, 1911, ad 1 (*A. Ap. S.*, III, 181).
[34] *Ibid.*
[35] S. C. Rel., Sept. 7, 1909, ad V (*A. Ap. S.*, I, 702 f).

Chant are called accessory branches.[36]   According to the
declaration of 1909, if private study embraces only a secondary branch, an examination made before the examiners
will suffice.   This examination may be taken at the end
of the school year together with the students who have
studied that branch in the school-room.   In the first part
of the decision mentioned it is laid down that a theological student who has missed school on account of sickness
or military service, may, if the time lost amounts to
no more than three months, supply the deficiency by private study, but he must pass the regular examination.[37]

ORDINATIONS PER SALTUM NOT PERMITTED

CAN. 977

**Ordines gradatim conferendi sunt ita ut ordinationes
per saltum omnino prohibeantur.**

Orders must be conferred successively, and ordinations *per saltum* are entirely forbidden.

Per saltum means by leaps and bounds, without keeping
the necessary intervals, or skipping an inferior order
which should precede the reception of a higher one.   The
Council of Sardica (can. 13) prescribes that the ascent to
the priesthood should be made by degrees, in order that
the candidate may be tested as to his faith, modesty,
character and reverence.   The object of successive or
gradual ordination, therefore, is to ensure due preparation and sufficient knowledge.[38]   An apprenticeship precedes every profession, and higher degrees are not con-

---

[36] S. C. Consist., July 16, 1912
(*A. Ap. S.*, IV, 491).

[37] S. C. Rel., March 1, 1915, ad
2 et 1 (*A. Ap. S.*, VII, 123 f.).   Although this is not expressly stated in
the code, the latter certainly is not
opposed to our explanation.

[38] Cfr. c. 1, Dist. 52; cc. 1, 4, 7,
Dist. 61; Propp. 51, 53 *Syn. Pistor.
damnatae*, "*Auctorem fidei*," Aug.
28, 1794 (Denzinger, n. 1414, 1416).

ferred on such as are barely initiated. Besides, there is also the succession of orders to be observed, as stated in the *Pontificale Romanum:* tonsure (*de clerico faciendo*), ostiariate, lectorate, exorcistate, acolythate, subdeaconship, deaconship, priesthood.[39]

The text says " *prohibeantur*," thereby intimating that this law is prohibitive, but not invalidating. Therefore the diaconate is validly conferred, even though the subdeaconship was omitted.[40] The priesthood could be validly received by one who had never been ordained a deacon[41] or ordained to deaconship invalidly. The H. O., in 1842, decided a case in point. One who had been invalidly ordained to the subdiaconate and the diaconate because of lack of consent, was finally ordained a priest. He received the priesthood with the right intention, but the question arose: Was he ordained validly? The Holy Office decided yes, but enjoined that he be secretly ordained to subdeaconship and deaconship.[42] Attention may be drawn to the *penalty* of suspension. This is not incurred unless the ordination *per saltum* is performed maliciously,[43] which, for instance, was not the case in the instance mentioned.

THE INTERSTICES

CAN. 978

§ 1. In ordinationibus serventur temporum interstitia quibus promoti in receptis ordinibus, secundum Episcopi praescriptum, sese exerceant.

§ 2. Interstitia primam tonsuram inter et ostiariatum vel inter singulos ordines minores prudenti Epis-

---

[39] *Trid.*, Sess. 23, cc. 11, 14 *de ref.*

[40] C. 1, Dist. 52 (Alex. II).

[41] C. nn. X, V, 29.

[42] S. O., March 2, 1842 (*Coll. P. F.*, n. 946).

[43] Can. 2374.

copi iudicio committuntur; acolythus vero ad subdia-
conatum, subdiaconus ad diaconatum, diaconus ad
presbyteratum ne antea promoveantur, quam acolythus unum saltem annum, subdiaconus et diaconus
tres saltem menses in suo quisque ordine fuerint ver-
sati, nisi necessitas aut utilitas Ecclesiae, iudicio Episcopi, aliud exposcat.

§ 3. Nunquam tamen, nisi de peculiari licentia Romani Pontificis, minores ordines cum subdiaconatu
duove sacri ordines uno eodemque die, reprobata
quavis contraria consuetudine, conferantur; imo nec
primam tonsuram conferre licet una cum aliquo ex ordinibus minoribus, neque omnes ordines minores una
simul.

§ 1. In ordaining, the intervals of time during which
the respective orders should be exercised, according to
episcopal prescription, must be observed.

The meaning of this law is that clerics should " exercise " the orders they have received, and although the
minor orders are generally not " practised," except in
religious institutions, yet our text, speaking as it does of
all intervals and all orders, certainly intends to inculcate
some kind of practice or exercise, at least of the higher
orders.[44] This is the very purpose of observing the interstices. How the " practice " is to be made is left to
the bishop.[45]

§ 2. It is left to the bishop also to *determine the intervals between the tonsure and the ostiariate,* and between the several minor orders. The interval between
the acolythate and subdeaconship must last one year;[46]

---

[44] Many, *l. c.*, p. 281 f., denies the
necessity of exercising the orders,
saying that the *ratio legis non cadit
sub lege.* Yes, if the *ratio* is not
stated in the law itself, the term

exerceant is expressly used in the
new Code.

[45] *Trid.*, Sess. 23, c. 11, *de ref.*

[46] A year, according to can. 32, §
2, means 365 days. But the eccle-

the interval between the subdiaconate and the diaconate, as also the interval between deaconship and the priesthood, must last at least three months, unless the bishop deems it necessary or useful for his diocese to shorten these intervals. Any plausible reason is sufficient. It may be added that it is the ordaining *bishop* who grants dispensation also in case of religious who may enjoy the privilege of being ordained without regard to the interstices.[47] The bishop, in ordaining such as are not his subjects, may also dispense from the intervals.[48]

§ 3. Minor Orders and subdeaconship, or two sacred orders, may never be conferred on the *same day*, without the express permission of the Roman Pontiff. Every contrary custom is hereby reprobated. Neither is it allowed to confer tonsure together with one of the minor orders, or all the minor orders at the same time.

The first clause is more severe than the second. For to receive two higher orders on one and the same natural day — for this is here to be understood — was always forbidden to all, exempt regulars not excepted.[49] The Code adds the reprobating clause in order at least to render contrary customs less admissible.

The second clause concerning tonsure and some or all minor orders repeats a Decretal, but apparently admits the contrary custom, which, as far as we are aware, was in vogue in several countries. The rule not to confer several sacred orders simultaneously also concerns the Oriental Rites.[50]

siastical year may here be admitted, on account of the *sacra tempora,* and was always acknowledged by Roman practice. (Many, *l. c.,* p. 280.)

47 S. C. C., May 17, 1593; May 31, 1597; Sept. 12, 1609 (Richter, *Trid.,* p. 200, n. 4 f.).

48 S. C. Sacr., Aug. 15, 1909 (*A. Ap. S.,* I, 656).

49 C. 2, X, V, 20.

50 S. C. P. T., April 13, 1807, n. XI; July 31, 1902, n. 8 (*Coll.,* nn. 692, 2149).

TITULUS ORDINATIONIS

Can. 979

§ 1. **Pro clericis saecularibus titulus canonicus est titulus beneficii, eoque deficiente, patrimonii aut pensionis.**

§ 2. **Hic titulus debet esse et vere securus pro tota ordinati vita et vere sufficiens ad congruam eiusdem sustentationem, secundum normas ab Ordinariis pro diversis locorum et temporum necessitatibus et adiunctis dandas.**

For the secular clergy the canonical title is that of an ecclesiastical benefice, or, where this is wanting, that of a patrimony or pension.

This title must be secure for the life-time of the ordinand, and entirely sufficient to support him properly, according to the regulations established by the Ordinaries to meet the needs and circumstances of places and times.

Title (*titulus*) originally signified an inscription placed on a house or property to show its owner, or the name of the place.[51] *Ecclesiastical language* has evolved two special meanings of the term, *viz.*, name for an oratory or a sepulchre of martyrs (*e.g., titulus pastoris* — S. Pudenziana). This name was later transferred to certain (25, then 49) churches of Rome, which in course of time became the so-called titular churches of the cardinals. As these churches had assigned to them a determined number of priests and clerics who lived from the revenues of these titles, the clergy itself was said to be "*intitulatus*" or "*incardinatus*."[52] Hence in this particular sense

---

51 Cfr. l. c. 2, 3, Cod. X, 10.

52 Armellini, *Lezioni di Archeologia Cristiana*, 1905, p. 192, 208,

269 f.; *Decreta Auth. S. Rit. C.,* Vol. IV, 342 f.

the word *title* meant service in a determined church which entitled a cleric to a decent living or support. This is the origin of the first and only exclusively ecclesiastical title called *beneficium*.

Later, especially in the 12th century, the practice arose of admitting aspirants to orders (from subdeaconship onward) on the *titulus* of means of their own, which title was known and canonically acknowledged as *patrimony*.[53] After the Council of Trent there were added to the two titles mentioned the *titulus pensionis*,[54] and others approved by custom and formally sanctioned by the later discipline of the Church.

A title may, therefore, be *defined* as a security given to a clergyman to insure his honorable maintenance, thereby enabling him to be promoted to higher orders. A title is thus needed for every order from subdeaconship onward. And from this general law no cleric, secular or religious, is excepted, for it is not becoming that those who devote themselves to the divine service should disgrace their sublime vocation by begging or exercising a trade not becoming to their state.[55]

Our code mentions *three titles* on which a *secular clergyman* may be ordained, but calls that of benefice *the canonical title par excellence*. This is quite intelligible, for although the other two titles were also admitted by the Church, they were extraordinary and tolerated only when a dispensation was granted. This at least was the Roman practice, as Benedict XIV says.[56] Now-a-days, however, no dispensation is required if there is no benefice available.

53 Cfr. cc. 4, 16, X, III, 5; Migne, *P. L.*, 210, 477; Benedict XIV, *De Syn. Dioec.*, XI, 2, 14.

54 Wernz, *Jus Dec.*, II, 114 (ed. 1).

55 *Trid.*, Sess. 21, c. 2, *de ref.*; c. 6, *Conc. Chalced.*

56 *De Syn. Dioec.*, XI, 2, 14.

1. The term *benefice* is to be understood of an ecclesiastical prebend which supplies its holder with a sufficient income to insure a permanent livelihood. A benefice must, according to our text, be *secure* and *sufficient*.

(a) It is judged to be *secure* if possessed actually, pacifically, and permanently, according to the requirements established by the Council of Trent.[57] The beneficiary, therefore, must not only be appointed to, but have actual possession of, his benefice. Besides, there must not be any litigation or dubious claims to the prebend, and, finally, it must be permanent.[58]

(b) A benefice must be *sufficient* to support its incumbent decently. The amount required to constitute a *congrua* is left to diocesan regulation. This was also the view taken by the Roman Court.[59] And most justly, for circumstances of time and place differ widely. Who could live now-a-days on forty scudi (forty dollars) per year? [60]

Residential and non-residential benefices are estimated differently. The amount of income accruing from a *residential benefice* depends on the regulations of the diocese in which the benefice is located, whereas that of a *non-residential benefice* depends on the rules of the diocese in which the beneficiary is to live.[61]

It may be added that *benefice* is here to be taken in its strictly canonical sense, and does not apply to most American parishes, unless they be considered as benefices.

57 Sess. 21, c. 2, *de ref.;* Many, *l. c.,* p. 337 f.

58 A benefice was considered permanent if bestowed for life, or at least for the respective order; S. C. C., July 8, 1690; April 14, 1696 (Richter, *Trid.,* p. 113, n. 2 f.).

59 S. C. C., July 1723 (Richter, *l. c.,* n. 4).

60 Benedict XIV, *Institut.,* 26, n. IV.

61 S. C. C., May 27, 1723 (Richter, *l. c.,* p. 112, n. 1). A deficient benefice could be supplied by a patrimony; S. C. C., Oct. 1589 (Richter, *l. c.,* n. 13).

2. *Patrimony*, properly speaking, is an inheritance received from one's ancestors, especially parents. Here
it means a subsidiary title, admitted for the needs or advantage of the Church. The conditions required are the
same as those demanded for a benefice. Hence the patrimony must be secure and sufficient. A secure patrimony
would be one consisting of real estate or other stable
and interest-bringing property, provided it is not
mortgaged. Mortgaged property is unsafe as it may be
sold at any time. The mere promise of parents or friends
to provide a patrimony would not be considered secure,[62]
nor the fact that the ordinand is by profession an artist,
a musician, a teacher, or possesses a doctor's degree.[63]
Much less would manual Mass stipends be considered a
source of secure income. Government, State, and muni-
cipal bonds, and shares in reliable and conservative firms
and companies [64] are in a different category. Live-stock,
grain and cotton or any marketable produce may also be
lawfully taken for patrimony.

As to *sufficiency*, what was said concerning the quantity or amount of a benefice also applies to a patrimony.
If the interest on a certain capital is assigned, the latter
must amount to about $15,000 or $20,000, which, invested
at 5%, would bring $750 or $1000 a year, which now-a-
days would just about afford a decent living.

If the ordinand assigns a portion of his own property as
a patrimony, this must clearly be determined and set aside
for the *titulus ordinationis*, and becomes inalienable. If
parents, relatives, or friends furnish a patrimony, they
must draw up a title-deed, donation, or note in legal form,
without fraud, condition, or liability. In other words,

---

62 S. C. C., Oct., 1589; Oct. 2,
1717 (Richter, *l. c.*, n. 16).

63 S. C. C., Oct., 1589; May 23,

1609 (Benedict XIV, *Institut.*, 26, n.
VII).

64 Many, *l. c.*, p. 345.

the claim must be clear and complete, so that it cannot be attacked under the civil law.[65]

A Roman decision says that the title of patrimony can not be used if one is to be ordained only for the solace and spiritual comfort of his parents, and there is no need or advantage on the part of the diocese to recommend his ordination.[66]

3. The *titulus pensionis* is of the same nature as that of patrimony, and must offer the same guarantees of security and sufficiency. Some writers take *pensio* in the sense of ecclesiastical pension only, excluding civil pensions,[67] though neither the Council of Trent nor our text restricts the term to a pension derived from an ecclesiastical benefice. Therefore other authors justly admit *any* pension, provided it is secure and sufficient.[68] This view is supported by a decision of the S. C. C., which admits an annual pension, if founded on immovable property and secure.[69] The main underlying idea always is safety and sufficiency. Hence even a State pension, provided it is sufficient, may be accepted as a *titulus ordinationis*, because such a title ordinarily is as safe as any other.

LOSS AND LACK OF A TITLE

CAN. 980

§ 1. Ordinatus in sacris, si titulum amittat, alium sibi provideat, nisi, iudicio Episcopi, eius congruae sustentationi aliter cautum sit.

[65] S. C. C., 1573, 1598, Nov. 29, 1670 (Richter, *Trid.*, p. 114, nn. 16, 17, 19); Benedict XIV, *Institut.*, 26, nn. XIII, XXVIII f.

[66] S. C. C., Sept. 9, 1679 (Richter, *l. c.*, n. 14).

[67] Many, *l. c.*, p. 348.

[68] *Trid.*, Sess. 21, c. 2, *de ref.*;

v. Scherer, *l. c.*, I, p. 362; Wernz, *l. c.*, II, n. 92, p. 115, who adds "*super bonis immobilibus fundatus sit*," according to S. C. C., Oct. 2, 1707 (Richter, *l. c.*, n. 20).

[69] Cfr. S. C. C., June 21, 1629; S. C. P. F., April 27, 1871, ad 2 (*Coll.*, n. 1369).

§ 2. Qui, citra apostolicum indultum, suum subditum in sacris sine titulo canonico scienter ordinaverint aut ordinari permiserint, debent ipsi eorumque successores eidem egenti alimenta necessaria praebere, donec congruae eiusdem sustentationi aliter provisum fuerit.

§ 3. Si Episcopus aliquem ordinaverit sine titulo canonico cum pacto ut ordinatus non petat ab ipso alimenta, hoc pactum omni vi caret.

§ 1. If a clergyman in holy orders *loses the title to which he was ordained*, he must procure another, unless in the judgment of the bishop, he is well provided for in some other way.

The title to which one is ordained is mentioned at the act of ordination and is not liable to alienation, as has been repeatedly declared by the S. Congregation.[70] Hence a change of whatever kind must be notified to the local Ordinary, whose subject the clergyman is. If we say *clergyman*, we include religious, for the text simply says: *ordinatus . . . si titulum amittat*, thus including all titles: benefice, patrimony, pension, service, mission, *mensa communis*, and religious profession. Hence (1) if one loses the title of benefice he must procure another title, *i.e.*, any one of those just mentioned. (2) This must be done with the *express permission of the bishop*, even though it is certain that the clergyman has a sufficient livelihood.[71] (3) The bishop may and should compel a clergyman who has lost the *titulus missionis* to procure another,[72] as stated above. (4) A religious who was ordained *ad titulum mensae communis* or *ad religiosam professionem* and loses this title must procure another; but in missionary countries such clergy-

---

70 Cfr. Richter, *Trid.*, p. 113 f.
71 S. C. C., Feb. 9, 1726; Nov. 28, 1686; July 1687 (Richter, *Trid.*, p. 113 f., nn. 7, 29).
72 S. C. P. F., April 27, 1871 n. 11 (*Coll.*, n. 1369).

men are only obliged to prove that they have sufficient means to live.[73] (5) If a patrimony assigned is changed into a benefice, the bishop's consent must be obtained, otherwise the change has no ecclesiastical effect.[74]

§ 2. Those who, without a previous Apostolic indult, have knowingly ordained, or permitted to be ordained, one of their subjects without a canonical title, are obliged to support the needy clergyman until he is otherwise provided with a living. This obligation also binds the successor of the prelate.[75]

The bishop who is here put under obligation is not the one who ordained the cleric, but the one of the subject ordained without a canonical title. The ordination must have been performed with full knowledge of the fact that there was no canonical title, *i.e.*, one acknowledged by the Church. If the bishop has been deceived by the ordinand or his parents, he is not obliged to support the cleric. On the other hand, if he was aware of the want of a canonical title, not only he himself, but his successor, is under that obligation. The term *successor* here includes the chapter, the Vicar Capitular or Administrator as well as the next bishop.[76] The obligation is limited by the condition of the clergyman and also as to duration. If the clergyman is *not really in need*, but has some other means of sustenance, no matter of what kind, so it be but becoming to the clerical state, the obligation ceases. It also ceases as soon as the state of need ceases. The bishop must defray this expense either from his personal income or from the *mensa episcopalis*, if there is such a one attached to his see.

---

[73] *Ibid.* and S. C. EE. et RR., Dec. 20, 1838 (Bizzarri, *Collect.*, p. 83 f).

[74] S. C. C., July 20, 1619; Nov. 16, 1686 (Richter, *l. c.*, nn. 21, 28).

[75] Cfr. c. 6, *Conc. Chalced.*, c. 1, Dist. 70; cc. 4, 16, X, III, 5.

[76] Reiffenstuel, l. I, tit. 11, n. 191 ff.

§ 3. If a bishop has ordained a cleric without a canonical title, with the mutual *agreement* that the ordinand should not demand any support of him, the stipulation is void.

Such a practice would savor of simony, and the text from which the Code took this law, actually belongs to the title on simony.[77] The penalty is suspension from conferring orders for one year and is reserved to the Holy See.[78]

TITULI SERVITII ET MISSIONIS

CAN. 981

§ 1. Si ne unus quidem ex titulis de quibus in can. 979, § 1, praesto sit, suppleri potest titulo servitii dioecesis, et, in locis Sacrae Congregationi de Prop. Fide subiectis, titulo missionis, ita tamen ut ordinandus, iureiurando interposito, se devoveat perpetuo dioecesis aut missionis servitio, sub Ordinarii loci pro tempore auctoritate.

§ 2. Ordinarius presbytero, quem promoverit titulo servitii ecclesiae vel missionis, debet beneficium vel officium vel subsidium, ad congruam eiusdem sustentationem sufficiens, conferre.

If none of the three titles,— benefice, patrimony, pension,— is available the title of the *service of the diocese,* or, in the provinces subject to the S. C. Propanda, the *titulus missionis* may be substituted. However, in both cases the ordinand must make oath that he will permanently serve the diocese or mission under the jurisdiction of the respective local Ordinary. The Ordinary owes to the one promoted to the title of service or mission either

---

77 C. 45, X, V, 3.   78 See can. 2373, n. 3.

a benefice or an office or a subsidy affording him sufficient support.

The *titulus servitii Ecclesiae* was first introducted under Eugene IV (1431-1447), who granted this privilege to the metropolitan of Florence. Later it was also permitted to the City of Mexico, under the title of administration, and as such was acknowledged by the Latin American Council of 1899.[79] The *titulus missionis*, which is only another form of the *titulus servitii Ecclesiae*, was first granted to the Irish College in Rome and then extended to other colleges under the Propaganda.[80] It was the usual title to which the clergy of the U. S. were ordained while we were under the jurisdiction of the said Congregation. When the S. C. Consistorialis, A.D. 1909, transferred the American, Irish and Scotch colleges in Rome to its own jurisdiction, it changed the *titulus missionis* into *titulus servitii*.[81] Since 1908, America and Great Britain also belong to the jurisdiction of the S. C. Consistorialis, and the *titulus missionis* is changed into that of service of the diocese, acknowledged not as canonical in the strict sense, but as legal or ecclesiastical; therefore no special faculties are needed to ordain one on this title.

1. Both the *titulus servitii* and the *titulus missionis* are *subsidiary* or extraordinary titles, which may only be used when there is none of the other three (benefice, patrimony, pension) available, and consequently should be employed only with discretion and for candidates who give manifest signs of a priestly vocation.[82]

---

79 Lingen-Reuss, *Causae Selectae*, p. 3; *A. S. S.*, 12, 569; *Acta et Decreta Conc. Lat. Am.*, 1900, p. 254, n. 582.

80 Urban VIII, "*Sacrosanctae*," April 12, 1631; May 18, 1638.

81 S. C. Consist., Nov. 12, 1908; Aug. 6, 1909 (*A. Ap. S.*, I, 148 ff; 678 ff.).

82 S. C. P. F. April 27, 1871, nn. 3, 6, 7 (*Coll.*, n. 1369).

2. Before they are ordained *subdeacons,* the ordinands must promise under *oath* to devote themselves to the permanent service of the diocese or mission for which they are ordained.

3. This oath, the formula of which has been re-modelled,[83] *excludes entrance into a religious community* without the special permission of the Holy See, which is granted either by the S. Cong. Consist., if one was ordained to the title of service, or by the S. Cong. Propaganda, if ordained to the title of mission.

4. By common law both titles are restricted to the respective diocese or the mission for which one was ordained, and the oath also is limited. In consequence no one could formerly, without a special indult from the S. Congregation, pass from one diocese or mission to another.[84] However, the bishops of England obtained an Apostolic indult that permitted one ordained for a certain diocese to be transferred to another diocese of the same ecclesiastical province without taking a new oath and without recourse to the Holy See. This indult was later extended to the dioceses of the U. S. and may still be made use of in both countries because it has not been expressly revoked by our canon.[85]

5. Either title may be *supplanted by another,* for instance, patrimony or pension. However, this change requires permission from the Holy See. If the title on which a priest was ordained is lost, and not supplanted by another, he is not suspended, but the Ordinary must compel him to procure another title.[86]

83 S. C. Consist., Aug. 6, 1909 (*A. Ap. S.,* I, 686).

84 S. C. P. F., April 27, 1871, n. 13; Feb. 4, 1873, ad 4 (*Coll.,* nn. 1369, 1394).

85 S. C. P. F., Aug. 18, 1885.

86 S. C. P. F., Aug. 18, Nov. 30, 1885 (*Coll.,* n. 1641); can. 4.

Can. 982

§ 1. Pro regularibus titulus canonicus est sollemnis religiosa professio seu titulus, ut dicitur, paupertatis.

§ 2. Pro religiosis votorum simplicium perpetuorum est titulus *mensa communis, Congregationis* aliusve similis, ad normam constitutionum.

§ 3. Ceteri religiosi, etiam ad ordinationis titulum quod attinet, iure saecularium reguntur.

§ 1. For *regulars,* the *canonical title* is that of *solemn religious profession,* or, as it is called, poverty.[87]

The Council of Chalcedon (can. 6) called this title *titulus monasterii,*[88] which is a juridical term, because under Justinian law [89] the monastery was a corporation responsible for the maintenance of its members. When the more centralized orders of the Mendicants arose, this title was necessarily transferred either to the province or to the order, and called religious poverty. *Salva reverentia* it may be permitted to say that this term has little justification in juridico-canonical language. It is for this reason, no doubt, that our Code adds: *ut dicitur.*

The title *paupertatis* is strictly limited to *regulars,* to wit, members of religious orders with solemn vows, and to solemn profession. Hence clerics belonging to orders whose members are only simply or temporarily professed, cannot be ordained on the title of religious profession.[90] This applies also to regulars working on the missions that are under the jurisdiction of the Propaganda.[91]

[87] S. C. P. F., April 27, 1871, n. 11 (*Coll.,* n. 1369).

[88] C. 1, Dist. 70.

[89] *Cod. Just.,* I, 3.

[90] *Auctis admodum,* Nov. 4, 1892, n. 1.

[91] S. C. P. F., April 27, 1871, n. 4 (*Coll.,* n. 1369).

§ 2. For *religious* of *simple perpetual vows,* the title is that of *mensae communis,* or *congregationis,* or a similar one, according to their own Constitutions.

This title is not called canonical in our text, but is legalized or acknowledged as valid for all congregations whose members take simple perpetual vows. Formerly it needed a special privilege or indult, for which each religious congregation, even though exempt, had to apply to the Holy See.[92]

This title signifies the same as that of religious profession, to wit, the claim to decent support. If it is lost, either by dismissal or withdrawal from the community, the Ordinary may suspend such an ex-religious, unless he has acquired another title sufficient for decent support.[93]

§ 3. All *other religious* fall under the common law of the Church, so far as the title of ordination is concerned. Hence

1.° Religious with purely *temporary vows* cannot be ordained subdeacons unless they have a canonical title, or one acknowledged by law, as prescribed for the secular clergy;[94]

2.° Novices are bound by the same law as the secular clergy;

3.° Members of religious societies without vows must obey the law laid down for the secular clergy, unless they have a special privilege.[95]

92 S. C. P. F., *ibid.,* Leo XIII, " *Conditae,*" Dec. 8, 1900, § 2, n. 6.

93 S. C. EE. et RR., Dec. 20, 1838 (Bizzarri, *Coll.,* p. 84).

94 S. C. super Statu Regul., Jan. 20, 1860 ad 1 (Bizzarri, *l. c.,* p. 858 f.).

95 As to the penalty, see can. 2373, 3°.

ART. II

CAN. 983

**Nullum impedimentum perpetuum quod venit no-
mine *irregularitatis*, sive ex defectu sit ex delicto, con-
trahitur, nisi quod fuerit in canonibus qui sequuntur
expressum.**

No permanent impediment which comes under the
name of *irregularity*, whether it arises from a mere defect or from a crime, is incurred, unless it is expressly
stated in the following canons.

The legislator has laid down (can. 968) a distinction
between irregularity and simple canonical impediment.
Now he determines the *source or origin* whence irregularity may be known or gathered — the *fons cognoscendi*.
This is the Code, and the Code only. Indirectly this
canon insinuates the power that may set up an irregularity. It is the common or *universal law*, or the Sovereign
Pontiff, the legislator of the universal Church, who alone
can lay down laws for all the clergy. The clergy is the
same wherever the Church exists, and requires essentially
the same qualities in all its members, and uniformity of
discipline in this very important matter is absolutely required, lest some should seek exemption or admission into
a laxer province.[96] The proposition that the Pope is the
sole competent law-giver must not be understood as
implying that custom[97] or particular synods did not
contribute to the establishment of irregularities. For,

[96] Phillips, *K.-R.*, 1845; Vol. I,
411 f.

[97] Wernz, *Ius Decret.*, Vol. II,
n. 97, p. 124 f. (ed. 1).

like any other merely ecclesiastical law, that concerning irregularities had its genesis and development. Since the completion of the Decretals no new irregularities have been added.

The enumeration of irregularities in our Code is to be understood *taxative, i.e.*, as full and complete. No others are admitted; nor can new ones be established by any bishop, for single bishops are not competent to make laws for the universal Church. And irregularities belong to universal or common law.

The canon distinguishes between irregularity *ex defectu* and *ex delicto*. This distinction is first found in a decretal of Innocent III, where the note or mark of crime, and the mark of mere defect, are clearly kept apart.[98]

Irregularities are, first and above all, a safeguard of the *dignity of the sacred ministry*, not a penalty. It is true that the cause of an irregularity may be a crime, and that the irregularity itself may therefore *appear* as a penalty. But still the penal element attached to an irregularity is not primarily intended by the Church, but only accessorily or secondarily[99] and *per modum concomitantiae*. The primary intent is to safeguard the sacred ministry from profanation, as stated above. This primary intention appears more clearly in the irregularities *ex defectu*, which are not imputable to those affected by them. The Church wants her ministers to be blameless in every respect, like the bodyguard of a king, whose members are " drafted " from among the most capable of his subjects.

Concerning the *historical development*, it may be noted that some irregularities were established from the very

---

[98] C. 14, X, V, 34, *de purgatione canonica.*   [99] Wernz, *l. c.*, II, n. 96, p. 121.

beginning of the Church, as the pastoral letters of St. Paul testify. No doubt the Mosaic Law furnished some prototypes for the priesthood of the New Testament, although the old ceremonial law could not essentially influence the New Dispensation.

IRREGULARITIES EX DEFECTU

CAN. 984

Sunt irregulares ex defectu:

1°. Illegitimi, sive illegitimitas sit publica sive occulta, nisi fuerint legitimati vel vota sollemnia professi;

2°. Corpore vitiati qui secure propter debilitatem, vel decenter propter deformitatem, altaris ministerio defungi non valeant. Ad impediendum tamen exercitium ordinis legitime recepti, gravior requiritur defectus, neque ob hunc defectum prohibentur actus qui rite poni possunt;

3°. Qui epileptici vel amentes vel a daemone possessi sunt vel fuerunt; quod si post receptos ordines tales evaserint et iam liberos esse certo constet, Ordinarius potest suis subditis receptorum ordinum exercitium rursus permittere;

4°. Bigami, qui nempe duo vel plura matrimonia valida successive contraxerunt;

5°. Qui infamia iuris notantur;

6°. Iudex qui mortis sententiam tulit;

7°. Qui munus carnificis susceperint eorumque voluntarii ac immediati ministri in exsecutione capitalis sententiae.

Irregular in consequence of a defect are:

1.° Those of *illegitimate birth, no matter whether their*

illegitimacy be public or occult, unless they have been legitimated or made solemn profession.

The tenth and eleventh centuries are known for disciplinary relaxation and for a low conception, or at least an imperfect practice, of sacerdotal celibacy. To check the evil, the *filii presbyterorum* were first excluded from entering the clerical state, or at least from succeeding their progenitors in ecclesiastical benefices.[1] Gradually, however, the note of illegitimacy was extended to all born out of lawful wedlock.[2] What illegitimacy means, as well as the mode of legitimation, has been explained elsewhere.[3]

Excepted from this rule are those who have been *legitimated* either by a subsequent marriage, or by a papal rescript. Note, however, that legitimation does not permit one to become a bishop or Cardinal,[4] whereas inferior prelacies are not excluded from its effects.

Besides, as the Decretals had already enacted, *religious profession* removes the stain of illegitimacy. But this effect only follows *solemn* profession and extends only to the priesthood inclusively, all, even regular prelatures being excluded.[5]

The text says: no matter whether the *illegitimacy be public or occult.* We here take these two terms in the same sense as public and occult impediments; the difference lying in the fact whether it can or cannot be proved in court.[6] The mere fact is sufficient to debar one from receiving orders. The judgment of the Church is milder if illegitimacy is *doubtful,* and canonists hold that *expositi* or foundlings, for instance, are not to be re-

---

1 C. 12, Dist. 56.
2 Cfr. X, I, 17; C. 13, X, IV, 17.
3 Cfr. can. 1114 f.
4 Cfr. can. 331, § 1, n. 1; can. 232, § 2, n. 1.

5 C. 1, X, I, 17: " *praelationem vero nullatenus habeant.*"
6 Can. 1037.

garded as illegitimate. Yet the practice rather favors *dispensatio ad cautelam.*[7] Illegitimacy is not to be extended to the second generation. If the son was born legitimately, it makes no difference whether his father was born legitimately or illegitimately.[8]

2.° Men who are *defective in body* or who, on account of weakness, cannot *safely,* or on account of deformity, cannot *becomingly* perform the functions of the altar. A greater defect is required to prohibit one from exercising an order already lawfully received, than for receiving a new order, nor are clerics forbidden by reason of such a defect to perform functions which they can properly perform.

The reason for this *defectus corporis* is incapability of ministering at the altar properly and the danger of exciting derision on the part of those present. The text simply says *corpore vitiati,* and refers every function to the ministry of the altar. Some examples may illustrate the text.

(a) If one has not the necessary stature to reach the altar properly, he would certainly be irregular.[9]

(b) One who is minus a *hand or a finger* which are necessary for handling the sacred species, is irregular. This is the case if thumb and index finger are missing. In cases where the hand was complete, but a great stiffness of the arm, caused by apoplexy or paralysis, rendered the breaking of the host or the making of the sign of the cross impossible, the S. Congregation denied a dispensation.[10]

7 C. un. X, V, 11; Phillips, *l. c.,* I, p. 530; Wernz, *l. c.,* II, n. 132, p. 184.

8 S. C. C., Nov. 9, 1647; Jan. 23, 1610 (Richter, *Trid.,* p. 465, nn. 6, 7).

9 Barbosa, *De Off. et Pot. Epi.,* P. II, alleg. 42, n. 53; but the S. C. C., July 12, 1721 (Richter, *l. c.,* 340, n. 13) in one case left it to the judgment of the bishop.

10 S. C. C., May 6, 1775; Dec. 19, 1772; July 28, 1770 (Richter, *l. c.,* nn. 18, 17, 16).

(c) Concerning the *eyesight*, irregularity certainly exists where there is complete blindness or loss of the *vis visiva*. Thus, if one had such feeble eyesight as not to be able to read the Missal, and if the defect were incurable, no dispensation for receiving holy orders would likely be granted, even though the petitioner would be useful and his services needed for the diocese or some charitable institution.[11] If the left or " canonical eye " is strong and sound, irregularity can not be asserted, but a man having the use of only one eye is certainly irregular.

(d) As to the sense of *hearing*, those who are completely deaf or dumb are irregular. The same is true of those who stammer in a very offensive manner.[12]

(e) A special class is that of the *deformed*, who are destitute of a limb and thereby rendered abnormal. To this class belong all who lack the nose, or an arm, or a leg, or who suffer from gout or paralysis so that they appear stooped or are unable to make a genuflection; also those who limp considerably, or are lame. In this latter case the degree of scandal or ridicule must be considered.[13]

The text says that the *defect* must be *greater* if one has been already promoted to sacred orders, to inhibit the exercise of that order.[14] But if the defect is too great, neither permission nor dispensation may be expected. Thus a dispensation was denied to a priest who

11 S. C. C., Sept. 17, 1814 (Richter, *l. c.*, n. 25); May 19, 1906 (*Anal., Eccl.*, XIV, 199 f.); see c. 7, X, I, 20; c. 2, X, III, 6.

12 S. C. C., April 14, 1832 (Richter, *l. c.*, n. 28): *notabiliter balbutiens*, fit neither for administering the Sacraments nor for teaching; S. C. C., Jan. 25, 1806 (Richter, *l. c.*, n. 22): " *auditus et vocis vitio*," unfit for chanting the Mass or hearing confessions.

13 S. C. C., Jan. 20, 1798; Jan. 28, 1832; May 25, 1833 (Richter, *l. c.*, nn. 20, 27, 29).

14 S. C. C., May 5. 1775, *et pluries* (Richter, *l. c.*, n. 12).

could stand on his feet only during the consecration,[15] whereas another who was blind and could say Mass with the assistance of another priest was granted a dispensation, since there was no other church to say Mass and the priest was poor.[16]

3.° *Epileptics, the insane and possessed, who are now or have formerly been in this condition.* If they have become afflicted after ordination and recovered their health, the Ordinary may permit them again to exercise the orders they had received. As to *epilepsy*, the medical authorities[17] tell us that it has many and different forms: convulsions in which patients fall down, attacks which occur only at night, epilepsy in which the physical signs are almost entirely lacking, ambulatory epilepsy, etc. All are attributable to nervous disease. The same is true of insanity.

Diabolic possession was in former times often confounded with epilepsy.

As to epilepsy, the S. Congregation, as a general rule, demanded the testimony of a conscientious physician regarding the nature and progress of the disease, and subsequent freedom from attacks, which has to continue from one to two years at least. In cases where the attacks occurred only at long intervals, dispensation was sometimes granted, sometimes refused.[18] Hence the rule stated above is safe to follow. The same may be applied to insanity and possession, though in one case the S. C. denied a dispensation even though the patient had had no attack for three years.[19] The term Ordinary here

15 S. C. C., Dec. 18, 1841 (*ibid.*, n. 31).

16 S. C. C., Aug. 23, 1727 (*ibid.*, 15).

17 See O'Malley-Walsh, *Essays in Pastoral Medicine*, p. 251 ff.

18 S. C. C., Aug. 25, 1905; Nov. 24, 1906 (*Anal. Eccl.*, L, XIII, 370 f.; L. XIV, 436 f).

19 S. C. C., Dec. 2, 1724 (Richter, *l. c.*, p. 340, n. 10); in one instance the S. C. C., April 27, 1816 (*Richter,*

includes the major superiors of exempt religious.

4.° *Bigamists,* who have validly and successively contracted two or more marriages. The reason for this law is stated in can. 1142. Note, however, that *bigamia interpretativa* or *simultanea* no longer entails irregularity. Those only are called bigamists, who after the first valid marriage has been dissolved, either by a dispensation *a matrimonio rato,* or by death, have married a second time and oftener. Whether the application of the Pauline Privilege would also count, seems doubtful.[20]

5.° *Those who have incurred infamia iuris,* loss of reputation or good name as stated in the law. *Infamia iuris* is a penalty inflicted on certain crimes expressly mentioned in the law,[21] either ecclesiastical or civil. The ecclesiastical law mentions several crimes as involving infamy *ipso facto.*[22] If a declaration is required to the effect that one is looked upon as infamous, infamy is not actually incurred until this declaration has been expressly made.[23] Infamy induced by civil law doubtless entails irregularity.[24]

6.° *A judge who has pronounced sentence of death.*

7.° *Those who have held the office of executioners and all their voluntary and immediate helpers in the execution of capital punishment.*

These two irregularities are styled *ex defectu lenitatis,* as they are supposed to indicate a lack of gentleness. It seems meet that the representatives of Christ, who was the meekest and gentlest of men, should be endowed with this preëminently Christian quality, which appears

---

n. 11) required ten years' freedom from attack, but the petitioner had followed a military career.

20 Because Baptism wipes out every stain, and bigamy certainly must be considered a personally contracted stain.

21 Can. 2293.

22 Canons 2320, 2328, 2343, 2351, 2356, 2357.

23 Canons 2314, 2359.

24 Cfr. Wernz, II, n. 130, p. 177; Gasparri, *l. c.,* n. 240 f.

notably wanting in all who coöperate, although without any fault of their own, in the infliction of capital punishment.[25] The Code restricts the defects formerly enumerated under this heading to strict coöperation in carrying out the death sentence. The assistants must act as helpers of the hangman or electrocutioner voluntarily, i.e., of their own accord, and immediately, whereas the job of the hangman is itself sufficient to involve irregularity. Soldiers or policemen who guard the place of execution do not incur irregularity; neither do priests and ministers of justice who assist or witness the act.[26]

IRREGULARITIES EX DELICTO

The pastoral letters of St. Paul form the foundation of the ecclesiastical discipline, which, however, wavered and changed considerably in course of time. "Having no crime,"[27] was the warning of the Apostle to Timothy when ordaining ministers of the New Dispensation. A crime in legal parlance always supposes a public or at least externally committed deed, which for one reason or another disturbs the public order and is offensive to those who witness it. Crime and sin must be and were distinguished from the beginning.[28] Baptism indeed wipes out sin and crime, but the *fomes peccati* remains. It seemed unbecoming that men who had committed one of the grosser crimes that were punished with special penances in the early Church, should be elevated to the sacred ministry. Three crimes (*apostasia, moechia,* and *homicidium*) were singled out as deserving of public

[25] Cfr. c. 8, Dist. 50; c. 1, Dist. 51; S. C. C., April 22, 1673, Zamboni, *Collect.,* II, 320, n. 3; May 14, 1825 (Lingen-Reuss, *Causae Selectae,* p. 113).

[26] Soldiers are here not mentioned, but they may fall under the following heading.

[27] Cfr. I, Tim. III, 10; Tit. 1, 6 f.; Phillips, *K.-R.,* I, 550 f.

[28] See the *Dictum Gratiani ad Dist. 25.*

penance, which latter almost automatically excluded one from embracing the ministry.[29] As the Church spread, her discipline grew milder and many aspirants to the clerical state did not measure up to the primitive, rather severe requirements. This compelled the Church to mitigate her former restrictions with regard to admission to the priesthood. Yet the principle of decency and blamelessness was retained intact.

CAN. 985

Sunt irregulares ex delicto:

1°. Apostatae a fide, haeretici, schismatici;

2°. Qui, praeterquam in casu extremae necessitatis, baptismum ab acatholicis quovis modo sibi conferri siverunt;

3°. Qui matrimonium attentare aut civilem tantum actum ponere ausi sunt, vel ipsimet vinculo matrimoniali aut ordine sacro aut votis religiosis etiam simplicibus ac temporariis ligati, vel cum muliere iisdem votis adstricta aut matrimonio valido coniuncta;

4°. Qui voluntarium homicidium perpetrarunt aut fetus humani abortum procuraverunt, effectu secuto, omnesque cooperantes;

5°. Qui seipsos vel alios mutilaverunt vel sibi vitam adimere tentaverunt;

6°. Clerici medicam vel chirurgicam artem sibi vetitam exercentes, si exinde mors sequatur;

7°. Qui actum ordinis, clericis in ordine sacro constitutis reservatum, ponunt, vel eo ordine carentes, vel ab eius exercitio poena canonica sive personali, medicinali aut vindicativa, sive locali prohibiti.

Irregularity arising from crime is incurred by

[29] Cfr. c. 4, Dist. 81 (Conc. Nic. I, can. 9).

1. *Apostates from the faith, heretics, and schismatics.*
These three classes were always barred from holy orders. Remark that the canon mentions only actual apostates, etc., and that can. 986 determines the extent of this crime.

2. *Whoever has allowed himself in any way to be baptized by non-Catholics, except in case of extreme necessity.* This cause of irregularity, which is now considerably modified, was formerly called *abusus baptismi.* The text says *siverunt,* who have permitted themselves,— which supposes that they were at least aware of the non-Catholic character of the Baptism. Therefore we may safely say that *adults* only are here to be understood. But the word "adults" must be interpreted according to can. 745, § 2, n. 2, which says that with regard to baptism all those are called adults who have attained the use of reason.[80] The term *siverunt* also excludes violent or fraudulent Baptism administered by a non-Catholic.

The expression *non-Catholic* includes the members of every heretical or schismatical sect, ministers as well as laymen, men and women, *vitandi* and *non-vitandi.*[81] *Quovis modo,* in whatever manner, refers to the mode of baptism, whether it be solemn or private, public or secret.

Extreme necessity is certainly present where there is danger of death and no other person than a non-Catholic is available. But even in that case the danger of perversion must be absent, or at least very remote.[82]

3.° *Those who have attempted marriage, or got married before the civil court whilst they were bound by marital ties, or by sacred orders, or by religious, even*

---

80 Cfr. c. 3, c. 1, q. 4.
81 Wernz, *l. c.,* II, n. 134, p. 191.
82 Thesaurus-Giraldi, *De Poenis*

Eccl., 1831, p. 107 (P. II, c. 5, *Baptis*).

though only simple or temporary vows, and also those (otherwise free) *who have attempted marriage before the civil court with a woman bound by the matrimonial tie or by a religious vow.*

This canon, as formulated, is to some extent new, though similar to the old law regarding *bigamia interpretativa* and *similitudinaria*, which were enumerated among the irregularities *ex defectu*. The two classes thus rendered irregular comprise:

(a) *Married* men who attempt marriage with another woman, whether a virgin or a widow, or legally divorced. The attempt, however, must be serious, and possess the semblance and figure of marriage. Note that the text does not require consummation of the marriage.[33] On the other hand mere concubinage does not constitute irregularity on this score.[34]

(b) *Clergymen in sacris*, or religious with simple, even only temporary, vows, who attempt marriage or to get married before the civil court. This was called *bigamia similitudinaria*, being a carnal marriage[35] contracted after a spiritual espousal. Here, however, a distinction must be made. Whereas the clergy in sacred orders and solemnly professed religious cannot validly contract, but at most *attempt* a marriage, *i.e.*, have the civil act performed, those with simple vows may contract validly, but incur irregularity unless they are dispensed from the simple vows and get married *in facie Ecclesiae*. It would be irreconcilable with the discipline of the Church, who dispenses from simple vows, to hold that irregularity follows religious who are lawfully dispensed from their vows, or who contract marriage after

---

[33] This was implied in most of the ancient texts; c. 15, Dist. 34; c. 1, X, I, 21.

[34] C. 6, X, I, 21.

[35] Wernz, II, p. 101, justly observes that the texts are not sufficiently clear to establish this irregularity.

the lapse of temporary vows (can. 637). Therefore the term *ligati* must be taken *in sensu composito,* not *in sensu diviso,* to use a well-known distinction.

(c) Men who attempt to contract marriage with any *woman* who is under religious or marital obligation to the same extent, *i.e.,* a religious with solemn or simple vows, as long as these bind, or a married woman, as long as the marital tie has not been duly dissolved. We say *men,* not clergymen, or religious, or married men, but men who are otherwise free to marry. This regulation was made for the preservation and honor of the sacred ministry no less than for that of the religious and the married state. Here, too, the old idea of similitudinarian bigamy may be traced.

4.° *Those who have committed voluntary homicide or procured the abortion of a human fetus, if these acts were effective; also all who have coöperated in these crimes.*

The Church has always had a special horror of homicide [86] and crimes of a similar nature. Our canon mentions two kinds, *viz.:*

(a) *Voluntary homicide,* which is a morally imputable action resulting in the death of a man. This definition includes within its scope all who, either personally or by command, kill another human being. Morally imputable means that the act was committed with deliberation and for a reason which cannot stand before the court of conscience.[37] Hence a mere accidental killing (*homicidium casuale*) cannot be imputed to the human agent. If a boy awkwardly handles a shotgun, which goes off and kills his sister, the boy is not irregular.[88]

---

[86] Cfr. X, V, 10–12; cc. 36 ff., Dist. 50; Gasparri, *l. c.,* n. 405 ff.

[37] Cc. 2, 3, 10, X, V, 12; c. 3, 6°, V. 4.

[88] S. C. C., July 3, 1677 (*Anal. Eccl.,* XIII, 134); cfr. c. 48, 51, Dist. 50.

But if one inflicts a wound with a knife, and the injured person dies from the effects of that wound, homicide must be imputed, because death immediately resulted from an illicit and unjust act, even though the intention of killing was absent.[39] If a man kills another in *self-defence*, if he neither intended the other's death nor could ward it off by any other expedient, he does not incur irregularity. However, since there is danger of excesses being committed in self-defense (*cum excessu moderaminis inculpatae tutelae*), provisional dispensation must be asked for in such cases. This is more readily granted if the assault was not provoked and no other way of escape was open.[40] But revengeful killing, although provoked by the assailant, would hardly be considered worthy of a dispensation. Irregularity is also incurred by knowingly and unnecessarily performing a dangerous action or engaging in a perilous amusement which results in the death of another.[41]

(b) Those who perform an *abortion* on a human being incur irregularity, provided, of course, the act is committed, not accidentally or unawares, but intentionally or through grievous culpability, even though by accident.[42] The aborted fetus must be a *fetus humanus,* and, as is generally added, *animatus, i. e.,* a living human fetus. We were surprised to see no reference, among Card. Gas-

39 S. C. C., May 21, 1763 (Richter, Trid., p. 92 f. n. 2). A passage reads: "*Homicidium voluntarium non est solum, quando occidens explicite vult occidere, sed etiam quando eius voluntas tendit in eum actum, ex quo per se ac immediate mors sequitur, non per accidens, uti contingit in eo, qui alium percutit, volens ei iniuriam irrogare, sed non occidere; si enim ex percussione mors sequatur, dicitur homicida voluntarius, cum voluntas percutientis feratur in percussionem, et in omne id quod immediate fuit secutum.*"

40 S. C. C., March 12, 1763; May 18, 1726; Aug. 6, 1808 (Richter, p. 92, nn. 6, 8, 9).

41 S. C. C., Sept. 24, 1718; April 19, 1738 (Richter *l. c.,* nn. 7, 10).

42 Sixtus V, "*Effraenatum,*" Oct. 29, 1588, § 2.

parri's quotations, to the Constitution of Gregory XIV, "*Sedes Apostolica,*" of May 31, 1591, which restricted irregularity and penalties to the *fetus animatus,* as the old law had it.[43]   However, said Constitution is quoted under can. 2350, § 1.   We believe that the unanimous teaching of the school should not be set aside, especially since the wording *fetus humanus* can only signify a living fetus. Animation, as stated before, takes place within the first week after conception.[44]   Theologians as well as canonists admit that the old theory concerning animation may still be held as far as the incurring of penalties and irregularities is concerned.   This theory is that between the conception and the animation of a male fetus forty days, and of a female fetus, eighty days elapse.   As long as no authentic declaration has been issued, the strict interpretation applied to penal laws may be followed here, and the period of forty, respectively eighty days be admitted.[45]   At any rate, we cannot scientifically speak of a human fetus before the lapse of six days after conception.

(c) *Effectu secuto* means that death must have actually resulted from the act of killing or abortion, because there must be a connection between cause and effect.

(d) The *cooperantes* are those who formally, not merely in a material way, command, counsel or assist in the act of homicide or abortion.   The coöperation must, therefore, be deliberate and external, and death must be foreseen.   The excuse that he did not intend to kill would not free anyone from the guilt of coöperation if his action

43 C. 2, X, V, 12 (quoted by Card. Gasparri).

44 Cfr. can. 746 f. We cannot accept Eschbach's assertion (*Disp. Phys.-Theol.*, p. 192) that there is no distinction between conception and animation; for it takes at least from four hours to six days until segmentation is complete, and only after six days the embryo becomes a fetus.

45 Cfr. c. 12, X, V, 12; Wernz, II, n. 147, p. 208.

was such that he could have foreseen that it would cause death. But the *cooperantes* incur irregularity only if their coöperation was efficacious, *i. e.*, if it really helped to bring about the death of the victim.[46] Physicians or druggists who give or sell medicine for the purpose of causing abortion are *cooperatores,* and in an even higher degree surgeons who perform an operation solely for that purpose. A midwife, husband, or father are guilty of coöperation if they give poison or strong medicine to a pregnant woman or beat or burden her so as to cause abortion.[47] On the other hand, the manufacture and sale of contraceptives, though criminal, does not induce irregularity. If several persons would plot against the life of another, but only one would actually kill him, all would be irregular if it were unknown who was the murderer.[48]

5. *Those who have mutilated themselves or others or have attempted suicide.* By mutilation authors generally understand the cutting off of a member which has a specific function to perform in the human body, *e. g.*, the nose, or an eye, or an ear, or a hand, or a foot. Hence it would not be mutilation to cut off a finger, or a knuckle, or to knock out a tooth.[49] By self-mutilation is here understood the *castratio sui ipsius,* which was so severely reprimanded in Origen.[50] But the term *seipsos* must not be pressed, as if irregularity would be incurred only if a person actually performed the operation on himself. To have it done by a physician is just as imputable, nor does it matter for what motive one perpetrates this foolish act. The " religious zeal " that inspires such an

---

[46] Reiffenstuel, V, tit. 12, nn. 27 ff.; cfr. can. 2209.

[47] Sixtus V, " *Effraenatum,*" Oct. 3, 1588, § 3.

[48] C. 5, X, V, 12; can. 2211, 2231; Wernz II, n. 147, p. 209. An

operation performed for the purpose of preventing pregnancy does not induce irregularity.

[49] Reiffenstuel, V, 12, n. 55 ff.

[50] C. 7, Dist. 55 (*Conc. Nic. I.,* c. 1); c. 4 f., Dist. 55; c. 4, X, I, 20.

act is deleterious. Yet we believe, in view of can. 986, which excuses from irregularity [51] when no mortal sin is involved, one who has castrated himself might *de facto* be declared immune from irregularity. But provisional dispensation would certainly be advisable.

As to attempts to commit *suicide* no comment is required except what we have just said in connection with can. 986. An attempt at suicide committed in an abnormal mental or nervous state, would be unimputable, and therefore would not involve irregularity.

It may have surprised the reader that not a word is said about *soldiers*, especially clergymen who served as such in the recent war. A decree of the S. C. Consistorialis, Oct. 25, 1918 ("*Redeuntibus*"), says the *defectus lenitatis* attaches to clergymen who were compelled to kill and mutilate,[52] but the Ordinary may grant a dispensation from it, unless the clergymen *volunteered* for active service in the war, in which case dispensation is reserved to the Holy See. By volunteering for military service these clerics have tacitly also resigned their office or benefice. The decree draws no distinction between just and unjust, offensive and defensive war. Formerly [53] it was generally thought that in an unjust war all soldiers, laymen as well as clerics, were irregular, if any one was killed. However, common soldiers are not easily persuaded that they are fighting in an unjust cause, and who is to be the impartial judge in such a case? It is therefore more reasonable to say that neither lay soldiers nor clergymen soldiers incur irregularity by the mere fact of fighting and killing if compelled to do so by

[51] Formerly this action induced irregularity *ex defectu*, and it may still involve it, if the two reasons hold; but *castratio* could not be styled such a defect.

[52] *A. Ap. S.*, X, 481 ff.

[53] Cfr. Benedict XIV, *Institut.*, 101, n. 16 f.

the public authorities, but a general *dispensatio ad cautelam* should be asked for or given as is done in the aforesaid decree. Can. 141 is not to be neglected, however.

6. *Clerics who practice medicine or surgery, both of which are forbidden to them, if death results from their practice.*

Can. 139, § 2, requires an Apostolic indult for the exercise of the medical profession by clerics. If they practice without an indult, they transgress the law of the Church, and therefore act illicitly. Hence if they kill any one, even accidentally and after due preparation, they become irregular.[54] Clerics who have obtained an Apostolic indult cannot be said to practice unlawfully, and therefore, even if death should occur at their hands, no irregularity would follow.

7. *Those who, without having received an order, perform an act which is reserved to clerics in higher orders, or who, without having received an order, or having been forbidden to exercise an order duly received, either by a canonical sentence inflicted on their person by a censure or vindictive penalty, or on the place where they exercise it.*

This number comprises the two irregularities called *abusus ordinis* and *ex capite violatae censurae*.

a) *Abuse of orders* is here strictly limited to *higher orders,* from subdeaconship onward. Hence if a layman exercises one of the minor orders, he is not now [55] irregular. A lector who exercises the office of acolyte is not irregular, even though he has not yet received the acolytate.[56] On the other hand if a layman, or a cleric in minor orders, would knowingly, solemnly, and seri-

---

[54] Cfr. c. 7, X, I, 14; c. 19, X, V, 12.

[55] Formerly he was; c. 1, X, V, 28; Gasparri, *l. c.,* n. 233 f.

[56] Cfr. cc. 1, 2, X, V, 28.

ously act as subdeacon; or if a subdeacon not yet ordained to the diaconate would act as deacon, they would incur irregularity. To serve as subdeacon without the maniple, or to serve as deacon at Mass without the stole, would not incur irregularity, because these vestments are the proper insignia of the respective orders.[57]

The *actus ordinis* is an act of a higher order. Such acts (priestly functions) are forbidden to clergymen in lower orders. Thus saying Mass is a strictly sacerdotal function. So is hearing confession, though it also involves an act of jurisdiction, and therefore a cleric not yet ordained a priest would be irregular if he were to attempt it.[58] A deacon solemnly baptizing without permission from the Ordinary or pastor would not be irregular.[59]

b) Irregular by violation of a *censure* or *vindictive penalty* are those who are *personally* under a canonical sentence. *Censures* are: excommunication, suspension from orders, and personal interdict. However, suspension may also be inflicted as a vindictive penalty.[60] But even in that case it must be declared as a suspension from orders, or as total suspension, *i. e.,* suspension simply so-called.[61] An interdict may affect *personally* a clergyman *in sacris,* inasmuch as this censure follows him everywhere. Or again the interdict may be local, affecting a certain territory only, and persons only indirectly. If the interdict is local only, can. 2271 f. must be consulted. If a local interdict permits the celebration of divine services, the priest who says Mass in accordance with said canons would certainly not be irregular, whereas a per-

57 How such clerics in minor orders should conduct themselves when acting as ministers of solemn Mass, see can. 1306.

58 C. 1, X, V, 28; Layman, *l. c.*

59 Gasparri, *l. c.,* n. 339; Wernz, *l. c.,* n. 137, p. 198

60 Can. 2298.

61 Can. 2278, § 2.

sonal interdict forbids the celebration of the divine office in any and every place. If, then, a clergyman *in sacris* thus censured or punished would seriously and solemnly exercise his order, he would incur irregularity.[62] This is also true if he were suspended *ex informata conscientia* and would exercise an act of orders while an appeal was pending, because such an appeal is permissible only *in devolutivo.*[63] But if a clergyman suspended *in sacris*, for instance, a deacon, would be ordained to the priesthood while suspended, he would not become irregular.[64]

HOW IRREGULARITY EX DELICTO IS INCURRED

CAN. 986

Haec delicta irregularitatem non pariunt, nisi fuerint gravia peccata, post baptismum perpetrata, salvo praescripto can. 985, n. 2, itemque externa, sive publica sive occulta.

These crimes do not produce irregularity, unless they are of the nature of a grievous sin committed after Baptism, and external, either public or occult, with due regard, of course, to can. 985, n. 2.

Hence *no* irregularity is incurred if the acts enumerated in can. 985 do not amount to a *grievous sin*,[65] as defined by theologians. For irregularity being a very serious, and if not a direct, at least an indirect penalty, the legislator naturally supposes a grievous fault. The text adds, "*committed after Baptism*," because Baptism wipes out every crime and sin.[66] The text makes an ex-

62 Cfr. c. 1, 6°, II, 14; cc. 1, 18, 20, 6°, V, 11; Gasparri, *l. c.,* n. 356 ff.

63 S. C. P. F., Oct. 20, 1884 (*Coll.,* n. 1628).

64 Layman, *l. c.,* c. 3, n. 5.

65 C. 1, Dist. 81 (S. Aug.): "*crimen est peccatum grave, accusatione et damnatione dignissimum.*"

66 C. 60, Dist. 50.

ception in favor of Baptism, which one may have administered to himself by a non-Catholic. But even this supposes a grievous fault, though naturally it could not be wiped out by Baptism, which has not yet been received.

The text further says: an *external* sin. Every crime is by its very nature external; *i. e.*, deserving of or liable to accusation. Hence one may be an apostate, a heretic, a schismatic and sin grievously in his heart,— as long as he does not manifest his apostasy or heresy by an external act, he is not irregular. It is *not* required, however, that the crime be *public, i. e.*, liable to be proved in an ecclesiastical court; even an occult crime suffices.[67]

CAN. 987

Sunt simpliciter impediti:

1°. Filii acatholicorum, quandiu parentes in suo errore permanent;

2°. Viri uxorem habentes;

3°. Qui officium vel administrationem gerunt clericis vetitam cuius rationes reddere debeant, donec, deposito officio et administratione atque rationibus redditis, liberi facti sint;

4°. Servi servitute proprie dicta ante acceptam libertatem;

5°. Qui ad ordinarium militare servitium civili lege adstringuntur, antequam illud expleverint;

6°. Neophyti, donec, iudicio Ordinarii, sufficienter probati fuerint;

7°. Qui infamia facti laborant, dum ipsa, iudicio Ordinarii, perdurat.

[67] The reason lies in the requirement of personal worthiness of the minister, which indirectly affects the public welfare of the Church; besides, an external act is liable to become known.

The following persons are incapable of receiving orders:

1.° *The sons of non-Catholics, as long as their parents remain in their error.* This was formerly called the *defectus fidei confirmatae* and comprised all male descendants of the paternal line to the second degree, and of the maternal line to the first degree. This was the Roman practice and obtained also in Germany and other countries where the prevailing religion was sectarian.[68] The Code, however, limits this impediment, which no longer involves irregularity, to the first degree, *i. e.*, to the parents. If the parents have become converted to the Catholic faith at the time when their son is to be ordained, no impediment prevents him from receiving orders. But it certainly is required that *both* be converts, for the name *parents* comprises father and mother.[68a]

The question may arise: What if the parents died as heretics before the ordination of their son? It would seem that the impediment still exists, because a decision of the Holy Office says: "and the sons of heretics who remain in heresy or who died in heresy."[69] But this very decision permits us to adopt a milder view. It, like our text, says *permanent*, *i. e.*, remaining or enduring until the time of the ordination. But when the parents are dead, their error cannot be said to remain. Besides the danger of perversion or returning to heresy by reason of filial attachment to the parents is precluded by their decease.

68 Clement VIII, *ad ep. Pac.*, Oct. 6, 1593 (Richter, *Trid.*, p. 339, n. 2); S. O., Dec. 4, 1890; March 6, 1891; Feb. 3, 1898, ad 2 et 3 (*Coll. P. F.*, nn. 1744, 1748, 1990).

68a This is now certain by decree of Oct. 16, 1919 (*A. Ap. S.*, XI, 478).

69 S. O., Dec. 4, 1890 (*Coll.*, n. 1744).

Non-Catholic means any sect, Christian, pagan, or Jewish.[70]

2.° *A man who has a wife* cannot embrace the clerical state while the wife lives. We say, the *clerical state,* because a married man may not even receive the tonsure, unless his wife consents.[71] This impediment, which is part of the former irregularity *ex defectu libertatis,* exists only in the Latin Church and is connected with the law of celibacy.[72]

The consent of the wife must be freely given, and she must, moreover, herself enter the religious state, if she is not yet advanced in years, and make profession there, to enable the husband to receive higher orders.[73] As tonsure and minor orders should not be conferred unless the subject intends to ascend to higher orders, it may be said, broadly, that the wife must make religious profession if her husband wishes to enter the clerical state with her express consent. But if she is of advanced age, say past fifty, she may remain in the world, provided she takes the simple vow of chastity, and provided also the husband is not suspected of incontinency.[74] The Holy Office refused to dispense a man of thirty-six who appeared to have all the necessary qualifications for the clerical state because his wife could not enter the religious state, there being no convent in that country.[75] The Holy See must declare whether the conditions are all verified in any given case, and if the decision is favorable, the wife must make the simple vow of chastity into the hands of the Ordinary or his delegate.[76]

---

[70] C. 1, Dist. 48; c. 10, Dist. 61; S. C. C., Jan. 25, 1749, etc. (Richter, *Trid.,* p. 339, nn. 3 ff.).

[71] C. 4, 60, I, 9.

[72] Cfr. c. 1, Dist. 77.

[73] C. 5, X, III, 32 mentions only higher orders.

[74] Benedict XIV, *De Syn. Dioec.,* XIII, 12, nn. 14 ff.

[75] S. O. Feb. 12, 1857 ad 4 (*Coll. P. F.,* n. 1057).

[76] Benedict XIV, *l. c.,* n. 16.

3.° *Those who are engaged in an office or administration forbidden to clerics, and of which they have to render an account, until they have given up the office and administration, settled their accounts, and thus become free.* This, too, is part of the former irregularity *ex defectu libertatis.* A chapter [77] of the Decree of Gratian mentions the *curiales, i. e.,* officers or rather employees of the various departments of civil administration who were engaged by the magistrates. To this class belonged also the mayors of small towns, who were responsible to the *fiscus* or State treasury. These Emperor Mauritius forbade to become clerics, and although Gregory I opposed the law on principle, he approved it, as far as rendering accounts was concerned. This is the idea underlying our canon; for the rest we refer to can. 139.[78]

4.° *Slaves, properly so-called, before they are given their liberty.* This belongs to the same *defectus libertatis.* Regarding slaves in the proper sense, *i. e.,* men who belong bodily to a master, the Church ordained that they should not enter the clerical state, partly because their admission would lower its dignity, and partly because they were not their own masters.[79]

5.° *Men bound to common military service by the civil law, before they are fully discharged.* This means all who are compelled by the law of the land to do military service.[80] Leave of absence, no matter whether for a definite or an indefinite time, does not free one from the military obligation. But if one is unconditionally discharged, his military duties may be regarded as " fully discharged," even though it is possible that the State will

---

[77] C. un., Dist. 53 (Greg. I): c. 3, Dist. 54.
[78] Vol. II, p. 88 ff.; see cc. 2, 4, X, III, 50.

[79] Cfr. Dist. 54, *passim;* can. 1083, § 2 and our commentary on the same.
[80] Cfr. Vol. II, p. 64 f.; p. 94, of our commentary.

call him again in case of necessity. The text of our canon certainly presumes that a soldier was discharged; extraordinary cases are not affected by this law.

6.° *Neophytes, until the bishop thinks their faith sufficiently tried.* The early ecclesiastical laws demanded a long and severe trial of neophytes, to prove their constancy and faith.[81]

Formerly the so-called *clinici* were also excluded from the clerical state. These were converts who delayed the reception of Baptism until they were sick.[82] Our canon leaves it to the discretion of the bishop to try converts and obtain moral certainty as to their sincerity and steadfastness.

7.° *Those who suffer from infamy* (not by law but) *in fact, as long as this blemish remains on the person according to the judgment of the Ordinary.* Infamy is here taken in a wider sense than *infamia iuris*, in can. 984, 5°, and signifies the loss of honor or the good reputation which men enjoy in the estimation of their fellows. The term may also signify the legal status of a person convicted of an infamous crime. This supposes a juridical sentence, or at least a crime branded as infamous by law. There are crimes which, though they do not entail legal infamy, are regarded by honest people generally as infamous.[83] Besides, there is a popular conviction that certain professions are mean or unbecoming to the clerical state. This is what was called the *levis nota.* Thus in former times actors (*histriones*) were branded with this stain.[84]

This infamy arising from *levis nota* cannot be meant in

---

[81] Cfr. 1, Tim. III, 6; c. 1, Dist. 48.

[82] Cfr. Benedict XIV, *De Syn. Dioec.,* XII, 6, 7; Armellini, *Lezioni del' Archeologia Crist.,* p. 290.

[83] Cfr. c. 17, c. 6, q. 1, which would include any sin against the Decalogue.

[84] Cfr. cc. 15, 16, X, III, 1.

our canon, as it was never looked upon as an irregularity in the proper sense, but rather as incompatible with the clerical state. Infamy must therefore be based upon a personal fact which degrades the perpetrator, and includes in its range those whom the civil law declares infamous,[85] or who have lost their civic rights. *Infamia facti*, says our Code, is contracted on account of a crime committed or because of immoral conduct which has deprived one of his good name among the faithful. This stain can only be removed by enduring amendment by which the lost reputation is re-established. *When* this is the case must be left to the judgment of the Ordinary.[86] But it may be added that infamy afflicting the parents or relatives of an ordinand does not affect the ordinand himself. Thus, if the father had been condemned to the galleys or capital punishment, the son would not be irregular on that account.[87]

IGNORANCE NO EXCUSE

CAN. 988

Ignorantia irregularitatum sive ex delicto sive ex defectu atque impedimentorum ab eisdem non excusat.

Ignorance of irregularities, whether resulting from defect or crime, and of impediments, does not excuse from incurring them.

Some authors held that certain irregularities were not incurred if one was ignorant of them. Thus it was maintained that the violation of the censure (can. 985, 7.°) would not render one irregular who had no knowledge of

---

[85] C. 2, c. 6, q. 1: "*omnes vero infames esse dicimus, quos leges saeculi infames appellant.*"

[86] Cfr. can. 2293, 2295.

[87] S. C. C., Aug. 11, 1759 (Richter, *Trid.*, p. 340, n. 8); can. 2293, § 4.

the same.[88] This may be true in the court of conscience.
But a logical application of the principle that irregularities are not properly called penalties would really seem to
exclude this opinion. All irregularities are directly intended to safeguard the dignity and reverence due to the
sacred ministry, and therefore the exterior fact, *i. e.*, the
quality of the minister as it ought to be in the face of the
Church, is considered, not his internal disposition. The
Code therefore says that ignorance, whether culpable or
inculpable, does not excuse from incurring the irregularities or contracting the canonical impediments. However,
it must be added that can. 986 requires a grievous sin to
induce an irregularity *ex delicto*. Therefore infants or
those who are not responsible for their acts cannot incur
irregularity from crime.[89]

MULTIPLIED IRREGULARITIES AND IMPEDIMENTS

CAN. 989

Irregularitates et impedimenta multiplicantur ex
diversis eorundem causis, non autem ex repetitione
eiusdem causae, nisi agatur de irregularitate ex homicidio voluntario.

Irregularities and impediments are multiplied if their
causes are different, but not by a repetition of the same
cause, except in case of irregularity from voluntary homicide.

The fundamental reason here again is the dignity of the
sacred ministry. If it is jeopardized or lost, the loss cannot be undone. The defect or crime may grow by degrees. A deliberate homicide increases the number of

88 Thesaurus-Giraldi, *De Poenis De Censuris*, disp. 40, sect. 5, n. 9
Eccl., P. I, c. 15 (ed. 1831, p. 15). f.; Gasparri, *l. c.*, n. 202; Wernz,
89 *Ibid.*, c. 17, p. 18; Suarez, *l. c.*, II, n. 100, p. 129.

irregularities because of the peculiar horridness of the crime. Hence if one has committed two homicides or two or more abortions, he has incurred as many irregularities as he has committed crimes.

The *cause* here understood is the *causa materialis, i. e.*, the occasion or *causa proxima* [90] of irregularity. This *causa materialis* or *proxima* is either a defect or a crime upon which the law has placed the penalty of irregularity. Such causes may differ either specifically or numerically. Thus one who is irregular by reason of illegitimacy may also become irregular on account of bigamy; one who is irregular because of apostacy may also contract irregularity by committing homicide; for all these are *specifically* different causes. The *numerical* difference consists in the repetition of the same act, for instance, if a judge inflicts the death sentence more than once, and thereby, as it were, multiplies or increases the irregularity. Here the Code adopts a different and more logical view than some canonists [91] by ruling that, with the exception of deliberately committed homicide, no irregularity is multiplied by repeated acts of the same species. In other words, the Code admits specific but rejects numerical multiplication, with the exception of homicide. Nevertheless those who are *corpore vitiati* (thus at least it seems to us), suffer from as many irregularities as there are defects, for instance, one deprived of an arm and deaf and blind is irregular for three separate and distinct causes. Therefore, these defects must all be mentioned in the petition for a dispensation, as per can. 991.

---

[90] Collet, *De Irregularitatibus*, in Migne, *Cursus Theol.*, Vol. XVII, col. 199.

[91] Suarez, *l. c.*, sect. 7, n. 5, ed.

Paris 1861, XXIII, 362 seems to admit multiplication analogously to suspension.

THE ORDINARY'S DISPENSING POWER

CAN. 990

§ 1. Licet Ordinariis per se vel per alium suos subditos dispensare ab irregularitatibus omnibus ex delicto occulto provenientibus, ea excepta de qua in can. 985, n. 4 aliave deducta ad forum iudiciale.

§ 2. Eadem facultas competit cuilibet confessario in casibus occultis urgentioribus in quibus Ordinarius adiri nequeat et periculum immineat gravis damni vel infamiae, sed ad hoc dumtaxat ut poenitens ordines iam susceptos exercere licite valeat.

This canon is a repetition of chapter 6, *Liceat,* Sess. 24, of the Council of Trent. The meaning is that *Ordinaries,* either by themselves or through delegates, may dispense from all irregularities arising from an *occult crime,* except the one mentioned in can. 985, n. 4, or any other brought before the ecclesiastical court.

a) The Ordinaries here mentioned are all those named in can. 198, including the higher superiors of exempt clerical institutes, who, of course, can make use of this power only in favor of their subjects. The special privileges accorded by various Pontiffs to diverse orders are not included in this power, but neither are they declared void by our canon. Pius V granted considerable faculties to the Theatines [92] and the Cassinese Congregation of the O.S.B.,[93] enabling the superiors to dispense even from homicide. This latter faculty, however, was valid only for the court of conscience. It would certainly not be advisable to stretch the privilege so as to include homicide. Besides, most authors exempt from these privi-

---

[92] *" Ad immarcescibilem,"* Feb. 6, 1567.

[93] *" Dum ad Congregationem,"* June 15, 1571.

leges dispensation from a notable bodily or mental defect. Furthermore this privilege would not avail for removing the inability for prelacies.[94]

Our text also says that Ordinaries who are entitled to dispense may either do so themselves or *delegate* some one to dispense in their name. For this is ordinary jurisdiction, which may be delegated to others, either habitually or for individual cases.[95] Therefore the Ordinary, the Vicar-General and the Vicar-Capitular (who needs no special faculties from the chapter)[96] enjoy the power of dispensing from these irregularities and may delegate another priest, either secular or regular, to impart it.

b) The canon mentions only *irregularities arising from an occult crime.* An *occult* crime, as stated elsewhere, is one which cannot be proved in an *ecclesiastical court.* The action of a civil court makes no difference. One declared guilty by a civil court but discharged as innocent by the ecclesiastical court would not be irregular and therefore would need no dispensation.[97] *All* irregularities arising from an occult crime may be dispensed from; this includes heresy, as to which a different opinion prevailed before the promulgation of the Code.[98]

c) Excepted are *homicide and abortion,* as explained under can. 985, n. 4, and any other irregularity from an occult crime which has been brought before the ecclesiastical court (*deducta ad forum iudiciale,* or *ad forum contentiosum,* as the Tridentine Council has it). An ecclesiastical trial begins when the summons (*citatio*) is duly made or the parties of their own accord appear be-

[94] Cfr. Ballerini-Palmieri, *Opus Theol. Moral.,* Vol. VII, p. 341; Piatus M., *Praelectiones Juris Regul.,* ed. 2, Vol. I, p. 578.

[95] Can. 199, § 1.

[96] Thus in S. C. C., Dec. 4, 1632 (Richter, *Trid.,* p. 338, n. 1).

[97] S. C. C., Jan. 25, 1726 (Richter, *l. c.,* p. 93, n. 4).

[98] S. C. C., June 18, 1796; Dec. 4, 1632 (Richter, *l. c.,* p. 339, n. 1); Gasparri, *l. c.,* n. 230.

fore the tribunal.[99]   Mere accusation or denunciation is
not sufficient to constitute a *casus deductus ad forum
iudiciale*.   But as soon as the ecclesiastical judge has
properly issued a summons, the matter has " taken a legal
turn," and after that the Ordinary can no longer dispense
from an irregularity arising from the crime which now
forms the matter of an ecclesiastical trial.   With the exception of these cases, however, Ordinaries may dispense
their *subjects* from said irregularities, not only at home,
but anywhere.

§ 2 extends this *same faculty* to all *confessors*, who consequently can absolve penitents in all occult *cases* of a very
urgent nature, when the Ordinary cannot be approached
and there is danger of a great loss or infamy.   But the
dispensation is valid only in that it enables the penitent
to exercise an order already received.   Notice the term,
eadem facultas, which doubtless means that the confessors
are subject to the same restrictions as the Ordinary, to
wit, that this faculty cannot be applied in case of deliberate
homicide and abortion, or of a crime that has been brought
before the ecclesiastical tribunal.   What *adire Ordinarium* signifies has been explained elsewhere.[1]   It is to
be understood of the usual and safe way of communication by letter, messenger or personal call.   A *grave
damnum* may be either material or spiritual, for instance,
a *pingue stipendium* needed for support, or the opportunity of gaining a plenary indulgence, or overcoming a
great temptation, or the chance of consulting a wise and
enlightened confessor.   *Infamia* is loss of reputation,
which might be incurred by a pastor or curate if he could
not say Mass on a festival day or a day appointed.   Note
that the canon does not require a *recursus* to the Ordinary or to the Holy See after dispensation has been

99 Can. 1725.   1 See Vol. V, p. 108. p. 294.

granted.[2] But this holds good only when there is question of exercising an order already received, not for ascending to a higher one.

PETITIONS FOR DISPENSATION

CAN. 991

§ 1. In precibus pro irregularitatum ac impedimentorum dispensatione, omnes irregularitates ac impedimenta indicanda sunt; secus dispensatio generalis valebit quidem etiam pro reticitis bona fide, iis exceptis quae in can. 990, § 1 excipiuntur, non autem pro reticitis in mala fide.

§ 2. Si agatur de irregularitate ex homicidio voluntario, etiam numerus delictorum exprimendus est sub poena nullitatis concedendae dispensationis.

§ 3. Dispensatio generalis ad ordines valet pro ordinibus quoque maioribus; et dispensatus potest obtinere beneficia non consistorialia etiam curata, sed renuntiari nequit S. R. E. Cardinalis, Episcopus, Abbas vel Praelatus *nullius*, Superior maior in religione clericali exempta.

§ 4. Dispensatio, in foro interno non sacramentali concessa, scripto consignetur; et de ea in secreto Curiae libro constare debet.

§ 1 rules that in petitions for dispensation from irregularities and impediments, *all existing irregularities and impediments* must be mentioned; else the general dispensation has no effect for those concealed if the concealment was made in bad faith, but only for such as have been concealed in good faith, except, however, homicide,

---

2 Neither was there a condition attached to the decision of the S. O., of Sept. 6, 1909 (*A. Ap. S.*, I, 677).

abortion, and other crimes brought before the ecclesiastical court.

The bodily defects must be mentioned as distinctly as the case permits, and especially must illegitimacy be explained as to its cause (*naturales, spurii, sacrilegi*) because the S. Congregation deals more severely with the latter than with the merely *naturales*. If a trial has taken place before the master of ceremonies, this fact, together with the judgment or opinion of the bishop, should be mentioned in the petition. But the dispensation proper is granted by the Holy See.[3]

If there is more than one irregularity all must be mentioned, and the rescript extends only to those expressly mentioned, unless a *bona fide* omission was made, in which latter case the irregularity which was not mentioned or forgotten is included in the dispensation, with the exception, however, of homicide and abortion or some other crime for which one was summoned before the ecclesiastical court. A wilful or deliberate omission of an irregularity would affect the rescript in so far as the concealed irregularity would remain, and consequently another dispensation would be required.

§ 2 requires that the *number* of homicides be mentioned under penalty of nullity of the rescript. Whether this affects also the number of abortions is not quite certain. The Roman practice includes abortion.[4] When the precise number cannot be given, an approximate one should be set down, or the plural number in general.

§ 3. A general dispensation is valid also for higher orders, and the one thus dispensed may obtain benefices which are not usually conferred in consistories, but he

---

[3] Cfr. Pyrrhus Corradus, *Praxis Dispensationum Apostolicarum*, l. III, c. 1; c. 6 (Migne, *Cursus Theol.*, t. XIX, p. 123, 161).

[4] *Idem*, l. V, c. 1 (*ed. cit.*, p. 287).

cannot be promoted to the cardinalate, the episcopate, an abbacy or prelacy *nullius,* nor to the office of higher superior in an exempt clerical institute.

A *general dispensation* is one granted for all orders and benefices or favors to be obtained, whereas a *particular* dispensation extends only to certain benefices or orders.[5] Thus a dispensation granted from the impediment of *defectus natalium ob haeresim parentum* (can. 987, n. 1) for tonsure and minor orders also avails for major orders,[6] and for the offices or benefices of pastor, curate, and canon. But a consistorial benefice, *i. e.,* one conferred in a public consistory, cannot be obtained in virtue of such a general dispensation. This is nothing else but the application of an old principle,[7] namely, that those affected with a blemish should not ascend to higher dignities.

§ 4. A dispensation granted in the internal forum but extrasacramentally, must be given in writing, and the diocesan court should keep a record thereof in a secret book. This rule is, or may be, of importance in cases where litigation concerning an office or benefice threatens or an accusation is brought before the ecclesiastical court.

REMARKS ON DISPENSATIONS FROM IRREGULARITIES [8]

1. The *sovereign Pontiff* may dispense from *all* irregularities, but is himself subject to none. The reason is because all irregularities exist by, and rest upon, positive ecclesiastical law. Dispensations from irregularities *pro foro externo* are granted by the *S. Congregatio pro Re Sacramentaria,* those for the internal forum by the *S.*

5 *Id.,* l. I, c. 3 (*ed. cit.,* p. 20).
6 S. O., Dec. 6, 1906 (*Coll. P. F.,* n. 2241).
7 Cfr. cc. 1, 18, X, I, 17; *Reg. Juris* 87 in 6°.

8 Cfr. Collet, *De Irregularitatibus* (Migne, *Cursus Theol.,* Vol. 17, coll. 317 ff.); Wernz, *l. c.,* II, n. 105, p. 133 ff.

Poenitentiaria. We must add that the *Roman Pontiff alone* is competent to grant dispensations, because all irregularities concern the common law of the Church. The *faculties* of *Ordinaries*[9] formerly granted in virtue of Form I, art. 2, can no longer be applied for the *external forum;*[10] and those *pro foro interno* are contained in can. 990. But we believe can. 81 may be lawfully applied here, provided the three conditions therein set forth are verified.

2. Some irregularities *ex defectu* cease if the cause entirely ceases. Thus if a bodily defect is cured or healed, the irregularity also ceases, because this was set up to safeguard the dignity of the sacred ministry and insure the physical ability of performing the sacred functions. Thus if one's eyesight is restored by an operation, the irregularity ceases *ipso facto,* and no dispensation is required. However, if a *doubt* exists as to the completeness of the cure, or the degree of deformity which may cause scandal or ridicule, the case must be referred to Rome, together with the statement of the master of ceremonies.[11] Dispensations are not easily granted if the applicant uses artificial limbs, even though the danger of scandal be remote.[12] Hence in every case of real doubt an authentic statement should be obtained from the S. Congregation.

The irregularities arising from bigamy, *infamia iuris,* or *defectus lenitatis,* can be removed only by dispensation

9 Cfr. Putzer, *Comment in Facult. Apost.,* ed. 4, p. 150 ff.

10 S. C. Consist., April 25, 1918.

11 Cfr. S. C. C., June 15, 1878 (*A. S. S.,* Vol. 11, 423). The S. C. required a photograph in case of a hunchback, whose size was 153 centimeters (= 5 feet), which was considered sufficient; but the S. C. also inquired into the moral qualities which were in favor of the petitioner. Hence the decision " *arbitrio et conscientiae episcopi, cum facultate dispensandi et habilitandi oratorem ad omnes ordines usque ad presbyteratum inclusive, facto verbo cum Ssmo.*"

12 S. C. C., Dec. 19, 1772; May 6, 1775; Nov. 18, 1837 (Richter, p. 340, nn. 17, 18, 30).

proper. However, if the *infamia iuris* arises from civil law, it ceases of itself as soon as the civil authority restores the subject to civil or civic rights.

Illegitimacy requires a dispensation, unless, as stated in the canon, it has been removed by subsequent marriage or solemn religious profession.

3. Irregularities *ex delicto,* if of a public nature, can be dispensed only by the Apostolic See; if *occult,* can. 990 applies. Clergymen who practice medicine or surgery with an Apostolic indult must abide by the conditions of time, place, or person laid down in the rescript. If they have extended the faculty beyond the time allowed, a provisional dispensation would be required for the period during which they practiced medicine unlawfully, even though they are morally certain that they caused no death.[13] In case of a *doubtful fact of homicide, i. e.,* when a cleric is uncertain whether he or another was the cause of a homicide, it is the common opinion of theologians that he must conduct himself as irregular,[14] and therefore abstain from exercising acts of the orders which he has received and in the meantime apply for a dispensation.

4. With regard to *impediments properly so-called,* it is evident that five of them (nn. 1–5) are conditional, *i. e.,* last only as long as the impediment itself. This is clearly expressed in the wording of the text. Concerning these, then, the attestation or proof of cessation is sufficient and no dispensation is needed. The two others depend on the finding or judgment of the bishop, who is the arbiter in such cases.

We may add that *infamia facti* is often removed by change of domicile combined with a lasting amendment of conduct.

---

13 S. C. C., Dec. 12, 1761   14 Collet, *l. c.,* p. 215.
(Richter, *l. c.,* p. 342, n. 34).

CHAPTER III

CAN. 992

Omnes tum saeculares tum religiosi ad ordines promovendi per se ipsi vel per alios Episcopo aliive qui Episcopi hac in re vices gerat, suum propositum ante ordinationem opportuno tempore aperiant.

All who wish to be ordained, seculars as well as religious, must either themselves or through others manifest their intention at some opportune time before ordination to their bishop or whoever holds his place with regard to ordination.

The Council of Trent [1] had ordered that the *ordinandi* should present themselves before the bishop one month before ordination. This rule was enacted so that the bishop might have time to give orders to the parish priest to make the public announcements and to select the examiners. But *manifestare propositum* may have another signification, namely, to make sure that the ordinand is not compelled to embrace the clerical state. The process is somewhat similar to the *exploratio voluntatis* required for female religious and may be called the first of the three scrutinies which were formerly demanded. The text says this manifestation of intention may also be made to the one who represents the bishop in the matter of ordination. In former centuries this was the archdeacon,

---

[1] Sess. 23, c. 5, *de ref.*

still mentioned in the *Pontificale*.[2] His place is now taken by the Vicar General, or in some dioceses by the Chancellor. The Code is not explicit on this point.

TESTIMONIALS

CAN. 993

Promovendi saeculares aut religiosi qui, quod pertinet ad ordinationem, saecularium iure reguntur, afferant:

1°. Testimonium ultimae ordinationis aut, si de prima tonsura agatur, recepti baptismatis et confirmationis;

2°. Testimonium de peractis studiis, pro singulis ordinibus, ad norman can. 976, requisitis;

3°. Testimonium rectoris Seminarii, aut sacerdotis cui candidatus extra Seminarium commendatus fuerit, de bonis eiusdem candidati moribus;

4°. Testimoniales litteras Ordinarii loci in quo promovendus tantum temporis moratus est ut canonicum impedimentum contrahere ibi potuerit;

5°. Testimoniales Superioris maioris religiosi, si cui religioni promovendus adscriptus sit.

CAN. 994

§ 1. Tempus quo promovendus potuit canonicum impedimentum contrahere est, regulariter, pro militibus trimestre, pro aliis semestre post pubertatem; sed Episcopus ordinans pro sua prudentia exigere potest litteras testimoniales etiam ob brevius commorationis tempus, et ob tempus quoque quod pubertatem antecessit.

---

2 Cfr. cc. 5, 9, X, I, 23, *de off. archidiaconi.*

§ 2. Si loci Ordinarius neque per se neque per alios promovendum satis noverit, ut testari possit eum, tempore quo in suo territorio moratus est, nullum canonicum impedimentum contraxisse, aut si promovendus per tot dioeceses vagatus sit ut impossibile vel nimis difficile evadat omnes litteras testimoniales exquirere, provideat Ordinarius saltem per iuramentum suppletorium a promovendo praestandum.

§ 3. Si post obtentas litteras testimoniales et ante peractam ordinationem, promovendus praedicto temporis spatio in eodem territorio rursus moratus sit, novae litterae testimoniales Ordinarii loci necessariae sunt.

Can. 995

§ 1. Etiam Superior religiosus suis litteris dimissoriis non solum testari debet promovendum professionem religiosam emisisse et esse de familia domus religiosae sibi subditae, sed etiam de studiis peractis, deque aliis iure requisitis.

§ 2. Episcopus, acceptis iis litteris dimissoriis, aliis testimonialibus litteris non indiget.

Seculars as well as those religious who in matters of ordination are governed by the rules laid down for seculars, must produce:

1°. A certificate of the *order they have received* last, or if tonsure is to be received, their baptismal and confirmation record;

2°. A certificate showing that they have completed the *studies* required for the several orders according to can. 976;

3°. Testimonials from the *rector* of the *seminary*, or from the priest to whose care the candidate had been entrusted during his stay outside the seminary, as to his good character;

4°. Testimonials from the *Ordinary* of the diocese in which the candidate has lived sufficiently long to contract a canonical impediment;

5°. Testimonials from the *higher superior*, if the candidate belongs to a religious community.

Can. 994, in § 1, determines the *time* which may be considered sufficient for one to contract a canonical impediment. It is, as a rule, *six months after the age of puberty*, and three months for those engaged in military service. However, the bishop may, if he thinks it prudent, demand testimonials for a shorter time, and also for the time before the age of puberty.

§ 2. If the Ordinary himself, or other responsible men of his surroundings or diocese, do not know the candidate sufficiently well to be able to testify to his freedom from canonical impediments for the time spent in the diocese, the Ordinary shall demand a supplementary oath from the candidate. This same oath shall also be demanded if the candidate has lived in so many dioceses that it is impossible, or extremely difficult, to obtain all the testimonials required.

§ 3. If, after the testimonials have been obtained and before the candidate is ordained, he again lives in the same territory for a space of time which may suffice for contracting a canonical impediment, new testimonials from the local Ordinary are required.

Can. 995 regulates the matter with regard to *religious superiors*. These, when giving the *litterae dimissoriae*, must testify that the candidate has made religious profession, and that he is a member of the religious house subject to the resp. superior, and has completed the required studies and complied with the other conditions demanded by law. Upon having received the *litterae dimissoriae* thus described, the bishop needs no other testimonials.

The first of these canons mentions (1°) the *certificate of ordination*, which was formerly called *litterae formatae*, or written statement of the order received. In Rome the Cardinal-Vicar issues such *litterae* after each ordination. The document contains the name of the ordaining bishop and the place and date of ordination. A similar attestation must be issued after tonsure has been conferred, and for receiving tonsure, the baptismal and confirmation certificates must be exhibited either to the *episcopus proprius* or to the ordaining bishop, together with the dimissorials. But after tonsure has been received and the certificate properly issued, the baptismal and confirmation records are no longer required.

(2°) The *contents* of the testimonials for the secular clergy refer to the studies, the moral character and freedom from canonical impediments.

(a) The *studies* must have been completed according to can. 976, and the testimonials must state that the terms required by law have been adhered to, unless a special indult permits one to be ordained to the priesthood after a three years' theological course, which fact should, we believe, be mentioned.

(b) The testimonials concerning *moral behavior* contain what was formerly called *de moribus et vita*.[3] Hence what we call conduct must be testified to, or, as the Council of Trent says, the candidates must be " *ita pietate ac castis moribus conspicui, ut praeclarum bonorum operum exemplum et vitae monita ab eis possint exspec-*

---

3 Innocent XII, " *Speculatores*," Nov. 4, 1694, §§ 3-6.

tari." [4] This testimony may be based upon the usual reports made by the director of the seminary.

(c) *Freedom from canonical impediments* means absence of the irregularities and canonical impediments mentioned in can. 987, and freedom from any censure or vindictive penalty which would prohibit the receiving of, or ascent to, a higher order.[5] Hence the phrase in these letters: "*et nullis, quantum scimus, censuris irretitum.*"

(3°) *Who are to give these letters?* The *certificate of orders* received should be issued by the bishop who conferred the same, or by his diocesan chancellor. The *baptismal certificate* is issued by the parish priest in whose parish the ordinand was baptized. The *confirmation certificate* by the bishop who confirmed the ordinand or by his officials. The testimonials concerning *studies* must be issued by the Ordinary in whose diocese these studies were made.[6] In that case, however, the director of the seminary shall testify to the time spent in the seminary, together with the result of the examinations passed by the candidate. To these the *director of the seminary* may add the testimonials concerning the *conduct* of the candidate, though these testimonials need not be given in writing, but may be given orally.

For the testimonials touching *canonical impediments several Ordinaries* may be required. The old law and practice insisted that the *episcopus proprius ratione originis* give the testimonials,[7] although any other competent bishop might ordain the candidate. Our Code, as far as we understand it, does not demand this, either in can.

---

[4] *Trid.,* Sess. 23, c. 14, *de ref.,* concerning the priesthood.

[5] An excommunicated Catholic cannot licitly receive the Sacraments, cfr. can. 2260, § 1.

[6] Many, *l. c.,* p. 323.

[7] Innocent XII, "*Speculatores,*" § 4; S. C. C., April 27, 1720; Feb. 7, 1733; May 29, 1824 (Richter, *Trid.,* p. 190 f., nn. 11, 16, 26).

956, or in can. 993, but, on the contrary, only states (can. 994, 1°) that the time for contracting a canonical impediment begins after the fourteenth year is completed. It makes no reference to the *episcopus originis*. Hence only those Ordinaries in whose dioceses the candidate has lived for six months after his 14th year, must give the testimonials; or in case of a soldier, the Ordinaries in whose dioceses the candidate has spent at least three months.[8] Note the term, "*pro militibus*," for soldiers, which sounds somewhat different from the wording found in the decree of the S.C.C., of Jan. 26th, 1895, which reads: "*pro clericis ordinandis iam militiae addictis*."[9] This meant that only clergymen soldiers had to bring testimonials from every Ordinary in whose diocese they had spent at least three months. The Code demands this of *all soldiers* whether they are about to receive tonsure or are already tonsured. The reason is palpable: they are supposed to have commenced their theological studies according to can. 976, 1°.

The Code, however, foresees the difficulty which was proposed in the above-mentioned decision of 1895, to wit, how to obtain the testimonials of all these Ordinaries. This may be impossible morally or physically, for lack of knowledge of the ordinand, or because of difficulties of communication, interrupted travel, etc. In that case the Ordinary competent for ordination must require a *supplementary oath* from the ordinand. This is taken upon the gospel book. Its object is to make sure of the candidate's freedom from canonical impediments, nothing more. The bishop is no longer [10] obliged to recur

---

8 *Trimestre* signifies a continuous sojourn of three months. Therefore, strictly speaking, Ordinaries are not obliged to ask for testimonials if a soldier clergyman would have stayed in various dioceses for less than three months; but they may ask for information.

9 *Urgelitana* (*Coll. P. F.*, n. 1886).

10 Formerly he needed a special

to the Holy See for taking the oath under such circumstances.

The text (can. 993, 4°) says "*ordinarii loci*," by which name are understood all those mentioned in can. 198. Therefore the Vicar-General and the Vicar-Capitular may issue these testimonials.

(4°) As to the testimonials required of *religious*, the following remarks may suffice (compare with can. 964):

(a) *Exempt religious superiors of higher rank, i. e.,* generals or provincials, are exclusively competent to grant testimonials to those who are subject to them, *for all orders*. They grant dimissorials, and with these may include the testimonials. No other testimonials are needed if the candidates have not been engaged in military service or made their studies outside their own study house.[11] The certificates of Baptism and Confirmation are not expressly required, because aspirants to the religious state must bring them along when they enter.

But if a religious has to undergo *military service* (as in France and Italy) the religious superior must obtain *litterae testimoniales* from each and every Ordinary in whose diocese the candidate spent at least three months.[12] However, in the case mentioned in can. 994, 2°, namely, when it is impossible or difficult to obtain all these testimonials, the religious superior — for he is the Ordinary of the *ordinandus* — may demand a supplementary oath from the candidate as to his freedom from canonical impediments. If the candidate has made his studies *outside* the study house of his order or congregation, the superior must ask for a *certificate of studies* properly completed, as required by can. 976, and *testimonials from the director*

faculty from the Ap. See; S. C. C. Jan. 26, 1895.

11 See can. 544, § 1.

12 S. C. *super Disciplina Regulari,* Nov. 27, 1892 (*A. S. S.*, Vol. 25, 638); this was issued for Italy, but may be applied to all countries with compulsory service for clergymen.

of the seminary or study house as to the moral character of the candidate. After the exempt religious superior has collected all these informations, *de quibus conscientia eius oneratur,* he may draw up *one document* containing the dimissorials and testimonials and present the candidate to the diocesan bishop, or to another if can. 966 admits. If the *episcopus proprius* ordains at the house of the religious, no writing is required, because everything may be done orally.

(b) *Non-exempt religious superiors* proceed similarly, with some little difference. Since they are allowed to grant dimissorials only for tonsure and minor orders, whilst for higher orders the competent bishop is the one according to can. 956, "*domicilii una cum origine aut domicilii solius,*" the onus of gathering the testimonials would seem to rest on the *episcopus proprius.* Yet it appears to be more conformable to the wording and intention of the law, as laid down in can. 993, 5°, and can. 995, that the religious superior perform this task, and then he has to proceed as stated above under (a). For the bishop may be satisfied with the testimonials presented by the religious superior, as can. 995, 2°, expressly states.[13]

(c) The *contents of these testimonials* are outlined in the same can. 995, 1°. They must contain the statement that the candidate has made simple temporary profession for tonsure and minor orders, or perpetual or solemn profession for major orders. The superior must furthermore testify that the candidate is an habitual,[14] not only a temporary, member of the community of which he is superior. Besides, the course of studies, as set forth in can. 976, must be testified to. And finally *de aliis iure*

---

13 Cfr. S. C. EE. et RR., March 1, 1895 (*apud* Many, *l. c.,* p. 425 f.).

14 *De conventu,* or *de familia,* to prevent fraud, see can. 967.

requisitis. This term indicates what we stated under (a) concerning military service and course; in other seminaries, from which latter the ordinand must have testimonials of the director as to his moral conduct. No other testimonials are required.[16]

EXAMINATIONS BEFORE ORDINATION

CAN. 996

§ 1. Quilibet promovendus sive saecularis sive religiosus debet praevium ac diligens examen subire circa ipsum ordinem suscipiendum.

§ 2. Promovendi vero ad sacros ordines in aliis quoque de sacra theologia tractationibus periculum faciant.

§ 3. Episcoporum est statuere qua methodo, coram quibus examinatoribus et quibus in tractationibus sacrae theologiae promovendi periculum facere debeant.

CAN. 997

§ 1. Hoc examen sive pro clericis saecularibus sive pro religiosis recipit loci Ordinarius qui iure proprio ordinat, aut dat dimissorias litteras; qui tamen potest quoque, ex iusta causa, illud Episcopo ordinaturo committere qui id oneris suscipere velit.

§ 2. Episcopus alienum subditum sive saecularem sive religiosum ordinans cum legitimis litteris dimissoriis, quibus asseritur candidatum examinatum fuisse ad norman § 1, et idoneum repertum, potest huic attestationi acquiescere, sed non tenetur; et si pro sua

---

[16] Thus testimonials from the bishops in whose dioceses they lived for six months before entering religion, are not required, being supplied by the testimonials required for entrance.

conscientia censeat candidatum non esse idoneum, eum
ne promoveat.

A synod of Nantes [16] set up the rule that those who
wished to enter the sacred ministry should present themselves, accompanied by their archpriest, before the bishop
on Wednesday before ordination day.   The bishop should
choose from among his priests and other prudent men
some examiners well versed in divine and ecclesiastical
law, who should carefully examine the *ordinandi* concerning their faith, morals, and education.   The substance
of this canon entered the decrees of the Council of
Trent,[17] whence it was adopted into our Code.

§ 1 of can. 996 enacts that all seculars as well as religious must, before ordination, be carefully examined concerning the order they are going to receive.   This information can best be obtained from the *Pontificale Romanum*, which should therefore be studied, together with the
practical exercises.

§ 2. Those to be promoted to higher orders shall also
undergo an examination in the one or other theological
discipline which they studied in school.

§ 3. The bishop has the right to determine the method,
the examiners and the subject-matter of these examinations.   The prelate before whom the secular as well as
religious clergy have to pass this examination (can. 997,
1°) is the *competent ordinary*, who either himself ordains them or grants them dimissorials.   The competent
ordinary may, for a just reason, entrust the ordaining
bishop with this examination, provided the latter is
willing.

Note that no distinction is made between exempt and

---

[16] C. 5, Dist. 24 (held probably in
658, Hefele, *Conc.-Gesch.*, III, 97;
IV, 537).

[17] Sess. 23, c. 14, *de ref.*

non-exempt religious. All have to undergo the examination, not before their religious superior, but before the examiners appointed by the bishop, and in his presence. Even those who claimed to be exempt, and who enjoyed many privileges, were told that the examination for ordination must be made either before the competent or the ordaining bishop.[18] The Council of Trent enjoined bishops to suspend from the exercise of orders all those who were presented as fit but were found to be unfit.[19]

§ 2°, can. 997, *permits* the bishop who ordains one not his subject, either secular or regular, to *abide by the attestation* of the *episcopus proprius*. But this statement, which is given together with the dimissorials, supposes that the candidate was duly examined according to § 1 of this canon and found fit. Yet the ordaining bishop is *not bound* to accept the attestation, and should not ordain the candidate if he in conscience regards him as unfit.

The question was once proposed to the S. Congregation [20] whether an auxiliary bishop may examine a candidate who has received dimissorials from his own bishop (or, *sede vacante*, from the Vicar-Capitular, after a year's vacancy), and reject him, if he finds him unfit. The answer was as stated in the text: he is not obliged to, but may, examine him. In that case the candidate may appeal to his bishop, who would be entitled to try another bishop, or have recourse to the S. Cong. Consistorialis. But if a religious, whether exempt or non-exempt, is rejected by his own bishop, *i. e.*, the bishop, in whose diocese the religious house is located, the superior is not allowed to send the religious to another bishop; [21] he may, however, appeal to the S. C. Religiosorum.

18 S. C. EE. et RR., July 13, 1730 (Bizzarri, *Coll.*, p. 341 f).
19 Sess. 14, c. 3, *de ref.*
20 S. C. C., Aug. 2, Aug. 23, 1720; Jan. 16, 1595; Jan. 17, 1693 (Richter, *Trid.*, p. 190 f. n. 12).
21 S. C. C., March 14, 1620; S. C. EE. et RR., Feb. 13, 1838; Piatus

PUBLICATION OF THE ORDINATION

CAN. 998

§ 1. Nomina promovendorum ad singulos sacros ordines, exceptis religiosis a votis perpetuis sive sollemnibus sive simplicibus, publice denuntientur in paroeciali cuiusque candidati ecclesia; sed Ordinarius pro sua prudentia potest tum ab hac publicatione dispensare ex iusta causa, tum praecipere ut in aliis ecclesiis peragatur, tum publicationi substituere publicam ad valvas ecclesiae affixionem per aliquot dies, in quibus unus saltem dies festus comprehendatur.

§ 2. Publicatio fiat die festo de praecepto in ecclesia inter Missarum sollemnia aut alia die et hora quibus maior populi frequentia in ecclesia habeatur.

§ 3. Si sex intra menses candidatus promotus non fuerit, repetatur publicatio, nisi aliud Ordinario videntur.

CAN. 999

Omnes fideles obligatione tenentur impedimenta ad sacros ordines, si qua norint, Ordinario vel parocho ante sacram ordinationem revelandi.

The Council of Trent [22] made a rule which was never put into practice or forgotten in many dioceses,[23] namely, that the names of *candidates for ordination should be publicly announced* in their respective parish churches. This rule the Code re-inforces for all aspirants to *higher orders*, with the exception of religious with either simple or solemn vows. The *church* in which these publications

M *l. c.*, II, p. 297; Many, *l. c.*,
P 389.
22 Sess. 23, c. 5, *de ref.*
23 Many, *l. c.*, p. 306; neither was

it observed in the U. S., and the contrary custom cannot be styled unreasonable.

are to be made is the *parish church* of the candidate, to which he belongs by reason of domicile or quasi-domicile on his own part or that of his parents. The *time* for these publications is the parochial service on some feast of obligation or any other day or hour when there is a large gathering of people.

If the candidate is not ordained within six months from the date of the publication, the latter must be repeated. The bishop may, for a just reason, dispense with this announcement, but he has a right to demand that the publication be made not only in the parish church of the candidate, but also elsewhere, or that, instead of a public announcement, the names be posted at the church door and left there for some days, one of which should be a holy-day of obligation.

Can. 999 enjoins *upon all the faithful the obligation* of revealing to the Ordinary or pastor, before the day of ordination, any impediments they may happen to know of.

The reader will readily perceive the similarity between these announcements and the publication of the banns (see can. 1022 ff.).

SPECIAL INFORMATION

CAN. 1000

§ 1. Parocho qui publicationem peragit, et etiam alii, si id expedire videatur, Ordinarius committat ut de ordinandorum moribus et vita a fide dignis diligenter exquirat, et litteras testimoniales, ipsam investigationem et publicationem referentes, ad Curiam transmittat.

§ 2. Idem Ordinarius alias percontationes etiam privatas, si id necessarium aut opportunum iudicaverit, facere ne omittat.

The Ordinary may ask the pastor who has made the publication, or, if he deems it expedient, any other person, to investigate the conduct and life of the candidate by questioning trustworthy persons, and to transmit the testimonial letters containing the results of that investigation and publication to the diocesan court.

The Ordinary may and should, if he deems it necessary or advisable, also make private inquiries.

The text is plain, and we need only add that, as the matter is a serious one, all who are called upon to give information should feel bound in conscience to testify faithfully and impartially.

SPIRITUAL EXERCISES OR RETREAT

CAN. 1001

§ 1. Qui ad primam tonsuram et ordines minores promovendi sunt, spiritualibus exercitiis per tres saltem integros dies; qui vero ad ordines sacros, saltem per sex integros dies vacent; sed si qui, intra semestre, ad plures ordines maiores promovendi sint, Ordinarius potest exercitiorum tempus pro ordinatione ad diaconatum reducere, non tamen infra tres integros dies.

§ 2. Si, expletis exercitiis, sacra ordinatio qualibet de causa ultra semestre differatur, exercitia iterentur; secus iudicet Ordinarius utrum iteranda sint, necne.

§ 3. Haec spiritualia exercitia religiosi peragant in propria domo vel in alia de prudenti Superioris arbitrio; saeculares vero in Seminario aut in alia pia vel religiosa domo ab Episcopo designata.

§ 4. De peractis spiritualibus exercitiis Episcopus certior fiat testimonio Superioris domus, in qua peracta fuerint; vel, si de religiosis agatur, attestatione proprii Superioris maioris.

What was formerly prescribed for the clergy to be ordained in Rome, for the suburbicarian and Italian clergy,[24] and was by way of pious custom observed elsewhere, has now become general law, *viz.:*

1. That a *retreat of three full days* precede tonsure and minor orders, and one of *six full days* each sacred order. If three major orders are received within a semester, or six months, the ordinary may reduce the time of the retreat for the diaconate to three days, but no less.

2. If for any reason ordination is *put off more than six months,* the retreat must be repeated; if the delay is less than six months, it is for the Ordinary to decide whether the retreat must be repeated.

3. *Religious* must make the retreat in their own house, or in such other place as the superiors deem proper; seculars, in the seminary or in a religious institution, convent, or monastery appointed by the bishop.

4. The bishop must be informed of the retreat by an attestation of the superior of the house in which the exercises took place; and in the case of religious by an attestation of their superiors.

We surmise the bishop who is entitled to be informed is the one who is to ordain the candidate. If he is not at the same time the *episcopus proprius,* he may abide by the attestation of the latter.

The candidate himself should see to it that all his papers are in proper shape, he being the one who should ask for the testimonials, unless this is done by the director of the seminary.[25]

24 Alex. VII, "*Apostolica Sollicitudo,*" Aug. 7, 1662; S. C. EE. et RR., Oct. 9, 1682 (Bizzarri, *Coll.,* p. 374 f).

25 Many, *l. c.,* p. 323 f.

CHAPTER IV

RITES AND CEREMONIES OF S. ORDINATION

CAN. 1002

In quovis conferendo ordine, minister proprios ritus in Pontificali Romano aliisve ritualibus libris ab Ecclesia probatis descriptos, adamussim servet, quos nulla ratione licet praeterire vel invertere.

The minister, in conferring orders, must carefully observe the rites prescribed in the *Pontificale Romanum* and other liturgical books approved by the Church, and he is not allowed to omit or change anything.

The venerable age [1] of these rites commands the greatest respect and the danger of exposing the Sacrament to nullity [2] by omitting an essential part of the form should caution the minister to follow the *Pontificale* closely. He should adhere scrupulously to the words and rubrics of the *Pontificale*, no matter what his personal opinion may be concerning the matter of the Sacrament of Orders. The Greeks must use their *Euchologia*, although these do not contain all the minor orders in vogue among the Latins.[3]

The *minister is not allowed to omit an order*, or any part of the prayers and ceremonies, nor to *invert* the order

---

[1] The oldest decuments relating to the rite of ordination are the *Sacramentarium Leonianum* and the *Gregorianum* (VIth and VIIth century) and the *Ordines Romani*, of the VIIIth and IXth.

[2] Leo XIII, "*Apostolicae curae*," Sept. 13, 1896; Many, *l. c.*, p. 530.

[3] Benedict XIV, "*Etsi pastoralis*," May 26, 1742, § VII, n. VI.

of the Roman *Pontificale*. Therefore, also, the anointings (*unctiones*) must be performed according to the rubrics. Thus if the Pontifical says: "*ungit totaliter palmas*," the whole interior palm of the hand together with the fingers is to be anointed.[4] It is not necessary to add the different requisites for conferring orders, as they are stated plainly enough in the liturgical books.[5]

THE ORDINATION MASS

CAN. 1003

Missa ordinationis vel consecrationis episcopalis semper debet ab ipsomet ordinationis vel consecrationis ministro celebrari.

The Mass of ordination or episcopal consecration must always be celebrated by the minister of ordination or consecration himself.

This law was so vigorously insisted upon that the S. Congregation never permitted an exception, though repeatedly requested to do so. Thus an old bishop afflicted with the gout asked to confer orders sitting on the *scamnum*. But though there was no other bishop within a radius of 300 miles, the S. Rit. C. answered: *nihil*, and the second time, *nihil indulgendum fere*.[6] Another bishop in the same condition was told: *non licere*.[7] Hence when a bishop is unable to say the ordination mass, nothing else remains to be done than either to call in another bishop or to send the candidate to another. Now-a-days there is no great difficulty in doing so, except perhaps in China and "darkest" Africa.

4 S. Rit. C., Jan. 12, 1917 (*A. Ap. S.*, IX, 351 f.).

5 See the very practical *Manual of Episcopal Ceremonies* by A. Stehle, O. S. B., 1916, p. 353 ff.

6 S. Rit. C., June 8, 1658; Jan. 24, 1660 (*Dec. Auth.*, nn. 1070, 1150).

7 S. Rit. C., Sept. 23, 1837 (*Dec. Auth.*, n. 2712).

We may add two other decisions of the same S. Congregation concerning the *rubrical Mass*. On Holy Saturday the ordination mass, even if the bishop confers orders in his domestic chapel, must commence with the prophesies. On the six Saturdays on which general ordinations are held, the *Missa* must always be *de feria occurrente*, even though the bishop may say Mass privately and without chant. The custom of saying the *Missa de Sancto* is not to be tolerated.[8]

ORIENTAL AND LATIN RITES

CAN. 1004

Si quis, ritu orientali ad aliquos ordines iam promotus, a Sede Apostolica indultum obtinuerit superiores ordines suscipiendi ritu latino, debet prius ritu latino recipere ordines quos ritu orientali non receperit.

If one has received some orders in an *Oriental rite* and afterwards obtained an Apostolic indult to receive the higher orders according to the Latin rite, he must first receive in the Latin rite those orders which he did not receive in the Oriental rite.

To understand this canon it must be remembered that the Greek *Euchologion*, as published in 1754, and more lately in 1873, by the Propaganda, contains no special formularies except for conferring the tonsure or clericate and the lectorate[9] among minor orders. But the Latin subdiaconate includes not only this order proper, but also the acolythate and ostiariate. Hence,—says Benedict XIV, from whose Constitution, " *Etsi pastoralis,*" May

---

[8] S. Rit. C., March 21, 1744; Feb. 11, 1764 (*Dec. Auth.*, nn. 2375, 2473).

[9] Two orders, lectorate and cantorate, are almost identical.

26, 1742, our text is taken,— if one has received the
clericate and lectorate according to the Greek rite, and
afterwards obtains an Apostolic indult to receive the
major orders according to the Latin rite, he must, before
he can receive subdeaconship, receive the ostiariate,
the exorcistate, and the acolythate. But if he was ordained in the Greek rite as far as subdeaconship inclusively, it is sufficient that he receive the exorcistate, since
the acolythate and the ostiariate are included in the Greek
subdiaconate. The same rule applies if one was ordained
according to the Greek rite as far as the diaconate or
presbyterate; to wit, only the exorcistate must be supplied according to the Latin rite.[10] The other Oriental
rites, like those of the Syrian Maronites and Copts, all
have the same number of minor orders as the Greek,
whereas the Armenians, whose ritual was published officially in 1807, have the full number of the Latin rite.[11]

HOLY COMMUNION IN S. ORDINATION

CAN. 1005

Omnes ad maiores ordines promoti obligatione
tenentur sacrae communionis in ipsa ordinationis
Missa recipiendae.

What the *Pontificale Romanum* prescribes, the Code
here emphasizes as a universal law, *viz.:* that all who receive *major orders* are obliged to go to holy Communion
in the ordination mass.

10 See § VII, n. VI.   11 Many, *l. c.*, p. 479 ff.

CHAPTER V

DAYS ON WHICH ORDINATIONS MAY BE CONFERRED

CAN. 1006

§ 1. Consecratio episcopalis conferri debet intra Missarum sollemnia, die dominico vel natalitio Apostolorum.

§ 2. Ordinationes in sacris celebrentur intra Missarum sollemnia sabbatis Quatuor Temporum, sabbato ante dominicam Passionis, et Sabbato Sancto.

§ 3. Gravi tamen causa interveniente, Episcopus potest eas habere etiam quolibet die dominico aut festo de praecepto.

§ 4. Prima tonsura quolibet die et hora conferri potest; ordines minores singulis diebus dominicis et festis duplicibus, mane tamen.

§ 5. Reprobatur consuetudo contra ordinationum tempora praecedentibus paragraphis praescripta; quae servanda quoque sunt, cum Episcopus latini ritus ordinat ex apostolico indulto clericum ritus orientalis aut contra.

§ 1. *Episcopal consecration* must be conferred during the solemnity of the Mass on a Sunday or the feast of an Apostle.

According to the Roman Pontifical,[1] a *missa cantata* is not required, hence a low Mass is sufficient.

1 De Consecratione Electi in Episcopum si Missa cantatur.

The *days* on which consecration may take place are the *Sundays* and the feastdays of the Apostles. This term is to be interpreted strictly, and hence episcopal consecration on a holyday of obligation during the week or on a suppressed feastday, is not permitted without a special Apostolic indult. The expression, "*feast of an Apostle*," is also to be taken in its strict sense, to the exclusion of the feasts of SS. Luke, Mark, and Barnabas.[2]

§ 2 and § 3. *Higher Orders* should be conferred during holy Mass on the four Ember Saturdays, on the Saturday "*Sitientes*," before Passion Sunday, and on Holy Saturday. However, the bishop may ordain to higher orders also on any Sunday or holyday of obligation if there be a grave reason for so doing.

The practice here mentioned dates back to the fifth century, at least as far as it concerns the four Ember days and Saturday before Passion Sunday, for these are mentioned in a decree of Gelasius I (492–496), part of which has found a place in Gratian's Decree.[3] Holy Saturday is mentioned only once, in a Decretal of Alexander III, but was assigned as Ordination Day[4] in Rome already by Pelagius II (579–590). The reason for assigning these days was that the solemn fast was protracted to midnight of the following Sunday, on which, as the first day of the week, God commenced to create the world, Christ arose and sent the Holy Ghost upon the disciples.[5] From this it may be understood why Sunday or a feastday is permitted.

The Code requires a *gravis causa* for conferring sacred orders on any other day besides the six Saturdays. The judgment as to the gravity of the reason is left to the

---

[2] S. Rit. C., April 4, 1913 (*A. Ap. S.*, V, 186).

[3] See c. 7, Dist. 75.

[4] C. 3, X, I, 11.

[5] C. 4, Dist. 75; Migne, *P. L.*, 54, 625; Many, *l. c.*, p. 238 f.

bishop. We may be permitted to add that the inconvenience of a "*magro*" (fast) could hardly be styled a grave reason.

Note that the Code is silent about the *fast*, which the *Pontificale Romanum* says should fitly be observed on the day before episcopal consecration. No such obligation is insinuated in our text. It is understood, of course, that ordination on one of the six Saturdays does not *per se* constitute an excuse for violating the fast. If a feast of obligation, together with the office, is by a special indult transferred to a Sunday, ordination may be held on that day.[6]

We note a few important decisions of the S. Congregations on kindred topics. The S.C. Concilii has always insisted that the bishop should not ordain candidates who have the privilege or an indult allowing them to be ordained *extra tempora*, on a day which is not a holyday of obligation.[7] The Congregation of Bishops and Regulars once answered, concerning exempt regulars who enjoyed the privilege of being ordained *extra tempora*, that the bishop may, but is not obliged to, ordain them on odd days.[8] However, even for exempt religious § 5 of our canon is binding.

§ 4. *Tonsure* may be given on any day and at any hour of the day, in the forenoon or in the afternoon.[9] *Minor Orders* may be conferred on *Sundays* and weekdays which have a feast celebrated or marked in the diocesan calendar as *duplex*. At least this seems the ob-

---

[6] S. Rit. C., March 6, 1896, I, 3 (*Dec. Auth.*, n. 389); but the bishop is not allowed to ordain on the *dies a quo.*

[7] Jan. 15, 1689. On half holidays the S. C. permitted ordination if an indult was given; S. C. C., May 11, 1782 (Richter, *Trid.*, p. 186, nn. 2, 3, 4); S. O., March 5, 1712 (*Coll. P. F.*, n. 280). Our text excludes such days.

[8] S. C. EE. et RR., July 18, 1732 (Bizzarri, *l. c.*, p. 343).

[9] S. C. C., April 13, 1720 (Richter, *l. c.*, n. 5).

vious sense of the term *festis duplicibus*, although it is true that certain decisions of the S. Rit. C. admit only feastdays of obligation or " double " feasts which were feastdays of obligation before they were suppressed; in other words feasts of Apostles and other suppressed holy-days.[10] However, the legislator, by using the term " *festa duplicia* " certainly wishes us to understand it in a general sense, and in this sense all the feasts marked as *duplicia* are days on which minor orders may be conferred. *Mane tantum* properly signifies an early morning hour, but in view of a decision which permitted the conferring of tonsure and minor orders in the afternoon,[11] we may safely say that *mane* includes the whole of the time during which it is permitted to say Mass.

§ 5. The *custom* of ordaining outside the times prescribed in the preceding sections is *reprobated*. These times must also be observed when a *bishop* of the *Latin Rite*, in virtue of an Apostolic indult, ordains a clergyman of an *Oriental rite*, and conversely. The reason for this latter enactment is the contrary practice of the Oriental bishops, who never received the decrees and decretals of the Western Church and still ordain on any day of the year.[12]

The *reprobation of the custom* of ordaining on other than the prescribed days also concerns our bishops, who must therefore relinquish the old custom. The faculties[13] which they formerly enjoyed are abrogated, even though they were granted as late as Jan. 1, 1918. The decree of April 25, 1918, has abolished them *in foro externo*. Exempt religious must also abide by this law.

---

10 S. Rit. C., Nov. 12, 1831, ad 1; March 16, 1833; Feb. 18, 1843 (*Dec. Auth.*, nn. 2682, 2705, 2852).
11 S. C. C., April 13, 1720 (Richter, *l. c.*, p. 186, n. 5).

12 Many, *l. c.*, p. 262.
13 See Putzer, *Comment.*, p. 144 ff.

DEFECTIVE ORDINATION

CAN. 1007

Quoties ordinatio iteranda sit vel aliquis ritus supplendus, sive absolute sive sub conditione, id fieri potest etiam extra tempora ac secreto.

Whenever ordination has to be repeated, or a rite has to be supplied, either absolutely or conditionally, this may be done outside of the appointed time and secretly.

This brief canon raises a number of incidental questions. Repetition of ordination may become necessary either by reason of a fault committed by the ordaining prelate or by reason of the candidate's disposition. Since ordination in the Latin Church *now* consists of the double *matter* of the imposition of hands and the delivery of the instruments, the question naturally arises whether both are essential to the validity of the episcopate, presbyterate, and diaconate. The answer is that, *theoretically* speaking, only one, namely, the imposition of hands, is essential. However, since in the administration of the Sacraments the safer view (*tutior opinio*) must be followed, it has been the practice of the Roman Court to order ordination to be repeated if an essential part either of the imposition of hands or the delivery of instruments has been omitted or corrupted. The same rule holds good also with regard to the form. Below we shall rehearse several decisions which illustrate the essential parts of the priesthood and the diaconate. As to the episcopate and the subdiaconate, decisions are scarce, but the practice of the Church may be deduced from analogy.

The *matter* of ordination to the *priesthood* comprises the imposition of hands and the delivery of the instruments.

(a) There are three *impositions* of hands. The first one, by the bishop and the priests present, is made silently by physical contact with the head of each ordinand; the second is made by the bishop and priests present with extended hands, but without physically touching the heads of the *ordinandi*, whilst the bishop recites: "*Oremus, fratres carissimi*," etc. The last one is performed after Communion, when the bishop, sitting in the middle of the altar, puts both hands upon the head of each ordinand and says: "*Accipe Spiritum Sanctum*."

The first imposition must be made by physically touching the head of the ordained, *i.e.*, the bishop at least must touch the head, or hair, or skullcap of the ordinand; if no physical contact has taken place, the whole rite must be repeated conditionally.[14]

In the *second imposition* the hands must be extended over the *ordinandi*, at least for a moment, otherwise the whole ceremony must be repeated conditionally.[15]

If the *third imposition* was made without physical contact, this one imposition, together with the prayer, must be repeated, but not the whole ordination.[16]

If the first and second impositions were omitted in their proper place, and supplied after Communion, before the "*Iam non dicam*," the whole ordination must be repeated conditionally.[17]

The same rule applies to the *diaconate*. If the imposition was made without physical contact, the whole ceremony must be repeated conditionally[18]

(b) Concerning the *delivery of the instruments* the

14 S. O., Aug. 19, 1851; Jan. 20, 1875; Jan. 26, 1898; July 4, 1900 (*Coll. P. F.*, nn. 1066, 1431, 1989, 2086).

15 S. O., July 6, 1898; July 19, 1899 (*ibid.*, nn. 2009, 2058).

16 S. O., Aug. 19, 1851 (n. 1066).

17 S. O., Aug. 22, 1900 (*ibid.*, n. 2092).

18 S. O., Jan. 20, 1875; Jan. 26, 1898 (*l. c.*).

following decisions may be cited: If this ceremony was *entirely* omitted, the whole ordination must be repeated.[19] In one case the imposition was duly made, but the ordinand had forgotten to touch the instruments. The rite had to be repeated.[20]

If the instruments were offered to the ordinand not by the bishop himself, but by another, for instance, the master of ceremonies, the whole ordination must be repeated conditionally.[21]

As to *touching the instruments*, the Holy Office, has answered in several instances with "*Acquiescat*," *i.e.*, the ordination is valid if the chalice and paten were touched, even though the host was not; or if the chalice only was touched, and not the paten; or if the paten only was touched, or the host only, without the paten; or if the ordinand touched the chalice first and then the paten, but not at the moment when the bishop pronounced the words; or if the bishop, when reaching the chalice and paten, for some moments interrupted the ceremony.[22]

As to the *diaconate*, the delivery of the Gospel Book, or the Missal [23] in its place, is required, together with the formula: "*Accipe potestatem legendi Evangelium.*" If this is omitted, or if no moral (not even a dubiously moral) connection was made between the delivery of the book and the act of pronouncing the words, this rite, and it alone, must be repeated secretly; the repetition may be made at the next ordination or, if it is inconvenient for the deacon to wait for the next ordination at any other time.[24]

19 *De Syn. Dioec.*, VIII, 10, 1.

20 S. O., Aug. 1, 1697; cfr. Many, *l. c.*, p. 563.

21 S. O., Jan. 17, 1900; July 6, 1898; Jan. 11, 1899; Sept. 7, 1892 (*Coll. P. F.*, nn. 2075, 2008, 2032, 1811).

22 S. O., Jan. 17, 1900; March 7, 1897; Dec. 14, 1898; April 20, 1898 (*Coll. cit.*, nn. 2075, 1963; *A. S. S.*, Vol. 30, 286, 750).

23 S. Rit. C., Sept. 27, 1873 (*Dec. Auth.*, n. 3315).

24 S. Rit. C., June 16, 1837 (*Dec. Auth.*, n. 2767).

Concerning the *episcopate,* the imposition of the hands with physical contact is required; but if this was omitted only by the co-consecrators, nothing is to be repeated or supplied. If the act of placing the Book of the Gospels on the neck of the bishop elect was omitted, it would be advisable to supply this ceremony.[25]

As to the *subdiaconate,* the delivery of the empty chalice and paten cannot be omitted without endangering the validity of the order. If the physical touch has been forgotten, the whole ordination must be repeated conditionally. But if a chalice containing wine or water would be reached instead of the empty chalice, nothing would have to be repeated.[26]

2. With regard to the *form* of ordination, it may be observed that the essential form of the *episcopal consecration* consists either in the prayer "*Propitiare,*" or, more probably, in the preface said after the "*Propitiare.*" The form for the *priesthood* probably is also contained in the preface, certainly not in the "*Propitiare.*" It is probable that the "*Exaudi nos*" may be considered as at least the partial form. For the *diaconate* the form is either the "*Accipe Spiritum Sanctum ad robur,*" or the Preface "*Emitte.*" But nearly every one of these points is controverted.[27] For the *subdiaconate* there is no imposition of hands, but only a delivery of the instruments, accompanied by certain formulas. The same holds good concerning minor orders.

From these controversial views it may be seen why the Church insists upon having everything performed according to the *Pontificale Romanum.* Any essential change of the form would render the ordination invalid.

[25] Many, *l. c.,* p. 568.
[26] *Ibid.,* p. 569.
[27] See Pohle-Preuss, *The Sacra-*
ments, III, p. 67; Many, *l. c.,* p. 499 ff.

If the formula for conveying the power of forgiving sins were mispronounced, this part would have to be supplied, but the whole rite of ordination would not have to be repeated. In one case a distracted bishop said: "Quorum *remiseris* peccata *retenta* sunt, et quorum *retinueris remissa* sunt," and the Holy Office decided that any bishop pontifically garbed should supply the words wrongly pronounced, and that this might be done at any time and in the bishop's private chapel.[28]

It may be added that the Holy Office, when answering questions as to the possible invalidity of an ordination which was ordered to be conditionally repeated, always employed the phrase: Let the ordination be secretly and conditionally repeated on any day, *facto verbo cum Ssmo.*, in order that he might supply the Masses celebrated [29] out of the treasury of the Church, as far as necessary. Therefore, the bishop [30] should use the conditional form, or have the intention of ordaining conditionally at the beginning, and then perform the whole ceremony as usual. The second part of the clause is added to assure the priest that he is not obliged to say again the Masses said during his dubious state.

If the *defects* are only *accidental,* and consequently do not affect the validity of the ordination, they are simply to be supplied. Thus if the anointings were omitted at an *episcopal consecration,* they must be supplied.[31] But if the anointings were performed and the mode only was defective, or if one kind of oil was mistaken for another, nothing is to be supplied. The same may be said concerning the *priesthood.* Thus if the master of cere-

---

28 S. O., May 27, 1840; S. Rit. C., May 22, 1841 (*Dec. Auth.*, n. 2836) S. O., Dec. 9, 1897 (*Coll. P. F.*, n. 1987).

29 For instance, S. O., July 4, 1900 (*ibid.*, n. 2086).

30 The clause "*a quocumque episcopo*" is sometimes added.

31 Cfr. c. 1, X, I, 15.

monies would offer the chrism instead of the *oleum catechumenorum,* and the bishop used the former instead of the latter, the ordination would not only be valid, but nothing need be supplied.[32] If the formula was slightly mutilated, for instance, by using the singular instead of the plural, or the feminine instead of the masculine gender, or if any words were needlessly repeated, there is no reason for entertaining scruples. In one case, where the bishop had forgotten to pronounce the words "*et nostram benedictionem*" at the anointing of the hand, the Holy Office answered: "*Acquiescat.*"[33]

3. As to the *other orders, the following ceremonies are not to be supplied:* for deacons, the putting on of the stole and dalmatic; for subdeacons, the handing of the cruets and putting on of the amice, maniple, and tunic; for ostiaries the opening of the gate and ringing of the bells.[34] But if the epistle book would not have been touched at the ordination of a subdeacon, this omission would have to be supplied.[35]

The validity of ordination furthermore depends on the *mental attitude of the ordinand. Compulsion* renders ordination null and void. *Grave fear* does *per se* not render it invalid, but conveys the right of having oneself declared free of the obligations attached to higher orders, as stated under can. 214. Fear may, moreover, be the cause of *not having the right intention.* For although a habitual intention is sufficient, fear may preclude even this, because the actual intention caused by fear of not being willing to be ordained, is contrary to the habitual intention. In one case a mother morally compelled her son to have himself ordained by threaten-

---

32 S. O., July 22, 1871 (*Coll. P. F.*, n. 1421).

33 S. O., Nov. 28, 1900 (*A. S. S.,* Vol. 33, 374).

34 Many, *l. c.,* p. 572.

35 S. C. C., Jan. 10, 1711 (Richter, *Trid.,* p. 178, n. 7).

ing to disinherit him. The son presented himself on the day of ordination together with the other *ordinandi*, and out of human respect permitted the ceremonies to be performed over him, though firmly determined all the while not to receive orders. He bowed his head to the imposition and touched the instruments, but with a reluctant jerk. This was a plain case of lack of proper intention, and the S. Congregation ordered conditional reordination.[36] If sufficient proofs could have been furnished, the S. Congregation would doubtless have decided in favor of absolute re-ordination. A surprising answer was given to a scrupulous priest by his confessor, who said: The external act was sufficient, because the candidate *in casu* had approached the bishop without compulsion to receive orders. *Distinguo:* there was no compulsion, *concedo;* there was the intention to receive orders, *nego.*

We said that a habitual intention is sufficient. We may add that it is also required. This means that the candidate must have *the will or desire to receive the Sacrament*, or the will to receive the respective order with its obligations. However, if he wishes the order, he also wishes the obligation, for the two cannot be separated. That the intention is required of receiving the Sacrament, and not the merely external rite, may be made evident from the necessity of distinguishing one Sacrament from another. And since the intention is absolutely required for Baptism [37] and other Sacraments, it follows that the intention must be directed towards the Sacrament of order. Thus if one positively refuses to receive an order now, although he desires to receive it

---

[36] S. C. C., Melivet., June 18, 1792 (Richter, *l. c.*, p. 175, n. 6).

[37] C. Majores 3, III, 42; Hallier,

De Sacris Electionibus et Ordinationibus, P. I, Sect. 5, c. 1 (Migne, *Cursus Theol.*, t. XXIV, p. 407 ff).

later on, and permits the ceremonies to be performed over him, such a one would not be ordained, but would have to be reordained, at least conditionally, says the Holy Office.[88]   If one would make up his mind not to receive orders as a Sacrament, but merely as a natural ceremony, because he looked upon the rites and Sacraments of the Church from a theosophic or a merely natural point of view, he would not be ordained, for the Sacrament of Orders cannot *de facto* exist without the supernatural order.   It is not, of course, required that an ordinand think explicitly of the supernatural order in the course of the ceremony of ordination.

The *intention of the ordaining bishop* must be virtually, if not actually, directed towards doing what the Church does.   If this intention is present and virtually exerts its influence, ordination is valid, even though the bishop may not believe in ordination .as a Sacrament or in the Church.   The public announcement of the archdeacon that those suffering from a canonical impediment should not present themselves for ordination, has no effect on the validity of ordination, even of those who are irregular.   However, if the bishop really had the intention not to ordain those who are irregular, the latter would not be validly ordained, provided it could be proved by a careful investigation that the ordaining prelate had this negative intention, and had not revoked it before or during the act of ordination.[89]

88 S. O., Nov. 28, 1900 (*Coll. P. F.*, n. 2096).

89 S. C. C., Feb. 13, 1682; Jan. 11, 1710, *apud* Bened. XIV, *De Sacrificio Missae*, l. III, c. 10, nn. 6–10.

ORDINATION OUTSIDE THE DIOCESE

CAN. 1008

Episcopus extra proprium territorium, sine Ordinarii loci licentia, nequit ordines conferre, in quorum collatione pontificalia exercentur, salvo praescripto can. 239, § 1, n. 15.

A bishop is not allowed, without the permission of the local Ordinary, to confer outside his own diocese any orders which require the exercise of pontificals.

This ruling, taken from the Council of Trent,[40] is as ancient as the local organization of the Church. The Oriental synods [41] were as rigorous as the Latin Church with regard to the exercise of pontifical rights. The reason is not far to seek, for the use of such rights presupposes jurisdiction, which (with some exceptions) is restricted to the territory of each Ordinary, and overlapping would cause confusion. Besides, there might be danger of intrusion on the part of candidates for ordination who were rejected by their own Ordinaries. Therefore our canon requires the *permission* of the bishop in whose diocese the pontificals are to be exercised. *Pontificals* in the strict sense are exercised only when sacred orders are conferred; for tonsure and minor orders may be conferred in rochette, stole, and simple mitre.[42] If clerics of another diocese join those of the diocese in which a strange bishop confers orders with the permission of the local Ordinary, they may be ordained, provided they have dimissorials from their own bishop.[48]

40 Sess. 6, c. 5, *de ref.*
41 Cfr. cc. 6, 7, 9, C. 9, q. 2; (c. 28, C. 7, q. 1, (Pseudo-Anaclete).

42 *Pont. Rom.*, "*De Ordinibus Celebrandis.*"
48 Benedict XIV, "*Ad Audientiam,*" Feb. 15, 1753, § 5 f.; S. C. C., 1753; June 25, 1599 (*ibid.*).

Cardinals, in virtue of can. 239, 1°, n. 15 enjoy the privilege of pontificating everywhere outside the city of Rome; but if they wish to exercise pontifical functions in a cathedral church, they must first inform the bishop of the diocese. If they wish to confer tonsure and minor orders in a cathedral church they must also demand dimissorials from the bishop.[44]

The suburbicarian cardinal bishops are not allowed to confer orders in their private chapels in Rome without the permission of the Cardinal Vicar.[45]

PLACE OF ORDINATION

CAN. 1009

§ 1. Ordinationes generales in cathedrali ecclesia, vocatis praesentibusque ecclesiae canonicis, publice celebrentur; si autem in alio dioecesis loco, praesente clero loci, dignior, quantum fieri poterit, ecclesia adeatur.

§ 2. Non prohibetur autem Episcopus, iusta suadente causa, ordinationes particulares habere in aliis etiam ecclesiis itemque in oratorio domus episcopalis aut Seminarii aut religiosae domus.

§ 3. Prima tonsura et ordines minores conferri possunt etiam in privatis oratoriis.

§ 1. *General ordinations* should be held publicly in the *cathedral church,* and the canons of that church should be called to and be present thereat. If these ordinations are held elsewhere in the diocese, a more prominent church should be selected and the local clergy should be present.

§ 2. The bishop, for a just reason, may hold *par-*

---

[44] Can. 239, § 1, n. 22.   [45] Benedict XIV, *Const. cit.,* § 1.

ticular ordinations in some other church, or in the chapel of the episcopal residence, or in the oratory of a seminary or convent.

§ 3. Tonsure and minor orders may also be conferred in private oratories.

By *general ordinations* were always understood those conferred on the six Saturdays assigned by law for conferring higher orders. However, can. 1006, § 3, apparently states that these general ordinations may now also be held on a Sunday or holyday of obligation, and therefore a general ordination may be defined as one which should [46] be held on the six Saturdays, but may be transferred to another day for a grave reason. A *particular* or special ordination is one held *extra tempora*, *i.e.*, outside the prescribed time. But can. 1006, § 3. does not exclude the time-honored practice and view of the school that general ordinations are really only those held on the six Saturdays, because said canon only says, ordinations for higher orders may be held on a Sunday or holyday of obligation. Therefore the bishop, to say the least, would have to state clearly that an ordination to be held on any other day than one of the six Saturdays, is a general one.

The reason why this must be made clear and manifest lies in the *compulsory presence of the canons or clergy*. For the Tridentine text [47] which has passed into the Code, as well as several decisions of the S. Congregation,[48] speak only of general ordination at which the clergy must be present. To such an ordination, if held in the cathedral church, the bishop may call the canons under threat of censures.[49] If the ordination is held in some

---

[46] Cfr. cc. 2, 3, X, I, 11; *Trid.*, Sess. 23, c. 8, *de ref.*

[47] *L. c.*

[48] S. C. C., Aug. 2, 1727; June

19, 1728 (Richter, *Trid.*, p. 184, n. 1).

[49] *Ibid.*, ad IX; the canons should chant their office at such a time

other prominent church of the diocese, the local clergy should be present, for the sake of honoring the bishop and out of respect for the sacred ceremony. But compulsory presence cannot be read into the text. The *Caeremoniale Episcoporum* prescribes that the Blessed Sacrament should be removed from the main altar, if preserved there,[50] during the ordination ceremony.

§ 2 is evident. Any reason may be called *just* which the bishop considers to be such. By the chapel of the episcopal residence is understood the oratory which bishops, like cardinals, are allowed to have in their residence. The *domus episcopalis* is the house in which the bishop habitually resides, but the term is not to be interpreted rigidly, as custom permits the bishop to make use, for instance, of a summer residence.[51] The *religiosa domus* is the one described in can. 488, 5.°, of our Code. Hence we translate it with *convent, viz.*: a house which belongs to any religious organization. By the name of *seminary* may be understood the preparatory as well as the grand (theological) seminary. The latter is *the* seminary *par excellence,* of course; but since the wording is general, the term may be taken in its broadest sense. What is meant by *private oratories* is explained in can. 1188, § 2.

as not to interfere with ordination; ibid, ad III.

50 Lib. I, c. 12, n. 8 (Ed. Typ. Pustet, 1886, p. 47).

51 Barbosa, *De Officio et Potestate Episcopi*, P. II, Alleg. 11, n. 24.

CHAPTER VI

CAN. 1010

§ 1. Expleta ordinatione, nomina singulorum ordinatorum ac ministri ordinantis, locus et dies ordinationis notentur in peculiari libro in Curia loci ordinationis diligenter custodiendo, et omnia singularum ordinationum documenta accurate serventur.

§ 2. Singulis ordinatis detur authenticum ordinationis receptae testimonium; qui, si ab Episcopo extraneo cum litteris dimissoriis promoti fuerint, illud proprio Ordinario exhibeant pro ordinationis adnotatione in speciali libro in archivo servando.

After ordination the names of those who have been ordained, as well as that of the ordaining minister, together with the place and day of the ordination should be entered in a *special book,* which must be carefully kept in the court of the place of ordination. Besides, all documents relating to the individual ordinations should be carefully preserved.

Each one who has been ordained should be given an authentic attestation of the order received. In case the candidates were ordained by a strange bishop, with dimissorials from their own ordinary, they must show the certificate to the letter, in order that it may be registered in the special book to be kept in the archives.

"*Curia loci ordinationis*" may have a twofold meaning: the diocesan court and the court of the place of ordination. That these two denominations are not entirely identical is evident from can. 1009, § 1, which mentions, besides the cathedral, some other prominent church of the diocese. Hence the obvious interpretation would be that in the place of ordination a book should be kept for the purpose of entering therein the names of the *ordinati*, the *ordinans*, and the place and date.

The Code, however, mentions another book to be kept in the *diocesan archives*. This book is intended not only for the ordinations performed by a strange bishop, but also for the ordinations which the diocesan bishop confers. Hence we may call it the *Liber Ordinandorum* or *Ordinationum*. It may also serve the purpose mentioned in § 1, but the Curia of the place where ordination takes place would not on that account be excused from keeping a separate record of its own.

CAN. 1011

Praeterea loci Ordinarius, si agatur de ordinatis e clero saeculari, aut Superior maior, si de religiosis ordinatis cum suis litteris dimissoriis, notitiam celebratae ordinationis uniuscuiusque subdiaconi transmittat ad parochum baptismi, qui id adnotet in suo baptizatorum libro ad normam can. 470, § 2.

In the case of the secular clergy the local Ordinary, and in case of religious ordained with his dimissorials, the religious superior must inform the pastor of the church in which the ordinand was baptized of his ordination to subdeaconship, in order that said pastor may enter the fact in the baptismal register.

The religious superior here mentioned is a superior of exempt religious, because none other can give dimissorials for sacred orders.

PROCEDURE IN ORDINATION CASES

(Lib. IV, Tit. 21)

For the sake of convenience and to complete the treatise on ordinations, six canons from Book IV may here find a place.

THE COMPETENT COURT

Can. 1993

§ 1. In causis quibus impugnantur obligationes ex sacra ordinatione contractae vel ipsa sacrae ordinationis validitas, libellus mitti debet ad Sacram Congregationem de disciplina Sacramentorum vel, si ordinatio impugnetur ob defectum substantialem sacri ritus, ad Sacram Congregationem S. Officii; et Sacra Congregatio definit utrum causa iudiciario ordine an disciplinae tramite sit pertractanda.

§ 2. Si primum, Sacra Congregatio causam remittit ad tribunal dioecesis quae clerico propria fuit tempore sacrae ordinationis, vel, si sacra ordinatio impugnetur ob defectum substantialem sacri ritus, ad tribunal dioecesis in qua ordinatio peracta fuit; pro gradibus vero appellationis standum praescripto can. 1594–1601.

§ 3. Si alterum, ipsamet Sacra Congregatio quaestionem dirimit, praevio processu informativo peracto a tribunali Curiae competentis.

§ 1. If the obligations arising from sacred ordination, or the validity of the ordination itself, are disputed, a petition must be filed with the *S. C. of Sacraments*. If the validity is disputed because of a substantial defect in the holy rites, the S. C. of the *Holy Office* is competent and shall decide whether the case is to be tried in a judiciary or disciplinary manner.

§ 2. If the *judiciary form* is chosen, the S. Congregation shall refer the case to the court of the diocese to which the clergyman belonged at the time of his ordination, or, if the case turns about a substantial defect of the holy rites of ordination, to the court of the diocese in which he was ordained. As to the various instances of appeal, canons 1594–1601 must be observed.

§ 3. If the case is to be settled in the *disciplinary way,* the S. Congregation itself shall render the decision, after having received the necessary documents from the competent diocesan court.

A petition may be filed to get rid of the obligations attendant upon valid ordination, or to impugn the validity of the ordination itself. In either case *vis et metus* may be alleged. Yet even *grave fear,* as can. 264 says, does not render an ordination invalid.

The validity of ordination may, however, be attacked on another score; namely, because of lack of intention, either in the person ordained or in the minister. However, as this defect is difficult to prove, the S. Congregations are very reluctant to declare ordination invalid on that score, although they sometimes take the obligations away. Here the *S. C. Sac.* is competent.

The question of validity is more readily answered if the *sacred rites* can be proved to have been defective, because the rites are outward and generally performed in the presence of witnesses. In such cases the *Holy Office* is competent, because the matter is connected with faith and morals.

Either congregation has first to decide how the peti-

tion should be answered. Our text mentions two ways:
the *disciplinary* and the *judiciary*. The former belongs
strictly to the Roman congregations, because it concerns
the discipline of the Church. But this is not the only or
chief point of distinction between the two ways of set-
tling a question concerning ordination. Another, and
the principal one is the fact that an ordination is *con-
tested* by the person ordained or by a third party inter-
ested in the case. When no one is particularly inter-
ested, or the matter has no far-reaching consequences
in the sacramental discipline, the question is generally
settled by the Congregation itself. A plenary session of
the Cardinals of the Congregation is required to give the
decisive vote, and very important matters furthermore
require the ratification of the Pope (*Ssms. approvavit*).

If either of the S. Congregations, namely, that of the
Sacraments or the Holy Office, declares in favor of the
judiciary way, the matter is referred to the S. R. Rota,[1]
which proceeds according to special norms. It may
be noted that neither the S. Congregation nor the S. R.
Rota easily pronounce in favor of the nullity of an ordination. The reason is that, with the exception of physical
compulsion, it is difficult to furnish convincing proofs.
In regard to dispensing from the obligation of celibacy
Cardinal Albitinus says of his time: " When I was as-
sessor I saw several pontiffs dispense from celibacy in
favor of subdeacons, but hardly ever in favor of deacons,
and never in favor of priests, let alone bishops." [2] This,
we may safely say, is equally true to-day.

Diocesan courts are requested to note that the Apostolic
See always expects either a verdict or at least documents

[1] Pius X, " *Sapienti consilio*,"
June 29, 1908 (*A. Ap. S.*, I, pp. 11,
87 ff.).

n. 134; S. C. C., Jan. 25, July 12,
1721 (Richter, *Trid.*, p. 202 ff., n.
2).

[2] *De Inconstantia in Fide*, c. 36,

relating to the case. A *verdict* or sentence is required
if the Roman tribunal is to take up the case. But no
verdict is to be given before the S. Congregation has notified the diocesan court that the case should be settled
ordine iudiciario. This must be expressly stated in the
document sent from Rome.

A noteworthy distinction is made in our text when it
says that if an ordination is impugned because of a substantial defect in the sacred rites (*i.e.*, the matter and
form of the Sacrament), the competent tribunal is the
*court of the diocese in which the ordination was per-
formed.* This is very logical and judicial, and we might
call the diocesan court *forum competens ratione delicti.*

But if the obligations or the validity of the ordination
are assailed, the competent court is the one of the diocese
to which the plaintiff belongs.

As to the various *instances of appeal,* the canons mentioned in our text should be observed. Can. 1597 says
the second instance is the metropolitan court. But this
does not preclude the plaintiff from appealing directly to
the Holy See.

For exempt religious the first instance is the provincial,
and the second the general, and the proper congregation
to appeal to is the S. C. Relig.

Note that if the case appertains to the Holy Office,
the religious superior may not interfere.

§ 3 refers to decisions rendered by the S. Congregation itself in the disciplinary way. Such a decision may
be couched either in the form of a solution of a doubt,
or a favor exempting from the obligations. The latter is
the more usual and the less expensive way. But even in
that case the diocesan court must furnish the necessary
documents (*processus informationis*), *i.e.*, the deposi-
tions of witnesses, the petition, and the recommendation of

the Ordinary. No verdict must accompany these papers, but the diocesan court may suggest or insinuate its opinion.

THE PLAINTIFF

CAN. 1994

§ 1. **Validitatem sacrae ordinationis accusare valet clericus peraeque ac Ordinarius cui clericus subsit vel in cuius dioecesi ordinatus sit.**

§ 2. **Solus clericus, qui existimet se ex sacra ordinatione obligationes ordini adnexas non contraxisse, potest declarationem nullitatis onerum petere.**

The clergyman himself, as well as the Ordinary to whom he is subject, or in whose diocese he was ordained, may attack the validity of an ordination.

No one but the clergyman who thinks that he has not contracted the obligations arising from sacred ordination, is entitled to ask for exemption from these obligations.

The two propositions are evident. The validity of ordination touches the public good, as the Sacrament of Orders is intended not so much for the individual cleric, as for the Christian populace at large. The assumption of the obligations involved is personal *in recto*, although secretly benefiting *in obliquo*. Hence the validity of an ordination may be attacked not only by the clergyman directly concerned, but also by the Ordinary, whereas exemption from the obligations of the clerical state may be asked for only by the cleric himself.

MODE OF PROCEDURE

CAN. 1995

Ea omnia, quae tum in Sectione Prima huius Partis, tum in peculiari titulo de processu in causis matrimonialibus sunt dicta, servari etiam debent, congrua congruis referendo, in causis contra sacram ordinationem.

CAN. 1996

Defensor vinculi sacrae ordinationis iisdem gaudet iuribus iisdemque tenetur officiis quibus defensor vinculi matrimonialis.

These two canons enact the same rules for the trial of cases concerning ordination which are laid down in the first section of Book IV for matrimonial cases, as far as they can be adapted for this purpose.

A novelty in Canon Law is the *defender of the ordination tie*, who, as can. 1996 rules, has the same rights and duties as the *defensor vinculi matrimonialis*. There was no text or papal constitution which demanded a defender in ordination trials, though it was customary with the S. Congregatio Concilii to employ a *defensor* as often as it proceeded *ordine iuris servato, i.e.*, in a judiciary way. The rights and duties of the defender are laid down in can. 1967–69 and have been explained in Vol. V of our Commentary.

SUSPENSION PENDING THE TRIAL

CAN. 1997

Quamvis actio instituta fuerit non super ipsamet sacrae ordinationis nullitate, sed super obligationibus

tantum ex ipsa sacra ordinatione exsurgentibus, nihilominus clericus est ad cautelam ab exercitio ordinum prohibendus.

A clergyman who brings suit for the purpose of being freed from the obligations arising from sacred ordination, even though he does not attack its validity, is provisionally suspended from the exercise of orders. This suspension or rather prohibition is not one in the strict sense of the word, *i.e.*, it is not penal, and consequently the cleric affected by it would not become irregular if he were illicitly to exercise the functions proper to his order.[3]

TWO SENTENCES REQUIRED

CAN. 1998

§ 1. **Ut clericus liber sit ab obligationibus quae a vinculo ordinationis manant, requiruntur duae sententiae conformes.**

§ 2. **Quod ad appellationem attinet, in his causis serventur praescripta can. 1986-1989 de causis matrimonialibus.**

Two identic sentences are required to free a clergyman from the obligations attached to sacred orders. Concerning *appeals*, canons 1986-1989 must be observed.

As is evident from these few canons, a trial in the proper sense of the word requires an appeal, which the defender has to make when the nullity of an ordination or freedom from its obligations has been declared. However, after the second court has ratified the sentence of the first, the defender is not obliged to appeal unless he is convinced, or morally certain (for absolute certainty is neither required nor always possible), that the de-

---

[3] See can. 985, n. 7.

cisions rendered were wrong, or if there has been a gross disregard of technicalities.

Having dealt with the Sacraments as far as it seemed necessary and opportune from the viewpoint of Canon Law, we now add the Title on the Sacramentals, because it is closely connected with the same subject.

TITLE VIII

THE SACRAMENTALS [1]

DEFINITION

CAN. 1144

Sacramentalia sunt res aut actiones quibus Ecclesia, in aliquam Sacramentorum imitationem, uti solet ad obtinendos ex sua impetratione effectus praesertim spirituales.

The Sacramentals are objects or actions resembling the Sacraments which the Church makes use of by way of intercession to obtain especially spiritual effects.

The word Sacramentals, it appears, was brought into use by Alexander of Hales. The Sacramentals resemble the Sacraments in this that they ordinarily consist of matter and form, or external signs which produce a spiritual as well as a temporal effect, though the former is chiefly intended. They differ from the Sacraments inasmuch as they do not convey sanctifying grace nor produce their effects *ex opere operato*, but *ex opere operantis* or through the intercession of the Church. But there is another even more important difference: unlike the Sacraments, the Sacramentals, though traceable to remote antiquity, cannot, as such, claim divine institution.

[1] See Arendt, S. J., *De Sacramentalibus*, Rome 1900; Pohle-Preuss, *The Sacraments*, Vol. I, p. 111 ff.

558

INSTITUTION, INTERPRETATION, CHANGE

CAN. 1145

Nova Sacramentalia constituere aut recepta authentice interpretari, ex eisdem aliqua abolere aut mutare, sola potest Sedes Apostolica.

The Apostolic See alone can institute Sacramentals, authentically interpret those in use, or abolish or change some of them.

This is not a dogma, as the Council of Trent [2] has not defined this power directly, but only negatively determined that the rites accompanying the administration of the Sacraments may not be arbitrarily condemned, omitted, or changed.

Our text claims the *exclusive power* of instituting Sacramentals for the *Holy See*. This is not surprising if we remember the general saying: *Lex orandi, lex credendi*. The Sacramentals are the living expression of the faith and hope that is in the Church. However, this does not mean that no Sacramentals were instituted without the concurrence of the Apostolic See. For more than one of them, especially the rites surrounding the administration of Baptism, are undoubtedly of Apostolic origin. This explains why the Holy See has consistently refused to depart from such practices as anointings, spittle, breathing, even among nations who were opposed to these rites.[3]

The legislative and ministerial power of the Church alone can declare which rites by their external sign signify the blessing or favor that God wishes to bestow.

---

[2] Sess. 7, can. 13, *de sacr.*
[3] S. O., Sept. 12, 1645 n. 2; March 23, 1656; Nov. 13, 1669; Bened. XIV, " *Omnium sollicitudinum* " Sept. 12, 1744, § 14 (*Coll. P. F.*, nn. 114, 126, 189, 347).

And it is the intercession of the Church which produces the effects of Sacramentals. That the supreme power invested in the Church is claimed for the Holy See does not, of course, conflict with the idea that God is the efficient cause.[4]

MINISTER OF THE SACRAMENTALS

CAN. 1146

Legitimus Sacramentalium minister est clericus, cui ad id potestas collata sit quique a competente auctoritate ecclesiastica non sit prohibitus eandem exercere.

The legitimate minister of the Sacramentals is any clergyman duly empowered and not forbidden to exercise his power by the competent ecclesiastical authority.

The general rule is that the minister of a Sacramental is the *priest,* although it is quite true that the sacerdotal character is not required for all Sacramentals.[5] What is absolutely necessary is power granted by the Church, because the latter by her intercession obtains the effects. Another requirement is the *clerical* state. Therefore a lay catechist cannot administer a Sacramental, for instance, bless a corpse or grave.[6] Much less is a woman, even though she be an abbess, entitled to function as minister of the Sacramentals. Hence the blessings of female religious superiors cannot be Sacramentals in the proper sense of the word.[7]

The power is withdrawn from the legitimate minister by complete suspension from office or excommunication, or the personal interdict.[8]

---

[4] Somewhat confused is Arendt's argumentation, *l. c.*, p. 385.

[5] *Rit. Rom.*, tit. VIII, c. 1, n. 1; *Pont. Rom.*, "*De Ordinatione Presbyt.*"

[6] S. Rit. C., July 5, 1893 (*Coll. P. F.*, n. 1801).

[7] Arendt, *l. c.*, p. 390, n. 362: *mera oratio et gratiarum actio.*

[8] Cfr. can. 2260, 2275.

DIVERSE CONSECRATIONS AND BLESSINGS

Can. 1147

§ 1. Consecrationes nemo qui charactere episcopali careat, valide peragere potest, nisi vel iure vel apostolico indulto id ei permittatur.

§2. Benedictiones autem impertire potest quilibet presbyter, exceptis iis quae Romano Pontifici aut Episcopis aliisve reserventur.

§ 3. Benedictio reservata quae a presbytero detur sine necessaria licentia, illicita est, sed valida, nisi in reservatione Sedes Apostolica aliud expresserit.

§ 4. Diaconi et lectores illas tantum valide et licite benedictiones dare possunt, quae ipsis expresse a iure permittuntur.

§ 1. No one who lacks the episcopal character can validly perform *consecrations,* unless he is allowed to do so by law or in virtue of an *Apostolic indult.*

A consecration is a blessing accompanied by anointing with holy oils, *e.g.,* of a church, an altar, a chalice and paten, a bell, etc. To perform such a consecration *validly requires* either the episcopal character, or a grant by law or papal indult. Consequently:

(a) *All* bishops may validly consecrate the objects mentioned above; but a titular bishop needs the permission or consent of the local Ordinary.[9]

(b) *Cardinals may by law* consecrate churches, altars, and sacred vessels anywhere, with the consent of the local Ordinary.[10] The same applies to *vicars Apostolic* and *prefects Apostolic,* even though they are not consecrated bishops, as well as to *proprefects and provicars,* who may consecrate chalices, patens, and portable altars

---

9 Can. 1157.   10 Can. 239, § 1, n. 20; can. 1157.

within the boundaries of their territory and during their term of office.[11]

By law, finally, *abbots or prelates nullius* may consecrate sacred vessels, churches, and altars, portable as well as immovable.[12]

(c) By *apostolic indult* all those may consecrate who have obtained the privilege directly and not by way of communication.

What about *governing abbots?* Our answer to this question is given in Vol. III, p. 353. A decree of the S. Rit. C., Sept. 27, 1659, as well as other decrees state that abbots who, according to can. 625, enjoy the right to use pontificals, provided they are *abbates regiminis* (to the exclusion therefore of titular abbots) may bless bells, chalices, and similar objects in which anointments are used, *but only for the use of their own churches.*[13] Nothing is said of altars, nor was this privilege ever included in the general grant;[14] it was not even given to chorepiscopi,[15] because consecration has always been considered a strictly episcopal function.[16] If the privilege has been directly granted to some order or congregation, it is indeed not taken away by the present code, but it remains to be seen whether communicated privileges will stand the test when they are brought up for examination. Here another decision may find a place. The Primate of Hungary had asked the S. Congregation whether in cities far removed from the episcopal residence, which have a bell-foundry, one of the dignitaries

---

11 Can. 294, § 2; can. 310, § 2.

12 Can. 323.

13 *Dec. Auth.*, 1133, n. XIX; S. Rit. C., Aug. 31, 1737, referring to a decree of Sept. 27, 1659, says: "*In decisis et amplius [non proponatur]*" for the Cistercians of Stams in the Tyrol; S. Rit. C., May 16, 1744 (*Dec. Auth.*, n. 2377)

14 Benedict XIV, "*Ex tuis precibus*," Nov. 16, 1748.

15 C. 4, Dist. 68.

16 C. 1, Dist. 25; cc. 2, 9, 11, 12, Dist. 1, de Consecr.

of the chapter or a prelate may be delegated to bless bells without anointing. The answer was, No, if the bells are intended for the use of churches and for announcing sacred functions.[17]

§ 2. *Any priest may perform blessings which are not reserved to the Roman Pontiff, to the bishops, or to others.*

§ 3. The blessing given by a priest, if given without the necessary permission, though reserved, is valid, but illicit, unless the Apostolic See has added an invalidating clause in the reservation.

Blessings *reserved to the Pope* are: those of the pallium, the Agnus Dei, the Golden Rose, and the swords of princes.[18] Blessings *reserved to bishops* are: the blessing of abbots, the consecration of virgins, the blessing of holy oils and chrism, the dedication of churches, the consecration of altars and sacred vessels (not vestments), the blessing of bells. These blessings are properly called *reserved*.[19]

Blessings *reserved to others* are those reserved to the pastor, as stated in can. 462.

The *benedictio mulieris post partum* is not a strictly parochial right, but may be imparted by any priest in any church or public oratory.[20]

Blessings reserved to religious orders and congregations are those contained in the appendix of the typical edition of the Roman Ritual.[21]

Not reserved are the blessings mentioned in the same

---

17 S. Rit. C., May 9, 1857 (*Dec. Auth.*, n. 3042).

18 Van der Stappen, *S. Liturgia,* Vol. IV, p. 342 ff.

19 We refer the reader to what will be said in Vol. VI and to the

Rit. Rom., tit. VIII, cc. 20–21; but cc. 20–22 are no longer reserved.

20 S. Rit. C., Nov. 20, 1893, ad II (*Dec. Auth.*, n. 3813).

21 Ed. Pustet, 1913, p. 95.

Ritual under title VIII, c. 1–19, and in the Appendix under: "*Benedictiones Non Reservatae.*"[22] Any priest may give these.

Observe that neither bishops nor vicars general are entitled to grant faculties to priests to impart all the blessings described as reserved in the Roman Ritual, and in which no anointment is employed. This would exceed their ordinary or customary power.[23] Nor may bishops, without an Apostolic indult, impart or delegate other priests to impart the blessings reserved to religious orders.[24] But if reservation is not explicitly accompanied by an *invalidating* clause, a blessing given without permission is valid, though illicit. An invalidating clause would be: "*aliter non valeant,*" or one expressed by a conditional apposition, or in the form of an ablative absolute. Therefore the rescripts must be carefully read. The clause, "*de consensu tamen Ordinarii loci,*" necessitates the (at least presumed) consent of the Ordinary for the valid use of the faculties. If only the words, "*de consensu Ordinarii,*" without the additional "*loci,*" are found in the rescript, the consent of the religious superior is sufficient for exempt religious, even though the clause contains the former formula, "*de consensu Ordinarii loci,*" provided the faculty is to be used only for the convent, not for a public church or public oratory.[25]

§ 4. *Deacons and lectors* may validly and licitly perform only such blessings as are allowed them by law. When a deacon confers solemn Baptism, he is not allowed to bless the salt and water.[26] Hence these must be blessed

22 *Ibid.*, p. 220–233; App., p. 26–71.

23 S. Rit. C., April 2, 1875 (*Dec. Auth.*, n. 3343).

24 S. Rit. C., Dec. 2, 1884 (*Dec. Auth.*, n. 3533).

25 See can. 198; Putzer, *Comment. in Fac. Ap.*, p. 74, n. 54.

26 S. Rit. C., Feb. 10, 1888 (*Dec. Auth.*, n. 3684).

for the purpose by the pastor or another priest. A deacon is not allowed, even though he has the permission of the parish priest, to bless houses on Holy Saturday with stole and surplice.[27] Although, if a priest can be had, a deacon is not allowed to accompany the funeral and bless the grave,[28] yet if no priest is at hand, and the Ordinary grants permission, a deacon may perform the funeral service, especially in private houses.[29] A right peculiar to deacons is the solemn blessing of the Easter Candle, after the five grains of incense have been blessed by a priest.

RITES TO BE OBSERVED

Can. 1148

§ 1. In Sacramentalibus conficiendis seu administrandis accurate serventur ritus ab Ecclesia probati.

§ 2. Consecrationes ac benedictiones sive constitutivae sive invocativae invalidae sunt, si adhibita non fuerit formula ab Ecclesia praescripta.

In performing or administering Sacramentals, the rites approved by the Church must be carefully observed.

Consecrations and blessings, those called constitutive, as well as those called invocative, are invalid if the formulas prescribed by the Church have not been employed.

Constitutive consecrations or blessings are those by which persons or objects are dedicated to the ministry or service of God or religion and become permanently separated from profane use, having received, as it were, a higher or sacred existence.[30] Thus, for instance, persons

---

27 S. Rit. C., Aug. 8, 1835 (*ibid.*, n. 27, 29).

28 S. Rit. C., Sept. 11, 1847, ad. 10 (*ibid.*, n. 29, 51).

29 S. Rit. C., Aug. 14, 1858 (*ibid.*, n. 3074).

30 Van der Stappen, *l. c.*, IV, p. 340, n. 321; *Reg. Juris 51 in 6°*.

become sacred by a blessing, as abbots and consecrated virgins.[81] Material objects, such as churches, chalices, and cemeteries, become sacred by being blessed and are withdrawn from common or profane use.

Invocative blessings are intended to confer a spiritual or temporal favor, through the bounty of God, upon persons or objects, without, however, changing their condition or natural state. Thus, *e. g.*, the nuptial blessing is given to a person, women are "churched," machines, ships, etc., are blessed, and so forth.

For most of these blessings the Church has prescribed certain rites or formulas, which are all contained in the Roman Ritual, and should be carefully and accurately followed, without any admixture of frivolous ceremonies or the use of unsuitable objects.[82] This applies especially to the prayers prescribed for exorcisms. Stole and surplice are prescribed for most of these blessings. Those who have the privilege of wearing the rochette may use it, together with the surplice and stole.[83] The priest who imparts the general absolution to secular Tertiaries — and we suppose also to Oblates of St. Benedict — must use the purple stole.[84]

SUBJECT OF SACRAMENTALS

CAN. 1149

Benedictiones, imprimis impertiendae catholicis, dari quoque possunt catechumenis, imo, nisi obstet Ecclesiae prohibitio, etiam acatholicis ad obtinendum fidei lumen vel, una cum illo, corporis sanitatem.

---

81 The *consecratio virginum* is only imparted to *moniales* with solemn vows, and is, as far as we know, not customary in our country.

82 Benedict XIV, "*Sollicitudini,*" Oct. 1, 1745, § 43.

83 S. Rit. C., March 11, 1871, ad II; July 11, 1892, ad I et II (*Dec. Auth.,* nn. 3237, 3784).

84 S. Rit. C., Dec. 22, 1905 (*ibid.,* n. 4176).

Blessings are to be bestowed chiefly upon Catholics; they may also be given to catechumens, and, unless the Church prohibits it, to non-Catholics in order to obtain for them the light of faith, or, together with it, bodily health.

Concerning the blessings which may be given to *non-Catholics* note that these persons should be instructed not to expect an absolutely sure effect from the use of them. Any superstition based on the number of words employed, or the kind of paper on which they are written, or some special hour must be discountenanced.[35] Relics or objects touched with the holy oils must not be left in the hands of unbelievers.[36] Priests may also bless the houses of schismatics or non-Catholics.[37] Non-Catholics may be admitted to public blessings, for instance, to receive candles, ashes, palms, etc.[38]

EFFECT OF CONSTITUTIVE BLESSINGS

CAN. 1150

Res consecratae, vel benedictae constitutiva benedictione, reverenter tractentur neque ad usum profanum vel non proprium adhibeantur, etiamsi in dominio privatorum sint.

Objects consecrated or blessed by a constitutive blessing should be treated reverently, and not be used for profane or foreign purposes, even though they may be in the possession of private persons.

This is true especially of churches, chapels, sacred vessels, and vestments, as will be seen under the proper heading.

[35] S. O., Dec. 11, 1749 (*Coll. P. F.*, n. 374).

[36] S. O., Aug. 11, 1768 (*ibid.*, n. 468).

[37] S. C. P. F., April 17, 1758 (*ibid.*, n. 411).

[38] S. Rit. C., March 9, 1919 (*Ephemerides Lit.*, Vol. 33, p. 771).

EXORCISMS

CAN. 1151

§ 1. Nemo, potestate exorcizandi praeditus, exorcismos in obsessos proferre legitime potest, nisi ab Ordinario peculiarem et expressam licentiam obtinuerit.

§ 2. Haec licentia ab Ordinario concedatur tantummodo sacerdoti pietate, prudentia ac vitae integritate praedito; qui ad exorcismos ne procedat, nisi postquam diligenti prudentique investigatione compererit exorcizandum esse revera a daemone obsessum.

CAN. 1152

Exorcismi a legitimis ministris fieri possunt non solum in fideles et catechumenos, sed etiam in acatholicos vel excommunicatos.

CAN. 1153

Ministri exorcismorum qui occurrunt in baptismo et in consecrationibus vel benedictionibus, sunt iidem qui eorundem sacrorum rituum legitimi ministri sunt.

These three canons deal with exorcisms. That the influence of demons over men is real, Holy Writ abundantly proves, most particularly the Gospel of St. Mark. But no less do historical documents prove the power of the Church over the spirits of darkness. The activity of the latter explains not only the peculiar charisma, but also the development of the exorcistate in the Latin and the lectorate in the Oriental Church during the third century. Early writers recommend the invocation of the name of Jesus of Nazareth, warn against unnecessary and curious questioning of the demons, and recommend fasting and prayer. As to the rites or ceremonies the same writers mention *exsufflatio,* laying on of hands, and reading portions of Holy Writ. Classes of obsessed or possessed were distinguished and a special discipline for *energumeni* was developed.[39]

Our Code says that no one who is endowed with the faculty or power of exorcizing, is allowed to pronounce an exorcism over a possessed person unless he has obtained special and express permission to do so from the Ordinary. The Ordinary may grant this permission only to such priests as are distinguished for their piety, prudence, and integrity of life. No priest shall pronounce an exorcism until he has by a careful and prudent investigation ascertained the fact of real obsession.

The *Ordinary* who is to give this permission is the one in whose diocese the exorcism is to take place, or the one to whom the priest is subject. For exempt religious he is the immediate *superior major,* for the text simply says: *Ordinarius.* That the exorcising priest should be irreproachable and endowed with the necessary qualities follows from the astuteness of the demons and the awful task laid upon the exorcist. The text employs the term *obsessos,* but we hardly believe that it means only those obsessed by demons in the strict sense of that term, *i. e.,* attacked bodily from without, but includes *possession, i. e.,* control of man's body from within.[40] A conscientious medical expert should be consulted before exorcism is decided upon.

Exorcisms, continues the Code, may be pronounced not only over faithful Catholics and catechumens, but also over non-Catholics [41] and excommunicated persons. The

---

[39] Cfr. Wieland, *Die Genetische Entwicklung der sog. Ordines Minores,* 1897, p. 114 ff.; Arendt, *l. c.,* p. 347 ff.

[40] See *Cath. Encycl.,* s. v. "Possession" (Vol. XII, 315 f.).

[41] S. O., Sept. 17, 1681 (*Coll. P. F.,* n. 225).

ministers of the exorcisms employed in Baptism, consecrations and blessings, are the same persons who administer these sacred rites.   Hence for these cases no special
permission from the Ordinary is required.

LATITUDES

DATES		0°	5°	10°	15°	20°	25°	30°	35°	40°	45°	50°	55°	60°	65°
		h.m.	h.m.	h.m.	h.m.	h.m.	h.m.	h.m.	h.m.	h.m.	h.m.	h.m.	h.m.	h.m.	h.m.
JANUARY	1	1.16	1.16	1.16	1.18	1.20	1.23	1.27	1.32	1.39	1.48	2.1	2.19	2.48	3.42
	16	1.15	1.15	1.15	1.17	1.19	1.21	1.25	1.30	1.37	1.46	1.58	2.14	2.39	3.22
	31	1.13	1.13	1.14	1.15	1.17	1.20	1.23	1.28	1.34	1.43	1.54	2.9	2.30	3.3
FEBRUARY	15	1.11	1.11	1.11	1.13	1.15	1.18	1.22	1.26	1.32	1.40	1.50	2.4	2.23	2.51
MARCH	13	1.10	1.10	1.11	1.12	1.14	1.17	1.21	1.25	1.31	1.39	1.49	2.3	2.21	2.49
	17	1.10	1.10	1.11	1.12	1.14	1.17	1.21	1.26	1.32	1.40	1.51	2.5	2.26	2.58
APRIL	1	1.11	1.11	1.12	1.14	1.15	1.18	1.22	1.27	1.34	1.43	1.55	2.13	2.41	3.35
	16	1.12	1.13	1.14	1.16	1.17	1.20	1.25	1.31	1.39	1.49	2.5	2.30	3.22	(1)
MAY	1	1.14	1.15	1.16	1.18	1.19	1.23	1.28	1.35	1.45	1.59	2.21	3.7	(1)	(1)
	16	1.15	1.16	1.18	1.20	1.22	1.26	1.32	1.41	1.53	2.11	2.47	(1)	(1)	(1)
	31	1.16	1.17	1.19	1.21	1.24	1.29	1.36	1.45	2.0	2.25	3.45	(1)	(1)	(1)
JUNE	15	1.16	1.17	1.18	1.21	1.25	1.31	1.38	1.48	2.5	2.35	(1)	(1)	(1)	(1)
	30	1.15	1.14	1.18	1.20	1.24	1.30	1.35	1.45	2.4	2.34	(1)	(1)	(1)	(1)
JULY	15	1.14	1.14	1.14	1.14	1.21	1.25	1.32	1.40	1.51	2.9	2.41	(1)	(1)	(1)
	30	1.12	1.13	1.14	1.16	1.19	1.22	1.28	1.34	1.44	1.57	2.18	2.58	(1)	(1)
AUGUST	14	1.11	1.11	1.12	1.18	1.17	1.20	1.24	1.30	1.38	1.49	2.4	2.27	3.12	(1)
	29	1.10	1.10	1.11	1.13	1.15	1.18	1.22	1.27	1.34	1.43	1.55	2.12	2.38	3.26
SEPTEMBER	13	1.10	1.10	1.11	1.12	1.14	1.17	1.21	1.25	1.32	1.40	1.50	2.5	2.35	2.56
	28	1.12	1.11	1.11	1.13	1.16	1.18	1.21	1.26	1.31	1.39	1.49	2.3	2.21	2.48
OCTOBER	13	1.12	1.12	1.12	1.14	1.16	1.18	1.22	1.26	1.33	1.40	1.51	2.5	2.24	2.52
	28	1.13	1.13	1.14	1.16	1.17	1.20	1.24	1.28	1.35	1.43	1.54	2.9	2.31	3.4
NOVEMBER	12	1.15	1.16	1.16	1.17	1.19	1.22	1.26	1.30	1.37	1.46	1.58	2.15	2.40	3.14
	27	1.16	1.16	1.16	1.18	1.20	1.23	1.27	1.32	1.39	1.48	2.1	2.19	2.48	3.44
DECEMBER	12	1.16	1.16	1.17	1.18	1.20	1.23	1.27	1.32	1.39	1.49	2.1	2.20	2.49	3.47
	27														

(1) The sun does not go down at 18° below the horizon

Can. 816

Unleavened or Leavened Bread*

In Missae celebratione sacerdos, secundum proprium ritum, debet panem azymum vel fermentatum adhibere ubicunque Sacrum litet.

This canon recalls part of the history of the Eastern Schism begun under Photius (IXth century) and completed under Michael Caerularius (XIth century), the latter of whom styled the Latins " Azymites " because they used unleavened bread for the Holy Eucharist. It is certain that unleavened bread was commonly used in the Western, or rather Latin, Church since the ninth century, and that the Churches of the Latin Rite made use of such bread also at Constantinople, where the controversy became accentuated under the Patriarch Michael.[1] The question whether leavened or unleavened bread should be employed for the Holy Eucharist affected every attempt at re-union between the Latin and the Greek Church, although there was no dogma directly involved. Indirectly, indeed, an article of faith is implied, inasmuch, namely, as the Greeks and all Orientals who make use of leavened

[1] See Hefele, *Conciliengeschichte,* IV, 733 f.; Hergenröther, *Photius,* III, 727 ff; *Cath. Encycl.,* II, 172. The historico-critical question concerning the dogmatical point at issue is whether Christ celebrated the Last, respectively the Eucharistic, Supper with unfermented bread. This is confidently asserted by Benedict XIV (*De Sacrif. Missae,* l. II, c. 10, n. 8). It depends on whether Christ died on the 14th or the 15th of Nisan; for on the latter day the observance of the azymes began; see Smith-Cheetham, *Dictionary of Christian Antiquities,* 1893, Vol. II, 601 f.; Valitutti, *Chronology of the Life of Christ,* 1918.

* By an oversight this canon was not inserted in its proper place.

bread *must believe* that leavened as well as unleavened bread is valid matter for the Sacrament.[2] This article of faith, of course, also concerns the Latins, *suo modo*. But in order not to mix up the different rites, the Church has, ever since the fight became acute, insisted that each Church should follow its own rite, provided only that the belief stated above was firmly held. At the same time the Popes always demanded that the Greeks should everywhere use the bread prescribed by their rite, *i. e.*, leavened bread, and that the Latins should everywhere use unleavened bread, as prescribed by their rite.[3] This is what our canon states when it says that *the priest in the Holy Sacrifice of the Mass, wherever he says Mass, must use either unleavened or leavened bread, according as his rite prescribes*. The obligation is *gravis*.[4] Since this matter plays quite a conspicuous part in the Oriental Churches, the S. Congregation of the Propaganda has laid down a rule for those of the Oriental Church who wish to be *transferred from one Oriental rite to another Oriental rite*. If the transfer concerns a change from a rite with unleavened bread to a rite with leavened bread, an Apostolic indult is required. Therefore, if a Melchite, a Copt, a Syrian or a Chaldaean wishes to be transferred to the Armenian or Maronite rite, he needs an indult of the Holy See (*S. C. pro Ecclesia Orientali*, can. 257). But where no such difference exists, the two bishops (*a quo*

---

2 Benedict XIV, " *Etsi pastoralis*," May 26, 1742, § I, n. II; " *Allatae sunt*," July 26, 1755, § 22; " *Nuper ad nos*," Mar. 16, 1743, § 5. The Armenians and Maronites, like the Latins, use unleavened bread; " *Allatae*," § 23; S. C. P. F., July 31, 1902, n. 1 (n. 2149).

3 " *Etsi pastoralis*," § VI, n. X.

4 *Constit. cit., l. c.*, enforced it under penalty of perpetual suspension. Lehmkuhl, II, n. 121, 3, says: " *A quo* [*praecepto*] *vix ulla ratio unquam excusat, exceptâ necessitate complendi sacrificium, si panis adhibitus deprehenditur corruptus, neque alius panis, qualem ritus requirit, potest haberi.*"

and *ad quem*) can settle the transfer.[5] This canon does not, of course, do away with special privileges or temporary papal indults.[6]

[5] *S. C. P. F.*, Nov. 20, 1838 (Coll., n. 878). But the decree says nothing concerning a transfer from an Oriental to the Latin Rite.

[6] Thus the Benedictines of the Greek College are permitted to say Mass in the Greek or Latin Rite; this privilege had already been granted formerly to other colleges; see Bened. XIV, " *Allatae*," § 20.